OILSEED BRASSICAS

Constraints and their Management

OILSEED BRASSICAS

Constraints and their Management

T.P. BHOWMIK

Principal Scientist (Retd.),
Division of Mycology & Plant Pathology,
Indian Agricultural Research Institute,
New Delhi, India

CBS

CBS PUBLISHERS & DISTRIBUTORS

4596/1-A, 11 Darya Ganj, New Delhi - 110 002 (India)
Website : http://www.cbspd.com

ISBN : 81-239-0877-6

First Edition : 2003

Published by :
Satish Kumar Jain for CBS Publishers and Distributors,
4596/1-A, 11 Darya Ganj, New Delhi - 110 002 (India)

Printed at :
Asia Printograph,
Shahdara, Delhi - 110 032

Affectionately
dedicated to
my wife
UMA
for her help and her
inspiration

Preface

India with its vast land surface and varied climate enjoys the distinction of growing as many as seven edible and two non-edible annual oilseed crops in addition to its numerous non-traditional perennial oilseed trees. Oilseeds are the second largest agricultural produce after food grains and major contributors to the agricultural economy of the country. Oilseed brassicas or mainly the rapeseed (*Brassica campestris*) and mustard (*B. juncea*) in India, are only next in importance to groundnut (*Arachis hypogaea*) as the source of edible oil in this country. Historically, from the position of net exporter of oilseeds and oils, India started facing their shortage after the sixties. Production of oilseed crops did not keep pace with our needs due to both rapid growth of population and their increased per capita consumption necessitating regular imports of oil and oilseeds at heavy cost to the national exchequer.

India leads the world in acreage under rapeseed and mustard but their productivity is low. Additionally, they also suffer serious losses in yield due to attack by large number of diseases, insect and non-insect pests, problem of soil salinity and alkalinity, and weed infestation, etc. Further, radical changes in cropping pattern in recent years, progressive emphasis on intensive cultivation and extension of cultivation of these crops to non-traditional areas to augment annual harvest, have vastly changed their diseases and pest scenario. Many diseases and pests which were either minor or rarely seen in the past, have become important and frequent. Higher demands for edible oils all over the world, have also led to spurt in research activities on both oilseed brassicas/crops and problems affecting them, in order to exploit their unique genetic potentialities for higher productivity. Notable advances have been made in research on host-parasite interaction, biologic races of pathogen, identification of resistance genes, inheritance of resistance and techniques of assessing host resistance, etc. Thus, information generated on diverse topics over the years, need compilation to update our knowledge.

Rapeseed and mustard are the short duration winter crops of this subcontinent, and their disease and pest problems are vastly different and more acute than those of long duration rape (*B. napus*) and turnip rape (*B. campestris*) of temperate countries like Canada and Europe where these crops are grown both in autumn and spring under different climatic conditions. A few books that have come out on oilseed brassicas in the recent past, give sketchy description of only a limited number of diseases and pests, and the information provided in many cases is not directly relevant to the problems affecting crops of this region.

This multidisciplinary book has attempted to provide under one cover, an up-to-date, complete, comprehensive and critical accounts of the biotic and abiotic factors that act as major constraints in the growth and productivity of rapeseed and mustard in this part of the globe, and occasionally of their counterparts in other countries as well. It includes accounts of diseases and pests that cause serious damage to the crops in temperature countries. The book comprises six independent chapters, each of which received full justice in treatment of the subject matter and all relevant research findings, which are vastly scattered, have been incorporated in a concised form and expressed in a lucid language. Research.areas needing further attention have been indicated. Each chapter is supported by complete references.

The introductory or the first chapter deals with oilseed brassicas. It furnishes information on species relationships, their nomenclature, origin and distribution, economic importance, agronomy, improved cultivars and seed quality. The second chapter deals with diseases caused by fungi, bacteria, viruses and phytoplasma. Topics covered are: symptoms, losses, the causal agent, perpetuation, epidemiology, biologic races, resistance, disease rating, resistant sources, and cultural and chemical methods of control. The third chapter is devoted to various insect pests, their damage, host range, life-history, natural enemies and management. The fourth chapter on non-insect pests is a special feature of the book. It provides information, for the first time, on the nature and extent of degradation caused by nematodes, slugs and snails, rodents, birds and other animals to rapeseed and mustard in India, and methods of their management. The penultimate chapter on soil salinity and alkalinty provides current information about salt-degraded soils, their characteristics, factors influencing salt-tolerance of plants, measurement of plant-tolerance to salts, salt-tolerant cultivars and management of saline and alkali soils. The sixth chapter provides information on weeds for the first time. Topics included are: the major weed flora of rapeseed and mustard in India, crop-weed competition, mechanical and chemical means of weed control, weed management in intercropping system, weed and fertilizer management, and integrated weed management.

The book is a complete, unsurpassed single source of information and references on the major constraints of oilseed brassicas and their management. It is essential for post-graduate students, teachers, Agronomists, Plant Pathologists, Entomologists, Agricultural Chemists, Weed Scientists, Plant breeders and all those who are dealing with these crops both in India and abroad.

I am extremely grateful to the Secretary, Department of Science and Technology, Government of India for financial grants for the preparation of this book, and to Dr. I. Ahmad, Principal Scientific Officer, for his generous help and cooperation. My sincere thanks are due to Prof. M. Amin, Head, Department of Bio-Sciences and the Registrar, Jamia Millia University, New Delhi for their help in initiating this project. I am greatly indebted to Dr. R.P. Sharma and Dr. I.P.S. Ahlawat, respectively the former and present Secretary, Indian Society of Agronomy, Indian Agricultural Research Institute (IARI), New Delhi for providing facilities and their cooperation and help in sundry ways.

Grateful thanks are due to Prof. A.N. Basu, Dr. A.K. Ganguli and Dr. Y.S. Ahlawat, IARI, New Delhi for their useful suggestions during the preparation of this volume. My special thanks to Prof. D.L. Deb, former Project Director, Nuclear Research Laboratory, IARI, New Delhi for critical scrutiny of the entire manuscript; Dr. (Mrs.) Bharati Bhattacharyya, Gargi College, Siri Fort, New Delhi for scrutiny of weed names and Dr. (Mrs.) Debjani Dey, IARI, New Delhi for her interest and help. I am thankful to Prof. A.L. Winfield, Wye, Ashford, Kent, UK; Prof. P.K. Sengupta and Dr. M.R. Ghosh, Bidhan Chandra Krishi Viswavidyalaya, Nadia, West Bengal and Dr. A.K. Chattopadhyay, Pulses and Oilseed Research station, Berhampore, West Bengal for providing reprints of their publication; Prof. P.H. Williams, Univ. of Wisconsin, USA for photocopy of visual white rust rating scale and Dr. P.R. Verma, Research Station, Agriculture Canada, Saskatchewan, Canada for transparencies of disease symptom. Sincere thanks are also due to Dr. V.H. Hedge and Dr. Bratin Pal and my student Dr. (Mrs.) Debashree (Choudhury) Chakraborty for help in screening of literature and Mr. D.S. Rawat for the excellent photographs. Finally, I greatly admire the gesture of cooperation and help extended by Mr. D.K. Arora.

T. P. Bhowmik

Contents

CHAPTER 2   DISEASES

CHAPTER 3   INSECT PESTS

CHAPTER 4   NON-INSECT PESTS

CHAPTER 5   SOIL SALINITY AND ALKALINITY

CHAPTER 6   WEEDS

Chapter 1

Oilseed Brassicas

1.1 ORIGIN, SPECIES RELATIONSHIPS AND DISTRIBUTION

Brassicas are members of the *Cruciferae* family. They occupy an unique position in world agriculture as the source of vegetable, oilseed, forage and fodder, green manure and condiment. Brassica seed oil is used for edible purpose, as industrial lubricants and as base for polymer synthesis. Oilseed brassica cake is used as organic manure and as source of protein in animal feeds.

Brassicas were known to the ancient Indians. Mention in Bengal of Siddharta and Rajika connoting respectively, the white seeded Sarson (*Brassica campestris*) and Rai (*B. juncea*) in ancient sanskrit "Upanisada" and "Brahamanas" (1500–1000 BC), and the presence of carbonized grains of mustard in the excavations at Harappa and Khokhrakat mount in Rohtak indicating its cultivation between 3600-1700 BC in Indian sub-continent, suggest their great antiquity in India (Mehra, 1966; Prain, 1898; Prakash, 1961; Rajan, 1973).

Oilseed brassicas comprise six species of which *B. nigra* ($2n = 16$, bb), *B. oleracea* ($2n = 18$, cc) and *B. campestris* ($2n = 20$, aa) are the primary species while *B. carinata* ($2n = 34$,bb cc), *B. juncea* ($2n = 36$, aa bb) and *B. napus* ($2n = 38$, aa cc) are the amphidiploids, which have arisen through inter-specific hybridization between primary diploid species in nature very long ago. The proof of their cytological relationship was provided by artificial synthesis of the derived species (*B. juncea*) by U (1935) and the scheme is commonly referred to U's triangle (Fig. 1.1). Subsequent cytological, biochemical and molecular investigations provided additional evidence in support of this hypothesis (Prakash & Chopra, 1990). Besides the species mentioned, there are other Brassicas whose relations are not very clear although they have the same chromosome numbers as the basic species in the triangle of U. They are the *B. tournefortii*, *B. barrelieri*, *B. oxhyrrina* ($2n = 20$), *B. arvensis* ($2n =18$) and *B. fructiculosa* ($2n = 16$). *Brassica tournefortii* is an oil yielding species (Bengtsson *et al.* 1972).

Brassica species are divided into subspecies, formae and varieties or cultivars. They exhibit wide adaptability, and can be successfully raised under diverse agroclimatic conditions. They can be grown at relatively low temperature as well as in the extremes of temperate regions (Downey, 1983). Rapeseed of commerce that is grown for oil represents several species and types of Brassicas and are differently named in different places (Table 1.1).

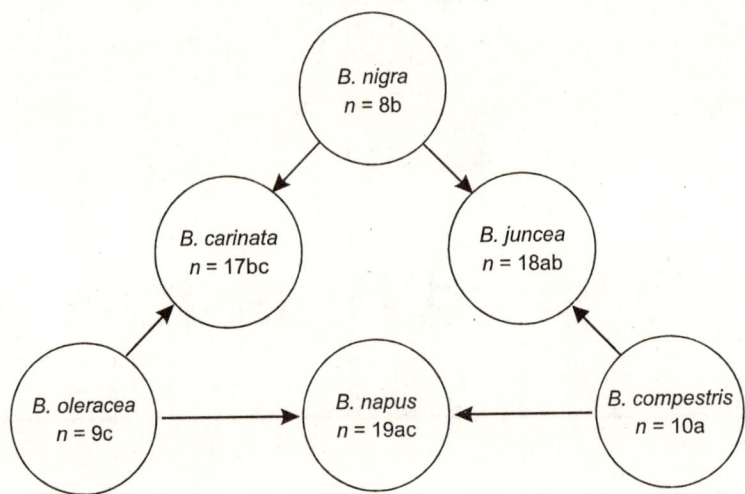

Fig. 1.1. Cytogenetical relationships between the *Brassica* species. (*Source*: U.N. 1935)

Table 1.1. Name, chromosome number and genome symbol of cruciferous plants grown in India for oil.

Botanical name	*n* Chromosome number	Genome symbol	Sub species, forma, variety	Common name	Indian name
Brassica nigra	8	b		Black mustard	Banarasi rai
Brassica campestris	10	a	ssp. *oleifera*	Rapeseed, Turnip rape	Rapeseed
			forma biennis	Winter turnip rape	
			forma annua	Summer turnip rape	
			var. Brown sarson		Brown sarson, Lotni, Tora
			var. Yellow sarson		Yellow sarson
			var. Toria		Toria, Lahia, Maghi lahi
Brassica tournefortii	10	t			Jangli rai
Eruca sativa	11	e		Rocket	Taramira, Tara
Brassica carinata	17	bc		Ethiopian mustard	Karan rai
Brassica juncea	18	ab		Brown mustard, Indian mustard	Rai, Raya, Laha Mustard
Brassica napus	19	ac	ssp. *oleifera*	Rapeseed, Oilseed rape, Swede rape	Gobi sarson
			forma biennis	Winter rape	
			forma annua	Summer rape	

Europe and Canada are the two major areas of rapeseed production. Both *Brassica napus* L. (rape) and *B. campestris* L. (turnip rape) are called rapeseed and each has summer (spring-sown) and winter (autumn-sown) types, which are morphologically alike but physiologically different. The winter types do not form seeds if not exposed to sub-zero temperature for a certain period (Bengtsson *et al.* 1972).

1.1.1 *Brassica napus* L. ssp. *oleifera*

Winter rape (*B. napus*) is widely grown in Europe under mild winter conditions (Fig. 1.2a). It is the pre-dominant crop in France, East and West Germany, UK, Poland and Czechoslovakia. It is also the major oilseed crop in China. Summer rape is found in Denmark, parts of Sweden and Canada.

Brassica napus is of relatively recent origin. It is believed to have developed in nature through inter-specific hybridization between *B. campestris* and *B. oleracea* in the Mediterranean region of South-West Europe where the two progenitors were growing in close proximity (Olsson, 1960; Prakash & Chopra, 1991; Tsunoda, 1980).

Brassica napus has been recently introduced into India because of its higher yield potential, tolerance to diseases, insect pests and frost. The crop, locally known as Gobi sarson, has become popular in Punjab and has a good scope in its central and sub-mountainous districts, and Ganganagar area of Rajasthan as an alternative to Indian mustard because of its prolonged vegetative phase and late bolting (Labana & Goomber, 1984; Singh & Kolar, 1987).

1.1.2 *Brassica campestris* L. ssp. *oleifera*

Winter turnip rape (*B. campestris*) is grown under very cold conditions in parts of Europe, Sweden and Finland (Fig. 1.2b). Summer turnip rape has two forms, the European and Asian. European summer turnip rape is grown in areas with short summer. It occupies the major area of the Canadian crop and the same is true for northern Sweden, Poland and northern region of German Federal Republic. Asian summer turnip rape, on the other hand, is extensively grown in China and Indian sub-contintent (Loof & Uppstrom, 1976; Williams, 1980).

Out of the European and Asian forms of oleiferous *B. campestris*, the former possibly evolved separately in European-Mediterranean area (Sinskaia, 1928), whereas the latter originated independently in the region comprising central Asia, Afghanistan and the adjoining North-West area of the Indian sub-continent (Prakash & Chopra, 1991; Prakash & Hinata, 1980; Sinskaia, 1928).

In India, *B. campestris* ssp. *oleifera* also called rapeseed, has three ecotypes viz., Brown sarson, Yellow sarson and Toria, out of which the former is considered to be the oldest (Singh, 1958). They differ from the European oleiferous types both in general morphology and in chemical make up of their seeds, by exhibiting a distinct pattern of fatty acid and glucosinolate composition (Downey, 1983). Russian workers consider Brown sarson to have evolved in North-West India but Alam (1945) considers its introduction into India from Iran.

Brown sarson has two distinct forms: (i) Lotni—a self-incompatible type cultivated mostly in Haryana and central Uttar Pradesh, and (ii) Tora—a self-compatible, bold seeded type grown in eastern parts of Uttar Pradesh (Singh & Chauhan, 1979).

(a)   (b)   (c)

Fig. 1.2. Distinguishing features of three important *Brassica* species: (a) *B. napus* ssp. *oleifera*: The upper leaf-blades partially clasp the stem. Flower buds above the open flower. (b) *B. campestris* ssp. *oleifera*: The upper leaf-blades fully clasp the stem. Flower buds lax and below the upper most open flowers. (c) *B. juncea*: The leaf-blades do not reach the stem (petiolate). Flower buds compact and below the upper most open flowers

Yellow sarson is believed to have originated as mutant of Brown sarson around 1200 BC either in North-Eastern India or plains of Punjab in the North-west (Hinata & Prakash, 1984; Prakash & Chopra, 1991). It is a self-pollinated crop with multivalved siliquae and is grown in a limited scale in eastern Uttar Pradesh, parts of Bihar but is popular in West Bengal and other eastern states because of consumers preference for its bolder yellow seed and pungency of oil.

Toria is believed to have evolved as mutant of Brown sarson in the foot hills of Himalayas (Hinata & Prakash, 1984; Prakash & Chopra, 1991). It is a self-incompatible, cross-pollinated and short duration crop (maturity 80-110 days) grown in almost all the rapeseed and mustard growing states of the country. The crop is, however, mainly concentrated to the foot hills of the Himalayas. It is mostly grown as catch crop between kharif and rabi seasons in intensive crop rotations with cereals like rice, wheat or as pure crop or also as mixed crop with sugarcane, gram, lentil and pea, etc. (Chauhan & Singh, 1992; Rai, 1979; Yadava, 1976). Toria may be yellow or brown seeded.

All these ecotypes of *B. campestris* are highly susceptible to Alternaria blight, aphids and frost but are somewhat tolerant to white rust disease. Toria usually escapes their attack when sown by the second week of September.

1.1.3 *Brassica juncea* (L.) Czern. & Coss.

The oleiferous form of *B. juncea* or the Indian mustard (Brown mustard in Europe) is extensively grown for its oil in Asia, with India, Pakistan, China, Bangladesh and Nepal constituting the principal growing centre (Fig. 1.2c). It is also cultivated in the Middle-East and East European countries. In recent years, commercial cultivation of *B. juncea* for oilseed production is on the rise in UK, Canada, USA and Australia.

There are conflicting views about the origin of *B. juncea*. Prain (1898) thought China to be the place of its origin from where it entered India through a North-Eastern route independent of any Aryan incursion. According to Vavilov (1949), Afganisthan and its adjoining regions (Central Asia) were the primary centre of its origin while central and western China, eastern India and Asia Minor with Iran comprised the secondary centre of origin. Others believed in multiple centres of its origin where its putative progenitors, *B. campestris* and *B. nigra* had geographic sympatry (Mizushima & Tsunoda, 1967; Olsson, 1960). Prakash and Chopra (1991), however, opined about two centres of its origin: a. Middle-East and India, and b. China. They believe that *B. juncea* reached North-West India from Middle-East through Afganistan between 500-2300 BC, underwent differentiation into various agro-ecotypes and spread to other parts.

Brassica juncea is known as Rai, Raya or Laha in India. It is a self-pollinated crop and is considered to be the most productive amongst all the Brassicas cultivated in India. It commands the major area in north and north-western India in contrast to *B. campestris* which is more common in eastern states. The area under *B. juncea* is steadily increasing in recent years at the expense of other Brassicas due to its higher productivity, wider adaptability, better tolerance to drought, frost, salinity, aphid pest (Labana *et al.* 1976; Singh *et al.* 1974) and Alternaria blight but it is highly susceptible to white rust and downy mildew diseases.

1.1.4 *Brassica nigra* Koch

Brassica nigra or Banarasi rai is grown on a very limited scale in some areas of India as gardencrop for use as spice due to pungency of its seed (Singh, 1958). It probably originated in Central- and South Europe (Bailey, 1922; Zeven & Zhukovsky, 1975) and was introduced into India later although it has been mentioned (as Sarshap) in our ancient scripture, Upanisada (Prakash, 1961).

1.1.5 *Brassica carinata* Braun.

Brassica carinata, called Karan rai in India, is presently grown mostly in research stations as part of crop improvement programme because of its high yield potential. It is the main indigenous oil and vegetable crop of Ethiopia. It may be both yellow and brown seeded. *Brassica carinata* is believed to have originated in Ethiopia as a result of hybridization between *B. nigra* and *B. oleracea* growing wild in nature (Prakash & Chopra, 1991).

1.1.6 *Brassica tournefortii* Gouan.

Brassica tournefortii occurs as weed in areas extending from the Iberian peninsula in the west to the north western regions of the Indian sub-continent in the east (Khan *et al.* 1987). It used to be grown in Punjab in the past but is now extinct.

1.1.7 *Eruca sativa* Mill.

Eruca sativa or Taramira or Tara (Rocket salad in Europe) is mostly cultivated for its oil in some pockets of Haryana and Western Uttar Pradesh. It is a native of south Europe and north Africa, and is of relatively recent introduction into India (Singh, 1958).

1.2 ECONOMIC IMPORTANCE OF RAPESEED AND MUSTARD IN INDIA

India enjoys the distinction of having one of the highest acreage (26.733 m.ha) under oilseed crops in the world. It produced 25.299 m.tonnes of oilseeds during 1998-99, the second largest agricultural produce after food grains and a major contributor to the agricultural economy of the country. Out of the nine annual oilseed crops that are grown in India, groundnut, rapeseed and mustard, soybean, sesamum, sunflower, safflower and niger comprise the edible group, and linseed and castor form the non-edible group. Rapeseed and mustard, the principal oleiferous Brassicas in India, occupying an area of 6.654 m.ha, producing 6.440 m.tonnes of seeds and with a productivity of 968 kg/ha are only next in importance to groundnut in terms of area (7.656 m.ha), production of seeds (8.776 m.tonnes) and productivity (1146 kg/ha), and act as the second main source of edible oil in the country (Table 1.2). According to FAO Statistics (1997), India ranks first in the world as far as its area (6.813 m.ha) under rapeseed and mustard is concerned, China (6.790 m.ha) being the second and Canada (4.813 m.ha) the third, and contributes about 19.83 per cent of world production of rapeseed (Table 1.3).

Rapeseed and mustard are extensively grown in the eastern, northern and north-western states of India. Cool moist climate of winter months, and the fertile alluvial soils of the Indo-Gangetic plains are very congenial for the luxuriant growth and productivity of these fast maturing crops. The states of Rajasthan, Uttar Pradesh, Madhya Pradesh, Haryana, Gujarat, West Bengal and Assam account for the major area under their commercial cultivation. Productivity of these crops is highest (1389 kg/ha) in Haryana, second best (1362 kg/ha) in Gujarat and lowest (600 kg/ha) in Assam (Table 1.4).

Paradoxically, the country which was once a net exporter of vegetable oils, started facing their shortage after the sixties. Production of oilseed crops did not keep pace with our national requirement due to both rapid growth in population and their increasing per capita consumption. Productivity of our oilseed corps is also low. Based on the minimum nutritional requirement of oils and fats at 18 g per capita per day, the Indian Council of Agricultural Research (ICAR) projected a demand of 26.0 m.tonnes of oilseeds by 2001 AD[1] when the population will exceed one billion mark.

In 1950-51, the all India acreage under nine oilseed crops and their production were, respectively 10.73 m.ha and 5.16 m.tonnes[2]. During that year, rapeseed and mustard group of crops occupied 2.07 m.ha (19.29%) area, produced only 0.76 m.tonnes (14.72%) of seeds with a productivity of 368 kg/ha. Nevertheless, due to the concerted developmental efforts undertaken by Commodity Committees, State departments and other research agencies since independence, there has been impressive gains in both production and productivity of these crops (Table 1.5). In 1966-67, for

1. *Bulletin*, Technology Mission on Oilseeds Production, Govt. of India.
2. Directorate of Economics & Statistics, Dept. Agri. & Co.op., Govt. of India.

Table 1.2. All India advance estimates of area, production and yield of nine oilseed crops 1998-99.

Crop	Area (m. ha)	Production (m. tonnes)	Yield (kg/ha)
Edible oilseeds			
Groundnut (Kharif + Rabi)	7.656	8.776	1146
Nigerseed	0.543	0.156	287
Sesamum	1.627	0.558	343
Rapeseed and mustard	6.654	6.440	968
Safflower	0.491	0.172	350
Sunflower	1.920	1.093	569
Soyabean	6.283	6.765	1076
Non-edible oilseeds			
Castor seed	0.693	1.010	1457
Linseed	0.866	0.324	374
Total (Nine oilseeds)	26.733	25.299	946

Source: Directorate of Economics & Statistics, Dept. Agri. & Co-op., Govt. of India.

Table 1.3. Area, yield and production of major rapeseed and mustard producing countries during 1995-1997.

	Area (1000 ha)			Yield (kg/ha)			Production(1000 mt)		
	1995	*1996*	*1997*	*1995*	*1996*	*1997*	*1995*	*1996*	*1997*
World	23873	22013	24198	1438	1392	1451	34338	30636	35103
Africa	170	171	172	1075	1079	1070	183	184	184
N/C America	5449	3594	5097	1229	1473	1300	6696	5294	6627
Canada	5273	3451	4813	1221	1467	1288	6436	5062	6198
South America	46	47	34	1473	1352	1557	67	63	54
Asia	13665	14074	14305	1173	1121	1191	16025	15779	17043
Bangladesh	337	336	336	728	732	742	245	246	249
China	6907	6734	6790*	1416	1366	1405	9777	9201	9540
India	6060	6659	6813	950	912	1022	5788	6071	6960
Pakistan	301	320	354	763	796	807	229	255	286
Europe	4165	3705	3931	2594	2340	2651	10805	8670	10422
France	864	875	988	3228	3328	3528	2789	2912	3486
Germany	974	854	918	3187	2308	3096	3103	1970	2843
Sweden	11	65	63	18500	2032	1905	196	133	120
UK	439	414	467	2813	3406	3231	1235	1410	1509
Australia	377	421	655	1479	1523	1174	557	641	769

Source: FAO Production Yearbook, Vol. 51, 1997;
* Unofficial.

Table 1.4. State-wise area, production and yield of rapeseed and mustard in India during 1998-1999.

State	Area	% of total area	Production (m.t.)	% of total production	Yield (kg/ha)
Rajasthan	2.791	41.94	2.571	39.92	921
Uttar Pradesh	1.136	17.07	1.050	16.30	924
Gujarat	0.425	6.39	0.579	8.99	1362
Haryana	0.576	8.66	0.800	12.42	1389
Madhya Pradesh	0.739	11.11	0.673	10.45	910
West Bengal	0.345	5.18	0.311	4.83	901
Assam	0.310	4.66	0.186	2.89	600
Bihar	0.101	1.52	0.900	1.40	891
Punjab	0.750	1.13	0.740	1.15	987
Others	0.156	2.34	0.106	1.65	—
All India	6.654	100.0	6.440	100.0	968

Source: Agricultural Statistics at a Glance. Directorate of Economics & Statistics, Dept. Agri. & Coop., Govt. of India.

example, the acreage under rapeseed and mustard rose to 3.01 m.ha (+45.41%) of which 20.3% of the area received irrigation, production peaked to 1.23 m.tonnes (+61.84%) with a productivity of 408 kg/ha (+10.86%).

Oilseed programme picked up the needed momentum in 1967, when the All India Coordinated Research Project on Oilseeds (AiCORPO) was established by the ICAR to initiate and coordinate research and development of major oilseed crops. The Project Directorate on Oilseeds Research was established in 1976 at Hyderabad, India and a separate Project Coordinator was provided exclusively for research and development of rapeseed and mustard group of crops. Besides, there are collaboration from International Development Research Centre of Canada and the Swedish Develoopment Agency for work on rapeseed and mustard. In 1994, the Rapeseed and Mustard Research Unit was elevated to an independent status, and the All India Coordinated Research Project on Rapeseed and Mustard [AICRP (R&M)] along with a Coordinating unit was established at Bharatpur, Rajasthan. The overall aim of these measures was to strengthen research, popularisation of improved cultivars and to enhance crop productivity and production through timely transfer of available advanced agro-production and protection technologies. As a result, there has been continued uptrend in growth rate of these crops. In 1998-99, after 22 years of the establishment of the AICORPO, the acreage under rapeseed and mustard stood at 6.65 m.ha (+221.25%), production increased to a high of 6.44 m.tonnes (+747.36%) and productivity to 968 kg/ha (+163.04%) compared to the situation during the base year 1950-51. The statistics on area covered with irrigation were not available. This high production achievement is attributed mainly to both significant increase in acreage and improvement in crop productivity due to various development efforts (Table 1.5). Even this productivity level (kg/ha) of rapeseed and mustard in India is considered low compared to that of the world or countries like France, Germany, Sweden and China (Table 1.3).

Table 1.5. All India area, production and yield of rapeseed and mustard during 1950-51 to 1998-99.

Year	Area (m.ha)	Production (m. tonnes)	Yield (kg/ha)	% Coverage under irrigation
1950-51	2.07	0.76	368	—
1952-53	2.11	0.86	408	—
1954-55	2.44	1.04	425	—
1956-57	2.54	1.04	411	13.5
1958-59	2.45	1.04	426	13.0
1960-61	2.88	1.35	467	12.1
1962-63	3.13	1.30	417	13.3
1964-65	2.91	1.47	507	15.2
1966-67	3.01	1.23	408	20.3
1968-69	2.87	1.35	469	18.4
1970-71	3.32	1.98	594	25.2
1972-73	3.32	1.81	545	26.7
1974-75	3.68	2.25	612	35.4
1976-77	3.13	1.55	496	34.4
1978-79	3.54	1.86	525	39.7
1980-81	4.11	2.30	560	43.7
1982-83	3.83	2.21	577	44.0
1984-85	3.99	3.07	771	53.3
1986-87	3.72	2.60	700	51.8
1988-89	4.83	4.38	906	60.0
1990-91	5.78	5.23	904	59.8
1992-93	6.19	4.80	776	60.0
1994-95	6.01	5.76	958	62.4
1996-97	6.86	6.94	1013	—
1998-99	6.65	6.44	968	—

Source: Agricultural Statistics at a Glance, Directorate of Economics & Statistics, Dept. Agri. & Coop., Govt. of India.
— Figures not available.

Nevertheless, it is commendable that a high 6.44 m tonnes seed yield of rapeseed and mustard has been obtained during the year 1998-99. This has also contributed greatly in achieving an all time high production of 25.299 m.tonnes for total oilseed crops during the year (Table 1.2), which is only 0.701 m.tonnes short of the production target for 2001 AD. The revised Nineth 5-Year Plan envisages a production of 30.00 m.tonnes during 2001-2002 AD.[3]

1.3 AGRONOMY

1.3.1 Climate and soil

Rapeseed and mustard are the rabi or winter crops in India which flourish well under relatively cool temperature and moderate rainfall of about 25 to 40 cm. They may be cultivated in wide range of soil types, from light loam to heavy clay but grow best in light to heavy loams. Soils having a tendency to form crust after rains should be avoided as they hinder the emergence of germinating seeds. The field should be well drained, water logging is detrimental to growth and development of the crop (Weiss, 1983). Brown sarson and Taramira are most drought tolerant and are suitable for sandy soils and rain-fed areas, whereas Toria is best cultivated under irrigated conditions and in high rainfall areas in loam to heavy loam soils. Mustard, on account of its deep root system with extensive lateral spread, can efficiently utilize both soil moisture and nutrients, and can be successfully grown under both rain-fed and irrigated conditions in practically all types of soils.

Rapeseed and mustard grow best in neutral soils although they can tolerate a wide range of soil reactions, acidic to saline and sodic (alkali). In West Bengal, Yellow sarson is cultivated in acid sandy loam and laterite soils with pH 5.2-6.4 (Chattopadhyay & Bagchi, 1989; Sinha *et al.* 1990) whereas, Indian mustard cultivars are grown in sandy loam/loamy sands with pH 8.2-8.4 in Haryana and Gujarat (Antil *et al.* 1986; Dobariya & Mehta, 1995). *Brassica juncea*, *B. campestris* (var. Yellow sarson, Brown sarson and Toria), *B. napus* and *E. sativa* are tolerant to both saline and sodic soils (CSSRI. 1982, 1985; Kumar, 1990). *Brassica carinata* and *B. juncea* perform well in saline alluvial sandy clay loam soils with pH 7.6-8.0 at the IARI, New Delhi (Malik, 1990), the former also grows well in alkali soil with pH 9.3 at Jodhpur, Rajasthan (AICORPDA. 1987).

1.3.2 Cultivation

Brassicas are small seeded crops and require a levelled fine seed bed for optimum germination. Two to four ploughings, depending upon the physical condition of the soil, with a soil-turning plough, and each followed by planking, are required for a fine seed-bed (Reddy, 1980). Excessive ploughings in sandy soil will make dry seed-bed. In rain-fed areas, disc-harrowing after every effective shower, is the best method of conserving soil moisture in kharif fellows. On the cessation of monsoon rains, harrowing followed by planking will make a fine and compact seed-bed (Kumar, 1983).

The ideal sowing time for rapeseed and mustard in northern states is mid-October when the mean daily temperature ranges between 25-28°C (Chatterjee & Ghosh, 1991; Gangasaran & Dey, 1979; Gangasaran & Giri, 1984). Kumar (1986) also recommends the same sowing time for Indian mustard when the maximum temperature is about 30°C, if the temperature is higher, the sowing should be delayed. High diurnal temperature at early sowing causes improper development of canopy and branching of stem, resulting in poor seed yield. Too early sowing also results in attack by pests like mustard sawfly and painted bug, whereas late sowing invites aphid infestation, reduction in seed oil content (Gangasaran & Giri, 1984) and higher disease incidence. Further, toomuch delay in sowing beyond mid-October causes significant reduction in seed yield (Patel *et al.* 1980a;

---

3. *Ninth Five-Year Plan Document.* Planning Commission, Govt. of India.

Yadava *et al.* 1988), the expected yield loss for each day delay in sowing of Brassica cultivars beyond the optimal sowing date (20th October) under Delhi conditions has been estimated at 4.97-7.94 g/m^2 per day (Bhargava, 1991).

The optimum temperature for germination of rapeseed is 20-30ºC and the highest emergence of seedlings is obtained with soil moisture at 40-60% field capacity (Kundu *et al.* 1989). Toria requires a moist seed bed for sowing but excessive moisture is detrimental. The second week of September is considered optimum time for sowing Toria. If the crop is to be followed by wheat, it should be sown earlier. Taramira performs best, if sown during the last week of October (Yadava, 1976). The optimum time for sowing Gobi sarson (*B. napus*) in Punjab is from mid-October to mid-November (Labana & Goomber, 1984). Early sown (October) Gobi sarson (cv. GSL) has higher oil content than late sown (November) crop [AICRP (R&M). 1996].

In the eastern region, the winter is short and mild, and rapeseed and mustard are sown as early as possible, between mid-October to first week of November (Chatterjee, 1984). At Assam, sowing of Toria between the third week of October to mid-November gave the highest yield and this also avoids infestation by aphid, flea beetle, mustard sawfly and other pests (Yein, 1985).

In mixed-cropping, sowing of rapeseed and mustard is adjusted along with the main crop.

Sowing should be timed in such a way that foraging activity of insect-pollinatars coincides with flowering stage of the crops. Foraging activity of insect pollinators, *Aphis cerana indica*, *A. mellifera*, *A. dorsata*, *A. florea* and other Hymenopterous, Lepidopterous and Dipterous insects on Indian mustard also depends on diurnal temperature. *Aphis cerana indica* with maximum number of visits (34 to 43%) between 9.00 and 16.00 h during December 1990 to January 1991 at Pusa, Bihar was the dominant pollinator followed by *A. dorsata* (20 to 26% visits) and others (< 13% visits). Activity of *A. cerana indica* was positively correlated with temperature while humidity had no significant effect (Chand *et al.* 1994).

Normally, a seed rate of 2.4 kg/ha is enough to give an optimum plant population (2-2.5 lakh/ha) but to cover the risk of poor germination due to their small size and variability in moisture in the surface soil layer, a seed rate of 4-5 kg/ha for rapeseed and mustard is recommended (Bhola & Yadava, 1982; Kumar, 1984). Sowing seeds pre-treated with metalaxyl (apron SD-35) @ 5-8 g a.i./ha against white rust and downy mildew (Mathur *et al.* 1992; Puzari & Saikia, 1997) or with mancozeb (0.2%), carbendazim (0.25%) or brassicol/captafol (0.4%), prevents seedling infection and improves stand and vigour of plants [AICRP(R&M). 1998; Chahal, 1982; Kumar & Singh, 1986]. Pre-soaking seeds in water or keeping them in moist soil over night improves both germination and seedling vigour in moisture-deficient soil (Chatterjee, 1984; Kumar, 1986). At the IARI, New Delhi, the usual practice is to provide a light irrigation following sowing and this ensures good and uniform germination.

Seeds are usually sown at a depth of 2-4 cm in the soil in irrigated areas (Saini, 1982) and at a depth of 4-5 cm in rain-fed areas (Kumar, 1986). Sowing should be done in furrows with a ridger seeder at 30-45 cm apart depending upon the Brassica species. Seeds may also be broadcasted but it does not give the desired depth, uniform germination or stand. Thinning and interculture operations are done 20-25 days after sowing to maintain plant to plant distance at 10-15 cm, remove weeds and conserve soil moisture. Heavy stand, particularly under rain-fed condition, results in inter-plant competition and concentration of fewer and smaller pods on the upper parts of plants (ICAR. 1986).

Indian mustard registered increased seed yield with the increase in row-spacing from 22.5 cm (4,44000plants/ha) to 37.5 cm (2,66000 plants/ha) but the yield response to spacing/plant density was significant only upto 30 cm row spacing (3,33000 plants/ha) (Sharma, 1991).

1.3.3 Fertilization

The yields of rapeseed and mustard are poor in India because these energy rich crops are mostly grown on marginal and sub-marginal lands with little or no fertilizer and water. Results of various experiments carried out with graded doses of fertilizers on these crops by different workers over the past several years, both under rain-fed and irrigated conditions, have amply demonstrated the beneficial effects of these inputs, though the magnitude of their response vary according to the nature of soil, type of the fertilizers used, the host species and agronomic practices followed. The effects of fertilizers are more when applied in conjunction with water. The yield responses are highly remunerative because the extra investment on fertilizers is more than neutralized by the additional yields obtained.

1.3.3.1 Nitrogen

Nitrogen encourages vigorous growth, leaf development and sustains their photosynthetic activity for longer durations. This encourages the flow of assimilates to flowers and developing pods, and ultimately the seed (Weiss, 1983).

Rapeseed and mustard are responsive to nitrogenous fertilizers, more under irrigated than under rain-fed conditions. The Indian mustard (cv. Varuna) responded linearly upto 120 kg N/ha on silty clay loam soil under irrigated conditions, which gave the highest increase in seed yield of 49.60% over control, and a response of 8.33 kg seed/kg N (Kumar *et al.* 1980). Pusa Bold (*B. juncea*) showed optimum yield with 80 kg N/ha on sandy loam soil under irrigated conditions. Its response with this fertilizer dose was 10.47 kg seed (4.3 kg oil)/kg N during 1987, and 10.23 kg seed (3.98 kg oil)/kg N during 1988 (Sharma, 1994). Dobariya and Mehta (1995) found 75 kg N/ha as optimum for the irrigated mustard cv. GH-1 on sandy loam soil. According to Ghatak *et al.* (1992), mustard (cv. Sarama) responded upto 160 kg N/ha under irrigated and upto 80 kg N/ha under rain-fed conditions on sandy loam soil, increasing the seed yield respectively, by 382 and 329% over control. However, the response/kg N, was 8.9 kg seed (3.7 kg oil) at 80 kg N/ha, which decreased to 5.2 kg seed (1.9 kg oil) at 160 kg N/ha.

Under rain-fed conditions, mustard (cv. Varuna) responded significantly upto 50 kg N/ha on clay soil, showing a response of 2.4 kg seed/kg N (Patel *et al.* 1980b). The mustard cvs. Prakash, RH-30 and RH-7513 showed optimum response at 90 kg N/ha on sandy loam soil, and their response was respectively, 7.6, 8.5 and 8.9 kg seed/kg N (Antil *et al.* 1986).

Thus, the optimum N rates for irrigated mustard seem to vary between 80-160 kg N/ha and that for rain-fed mustard, 50-80 kg N/ha depending upon the field condition.

Brown sarson responded upto 70 kg N/ha under dry land conditions (Gangasaran & Dey, 1979). Toria (cv. T-9) showed increased seed yield upto 90 kg N/ha under irrigated conditions beyond which the yield remained static (Kumar *et al.* 1980; Mahal *et al.* 1997). The economic optimum rates of N for Toria are 60-90 kg/ha whereas for Yellow sarson and Taramira, the optimum rate is about 30 kg/ha (Sahota & Saini, 1989).

The entire dose of N can be applied at sowing but the best result will follow if half of the fertilizer is drilled 7-10 cm below the soil surface, about 3-5 cm deeper than the seed to avoid its adverse effect on germination (Chatterjee, 1984; Kumar, 1986) and the remaining quantity applied as one or two foliar spray (with a 1.5 to 2.0% high-volume or 10 to 15% low-volume micronet-35 sprayer). The first spray should be given at flower-initiation period (Kumar, 1986). For Toria, application of N in two splits (half N at sowing time and the remaining half, 25 days after sowing) is practised (Sahota & Saini, 1989).

1.3.3.2 Phosphorus

Phosphorus helps plants in the development of deeper and proliferous root system leading to the extraction of water and nutrients from deeper soil profiles. Adequate P fertilization improves the seed weight, oil percentage and balances the ill effects of high N-dose. Phosphorus deficiency in plants, on the other hand, makes them dwarf, with smaller leaves and little or no flowering (Holmes, 1980).

Rapeseed and mustard show poor response to phosphatic fertilizers in soils with medium to high in available P (Kumar, 1980; Yadava, 1976) but in soils with very low in available P, below 34 kg P_2O_5/ha, relatively large increase in seed yield can be realized from their application (Kumar & Singh, 1988).

In general, the optimum P-rates for rapeseed and mustard are one-half of N-rates. Addition of P along with N results in higher seed yield than P alone (Pasricha *et al.* 1987). The economic optimum rate of P for the Indian mustard cv. Varuna is 40 kg P_2O_5/ha. It resulted in significantly higher seed yield, which was at par with that of 60 kg P_2O_5/ha. It also gave the highest oil yield (Punia *et al.* 1993). Pusa Barani (*B. juncea*) showed significant increase in seed yield over control when supplied with 40 kg N + 11 kg P_2O_5/ha (Gangasaran & Giri, 1990).

The optimum P rate for Toria is also 40 kg P_2O_5/ha. It gave significantly higher seed yield than that with 20 kg P_2O_5/ha but the yield was at par with that of 60 kg P_2O_5/ha (Narang *et al.* 1993).

The average yield response of P in irrigated and rain-fed areas is almost similar. On average, rapeseed and mustard need 40 kg P_2O_5/ha for optimum economic response, yielding 7.5 kg seed/kg P_2O_5 (Kumar & Singh, 1988). The entire dose of P should be applied at sowing, preferably drilled into the soil for better effects (Yadava, 1976).

1.3.3.3 Potassium

Potassium is a major nutrient for crops, which also regulates the utilization of other nutrients in the plant system. Potassium deficiency in oilseed rape reduces its growth with shortened internodes, smaller leaves and thinner stems (Holmes, 1980).

Potassic fertilizer is relatively less used in India because of high K-content in most of our soils. There are, however, reports of good response of K application on rapeseed and mustard in soils having low available K (Gangasaran & Giri, 1984; Ghosh *et al.* 1984; Pasricha & Bahl, 1996). In most fertilizer recommendations for rapeseed and mustard, the ratio of N:P:K is 2:1:1.

The most significant response of K is observed when it is applied in conjunction with high level of N, 60 kg/ha (Singh *et al.* 1974). At Kanpur, Uttar Pradesh, the Indian mustard cv. RH5 gave the highest seed yield when fertilized with 90 kg N + 40 kg P_2O_5 + 45 kg K_2O/ha (Tripathi & Abidi,

1976). The seed yield of mustard increased significantly upto 60 kg K_2O/ha on a medium available K status soil (2311.1 kg K_2O/ha) of Kalyani, West Bengal. The optimum dose worked out was 62.52 kg K_2O/ha which yielded 14.45 q seed/ha (Mondal *et al.* 1990). Under rain-fed conditions, in soils low in P and K, it is essential to apply at least 40 kg N/ha as basal, in conjunction with 20 kg P_2O_5 + 20 kg K_2O/ha to make it balanced for mustard (Chatterjee & Ghosh, 1991).

The basal application of K at sowing is most beneficial.

1.3.3.4 Sulphur

Sulphur is only next to NPK in importance. Amongst the oilseed crops, rapeseed and mustard have the highest requirement for S (Tandon, 1986). Sulphur promotes oil synthesis, it is an important constituent of seed protein amino acids, enzymes, glucosinolates and is needed for chlorophyll formation (Holmes, 1980; Tisdale & Nelson, 1975). Sulphur deficiency checks the growth of oilseed rape, plants turn pale green, leaves show interveinal chlorosis, flowers become pale yellow and flowering indeterminate. Pods contain fewer or no seeds or tips of pods become desiccated (Holmes, 1980).

The S-fertility status of soils in oilseed growing regions of India is poor and widespread, and as many as 120 districts have been found deficient in S throughout the country (Tandon, 1991). Sulphur increased the yield of mustard by 12 to 48% under irrigated, and by 17 to 124% under rain-fed conditions (Aulakh & Pasricha, 1988). In terms of agronomic efficiency, each kilogram of S increases the yield of mustard by 7.7 kg according to TSI report as quoted by Katyal *et al.* (1997).

Response of Toria to S varies from 20-50 kg/ha according to locations. Sulphur (@ 20 kg/ha) increased the seed yield, oil and protein content of Toria by 22.7%, 9.85% and 21.9%, respectively over no S in rain-fed sandy loam soil at Orissa (Mohapatra & Chandrajee, 1992), whereas on silty clay-loam acidic soil at Shilangani, Assam, 45 kg S/ha increased the seed yield and oil content by 23.1% and 12.5%, respectively over control (Das & Das, 1995). At Ludhiana, Punjab, application of 50 kg S/ha to Toria crop increased the seed protein content from 24.5 to 25.1%, oil content from 41.1 to 42.2% and seed yield by 1.6 q/ha over control (Narang *et al.* 1993).

Application of 60 kg S/ha increased the protein and oil content in Brown sarson by 5.1 and 5.5%, respectively (Pasricha *et al.* 1987). Yellow sarson (cv. Benoy) responded to 20 kg S/ha by 32% increase in seed yield (Sinha *et al.* 1990). Taramira responded to 90 kg S/ha with a mean increase of 3.7 kg seed/kg S (Tandon, 1986).

1.3.3.5 Nutrient interaction

There exists a strong positive interaction amongst N,P,K and S in respect to their utilization in rapeseed and mustard (Sahota & Saini, 1989). A positive interaction between N x P was observed when mustard produced the maximum yield (24.7 q/ha) with a dose of 80 kg N + 30 kg P_2O_5/ha in Delhi soil (Reddy & Sinha, 1988). Mustard utilized only 27-31% of applied S fertilizer without N application but the utilization increased to 37-38% following the addition of 60 kg N/ha (Sachdev & Deb, 1990). Transplanted Gobi sarson showed significant increase in seed yield with N dose upto 100 kg/ha. Likewise, S also increased the seed yield of Gobi sarson, and a dose of 20kg S/ha in combination with different levels of N gave higher seed yield than N alone. But a combined dose of 100 kg N +20 kg S/ha increased the seed yield by 2.16 times compared to that of control indicating

100 kg N + 20 kg S/ha as the best fertilizer combination for Gobi sarson (Aulakh *et al.* 1995). Synergistic interaction between applied S and P fertilizers in soil also leads to their increased uptake in mustard plants. Mustard crop grown on soil having 5-7 ppm availale S, recovered 17% of the applied S in the absence of P fertilizer but the recovery of applied S increased to 31% when the crop received 60 kg P_2O_5/ha (Lal & Dravid, 1991). Mustard showed increased dry matter yield with upto 40 kg P_2O_5 +50 kg S/ha. The uptake of N, P, K and S also increased in seed and stover due to the application of P and S (Jain *et al.* 1995). Hence, a combined application of all these nutrients in proper amounts based on soil test-crop response results is needed not only for realizing the maximum seed and oil yield but also for maintaining the balanced soil fertility both under irrigated and rain-fed conditions.

1.3.3.6 *Micronutrient*

Zinc (10 kg/ha) and B (1 kg/ha) applied either singly, in the form of zinc sulphate and borax respectively, or their combined dose results in significant increase in the yield of mustard on sandy loam soil (Verma *et al.* 1985). Boron (1.2 kg/ha), S (20 kg/ha) and Mo (0.5 kg/ha) caused respectively, 36, 32 and 20% increase in the yield of Yellow sarson (cv. Benoy) on acid sandy loam soil at Cooch Behar, West Bengal (Sinha *et al.* 1990). On the other hand, a combined dose of S (20 kg/ha) and B (1.0-1.2 kg/ha) resulted in the highest seed yield of both mustard and Yellow sarson over control in their respective locations indicating a positive interaction between S x B in rapeseed and mustard. This combination (20 kg S + 1.0 – 1.2 kg B/ha) can be used as basal dose in soil deficient in these nutrients.

1.3.4 Irrigation

Rapeseed and mustard have low water requirement. In India, they are usually grown in low rainfall areas and under conserved moisture conditions but they respond positively to irrigation with increased productivity. Crops raised under irrigated conditions yielded 43 to 88 per cent higher than those raised under rain-fed conditions (Saini *et al.* 1989). They can be successfully raised with only one irrigation at peak flowering stage but full productive potential of the crop will be realized with a maximum of two irrigations after sowing on conserved moisture (Yadava, 1976), such plants support lower aphid population, and have greater number of primary branches and pods (Singh *et al.* 1994).

The best time for first irrigation is 25 days after sowing when flowering has sufficiently advanced. It is better to delay the first irrigation as much as possible, preferably upto about a month. This stimulates root extension into deeper soil layer for greater extraction of water from lower soil profile and helps plants to branch well resulting in profuse flowering and fruiting. The second irrigation should be given at the fruiting stage, which is 55 days in Toria and 60 days in mustard (Kumar, 1986).

The crop of Pusa Bold (*B. juncea*) irrigated at 30 and 90 days after sowing, respectively at pre-flowering and pod-formation stages produced 33 per cent more yield over non-irrigated crop at Delhi (Gangaswaran & Giri, 1984). At Pantnagar, application of two irrigations, one at rosette and the other at pod development stage, resulted in significantly higher seed yield of Toria and mustard but this remained at par with treatment where only one irrigation was given (Kumar *et al.* 1980). However, in situations such as in Gujarat and West Bengal, best result was obtained, respectively with six and three irrigations (Kumar, 1986; Ghatak *et al.* 1992). In a field trial during 1986-88 seasons at the IARI, New Delhi, irrigation scheduled at 75 mm cumulative pan evaporation (CPE) and at 100 mm CPE were at par and significantly superior to irrigation given at 150 mm CPE in affecting the branches and pods/plant, pod length, seeds/pod, 1000-seed weight, seed and stover yields, oil yield/ha and net income/ha (Sharma, 1994).

Fertilizers improve the water use efficiency in plants. Seed yield of mustard did not increase with increase in soil moisture under nutrient deficient conditions but significant response to moisture was obtained with 60 kg N + 40 kg P_2O_5/ha (Saini *et al.* 1989). Nitrogen and P uptake, consumptive use of water and water-use efficiency in Indian mustard were significantly higher under 120 kg N + 60 kg P_2O_5 + 60 kg K_2O/ha than under lower levels of fertility on sandy-loam soil but the water-use efficiency increased upto one irrigation applied at pre-flowering and this gave additional returns per rupee invested on fertilizers (Tomar *et al.* 1992).

1.3.5 Harvesting

The crop should be harvested when most of the pods have turned yellow, the seeds are sufficiently hard and their moisture content is around 40-45 per cent. The oil content of seeds is maximum at full maturity. Pre-mature harvesting, with seeds containing more than 45 per cent moisture, will lower the crop yield, seed oil content and their viability (ICAR. 1986). The highest percentages of oil in seeds, 43.98% in Yellow sarson and 41.78% in Indian mustard are attained, respectively 47 and 61 days after flowering. Delay in harvesting will also reduce the seed oil content in addition to losses of seeds due to shattering of pods (Chatterjee & Ghosh, 1991). Harvesting should be done in the morning when the pods remain moist with dew to minimize shattering losses. Gobi sarson is very prone to shattering. It should be harvested at the proper time and stacked for seven to ten days before threshing (Labana & Goomber, 1982).

Harvested plants should be made into bundles and dried in the sun for a few days. Threshing is done by beating the seed bearing branches of the plant with a wooden stick or by trampling of bullocks or by running a tractor over them. Seeds are cleaned by winnowing and then dried in the sun to less than 8 per cent moisture level before their storage in gunny bags or bins (Reddy, 1980).

1.4 IMPROVED VARIETIES

Rapeseed and mustard are grown both as monocrop in areas of advance agronomy with adequate water and fertilizers, and as mixed crop in areas of marginal productivity under moisture and fertilizer stress conditions (Anand & Rawat, 1984). Therefore, high yielding varieties suitable for early (especially in Toria), normal and late sowing are required under both high and low fertility levels. Additionally, these improved varieties should also possess built-in resistance to major diseases and pests (aphid), drought and frost, and shattering of pods for superior performance (Labana *et al.* 1977; Labana & Goomber, 1982).

Work carried out at different research centres following the establishment of the AICORPO in 1967, has led to the release of a large number of excellent, high yielding varieties suitable for different regions (Table 1.6) besides identification of resistance to diseases and pests (Chapter 2,3). Generally, the improved varieties of mustard yield 9.0 to 32.0 per cent more under irrigated conditions, and 8.9 to 20.0 per cent more under rain-fed conditions over their respective standard control. In Toria and Yellow sarson, the increase in seed yield is 9.0 to 31.0 per cent (AICORPO. 1984). Release of these varieties for general cultivation has greatly helped in achieving significant increase in the annual production of rapeseed and mustard seeds (Table 1.5). However, none of these varieties is resistant to any specific disease or pest, although they may exhibit some tolerance under field conditions. Transference of disease and pest resistance from cultivated or wild crucifers to commercial cultivars of rapeseed and mustard will ensure stability in their productivity (Anand *et al.* 1976; Gupta *et al.* 1995; Singh & Yadava, 1988).

Table 1.6. Some released rapeseed and mustard varieties and their salient features.

Variety	Area of adaptability	Av. yield (kg/ha)	Oil (%)	Maturity (days)
		Mustard		
Seeta (B85)	WB	1200-1400 (R, I)	38.0	90
Varuna	UP	2000(R, I)	39.8	130
Kranti(PR 15)	UP	1500-1800 (R, I)	40.0	135
Patan-67	Gujarat	1900 (I)	38.0	119
Durgamati	Rajasthan	1000-1200 (R, I)	39.0	135
Pusa Bold	Delhi	1800 (I)	40.0	140
Prakash	Haryana	1500-2000 (R, I)	39.0	150
RH-30	Haryana	1600 (R, I)	40.0	——
RLM 198	Punjab	1700-1800 (R, I)	38.0	152
RLM 514	Punjab	1500-2000 (R, I)	40.0	152
RLM 619	Punjab	1500 (R)	43.0	140
Narendra Rai	Haryana, UP	853 (I)	41.0	128
Vardan	UP, MP	852 (I)	40.9	130
Rohini	UP, MP, Rajasthan	1550 (I)	38.7	130
CS-52	Haryana, UP	935	38.3	116
RL-1359	Punjab, Haryana, Rajasthan	1520 (I)	39.0	142
Pusa Jai Kishan (Bio-902)	Maharashtra, Gujarat, Rajasthan	1893 (I)	39.5	124
Pusa Bahar	Orissa, WB, Bihar, Assam	1013 (I)	41.2	119
Pusa Agrani (SEJ-2)	Punjab, Haryana, Rajasthan	1718 (I)	40.8	92
		Toria		
T-29	Assam, Orissa	1200 (R)	44.0	85
BR-23	WB, Assam	900-1000 (R)	43.0	100
T-9	UP, MP, Rajasthan	1200-1500 (I)	44.3	100

(Contd.)

Variety	Area of adaptability	Av. yield (kg/ha)	Oil (%)	Maturity (days)
T-36	UP, MP, Rajasthan	1200-1500 (I)	43.0	100
Sangam	Haryana	1500 (I)	44.2	105
TL-15	Punjab	1000 (I)	44.0	85
DK	HP	800-1000 (I)	44.0	75
PT 303	UP, MP, Rajasthan	1596 (I)	42.3	94
KS 101	HP, Kashmir	663 (I)	—	209
Bhawani	UP, MP	670 (I)	41.6	90
Brown Sarson				
BS-2	UP	1200-1500 (R)	44.5	115
BS-70	UP	1200-1500 (I)	45.0	130
Pusa Kalyani	UP	1300-1500 (I)	45.0	135
BSH-1	Haryana	1200-1500 (I)	45.0	135
KOS-1	Kashmir	1000 (R)	44.0	230
Yellow Sarson				
66-197-3	Bihar	1400-1600 (I)	42.0	120
T-151	UP	1400-1500 (I)	46.0	120
K 88	UP	1400-1800(I)	43.0	130
Patna Sarson-66	Gujarat	1200 (I)	42.0	110
YS Pb-24	Gujarat	1000 (I)	46.0	145
YST-151	UP, MP, Delhi, Bihar	1281 (I)	39.8	119
NDYS-2	UP, MP, Delhi, Bihar	1398 (I)	40.4	116
Benoy (B-9)	WB	1771 (I)	43.3	114
Gobi Sarson (*B. napus*)				
GSL-1	Punjab, HP	903 (I)	39.1	155
Karan Rai (*B. carinata*)				
Pusa Gaurav	Punjab, HP, Rajasthan, Delhi	1717 (R, I)	40.0	171
Taramira (*Eruca sativa*)				
T-27	Haryana	650 (R)	36.0	150
RTM-314	MP, Rajasthan	1161 (R)	37.9	128

I = Irrigated; R = Rain-fed; HP = Himachal Pradesh; MP = Madhya Pradesh; UP = Uttar Pradesh; WB = West Bengal
Source: AICRP (R&M). 1995-97; Yadav, 1984.

1.5 OIL AND SEED MEAL QUALITY

1.5.1 Oil

Research is needed for the improvement of both seed oil content and seed meal quality of rapeseed and mustard. Oil content is influenced by factors like temperature and moisture during seed development, nitrogen doses, and crop species and variety grown. Generally, cool, moist conditions favour high oil contents, while high nitrogen rates reduce oil percentage but increases oil yield/ha (Downey, 1983). Enhancement of oil content in seeds and simultaneous improvement in their quality will increase the total oil yield/ha of higher nutritive value.

The total seed-oil content in Indian rapeseed and mustard varies from 38-46 per cent and the meal or oil cake constitutes nearly 50 per cent of the whole seed. The protein content ranges between 24-30 per cent of the whole seed or 35-40 per cent of the meal (Anand *et al.* 1976). One of the easiest way to achieve rapid increase in total oil yield/ha is by raising the per cent oil content in seeds of the existing improved cultivars, rather than by raising their seed yield since seed oil content is less influenced by environment and is controlled by fewer genes than seed yield according to Reimann (1963) and Schuster (1967), quotes Anand *et al.* (1976). The higher content of oil in seeds implies a greater technical output and consequently lower production costs per unit weight of oil.

Erucic acid and glucosinolates are the two major deterrents respectively, of oil and seed meal in oilseed brassica. Indian rapeseed and mustard oils are inferior in quality as they contain high amounts of erucic (28.0-53.0%) and linolenic (8.5-22.7%) acids although they also contain linoleic (12.0-21.0%) and oleic (10.0-24.0%) acids which are nutritionally good (Table 1.7). High erucic acid (upto 50% of total fatty acids) oil is water-repellent and is used in making lubricants for marine engines, etc. (Bunting, 1986). High erucic acid rapeseed oil (eg. *B. campestris* var. Yellow sarson) is a preferred cooking medium for its pungency especially in the preparations of pickles, vegetables and fish items, etc. in eastern India. Fish prepared with Sarson-paste, "Sarson-maach", is considered a delicacy. Consumption of such oil in high level may lead to myocardial damage although at the level of intake of rapeseed and mustard oil presently prevalent in India, the risk of developing myocardial fibrosis is considered low (Shenolikar, 1988). Low erucic acid-oil, on the other hand, is more palatable and nutritive. The European Economic Community (EEC) has set the limit of erucic acid in edible oil for human consumption at less than 5 per cent since 1979 (Thompson & Hughes, 1986). The rapeseed varieties that are now being produced in Canada and European countries have even lower content (<1%) of erucic acid (Bunting, 1986).

Oils should also be low in linolenic acid and high in linoleic acid (Vit F) content, since the former easily gets oxidised to impart unpleasant smell to the oil while the latter is a polyunsatuated fatty acid which reduces the cholesterol content in the blood and is also an essential component of cell membranes. Therefore, low linolenic acid oils are more palatable and nutritive. Reduction in linolenic acid content and simultaneous increase in oleic acid content in the oil will render it more resistant to both oxidative and thermal break down, and thereby will impart good frying quality to it (Thompson & Hughes, 1986). Rapeseed (*B. napus*) lines with a low of 3-5 per cent linolenic acid, and lines with more than 40 per cent linoleic acid are known (Jonsson & Persson, 1984). Indian mustard lines TERI (OE) M-21-1, TERI (OE) M-12, TERI (OE) M-10, TERI (OE) M-07 and PBCM-326 contain zero erucic acid. The entries EC 287711, Shiva, Nihal, QM-40 and PBCM-3590 are the other promising strains with low erucic acid [AICRP (R&M). 1997]. The lines 2-6, 20-2, 22-2, 24-5 and 39-3 of Kanpur, Uttar Pradesh and lines, CM-6-3, CM-10-2, CM-10-7, CM-21-4, CM-21-8, CM-21-13 and CM-21-5 of Ludhiana, Punjab contain as high as 38-41 per cent oleic acid [AICRP (R&M). 1998].

Table 1.7. Fatty acid composition of oil of four *Brassica* species.

Crop variety	Fatty acids (percentage)							
	LA	16:0	18:0	18:1	18:2	18:3	20:1	22:1
*B. campestris**								
var. Toria	—	2.37	1.15	11.90	13.98	10.34	8.00	52.01
var. Yellow sarson	—	2.52	1.27	13.06	13.47	8.52	6.16	53.19
var. Brown sarson	—	2.57	1.42	14.65	12.49	9.83	8.04	49.95
*B. juncea**	—	2.07	1.14	10.46	16.40	12.00	6.91	49.72
B. juncea								
cv. RH 30	1.13	9.34	1.97	16.95	19.12	22.73	—	27.97
cv. RH 8812	0.97	8.41	1.56	15.95	20.12	21.15	—	29.12
cv. Varuna	1.32	9.12	1.81	16.42	21.46	19.53	—	28.35
*B. napus cv. target**	—	3.81	0.94	19.80	13.92	8.61	8.68	44.20
B. napus								
cv. HNS 9105	0.20	4.92	1.59	21.26	14.43	19.01	—	38.22
cv. HNS 9102	0.55	5.15	1.62	21.00	15.36	22.32	—	33.38
cv. HNS 9101	0.35	4.15	2.00	23.80	12.45	18.36	—	36.32
B. carinata								
cv. HC 2	0.86	7.56	1.47	17.62	20.82	19.34	—	31.42
cv. HC 9002	0.66	8.35	1.33	18.81	19.22	20.55	—	30.68
cv. HC 9003	0.81	7.54	1.42	18.40	19.37	21.16	—	30.38

LA = Lower fatty acids; 16:0 = Palmitic acid; 18:0 = Stearic acid;
18:1 = Oleic acid; 18:2 = Linoleic acid; 18:3 = Linolenic acid;
20:1 = Eicosenoic acid; 22:1 = Erucic acid; — Figures not available.
Source: *Anand *et al.* 1976; AICRP (R&M). 1996, part of Table 7.2.5, pp.266-267.

1.5.2 Seed Meal or Oilcake

Rapeseed and mustard plants contain strong flavoured sulphur compounds, the glucosinolates in their seeds and vegetative parts. Glucosinolates stay in the seed meal after extraction of oil and are broken down by the enzyme myrosinase into bitter tasting, toxic and goitrogenic compounds reducing the nutritive value and palatability of the meal (Bowland *et al.* 1965), and inhibit functioning of the thyroid gland of live stocks (Greer, 1950). Brassica seed low both in erucic acid (< 5% of total fatty acids) and glucosinolates (< 3 mg/g glucosinolates measured as 3-butenyl isothiocyanate in the oil-free meal) has been registered as "Canola" seed in Canada and its oil is called Canola oil. Now a days, the emphasis is to develop "double-low", low erucic acid (< 1%) and low glucosinolate (< 30 mg/g) or "double-zero" (0,0) cultivars. Elimination of the major glucosinolates from Indian commercial cultivars is essential to increase the value of their seed meal as protein source and animal feed. The *B. juncea* entries, KG-18, KG-19 and KG-20 have both low erucic acid and low glucosinolate content seeds and these can be used in the varietal improvement programme [AICRP (R&M).1998].

The quality of seed meal can be also improved by developing yellow-seeded cultivars. Yellow-seeded cultivars have higher oil and protein content, and about 4 per cent less fibre in the whole seed than brown-seeded cultivars (Stringam *et al.* 1975) mainly due to thinner seed coat with smaller cells. Seed meal with less fibre and absence of tannins in the seed coat is also more palatable to livestock (Thompson & Hughes, 1986).

1.6 PRODUCTION CONSTRAINTS

Oilseed production should keep pace with their growing demands for country's self-reliance in edible oils. Rapeseed and mustard have registered a high production of 6.44 m.tonnes during 1998-99 and this production has been achieved due to increase both in their area of cultivation and productivity (kg/ha). Our arable land area is limited and there is not much scope for further extension in oilseed crop area. Therefore, greater emphasis should be laid on stepping up of crop productivity, which is low compared to many other countries (Table 1.3).

A number of biotic and abiotic factors act as constraints in realizing the yield potential of commercial cultivars of rapeseed and mustard in India. Diseases incited by fungi, bacteria, viruses and phytoplasmas as well as by various insect and non-insect pests cause considerable damage to these crops from their sowing time to harvest. Further, the practice of augmentating production through extension of these crops to non-traditional areas, replacement of local cultivars with new high yielding (mostly susceptible) cultivars and crop species, progressive emphasis on intensive cultivation using higher inputs of water and fertilizers, etc., but without adequate plant protection cover, has greatly disturbed the ecological balance and effected dramatic changes in their disease and pest scenario in recent years. There are not only frequent epidemics of major diseases and pests, but those which were considered minor or were rarely seen in the past, are now becoming more prevalent and important. Moreover, the problem of soil salinity/alkalinity in certain tracts, changes in weed flora and increasing crop-weed competitions are the important abiotic constraints, among others, that hinder crop productivity. These emerging challenges need adequate attention.

Rapeseed and mustard are the fast maturing winter crops of the Indian sub-continent, and their disease and pest problems are radically different from those of rape and turnip rape in Canada, Europe and China, where they are grown under different environments. In India, Alternaria blight (*Alternaria brassicae* and *A. brassicicola*), white rust (*Albugo candida*) and downy mildew (*Peronospora brassicae*) are the major diseases, and aphid (*Lipaphis erysimi*), mustard sawfly (*Athalia proxima*) and painted bug (*Bagrada hilaris*) are the most serious pests. Development of integrated strategies for economic management of these constraints is the high priority area of research in India.

Rapeseed and mustard are input-responsive crops. Planning for increasing their productivity to meet the growing demands for vegetable oils, should comprise breeding high yielding superior cultivars with built-in resistance to major biotic and abiotic stresses, adoption of improved crop production technology, correcting soil reaction/fertility, timely application of need-based plant protection measures, elimination/reduction of crop-weed competitions and other local constraints, if any, and adequate market support.

REFERENCES

AICORPDA. 1987. Annu. Prog. Rept. 1987. *All India Coord. Res. Proj. Dryland Agric.*, Main Centre, Jodhpur, Rajasthan.

AICORPO. 1984. Annu. Prog. Rept. 1984. *All India Coord. Res. Proj. Oilseeds*, Direct. Oilseeds Res., ICAR, Hyderabad, India.

AICRP (R&M). 1996-98. Annu. Prog. Rept. 1996 to 98. *All India Coord. Res. Proj. Rapeseed & Mustard*, Natn. Res. Centr. Rapeseed & Mustard, ICAR, Bharatpur, Rajasthan.

Alam, Z. 1945. Nomenclature of oleiferous Brassicas cultivated in Punjab. *Indian J. Agric. Sci.* 15: 173-181.

Anand, I.J., Malik, R.S. and Rawat, D.S. 1976. Breeding rapeseed-mustard oil crops for productivity and improved quality pp. 58-69. *Proc. Symp. Rapeseed and Mustard*, Nov. 22-24, 1976, Central Food Technological Research Institute, Mysore.

Anand, I.J. and Rawat, D.S. 1984. Recent plant breeding efforts towards productivity break through in rapeseed-mustard, pp. 127-133. In: H.C. Srivastava, S. Bhaskaran, B. Vatsya and K.K.G. Menon eds., *Oilseed Production: Constraints and Opportunities*, Oxford & IBH Publishing Co., New Delhi.

Antil, R.S., Kumar, V. and Singh, M. 1986. Effect of nitrogen on yield and its uptake at different growth stages of raya (*Brassica juncea* Coss.). *Indian J. Agron.* 31(1): 37-44.

Aulakh, M.S. and Pasricha, N.S. 1988. Sulphur fertilization of oilseeds for yield and quality. *TSI-FAI Symp. Sulphur in Agriculture* S-11/3, Fertiliser Association of India, New Delhi.

Aulakh, M.S., Pasricha, N.S. and Ahuja, K.L. 1995. Effect of nitrogen and sulphur application on grain and oil yields, nutrient uptake and protein content in transplanted Gobi sarson (*Brassica napus* sub.sp. *oleifera* var. annua). *Indian J. Agric. Sci.* 65(7): 478-482.

Bailey, L.H. 1922. The cultivated Brassicas I. *Genets. Herb.* 1: 53-108.

Bengtsson, L., Hofsten, A.V. and Loof, B. 1972. Botany of Rapeseed. pp. 36-59. In: L.A. Appelqvist and R. Ohlson eds., *Rapeseed*. Elsevier, Amsterdam, The Netherlands.

Bhargava, S.C. 1991. Physiology. pp. 161-193. In: V.L. Chopra and S. Prakash eds., *Oilseed Brassicas in Indian Agriculture*. Vikas Publishing House, New Delhi.

Bhola, A.L. and Yadav, T.P. 1982. Management practices for rapeseed-mustard. *Indian Fmg.* 32: 48-50.

Bowland, J.P., Clandinin, D.R. and Wetter, L.R. 1965. *Rapeseed meal for livestock and poultry — A review. Cand. Dept. Agri. Publ.* No.1257.

Bunting, E.S. 1986. Oilseed rape in perspective. pp. 1-31. In: D.H. Scarisbric and R.W. Daniels eds., *Oilseed Rape*, Collins, London.

Chahal, A.S. 1982. Diseases of rapeseed and mustard. *Indian Fmg.* 32(6): 27-32.

Chand, H., Singh, R. and Hameed, S.F. 1994. Population dynamics of honey bees and insect pollinators on Indian mustard, *Brassica juncea* L. *J. Entomol. Res.* 18(3): 233-239.

Chatterjee, B.N. 1984. Oilseed production in eastern India, with particular reference to West Bengal, pp. 347-358. In: H.C. Srivastava, S. Bhaskaran, B. Vatsya and K.K.G. Menon eds., *Oilseed Production: Constraints and Opportunities*, Oxford & IBH Publishing Co., New Delhi.

Chatterjee, B.N. and Ghosh, R.K. 1991. Agronomy. pp. 138-160. In: V.L. Chopra and S. Prakash eds., *Oilseed Brassicas in Indian Agriculture*. Vikas Publishing House, New Delhi.

Chattopadhyay, A.K. and Bagchi, B.N. 1989. Occurrence of club root disease on rapeseed and mustard in West Bengal. *Indian J. Mycol. Res.* 27(1): 83-84.

Chauhan, Y.S. and Singh, D. 1992. Genetic and agronomic improvements in toria (*Brassica campestris* (L.) var. toria), pp. 275-311. In: D. Kumar and M. Rai, eds., *Advances in Oilseeds Research, Vol.1*, Scientific Publishers, Jodhpur.

CSSRI. 1982. Annu. Prog. Rept. 1982. Cent. Soil Salinity Res. Inst., Karnal.

CSSRI. 1985. Annu. Prog. Rept. 1985. Cent. Soil Salinity Res. Inst., Karnal.

Das, K.N. and Das, K. 1995. Effect of sulphur and nitrogen fertilization on growth and yield of toria (*Brassica campéstris* sub.sp. *oleifera* var. toria). *Indian J. Agron.*40(2): 329-331.

Dobariya, D.K. and Mehta, H.M. 1995. Effects of irrigation, nitrogen and ascrobic acid on Indian mustard (*Brassica juncea*). *Indian J. Agron.* 40(3): 522-524.

Downey, R.K. 1983. The origin and description of the Brassica oilseed crops, pp. 1-20. In: J.K.G. Kramer, F.D. Sauer and W.J. Pigden eds., *High and Low Erucic Acid Rapeseed Oils: Production, Usage, Chemistry and Toxicological Evaluation*. Academic Press, Canada.

Gangasaran, and De, Rajat. 1979. Influence of seeding dates, varieties and rates and methods of nitrogen application on the seed yield and quality of rapeseed grown on rainfed land. *Indian J. Agric. Sci.*, 49: 197-201.

Gangasaran and Giri, G. 1984. Agronomic manipulations for increasing yields of edible oilseeds, pp. 285-292. In: H.C. Srivastava, S. Bhaskaran, B. Vatsya and K.K.G. Menon eds., *Oilseed Production: Constraints and Opportunities*. Oxford & IBH Publishing Co., New Delhi.

Gangasaran and Giri, G. 1990. Influence of nitrogen, phosphorus and sulphur on mustard under semi-arid rain-fed conditions of north-west India. *Indian J. Agron.* 35(1&2): 131-136.

Ghatak, S., Sounda, G. and Jana, P.K. 1992. Effect of irrigation and nitrogen on seed and oil content of Indian mustard (*Brassica juncea*). *Indian J. Agri. Sci.* 62(10): 664-668.

Ghosh, D.C., Mazumder, S.K., Bagdi, P.R. and Bera, P. 1984. Growth and yield of rape and mustard as influenced by potassium nutrition. *Fert. News.* 29(11): 26-30.

Greer, M.A. 1950. Nutrition and goiter. *Physiol. Rev.* 30: 513-548.

Gupta, S.K., Sharma, T.R. and Chib, H.S. 1995. Evaluation of wild allies of Brassica under natural conditions. *Eucarpia Cruciferae Newsl.* (Fr.) No. 17: 10-11.

Hinata, K. and Prakash, S. 1984. Ethnobotany and evolutionary origin of Indian oleiferous Brassicae. *Indian J. Genet.* 44: 102-112.

Holmes, M.R.J. 1980. *Nutrition of the Oilseed Rape Crops*. Applied Science Publishers Ltd. Essex, England, pp. 158.

ICAR. 1986. Rapeseed-mustard production technology. *Technology for Better Crops*, 27: 1-23, ICAR, Krishi Bhavan, New Delhi.

Jain, G.L., Sahu, M.P. and Somani, L.L. 1984. Secondary nutrient research in Rajasthan-retrospect and prospect, pp. 147-174. *Proc. FAI-NR Seminar*, Jaipur, India. Mar. 30-31, 1984.

Jain, N.K., Vyas, A.K. and Singh, A.K. 1995. Effect of phosphorus and sulphur fertilization on growth and nutrient uptake by mustard (*Brassica juncea* L. Czern. & Coss.) *Ann. Agric. Res.* 16(3): 389-390.

Jonsson, R. and Persson, C. 1984. Breeding for improved fatty acid composition in rapeseed. *Proc. Sixth Inter. Rapeseed Conf.*, Paris, 1983, 1: 311-314.

Katyal, J.C., Sharma, K.L. and Srinivas, K. 1997. Sulphur in Indian Agriculture. pp. KS-2/1-2/12. In: *TSI/FAI/IFA Symp. Sulphur in balanced Fertilisation*, New Delhi, Feb. 13-14, 1997. The Sulphur Institute, Washington D.C., USA, The Fertiliser Association of India, New Delhi and International Fertiliser Industry Association, Paris.

Khan, A.R., Munir, M. and Yousuf, M.A. 1987. *Rape and Mustard in Pakistan*. Pakistan Agri. Res. Coun., P.O. Box 1031, Islamabad.

Kumar, A., Singh, R.P. and Vasi, M. 1980. Agronomic studies on rapeseed and mustard, 1979-80. In: *Annu. Res. Rept., Rapeseed and Mustard* 1980. G.B. Pant Univ. Agric. & Tech., Pantnagar, UP.

Kumar, A. and Singh, Y. 1988. Response of oilseeds to P in northern India. pp. 57-62. Proc. FAI (NR)—PPCL Seminar on importance of P fertilization with special reference to Oilseeds and Pulses in Northern India, Lucknow, June 21-22, 1988.

Kumar, D. 1990. Screening of related Brassica species for seedling emergence and seed yield under saline conditions, pp. 5, *Natn. Seminar on Genetics of Brassicas*. RAU, Agri. Res. Stn., Durgapura, Jaipur, August, 1990.

Kumar, K. and Singh, D.P. 1986. Control of *Alternaria brassicae* infection in mustard and rapeseeds. *Pesticides* 20(6): 22-23.

Kumar, P.R. 1980. Obtain higher yields of rape and mustard. *Indian Fmg.*, 29(12): 9.

Kumar, P.R. 1983. Package of practices for rapeseed-mustard in India. *Annu. Rabi Oilseeds Workshop, Rapeseed-Mustard*, HAU, Hissar, Aug.18-20, 1983.

Kumar, P.R. 1984. Studies on agricultural production aspects of rapeseed-mustard under the Indo-Swedish Collaboration Project. *Annu. Rabi Oilseeds Workshop*, Durgapura, Jaipur, Aug. 6-10, 1984.

Kumar, P.R. 1986. Technology package for increasing rapeseed-mustard production. *Annu. Rabi Oilseeds Workshop*, G.B. Pant Univ. Agri. & Tech., Pantnagar, UP., Aug. 11-14, 1986.

Kundu, P.B., Roy, K.M. and Paul, N.K. 1989. Germination and seedling growth of rapeseed (*Brassica campestris*L.)cultivars under different levels of soil moisture, temperature and urea. *Crop Res.* (Hissar) 2(2): 131-136.

Labana, K.S. and Goomber, T.S. 1982. New mustard varieties to boost oilseed production. *Indian Fmg.* 32: 3-5, 16.

Labana, K.S. and Goomber, T.S. 1984. Increasing oilseed production in Punjab—Constraints and opportunities pp. 311-321. In: H.C. Srivastava, S. Bhaskaran, B. Vatsya and K.K.G. Menon eds., *Oilseed Production: Constraints and opportunities*. Oxford & IBH Publishing Co, New Delhi.

Labana, K.S., Gupta, M.L. and Singh, M. 1977. Taramira—a cash crop under constrained inputs. *Prog. Fmg.* 15: 11.

Labana, K.S., Gupta, S.K. and Singh, B. 1976. Induced variability in different traits of Raya (*Brassica juncea* (L.) Czern. & Coss.). In: *Proc. symp. Rapeseed and mustard*, Nov.22-24, 1976, Central Food Technological Research Institute, Mysore.

Lal, K. and Dravid, M.S. 1991. Phosphate-sulphate-silicate and FYM interaction on P utilization by mustard. *J. Nuclear Agric. Biol.* 19(4): 232-235.

Loof, B. and Uppstrom, B. 1976. Brassica oilseeds of importance in the world production and possibilities of their improvement with special consideration of the situation in India, pp. 19-21. In: *Proc. Symp. : Rapeseed and Mustard*, Nov. 22-24, 1976. Central Food Technological Research Institute, Mysore.

Mahal, S.S., Gill, M.S.and Singh, P. 1997. Response of Toria (*Brassica campestris* sub sp. *oleifera* var. Toria) to irrigation, nitrogen and sulphur. *Indian J. Agron.* 42(4): 670-674.

Malik, R.S. 1990. Prospects of *Brassica carinata* as an oilseed crop in India. *Exptl. Agric.* 26: 125-129.

Mathur, Sneh., Bhatnagar, M.K. and Mathur, S. 1992. An effective chemical control for white rust *Albugo candida* (Pers.). *Indian J. Plant Prot.* 20(2): 144-149.

Mehra, K.L. 1966. History and ethnobotany of mustard in India. *Adv. Front. Plant Sci.* 19: 51-59.

Mizushima, U. and Tsunoda, S. 1967. A plant exploration in Brassica and allied genera. *Tohoku J. Agric. Res.* 17: 249-277.

Mohapatra, A.K. and Chandrajee, R. 1992. Effect of sulphur application on yield, quality and nutrient uptake of unirrigated Indian rape (*Brassica napus*). *Indian J. Agron.* 37(1): 201.

Mondal, S.S., Das, S.K., Pradhan, B.K. and Goswami, S.B. 1990. Effect of potassium on the growth and yield of mustard at varying plant density. *J. Pot. Res.* 6: 119-123.

Narang, R.S., Mohal, S.S. and Gill, M.S. 1993. Effect of phosphorus and sulphur on growth and yield of Toria (*Brassica campestris* sub sp. *oleifera* var. Toria). *Indian J. Agron.* 38(4): 593-597.

Olsson, G. 1960. Species crosses within the genus Brassica. I. Artificial *B. juncea* Coss. *Hereditas* 46: 171-222.

Pasricha, N.S., Aulakh, M.S., Bahl, G.S. and Baddesha, H.S. 1987. Nutritional requirements of oilseed and pulse crops in Punjab (1975-86). *Res. Bulletin* No.DR/Pub/87/15, pp. 30-35, Dept. Soils, PAU, Ludhiana.

Pasricha, N.S. and Bahl, G.S. 1996. Response to applied potassium for yield and quality in oilseed and pulse crops. *Fert. News* 41(5): 27-37.

Patel, J.R., Parmar, M.T. and Patel, J.C. 1980a. Effect of different spacings and plant populations on yield of mustard. *Indian J. Agron.* 25(3): 526-527.

Patel, J.R., Parmar, M.T. and Patel, J.C. 1980b. Response of mustard to different spacings, and levels of nitrogen and phosphorus. *Indian J. Agron.* 25(3): 524-525.

Prain, D. 1898. The mustards cultivated in Bengal. *Agr. Ledger* 5: 1-80.

Prakash, O. 1961. *Food and Drinks in Ancient India*. Munshi Ram Manohar Lal, Delhi.

Prakash, S. and Chopra, V.L. 1990. Cytogenetics of crop Brassicas and their allies. pp. II.161-180. In: T. Tsuchiya and P.K. Gupta eds., *Chromosome Engineering in Plants—Genetics and Breeding*. Elsevier Science Publishers, The Netherlands.

Prakash, S. and Chopra, V.L. 1991. Origin and evolution, pp. 60-85, In: V.L. Chopra and S. Prakash eds., *Oilseed Brassicas in Indian Agriculture*. Vikas Publishing House, New Delhi.

Prakash, S. and Hinata, K. 1980. Taxonomy, cytogenetics and origin of crop Brassicas, a review. *Opera Botanica* 5: 1-57.

Punia, B.S., Porwal, B.L. and Gaur, B.L. 1993. Response of mustard (*Brassica juncea*) to phosphorus on vertisols of Rajasthan. *Indian J. Agron.* 38(1): 142-143.

Puzari, K.C. and Saikia, U.N. 1997. Efficacy of fungicides for controlling downy mildew of rapeseed. *Indian Phytopath.* 50(4): 520-523.

Rai, B. 1979. Breeding strategy for developing high-yielding varieties of toria (*Brassica campestris* (L.) var. toria). *Proc. Natn. Symp. : Research and development strategies for oilseed production in India*, Nov. 7-9, 1979, IARI, New Delhi.

Rajan, S.S. 1973. *Report of the study team No.8 on Oilseeds, Natn. Commission on Agriculture,* Govt. of India, pp. 211.

Reddy, B.N. and Sinha, M.N. 1988. Yield and phosphorus utilization of mustard as influenced by phosphorus at various levels of nitrogen and moisture regimes. *Fert. News.* 33: 31-37.

Reddy, M.V. 1980. Commercial crops — Oilseed crops (rapeseed and mustard), pp. 933-945. In: *Handbook of Agriculture.* Revised edition, 1980, ICAR, New Delhi.

Sachdev, M.S. and Dev, D.L. 1990. Nitrogen and sulphur uptake, and efficiency in the mustard-moong-maize cropping system. *Fert. News.* 35: 45-55.

Sahota, T.S. and Saini, J.S. 1989. Agronomic research on rapeseed and mustard with special reference to fertiliser use. *Fert. News.* 34(9): 31-43.

Saini, J.S. 1982. Production technology for mustard. *Indian Fmg.* 32: 7-10.

Saini, J.S., Sahota, T.S. and Dhillon, A.S. 1989. Agronomy of rapeseed and mustard and their place in new and emerging cropping systems. *J. Oilseeds Res.* 6: 220-267.

Sharma, J.P. 1994. Response of Indian mustard (*Brassica juncea*) to different irrigation schedules, and nitrogen and sulphur levels. *Indian J. Agron.* 39(3): 421-425.

Sharma, M.L. 1991. Yield and oil content of mustard varieties in relation to plant population. *J. Oilseeds Res.* 8: 237-239.

Shenolikar, I.S. 1988. Toxicological studies on mustard oil. In: V.R. Rao and M.V.R. Prasad, eds., *Proc. Natn. Seminar on Strategies for making India self-reliant in vegetable oils*. Sept. 5-9, 1988. Indian Soc. Oilseeds Res., Direct. Oilseeds Res., Hyderabad, ICAR.

Singh, D.P. 1958. *Rape and Mustard*. The Indian Cent. Oilseeds Committee, Hyderabad, pp. 105.

Singh, B. and Kolar, J.S. 1987. Performance of Gobi sarson (*Brassica napus*) under different dates of sowing. *J. Res. Punjab Agric. Univ.* 24(2): 215-216.

Singh, H. and Yadava, T.P. 1988. Integrated management of aphid pest in rapeseed-mustard crops, pp. 150-157. In: V.R. Rao and M.V.R. Prasad, eds., *Proc. Natn. Seminar on strategies for making India self-reliant in vegetable oils.* Sept. 5-9, 1988. Indian Soc. Oilseeds Res., Direct. Oilseeds Res., Hyderabad, ICAR.

Singh, H.G. and Chauhan, Y.S. 1979. Factors limiting rapeseed-mustard production in North-Eastern part of India. *Proc. Natn. Symp. : Research and development strategies for Oilseed production in India.* Nov. 7-9, 1979, IARI, New Delhi.

Singh, I., Brar, K.S. and Ahuja, T.S. 1994. Effect of irrigation on the incidence of mustard aphid, *Lipaphis erysimi* (Kalt.). *Indian J. Ent.* 56(1): 63-66.

Singh, K.N., Joshi, Y.C. and Singh, T.N. 1974. In saline sodic soils — Raya better than other oilseed crops. *Indian Fmg.* 24(2): 9, 23.

Singh, U.B., Tomar, S.P. and Tomar, P.S. 1974. Comparative performance of different oilseed crops and their response to irrigation and fertilizer application. *Indian J. Agron.* 19: 1-5.

Sinha, A.C., Jana, P.K. and Mandal, B.B. 1990. Effect of micro-nutrients on rapeseed grown on acid soils of Eastern India. *Indian J. Agron.* 35(1&2): 126-130.

Sinskaia, E.N. 1928. The *oleiferous* plants and root crops of the family Cruciferae. *Bull. Appl. Bot. Genet. Pl. Breed.* 175: 3-166.

Stringam, G.R., McGregor, D.I. and Pawlowski, S.H. 1975. Chemical and morphological characteristics associated with seed color in rapeseed. pp. 99-108 *Proc. 4th Inter. Rapeseed Conf.*, Giessen, 1974.

Tandon, H.L.S. 1986. *Sulphur Research and Agricultural Production in India. Second Edition.* Fertiliser Development
• and Consultation Organisation, New Delhi, pp. 160.

Tandon, H.L.S. 1991. *Sulphur Research and Agricultural Production in India. Third Edition.* The Sulphur Institute, Washington, D.C., USA, pp. 140.

Thompson, K.F. and Hughes, W.G. 1986. Breeding and Varieties, pp. 32-82. In: D.H. Scarisbrick and R.W. Daniels eds., *Oilseed Rape.* Collins, London..

Tisdale, S.L. and Nelson, W.L. 1975. *Soil Fertility and Fertilizers.* pp. 83-88. McMillan Publishing Co. Inc., New York.

Tomar, S., Tomar, Sunita and Singh, S. 1992. Effect of irrigation and fertilizer on nutrient uptake and moisture use of mustard (*Brassica juncea*). *Indian J. Agron.* 37(1): 97-99.

Tripathi, R.D. and Abidi, A.B. 1976. Studies on the effect of sowing dates and fertilizer doses on the biochemical composition of some newly introduced oil rich varieties of Rai, *Brassica juncea* (L.) Czern and Coss. *Proc. Symp. : Rapeseed and mustard*, Nov. 22-24, 1976. Central Food Technological Research Institute, Mysore.

Tsunoda, S. 1980. Ecophysiology of wild and cultivated forms in Brassica and allied genera, pp. 109-120. In: S. Tsunoda *et al.* eds., *Brassica Crops and Wild Allies.* Japan Scientific Societies Press, Tokyo.

U.N. 1935. Genome analysis in Brassicae, with special reference to the experimental formation of *Brassica napus* and peculiar mode of fertilization. *Japan J. Bot.* 7: 389-452.

Vavilov, N.I. 1949. The origin, variation, immunity and breeding of cultivated plants. *Chron. Bot.* 13: 1-364.

Verma, K.P., Srivastava, A.N. and Pathak, R.K. 1985. Sulphur, zinc and boron nutrition of Indian mustard. *J. Oilseeds Res.* 309-314.

Weiss, E.A. 1983. *Oilseed crops.* Longman, New York, pp. 660.

Williams, I.H. 1980. Oilseed rape and beekeeping particularly in Britain. *Bee World* 61(4): 141-153.

Yadava, T.P. 1976. Present available status of production technology of rapeseed and mustard, and future programme of work, pp. 22-30. *Proc. Symp. : Rapeseed and mustard*, Nov.22-24, 1976. Central Food Technological Research Institute, Mysore.

Yadava, T.P. 1984. Higher production of oilseeds through research and developoment — An overview. pp. 41-71. In: H.C. Srivastava, S. Vaskaran, B. Vatsya and K.K.G. Menon eds., *Oilseed Production: Constraints and opportunities.* Oxford and IBH Publishing Co., New Delhi.

Yadava, T.P., Yadava, J.S. and Yadav, A.K. 1988. Current status and future perspective of rapeseed and mustard in Haryana, pp. 133-148. In: V.R. Rao and M.V.R. Prasad eds., *Proc. Natn. Seminar on strategies for making India self-reliant in vegetable oils.* Sept. 5-9, 1988. Indian Soc. Oilseeds Res., Direct. Oilseed Res., Hyderabad, ICAR.

Yein, B.R. 1985. Effect of date of sowing on the incidence of insect-pests of Toria *(Brassica campestris).* *J. Res. Assam Agri. Univ.* 6(1): 68-70.

Zeven, A.C. and Zhukovsky, P.M. 1975. *Dictionary of Cultivated Plants and their Centres of Diversity*, pp. 29-30, Pudoc.

Chapter 2

Diseases

2.1 INTRODUCTION

Diseases are the major cause of low productivity of oilseed brassicas especially when one or more of them appear in epiphytotic form. A number of fungal, bacterial, viral and phytoplasma diseases attack these crops at all stages of their development but all of them are not economically important in India (Table 2.1).

Table 2.1. Diseases of rapeseed and mustard in India.

Name of disease	Causal agent	Reference
Fungal diseases		
1. Alternaria blight***	*Alternaria brassicae* (Berk.) Sacc.	Butler (1918)
	A. brassicicola (Schw,) Wiltshire	Dey (1948)
2. White rust***	*Albugo candida* (Lev.) Kuntze	Butler (1918)
3. Downy mildew***	*Peronospora parasitica* (Pers.) ex.Fr.	Butler (1918)
4. Powdery mildew***	*Erysiphe polygoni* DC.	Butler (1918)
	E. cruciferarum	Sharma (1979)
5. Stem rot**	*Sclerotinia sclerotiorum* (Lib.) de Bary	Shaw and Agrekar (1915)
6. Collar rot*	*Sclerotium rolfsii* Sacc.	Rai *et al.* (1974)
	(*Pellicularia rolfsii*)	Upadhyay and Pavgi (1967)
7. Rhizoctonia rot*	*Rhizoctonia solani* Kuhn	Srivastava (1968)
	R. bataticola (Taub.) Butler	Rai *et al.* (1974)
	[*Macrophomina phaseolina* (Tassi) Goid]	Rai and Singh (1973)
8. Wilt*	*Fusarium oxysporum* f sp.*conglutinans*	Rai and Singh (1973)
9. Club root**	*Plasmodiophora brassicae* Wor.	Laha *et al.* (1985)
10. Root gall smut*	*Urocystis brassicae* Mundkur	Mundkur (1933)
11. Damping off*	*Pythium aphanidermatum* (Eds.) Filtz.	Mahmud (1950)
	P. butleri Subramanian	Aulakh (1971)

(Contd.)

Name of disease	Causal agent	Reference
12. Other leaf spots*	*Alternaria longipes* (Ell.&Ev.) Mason	Rao (1977)
	A. napiformae novo	Purkayastha & Mallik (1976)
	Cercospora cheiranthis var. *brassicae* Gov. & Thiru.	Govindu and Thirumalachar (1955)
	C. brassicicola	Mukherjee *et al.* (1983)
Bacterial diseases		
13. Black rot*	*Xanthomonas campestris* pv. campestris (Pammel) Dowson	Satyavir *et al.* (1973); Patel *et al.* (1949)
14. Stalk rot**	*Erwinia carotovora* (Jones) Holland	Bhowmik & Trivedi (1980)
15. Bacterial wilt*	*Pseudomonas solanacearum* Smith	Singh (1992)
Virus and Phytoplasma diseases		
16. Sarso mosaic*	Mosaic virus	Azad and Sehgal (1959); Vasudeva (1957)
17. Rai mosaic*	Mosaic virus	Sharma (1973)
18. Radish mosaic*	Poty virus	Verma *et al.* (1969)
19. Sesamum phyllody*	Phytoplasma	Bindra & Bakhetia (1967)

***Major diseases of all India importance; **Diseases of regional importance; *Diseases of minor importance.

Earlier, the area under these crops was comparatively low, they used to be grown in marginal lands with local cultivars with little or no manure and irrigation, often as mixed crop with others, and the occurrence of diseases was of little economic significance. After independence, with the increasing demand for edible oil, the crop area has increased steadily (Table 1.5), new crop species and varieties introduced, and there has been progressive emphasis on their intensive cultivation. Improved cultivars (both single low and double low) with reduced antinutritional factors (erucic acid and glucosinolates) are often more prone to diseases (Doughty *et al.* 1991; Nashaat & Rawlinson, 1994). All these factors have vastly changed the disease scenario. Serious incidence of the disease like Alternaria blight (*Alternaria* spp.) has become almost an annual feature. White rust (*Albugo candida*), which was sporadic in the past (Vasudeva, 1958), has become widespread and destructive. Clubroot (*Plasmodiophora brassicae*) in West Bengal and the new bacterial stalk rot (*Erwinia carotova*) disease in Rajasthan, Delhi, UP, Haryana and adjoining areas have emerged as serious threats. Diseases such as stem rot (*Sclerotinia sclerotiorum*), Rhizoctonia root rot (*Rhizoctonia* spp.) and Collar rot (*Sclerotium rolfsii*), which were obscure in the past are now being observed on the crop in many areas [AICRP (R&M). 1996].

Nevertheless, the disease situaiton in India is quite different from that of Canada, Europe and other countries where stem rot (*S. sclerotiorum*), black-leg/stem canker (*Leptosphaeria maculans*), light leaf spot (*Pyrenopeziza brassicae*), verticillium wilt (*Verticillium dahliae*) and grey mould (*Botrytis cinerea*), etc. cause serious damage to oilseed brassicas. The present chapter provides information on diseases that are important on rapeseed and mustard in India besides a brief account on stem rot and black-leg that are very destructive to oilseed rape elsewhere.

2.2 FUNGAL DISEASES

2.2.1 Alternaria Blight

Alternaria blight is one of the most widespread and destructive disease of rapeseed and mustard in India, particularly in the Indo-Gangetic plains (Vasudeva, 1958). The disease is also called the dark spot (Louvet, 1958) or grey spot (McDonald, 1959) based on symptoms produced on the host. In India, it was probably first noted on Sarson (*Brassica campestris* var. Sarson) in 1901 at Tirhoot (Trihut) near Pusa, Bihar (Butler, 1918).

The disease is caused predominantly by the fungus *Alternaria brassicae* (Berk.) Sacc. which is highly destructive and widespread, the world over. *Alternaria brassicicola* (Schw.) Wilts. is the other species that attacks the crop in India, but is of lesser economic significance. The latter named pathogen is more commonly associated with late season lesions and the level of infestation depends upon the host species involved and the prevalence of warm-humid weather. It was reported to be the predominant species on mustard (*B. campestris*) in West Bengal (Sarkar & Sengupta, 1978). The author, however, found *A. brassicae* is more important, the confusion seems to be due to simultaneous occurrence of the two species on the same spot, and *A. brassicicola* having the faster growth rate than *A. brassicae*. Generally, both the species may occur on the same host but *A. brassicae* is most frequently associated with the oleiferous *B. juncea*, *B. napus* and *B. rapa* (*B. campestris*), and *A. brassicicola* with *B. oleracea* (Humpherson-Jones, 1992).

Other species of Alternaria pathogenic on Brassica spp. are: *A. raphani* Grover and Skolko, *A. alternata* (Fr.) Keissler and *A. japonica* Yoshii (Degenhardt *et al.* 1974, 1982; Humpherson-Jones, 1992; Paul & Rawlinson, 1992; Seidel *et al.* 1995; Simmons, 1992; Vaartnou & Tewari, 1972) but none of these is important in India. In Canada, *A. brassicae* in association with *A. raphani* causes serious damage to oilseed brassicas (Degenhardt *et al.* 1974, 1982).

2.2.1.1 Symptoms

Alternaria blight attacks all the green parts of the plant reducing its photosynthetic area and vigour. In north India, the disease is usually seen during mid-December to early January as minute dark-brown or black spots on lower leaves of young plants. As the leaves age, the spots turn into circular, dark-brown sunken necrotic lesions surrounded by light yellow halo and bear conidiophores and conidia in concentric rings at the greyish-white centre giving them a target board appearance (Fig. 2.1). Under congenial weather, the lesions enlarge, coalesce with each other resulting in chlorosis and defoliation of leaves due to the production of senescing promoting compounds like abscisic acid, N-methyl-2,5-dimethyl-N'-cinnamoyl-piperazine, and 3-carboxy-2-methylene-4-pentenyl-4-butenolide by *A. brassicae* (Dahiya *et al.* 1988; Dahiya & Tewari, 1991). Gradually, the disease progresses to the upper leaves, stems and pods (Fig. 2.2). The spots on young stems and green pods appear as black specks. On stem, they turn into dark-brown elongated lesions with pointed ends while on pod, they become round to elliptical and sunken but they rarely encircle the stem or pod. Normally, lesions are seen only on that surface of the stem or pod that

Fig. 2.1. *A. brassicae* lesions on a leaf of *B. juncea*

Fig. 2.2. *A. brassicae* lesions on seed pods of *B. campestris* var. Yellow sarson

mostly faces the air currents (Fig. 2.3). The greyish-white centre of mature lesions becomes laden with dark spore mass to disseminate the disease within and between the fields. Late winter rains coinciding with pod maturation stage increase pod infection and this is more important than leaf infection in reducing seed yield (Chahal & Kang, 1979b; Dey, 1948; Stankova, 1972).

Infected pods show pre-mature ripening, they shrink and shatter easily. Seeds, particularly those directly below the pod-surface lesions show dark-brown spots on seed coat, become under sized, deformed, discoloured and infected. Such seeds, when peeled show dark-brown speaks on their cotyledons. Alternaria infection increases green seed counts in *B. rapa* (Seidel *et al.* 1995).

Alternaria blight results in both quantitative and qualitative losses in yield, and the extent of reduction depends upon the severity of attack, the crop species and variety involved. In India, the commercial cultivars of *B. juncea* are comparatively more tolerant to *A. brassicae* than the cultivars of *B. campestris* var. Brown sarson, *B. campestris* var. Toria and *B. campestris* var. Yellow sarson (Butler, 1918; Hussain & Thakur, 1963). The reduction in yield due to the disease has been differently reported from different locations. Losses in seed yield may be upto 71 per cent (Chahal &

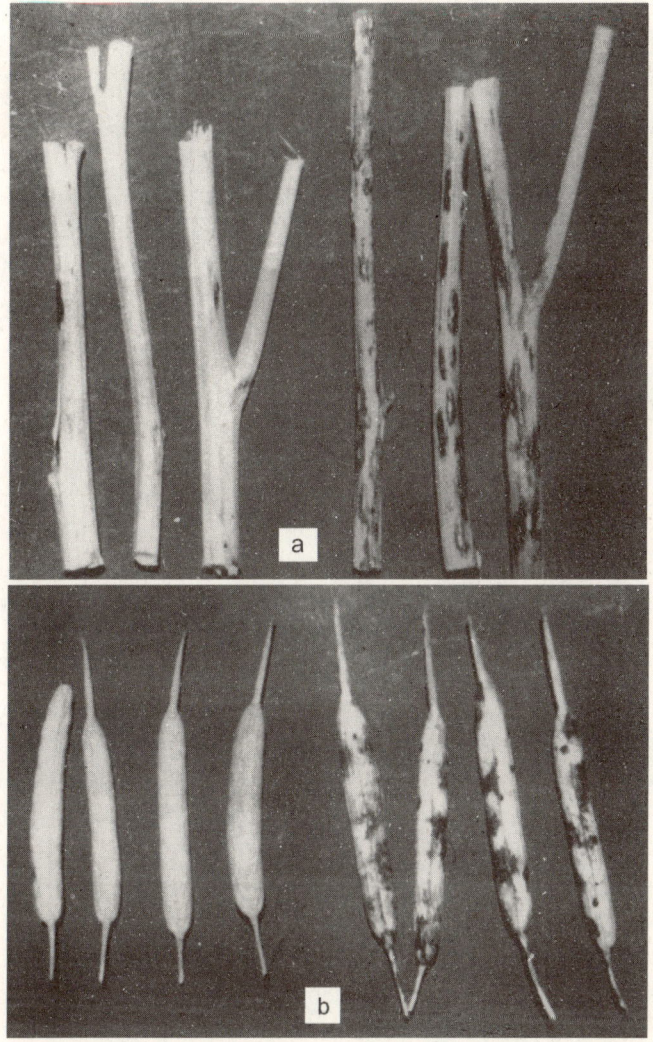

Fig. 2.3. *A. brassicae* lesions on (a) stem and (b) pod surface of *B. campestris* var.
Yellow sarson exposed to air currents

Sekhon, 1980; Kolte *et al.* 1987; Singh & Bhowmik, 1985; Shivanna & Sawhney, 1993). Infected seeds show poor germinability, and loss in oil and protein content (Bandopadhyay *et al.* 1974; Chahal & Kang, 1979c; Degenhardt *et al.* 1974; Nijhawan & Hussain, 1964; Vasudeva, 1958). The extent of reduction in seed oil content also varies with the crop species and variety involved, reduction is higher in rapeseed than in Indian mustard, and varied between 4.7 and 36%, and 2 and 29%, respectively (Ansari *et al.* 1988a; Kaushik *et al.* 1984). According to Stovold *et al.* (1987), the quality of rapeseed samples is not affected by the levels of seed borne *A. brassicae* but recent reports [AICRP (R&M). 1996; Gupta *et al.* 1998a] indicate change in the fatty acid composition of Brassica seeds.

2.2.1.2 The pathogens

Alternaria brassicae is found in the host tissues underlying the lesions, in the pod cavity and around the seed. The hyphae are intercellular, olive brown to dark olive buff, septate and measure 3-8 µm in diameter. After a limited growth within the host tissue, the hyphae collect in stromatic masses and give rise to conidiophores which pierce through the epidermis usually in bundles. On natural media, they are simple, erect, flexuous, measure 10-48 × 6-13 µm, often geniculate and show conidial scars. Conidia are solitary, rarely in chains of 2-3, obclavate, mostly straight with a very long beak, pale to dark olive buff, measure 37-147 × 9-23 µm with 3-18 transverse septa, and 0-15 longitudinal septa. The beak is 9-148 × 3.75 µm, often show 1-2 scars and 0.7 transverse septa. Total length of the spore is 39-356 µm (Butler, 1918; Neergaard, 1945). At Delhi, Munde (1983) recorded conidia on host surface measuring 104-128 × 11-17 µm, transverse septa 8.6-9.0, longitudinal septa 3-3.7 and beak length 25-32 µm. *Alternaria brassicae* makes slow growth in artificial media and there is gradual decline in its growth rate and sporulation with the passage of time. Culture preserved under mineral oil showed good growth and sporulation even after 10 months. Non-sporulating isolates of *A. brassicae* is induced to sporulate when grown on Richards medium supplemented with nicotinic acid (0.1 mg/litre) and glycine (0.15 mg/litre) (Sharma & Singh, 1994).

Occurrence of *A. brassicae* in distinct virulent races has been reported (Awasthi & Kolte, 1989; Mridha, 1983; Saharan & Kadian, 1983a), but in the absence of information on nuclear behaviour of the pathogen during spore delimitation and on genetic make up of nucleus in conidial cells in respect to pathogenicity, it is difficult to confirm whether virulence is a stable character with these isolates.

The hyphae of *A. brassicicola* in the host tissues are intercellular, olivaceous grey or black, septate and measure 1.5-7.5 µm in diameter. The conidiophores emerge through the stomata singly or in bundles of 2-12 or more, 0-3 septate, basal cell somewhat swollen, olivaceous grey, straight or curved, branch rarely, geniculation not always distinct, usually with a terminal scar and sometimes with lateral scars, and measure 20-70 × 5-8 µm. Conidia arise through pores in conidiophore wall, straight, pale to dark olivaceous brown, smooth or finely warted, cylindrical to oblong, muriform without beak and are borne in chains of 8-10 or more. Conidia measure 45-55 × 11-16 µm with 5-8 transverse septa and 0-6 longitudinal septa. The total spore length is 45-55 µm (Changstri & Weber, 1963; Holiday, 1981; Wiltshire, 1947). In artificial media, it grows faster than *A. brassicae* producing black mycelial colony and huge spore mass.

2.2.1.3 Perpetuation

Alternaria blight pathogens of oilseed brassicas are seed borne (Humpherson-Jones & Maude, 1983; McDonald, 1959; Petrie, 1975). Alternaria may remain confined on the coat of mature seeds but when infection occurs at an early stage of maturation, both *A. brassicae* and *A. brassicicola* may reach the deeper seed tissue and penetrate the embryo (Maude & Humpherson-Jones, 1980; Prasanna, 1993). According to Sharma *et al.* (1997), *A. brassicicola* is both extra- and intraembryonal in mustard seeds, the mycelium is found in all parts of discoloured, both bold and shrivelled seeds. They survive on crop and weed hosts, and on infected plant debris in soil. *Alternaria brassicae* attacks all the species of Cruciferae family and the two non-cruciferous plant species, *Godetia hybrida* and *Lactuca sativa* (Neergaard, 1945). Both *A. brassicae* and *A. brassicicola* infect the same cruciferous plants (Huang & Chung, 1993), neither of them is host-specific and cross infection occurs between different crops (Humpherson-Jones *et al*. 1983).

In temperate region, the primary infection arises from sowing of infected seeds or from spores arising from diseased plant debris or forage or vegetable brassicas (Davies, 1986). *Alternaria brassicae* and *A. brassicicola* remained viable on infected leaves of oilseed rape and cabbage for 9-12 weeks, till their tissues remained intact, and on their stem pieces upto 23 weeks in out doors on soil under UK conditions (Humpherson-Jones, 1989).

In India, *A. brassicae* possibly survives on both cultivated and wild species of crucifers. It also survives on weeds like *Anagallis arvensis* L., *Convolvulus arvensis* L. (Saharan *et al*. 1982) and *Chenopodium album* L. (Tripathi & Kaushik, 1984). Seed-borne inoculum does not seem to be important for its survival under our sub-tropical climate as the pathogen loses viability within a few months of storage at room temeprature after harvest (Bhowmik, 1980; Chahal, 1981; Kolte, 1980; Shivpuri & Siradhana, 1989; Tripathi & Kaushik, 1984). *Alternaria brassicae* was eliminated in 75 days from seeds and in 45 days from infected leaf and stem pieces when kept out doors while at 21°C, it was eliminated from stem pieces in 120 days, and from seeds and leaf pieces in 165 days indicating that they are unlikely to play any role in perpetuation of the pathogen during non-crop season in north Indian plains (Bhowmik, 1980). It may, however, survive in infected host materials at cooler places in higher altitudes since seed infection was reduced but not eliminated under cold storage (5 ± 2°C) condition during March-July (Shivpuri & Siradhana, 1989; Vishnuavat *et al*. 1985).

Alternarias produce resistant bodies like chlamydospores and micro-sclerotia to survive under adverse conditions (Vaartnou & Tewari, 1972). Transformation of *A. brassicae* conidia into micro-sclerotial bodies was reported by Tsuneda and Skoropod (1977). They were mostly found on partly decayed infected host tissues, which on germination give out new crop of conidia to disseminate the pathogen. Role of such bodies in the perpetuation of leaf blight pathogens has not been determined in India.

2.2.1.4 Epidemiology

The initiation of Alternaria blight starts with primary infection of cotyledonary and lower leaves which remain moist with dew during early hours of the day and these in turn act as the source of inoculum for its secondary infection. The relative humidity (RH) during this period of crop growth was found to range between 46-96 per cent during the day and 73-92 per cent during the night at Lucknow, UP (Wadhani & Dudeja, 1982).

Alternaria brassicae enters the leaves through stomatal opening and the newly formed spots bear spores in 3-4 days after infection (Butler, 1918). *Altenraria brassicicola* enters the host directly, by forming appressoria (Huang & Chung, 1993). The conditions necessary for conidial germination and infection of the host by these two pathogens have been differently reported from different places but these are not of great significance epidemiologically.

The optimum temperature for germination of conidia of *A. brassicae* is 20-23°C (Munde, 1983; Ansari *et al*. 1988) and that of *A. brassicicola,* 22-32°C (Sarkar & Sengupta, 1978) in artificial media. In general, *A. brassicicola* requires about 4°C higher temperature than *A. brassicae* for optimum growth (Huang & Chung, 1993). Probably, it is because of this higher temeprature requirement, that *A. brassicicola* is more common on end-season lesions than on those formed earlier (Degenhardt *et al*. 1982). Both *A. brassicae* and *A. brassicicola* require free water with optimum temperature of 15°C and 25°C, respectively for infection of cabbage plants. A minimum of 16 h is required for initiation of infection and 48-72 h for optimum disease development (Humpherson-Jones *et al*. 1983).

Sporulation in *A. brassicae* and *A. brassicicola* on naturally infected leaf discs of oilseed rape and cabbage requires RH $\geq$ 91.5 and 87 per cent, respectively. The optimum temperature for sporulaion is 18-24°C for *A. brassicae*, and 20-30°C for *A. brassicicola* at which temperature both the pathogens produce spores in 12-14 hours. Above 24°C, sporulation in *A. brassicae* is inhibited. Interrupting a 16 h wet period at 20°C with a dry period of 2 h at 70 or 80 per cent RH does not affect sporulation in either fungus but a dry interruption of 3 to 4 h inhibits sporulaion in both. Exposure of both fungi to alternating wet (18h at 100 per cent RH, 20°C) and dry periods (6 or 30h at 55-65 per cent RH, 20°C) does not affect the concentration of spores produced in each wet period. Sporulation times are not affected by either the host type or the age of the host tissue (Humpherson-Jones & Phelps, 1989). Alternate light and darkness is better for growth than continuous light or complete darkness (Ansari *et al*. 1989).

Susceptibility of oilseed brassicas to *A. brassicae* increases with plant age, prevailing temperature and duration of host surface wetness (Chahal, 1986a; Hong & Fitt, 1995; Mridha & Wheeler, 1993). According to Sinha and co-workers (1992), the disease intensity increased with the age of rapeseed and mustard plants, from a low on 21d old plants to highest on 71d old plants. Maximum leaf disease severity is seen during rosette and flowering stage of the crop (Awasthi & Kolte, 1994). On older leaves of oilseed rape (*B. napus*), infection was optimum at 25°C. On pods most infections were observed at 20°C, the highest temperature studied. The duration of minimum-wetness period required for infection of leaves and pods is longer at lower temperature than at higher temperature. A minimum wetness period of 4h was needed for infection by *A. brassicae* at 18°C and increase in the duration of wetness upto 12h increased disease severity. On leaves, dry periods interrupting wet periods limited lesion development to that obtained with initial wet peiod only, but on pods some further infections developed when pods were re-wetted (Mridha & Wheeler, 1993). In rapeseed and mustard, a 16-24 h period of leaf wetness is necessary at critical temperature of 25°C for high blight infection (Kadian & Saharan, 1984).

The concentration of inoculum also influences the disease incidence. The incidence of the disease on pods of spring rape, *B. napus* (cv. Starlight) increased as the inoculum concentration was increased from 80 to 104 spores/ml, further increase in inoculum concentration inceased only the severity of disease but not its incidence (percentage of pods diseased). The incubation period decreased as infection and incubation temperature increased from 6 to 20°C. The incubation period also decreased as wetness period increased from 2 to 12 h, as inoculum concentration increased from 80 to 2×10^3 spores/ml and as leaf age increased from 4 to 10d. The incubation period usually decreased sharply with increasing lesion density (Hong & Fitt, 1995, 1996).

In a study on seasonal and diurnal variations in microbial populations of the air during 1973-74 winter at Agra, India, the spores of *A. brassicae* and *A. brassicicola* were detected over the Brown sarson field from October to April, the entire period of crop growth. Their maximum populations were detected during the month of March, coinciding with maximum manifestation of the disease in the field. The maximum populations of these propagules were trapped, either in the afternoon or at noon, which appeared to be the effect of low humidity and high temperature whereas their minimum concentration was noted either at mid night or in the early morning (Sharma & Gupta, 1978).

Foggy weather is generally followed by severe Alternaria blight attacks in India (Butler, 1918). There is a positive correlation between weather factors and disease progress. Severe blight disease is associated with low temperature (minimum 2-12°C, maximum 16-26°C), high RH (80-96 per cent), average rainfall of 30 mm and wind velocity of 2-6 km/h (Dang *et al.* 1995; Sinha *et al.* 1992). According to Chahal and Kang (1979b), and Chahal (1982), average temperature of 18°C, prevalence of frequent rains, atmospheric humidity of 80 per cent or above, stormy weather coupled with high wind velocity during flowering and pod formation stage led to the development of the disease in epiphytotic form at Ludhiana, Punjab, India.

2.2.1.5 *Alternaria brassicae* toxin

Indications about the possible role of a toxin produced by *A. brassicae* inciting leaf blight of rape-seed and mustard came from Hussain and Thakur (1966) when they reported that the culture filtrates of the pathogen induce severe wilting beside causing water soaked spots in Yellow mustard cuttings within 12h. The culture filtrate increased the permeability of host cells and loss of electrolytes (Dube *et al.* 1980). According to Degenhardt (1978), the semipurified preparation of culture filtrates contain two groups of non-specific toxins which cause disease symptoms in leaves. Later, a purified preparation of the toxin was obtained which tested host-specific and was found identical to the cyclodepsipeptide destruxin B (Ayer & Pena-Rodriguez, 1987; Bains & Tewari, 1987), reported earlier from the culture filtrates of *A. brassicae* (Pena-Rodriguez, 1985). Both the fungus and the toxin cause symptoms of different severities on different Brassicas, ranging from severe chlorosis and necrosis to almost no visible chlorosis. The order of sensitivity of different Brassicas to the phytotoxin is similar to their order of susceptibility to *A. brassicae* (Bains & Tiwari, 1987).

The phytotoxin destruxin B of *A. brassicae* was not found host-specific on 30 different plant species tested. It caused necrotic and chlorotic symptoms both on host and non-host plants. But there were significant differences between taxonomic plant groups in their sensitivity to destruxin B. Brassica spp. were most sensitive to the toxin, and sensitivity decreased as relatedness of plant groups became more distant. No genotype within the Brassica species has been found specifically sensitive to destruxin B suggesting it to be host-selective in nature. It is considered to be a virulent factor that contributes to the aggressiveness of the pathogen by conditioning the host tissue and thereby determining the susceptibility of the host (Buchwaldt & Green, 1992).

Two other destruxins viz., homodestruxin B (Ayer & Pena-Rodriguez, 1987) and destruxin B_2 (Buchwaldt & Jensen, 1991) elaborated by *A. brassicae*, are also phytotoxic to leaves of oilseed rape. Like destruxin B, homodestruxin B also causes symptoms of different severities on leaves of various non-host plant species and therefore, is non-host specific in nature (Bains *et al.* 1993).

A plant growth regulator antagonistic to dextruxin B is found in *B. napus* leaves infected with *A. brassicae* (Agarwal *et al.* 1994).

2.2.1.6 Resistance

Among the cultivated oleiferous Brassicas, the digenomic species, especially *B. carinata* exhibits high resistance to diseases incited by fungi. Even though a high level of resistance to Alternaria blight is rare in cultivated species, the existence of wide inter- and intraspecific variations in reaction to the disease is a common feature. Lesion type and sporulation capacity seem to indicate the levels of resistance (Fig. 2.4a, b) in Brassica spp. (Bansal *et al.* 1990; Bhowmik & Munde, 1987; Kolte, 1987; Saharan & Kadian, 1983b; Sharma & Singh, 1992a). Based on these characteristics, Bhowmik and Munde (1987) defined four broad reaction types of Brassica species towards *A. brassicae,* and their general rank in order of most to least resistance is: *B. carinata* and *B. napus* > *B. tournefortii, B. nigra* and *B. fructiculosa* > *B. juncea* > *B. campestris* spp. *oleifera* (vars. Brown sarson, Toria and Yellow sarson) (Table 2.2). According to Sharma and Singh (1992a), out of *B. juncea, B. carinata, B. napus, B. rapa* and *B. hirta*, the latter has high degree of resistance as is evident from small spot size and minimum sporulation on both the surfaces of spot and absence of yellow halo. Intra-varietal differences in both lesion size and sporulation are also commonly discernable.

Resistance to *A. brassicae* in crucifers is layered and multicomponent (Tewari, 1991). *Alternaria brassicae* shows no difference in its interaction with resistant and susceptible hosts at

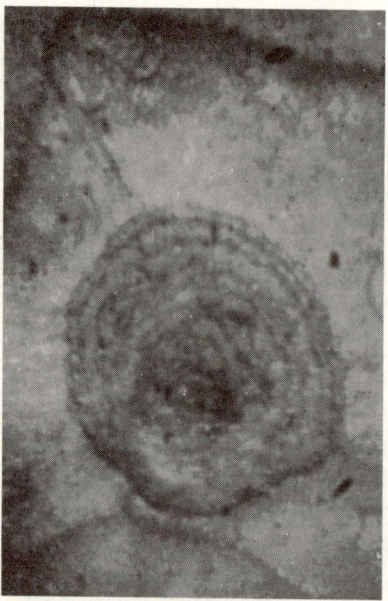 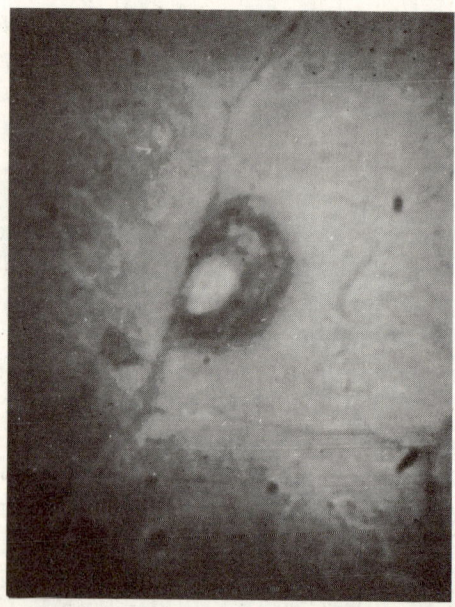

Fig. 2.4. (a) A susceptible lesion with concentric zonations on a leaf of *B. juncea* (cv. Pusa Bold) caused by *A. brassicae*

Fig. 2.4. (b) A resistant lesion with pigmented halo on a leaf of *B. napus* (str. art.) caused by *A. brassicae*

the early stages of infection. The histology of *A. brassicae* infection in leaves of susceptible *B. campestris* cv. Candle and moderately susceptible *B. napus* cv. Alex is similar, the pathogen becomes sub-cuticular after direct penetration and then colonizes the epidermal and mesophyll cells indicating that differential susceptibility of cultivars does not reside in the early stages of host-pathogen interaction (Tewari, 1986). The percentage conidial germination does not also vary significantly for any Alternaria pathogens of Brassica species between the host and non-host plants. The pathogens are affected by interactions occurring at the plant surface and inhibition of conidial germination is not a feature of resistance in oilseed brassicas (McRoberts & Lennard, 1991).

The presence of epicuticular wax in some cultivars of *B. napus* and *B. oleracea* var. *alboglabra* confers a physical type of resistance to *A. brassicae* (Munde & Bhowmik, 1985; Tewari & Skoropod, 1976). Wax layer being hydrophobic, may affect conidial germination by impeding movement of foliar exudates to surface, by preventing water droplets to stay on the leaf surface beside providing a sort of mechanical barrier to the invading pathogen but it has apparently no effect on the pathogen after its entry into the host (Berry & Lennard, 1988; Conn & Tewari, 1989; Munde & Bhowmik, 1985; Skoropod & Tewari, 1977).

Plants more distantly related to cuciferous species are often resistant to Alternaria blight (Conn *et al.* 1988; Tewari *et al.* 1987). *Sinapis alba* (*B. alba*), accessions of *Eruca sativa, Camelina sativa, Capsella bursa-pastoris* and *Neslia peniculata* possess high degree of resistance to *A. brassicae. Eruca sativa* exhibits a hyper sensitive type of reaction against infection by *A. brassicae* (Bhander & Maini, 1965; Brun *et al.* 1987a; Conn *et al.* 1988; Downey & Rimmer, 1993; Grontoft, 1986; Tewari & Conn, 1993). Both *C. sativa* and *C. bursa-pastoris* produce phytoalexins following inoculation with conidial suspension of the pathogen (Conn *et al.* 1988). *Camelina sativa* produces phytoalexin even when very few conidia are deposited on leaves. The phytoalexin accumulates within leaf areas under and in conidial droplets. The rapid rate of phytoalexin accumulation shortly after inoculation is considered responsible for inhibition of fungal growth on the leaf surfaces (Jejelowo *et al.* 1991). Two thiazoyl substituted indole phytoalexins, camalexin ($C_{11}N_8N_2S$) and 6-methoxycamalexin ($C_{12}H_{10}N_2SO$) are produced in leaves of *C. sativa* following elicitation by the pathogen (Browne *et al.* 1991).

Capsella bursa-pastoris elicits Camalexin, 6-methyoxycamalexin and N-methylcamalexin ($C_{12}H_{10}N_2S$) upon infection by the pathogen (Jimenez *et al.* 1997). Similarly, *A. brassicae* or its phytotoxin, destruxin B may induce production of the phytoalexin, "sinalexin" in *S. alba* (*B. alba*) for resistance to the pathogen (Pedras & Smith, 1997). It is believed that qualitative and/or quantitative differences in elicitation of phytoalexin may account for differences in resistance observed in plants (Conn *et al.* 1988).

Young brassica plants show a high degree of resistance to *A. brassicae* but they become susceptibile with age (Chahal, 1986a; Sarkar & Sengupta, 1978). Quantitative measurements of necrosis in leaf and pod tissue of oilseed rape after inoculation with *A. brassicae* and *A. brassicicola* showed that active defence mechanisms are involved in young tissue and susceptibility of plants to infection increases greatly by senescence and physiological stress. This was also evident from the fact that field application of BAS 11104 W, a growth regulator of the triozole group, retarded the aging of rape tissue and delayed infection by Alternaria spp. (Kohle & Hoffman, 1989). The changes in glucosinolate content in leaves of oilseed rape following infection by *A. brassicae* may restrict the spread of existing infection or inhibit subsequent attempted infections, especially in younger leaves. It has been observed that *B. campestris* (*B. rapa*) seedlings release alkenyl isothiocyanates for catabolism of glucosinolates during infection, which is a pre-requisite for their involvement in resistance to the invading pathogen (Doughty *et al*. 1991, 1996).

Resistance to *A. brassicae* in some Brassica genotypes has been associated with quantitative changes in certain biochemical compounds following infection. According to Munde (1983), one *B. napus* (art.) strain resistant to blight, recorded higher total phenols, polyphenol and peroxidase activities, higher content of free amino acids and sugars than its susceptible counterpart, *B. napus* (BO-54) strain, following inoculation with *A. brassicae*. The resistant strain showed higher accumulation of anthocyanins in the halo area surrounding the disease lesion and had scanty sporulation. Similar changes in the levels of total phenols, sugars, nitrogen and ascorbic acid, etc. in rapeseéd and mustard cultivars following infection with *A. brassicae* have been also correlated with their resistance or susceptibility to the disease by other workers (Begum *et al*. 1993; Chattopadhyay, 1989; Gupta *et al*. 1984, 1995b).

The *A. brassicae* tolerant *B. juncea* cultivars RC-781, PHR-1 and KRV-tall have violet coloured leaves. The cv. Pusa Bold with normal leaves is susceptible to *A. brassicae*. In F$_1$ populations derived from non-coloured (cv. Pusa Bold) × coloured (cv. RC 781) parents, only the coloured individuals showed more tolerance to infection (Bhowmik, 1984, 1985a). This may be due to higher levels of total phenols, glucosinolates and sugars in leaves of RC 781 compared to that in susceptible cultivar, like Varuna (Garg *et al*. 1999; Gupta *et al*. 1998b).

Resistance to *A*. brassicae in cv. RC 781, is governed by a single dominant gene (Tripathi *et al*. 1980). Saharan and Kadian (1983b) reproted high horizontal resistance in cultivars, Tower and RC 781. Sharma and Singh (1992b) transferred resistance to *A. brassicae* in *B. juncea* through interspecific hybridization and ovary culture technique on modified MS-medium. Hybrids of *B. juncea* × *B. hirta*, *B. juncea* × *B. napus* and *B. juncea* × *B. rapa* showed the same resistant reaction to *A. brassicae* as their respective male parents. Interspecific transfer of the *S. alba* resistance into *B. napus* was affected by manual pollination using reciprocal crosses and by somatic hybridization from protoplast fusion. Subsequently, embryo rescue and cytogenetic analysis led to the generation of normal *B. napus* plants with resistance to *A. brassicae* similar to that of *S. alba* (Chevre *et al*. 1991). Katiyar and Chamola (1994), on the other hand, transferred *A. brassicae* resistance from a *B. carinata* accession to the susceptible *B. juncea* cv. Varuna by interspecific hybridization and continuous selection. This led to the isolation of a fully fertile and productive genotype which was superior in resistance to all other commercial mustard varieties tested under natural incidence of *A. brassicae* in the field. The feasibility of transferring disease resistance genes of the wild *B. maurorum* Dur. to the cultivated *B. juncea* plants was reported by Bijral and co-workers (1995).

Cytoplasm also plays a role in conferring resistance to *A. brassicae* in *Brassica* spp. Alloplasmic lines of *B. juncea* having cytoplasm of either *B. napus* or *B. carinata* are comparatively more resistant to leaf blight under field conditions than euplasmic lines. On the other hand, *B. juncea* lines with cytoplasm of *B. rapa* (*B. campestris*) are more susceptible (Banga *et al*. 1984).

Synthetic *B. napus* developed by chromosome duplication of *B. campestris* × *B. oleracea* displayed resistance to both Alternaria and white rust diseases (Prakash & Raut, 1983a,b). Mutants of

B. juncea induced by exposign the cvs. Varuna, PR 5 and RS 3 to 60 kr gamma rays had resistance to both *A. brassicae* and *A. brassicicola* (Verma & Rai, 1980). Similarly, mutants recovered from M_2 populations of *B. juncea* cvs. Varuna and Kranti following mutations, were resistant to Alternaria (Sharma, 1990).

However, in the absence of major genes for resistance to *A. brassicae* in crucifers, it will be prudent to concentrate dispersed minor genes through techniques like diallel selective mating system besides attempting to incorporate non-host type of resistance in cultivated oilseed brassicas [AICRP (R&M). 1996]. The latter is a difficult task but the use of conventional breeding methods, mutation, polyploidy and biotechniques/genetic engineering may provide the desired result.

2.2.1.7 *Evaluation of germplasm*

Evaluation of germplasm lines for resistance to *A. brassicae* is usually made on the basis of disease ratings following artificial inoculation with the pathogen isolate and comparing the results with ratings obtained in the field from natural infection/and with supplementary artificial inoculation.

a. *Disease rating scale*

Brassica cultivars are rated for disease intensity by assigning arbitrary numerical scores on 0-5 rating scale where, 0 = no lesion and 5 = 50 per cent or more leaf area damaged (AICORPO. 1984; Bhowmik & Munde, 1987; Conn *et al.* 1990; Hussain & Thakur, 1963; Rai *et al.* 1976). The disease index is calculated by the formula (Townsend & Heuberger, 1943),

$$\text{Disease Index} = \frac{\text{Sum of all numerical ratings}}{\text{No. of leaves examined} \times \text{Maximum rating score}} \times 100$$

The numerical scale is essentially based on the extent of leaf area damaged, which is primarily related to the quantity of spores deposited on its surface at a particular point of time. This type of visual scale is useful only at the initial stage of screening in discarding the highly susceptible materials,but classification of cultivars into various disease reaction categories on the basis of such scale is not comparable and does not give a reliable estimate of their reaction to the disease (Bhowmik & Munde, 1987). Hong and Fitt (1995) also noted increasing number of lesions/cm^2 (severity) of dark leaf spot with the increase in inoculum concentration.

Bhowmik and Munde (1987) defined four reaction groups for Brassica cultivars towards *A. brassicae* on the basis of lesion type and sporulation capacity. Using these criteria, the degree of resistance of cultivars could be identified reliably (Table 2.2).

b. *Screening techniques*

Screening techniques usually employed to identify sources of resistance to *A. brassicae* are:

i. Screening at the cotyledonary stage Seeds are sown on small pots or trays filled with compost-mixed garden soil. The cotyledons of young seedlings are wounded on the seventh or eighth day of seeding with a sterile needle or pin. Using a 10 microlitre pipette, a 10 μl drop of inoculum of *A. brassicae* (5×10^4 conidia/ml) made from a freshly isolated culture of the pathogen

Table 2.2. Reaction of Brassica species to Alternaria blight caused by *A. brassicae*.

Reaction category	Nature of lesions[1]	Size (mm)	Sporulation/ml
Highly resistant			
B. carinata Br.	Dark brown or black specks with liver brown to carob brown halo.	< 0.50	$< 2 \times 10^4$
B. napus L.(Str. art.)	Leaves turn coppery red with age in *B. napus*		
Resistant			
B. tournefortii Goun *B. nigra* (L.) Koch	Round necrotic spots with ash-grey centre and light yellowish-brown halo.	< 0.50 to 1.00	$> 2 \times 10^4$ to 5×10^4
B. fructiculosa Cyr.	Halo deep violet in *B. tournefortii*		
Susceptible			
B. juncea (L.) Czern.	Round to circular necrotic spots with ash-grey centre and concentric zonations; halo light chlorotic; slow spreading	> 1.00 to 1.50	$> 5 \times 10^4$ to 15×10^4
Highly susceptible			
B. campestris ssp. *oleifera* (Metzg.) Sinsk. (vars. Brown sarson, Toria, Yellow sarson)	Lesion same as above; halo deep chlorotic; fast spreading	> 1.50	$> 15 \times 10^4$

[1]Colour according to Ridgeway (1912).
Source: Bhowmik and Munde (1987).

is placed over the wound of each cotyledon. Inoculated seedlings are transferred to growth chambers at 18°C, 80% relative humidity and 14 h light, and are rated for disease development after 2-4 days. Seedling reaction highly correlates with adult plant reaction. The technique is very useful for rapid screening of large population at the early stage without sacrificing the test plants (Brun *et al.* 1987; McNabb *et al.* 1993).

ii. Screening with detached leaves   Fully expanded fourth leaves from 3-week old plants of the test cultivars are placed on a small tray lined with moist paper towel. A small hole of about 3 mm diameter is made on either side of the mid-rib of each leaf with a sterile needle. A drop of conidial suspension made from young culture of *A. brassicae* and mixed with Rose Bengal (0.4 mg/l), is placed over each wound. The tray is sealed and then incubated at room temeprature under continuous light for lesion development. Observations on lesion diameter and halo are taken on the fourth day following inoculation (Bansal *et al.* 1990; Gugel *et al.* 1990).

iii. In-vitro selection of pollen grains   The effects of the toxin destruxin B of *A. brassicae* is tested on *in-vitro* pollen germination and pollen-tube growth of Brassica species to ascertain their relative sensitivity to the toxin. The effects of the toxin are also seen on leaves of the host species, and the degree of sensitivity of leaves of different species is comparable to that of their pollen grains. The results on the responses of pollen grains and leaves to the toxin agree with the degree of susceptibility/resistance of these species to *A. brassicae* determined earlier in the field. The technique offers a simple and effective method of application of selection pressure to eliminate pollen grains susceptible to the toxin for effecting fertilization (Shivanna & Sawhney, 1993).

iv. Screening of young plants   Test plants are raised in small pots. A hole of about 4 mm diameter is made on either side of the mid-rib of the second leaf of each plant. Small agar disc contianing *A. brassicae* is placed with the infected side against the upper side of the leaf over one hole, the other hole serves as control. The inoculated plants are transferred into moist chamber maintaining high humidity for symptom development. Disease reaction is rated by the size of the lesion developed (Grontoft & O'Connor, 1990).

Another efficient method of evaluation is to raise plants in 25 cm pots, four in each and five pots for every test cultivar. Plants when 60 days old, are inoculated uniformly with equal amounts of inoculum (10 ml) of *A. brassicae* and then incubated in moist chambers for 48 hrs. The minimum and maximum temperature, and relative humidity during the experimental period are maintained between 9-16°C and 80-100 per cent, respectively. Data on the nature and size of lesions developed · on the lower 4th to 6th leaves, and their sporulation are taken to assess the reaction of cultivars (Bhowmik & Munde, 1987).

v. Screening of adult plants   Germplasm lines are exposed to heavy disease pressure under natural conditions in the field. Sowing is usually done towards the third week of October under north Indian conditions in 10-15 m long rows, keeping 30-40 cm between rows and 10-15 cm between plants depending upon the growth habit of cultivars. A highly susceptible cultivar such as the Yellow sarson cv. YS-8 (*Brassica compestris* var. Yellow sarson) is grown at regular intervals between the test cultivars as infector rows, and around the experimental area as border rows. The disease, which normally appears on the lower leaves towards the first week of January, develops in severe epiphytotic form by mid-February, when the reaction of cultivars is rated (Bhowmik & Munde, 1987). To ensure high disease development, one or two extra irrigations and artificial inoculation may also be needed. The inoculum for artificial inoculation is prepared from a 10 d old growth of *A. brassicae* in nutrient medium or from washings of Alternaria infected leaves (Tripathi *et al*. 1980).

Screening of Brassica germplasm under the AICORPO is carried out at multilocational disease nurseries using uniform procedures of sowing, and interplanting a highly susceptible cultivar at regular intervals as infector rows. Rating of leaf infection is based on the average of three observations on 0-5 scale. Pod infection is also rated on 0-5 scale, about one week before a cultivar is harvested (AICORPO. 1990).

2.2.1.8 *Sources of resistance*

None of the improved commercial varieties of rapeseed and mustard released in India is resistant to major diseases (AICORPO. 1990). However, genotypes reported highly tolerant to *A. brassicae* under artificial inoculations are: *Brassica* (*Sinapis*) *alba*; *B. hirta*; *B. napus* lines Lethbridge,

Westar, WRG-1, Midas, HNS-3, UP 75-BN-5403, Target-84, Exotic-131 and *B. napus* (str. art.); *B. carinata* lines PC-3 and -5, BCON-1, CE-8 and -9, and PPSC-1; *B. tournefortii*; *B. nigra*; *B. oleracea* var. *alboglabra*; *B. fructiculosa*; *B. juncea* lines BC-115, CSR-448, DIRA-251, PHR-2, Zem-1, RC-781, RH-8312, RS-104, RSK-21, RW-5453, B-2, K-41732; and *B. campestris* lines Tobin and PYS-3 [AICORPO. 1988, 1990; AICRP (R&M). 1996; Bhowmik & Munde, 1987; Chahal & Jaura, 1994; Hussain & Thakur, 1963; Munde & Bhowmik, 1985; Saharan *et al*. 1981; Sharma & Singh, 1992a; Rai *et al*. 1976; Tripathi *et al*. 1980].

The cultivars Gulivar, Tower, GSL-1 and EC-126743 of *B. napus*; PC-5 and HC-1 of *B. carinata*; TM-7, TMV-2, YRT-3, KRV-Tall, PHR-1, Vardan, Saurabh, RC-1401, CSR-43, -142, -142-2, -343, -622 and -741, RH-8113 and -8114, and B-108(3) of *B. juncea*; and Torch, T-8 and -22, DYS-1 and Jata sarson of *B. campestris* have consistently performed tolerant to *A. brassicae* under field conditions over several years at different locations in the country [AICORPO. 1979-1993; AICRP (R&M). 1994-1996; Dikshit and Srivastava, 1991; Kolte, 1987; Saharan & Chand, 1988; S.C. Gulati, per. commun.)].

The *B. napus* cvs. Midas and Tower in Canada (Tewari & Skoropod, 1976), cvs. Norde and Vestal in Poland (Rozej, 1974); *B. juncea* cv. Picra, *B. carinata* cv. Awassa, *B. nigra* cv. Junius and the *Sinapis alba* cv. Emergo in France (Brun *et al*. 1989) have been reported resistant. In China, the *S. alba* cv. J-10 is immune to *A. brassicae* (Gong *et al*. 1994).

2.2.1.9 *Control*

A number of cultural practices or their modifications that are usually followed by farmers, a variety of chemical pesticides, and especially a suitable combination of agro-practices and chemicals may provide effective control of Alternaria blight.

a. *Cultural practices*

The field and its neighbourhood area should be cleared of weeds before taking up sowing operations. Sound and bold seeds of the recommended cultivar that are free from discoloured ones should only be sown. Usually, rapeseed and mustard sown by mid-October escapes severe attack of Alternaria blight in north India. In the eastern part, delay in sowing of Indian mustard by one month beyond 22nd October under West Bengal conditions increased the incidence of *A. brassicae* and *A. brassicicola* on leaves by 37 per cent and on pods by 31 per cent. The consequent reduction in seed yield was 38 per cent and that of seed oil content 14 per cent (Das Gupta, 1991).

Use of correct seed rate at sowing is also essential as crop density per unit area directly affects the disease incidence and yield. Results of field trials conducted during 1980-1982 seasons on the effect of plant density on disease intensity and crop yield, showed that an increase in plant population through a reduction in both inter- and intrarow distances, increases the disease intensity, reduces the per plant yield but increases the total per plot yield because of higher number of plants per unit area. Sowing of Yellow sarson cv. YS-8 at 30 × 10 cm inter- and intrarow spacings gave the highest per plot yield than other spacing combinations used, although this resulted in lowest per plant yield (Munde, 1983).

High fertilizer doses, especially of nitrogen increase the severity of Alternaria blight in oilseed rape (Stankova, 1972). In both pot and field experiments at Pantnagar, UP, rape plants (*B. campestris*) fertilized with potash (40 kg K_2O/ha) were resistant to lodging, and produced seeds with low infection, increased weight and germinability. Application of nitrogen and potash (90 kg N/ha + 40 kg K_2O/ha) decreased the disease severity and consistently increased the seed yield, 68 per cent more than those of control and other treatments (Sharma & Kolte, 1994). Significant reduction in disease severity and highest yield of mustard were obtained under field conditions at Faizabad, UP when NPK were used at 100:40:40 kg/ha along with three sprays of Indofil M-45 (Singh & Chauhan, 1997). In general, balanced fertilizer dose (N:P:K:: 40:40:80) coupled with prophylectic sprays of fungicide (eg. mancozeb) provide maximum increase in yield [AICRP (R&M). 1996].

b. Chemical control

With the ready availability of an array of highly effective broad spectrum pesticides over the past decades, the use of chemicals has become the most important component of pest management strategy in rapeseed and mustard.

Seed treatment with brassicol or captafol at 4 g/kg seeds (Chahal, 1982; Chahal & Sekhon, 1980; Saini, 1982), iprodione at 1.25g a.i./kg seeds (Stovold *et al.* 1987), bavistin (carbendazim) at 2.5 g/kg seeds or dithane-M 45 (mancozeb) at 2 g/kg seeds eradicate the seed borne infection of *A. brassicae*. At least 24 h storage period after their treatment is needed for effective eradication of infection (Kumar & Singh, 1986). Seed treatment ensures emergence of healthy seedlings in temperate countries with cooler climate such as in UK (Evans *et al.* 1984) but it is not essential under our sub-tropical climate as the seed borne inoculum of *A. brassicae* gets eliminated during storage in summer months.

Spray application of copper fungicides reduces the incidence of Alternaria blight of rapeseed and mustard. A minimum of four sprays with 0.5 per cent bordaux mixture are required to reduce the diease incidence and increase the crop yield significantly. Losses in seed yield were negligible when the disease intensity on pods was reduced to 10.7 per cent with six sprays of bordaux mixture (Chahal & Kang, 1979a). Copper oxychloride, cupravit, blitox or fytolan are also effective but phytotoxic (Howlider *et al.* 1985; Mridula *et al.* 1994; Shivpuri *et al.* 1988; Singh & Bhowmik, 1985). Chahal (1986b) reported the best cost/benefit ratio with copper oxychloride applied four times, spray starting when the crop was 75 days old.

Among the more popular chemicals, spraying with difolatan (captafol); dithane-M45, dithane-Z78 and cuman L(dithiocarbamates); bavistin (carbendazim); panolil (guazatin); baycor (bitertanol); syllit (dodecyl guanidine acetate); daconil (chlorothalonil); wettable sulphur; dueter (fentin hydroxide); fentin acetate; Topsin-M (thiophanate-methyl) and TPTH (triphenyl tin-hydroxide) at 0.2-0.25 per cent provide effective control of the disease and result significant increase in crop yield (Chahal, 1986b; Chahal & Sekhon, 1980; Chattopadhyay & Bagchi, 1994; Das Gupta, 1991; Gupta *et al.* 1997; Kaushik *et al.* 1983; Kolte *et al.* 1987; Mridula *et al.* 1994; Singh & Bhowmik, 1985; Tripathi *et al.* 1987).

In a comparative study on the persistence and efficacy of fungicides against *A. brassicae* on Indian mustard cv. Pusa Bold during 1978-80 crop seasons, Singh and Bhowmik (1985) found that fungicides which are more toxic are also more persistent on the host surface and that the rate of decline in their toxicity is more rapid in the beginning than afterwards. Out of eight fungicides tested, difolatan was the most persistent and effective in both reducing the disease intensity and increasing seed yield of plants. Dithane-M 45 was the next best. High efficacy of these two chemicals has also been confirmed from other field trials (AICORPO. 1986; Chattopadhyay & Bagchi, 1994; Gupta *et al.* 1985; Kaushik *et al.* 1983).

Iprodione is also highly effective. In a field trial during 1986-87 at Jaipur, India the efficacy of iprodione (rovral) against *A. brassicae* was compared with five other fungicides on Indian mustard cv. Varuna. All the chemicals controlled the disease but iprodione (0.2 per cent) was the best, though captafol, mancozeb (dithane-M 45), indofil M-45 (mancozeb + thiophenate methyl) and ridomil MZ (mancozeb + metalaxyl) were also highly effective. Iprodione caused minimum defoliation (Kumar, 1996; Shivpuri *et al.* 1988) and increased the crop yield by 20.2 and 10.0 per cent over control, respectively during 1991-92 and 1992-93 seasons. Seed oil content in iprodine treated crop was 39.37 per cent as compared to 36.75 per cent in control crop (Brar & Chahal, 1993). In spray trials at different locations in the country during 1994-96 seasons against Alternaria blight, iprodione (rovral 50 WDP) at 0.2 per cent was 15-60 per cent more effective over mancozeb (dithane-M 45) and resulted in corresponding yield increase of 6-35 per cent. The amount of residues of iprodione in edible commodity (seeds) was less than the recommended MRL (0.5 mg/kg) safety level [AICRP (R&M). 1995, 1996; Chatterjee *et al.* 1997].

Spray operatons with fungicides should be taken up with the first appearance of disease spots and then repeated two to three times at 10 to 15 days intervals depending upon the crop variety, its growth stage and the severity of infection (Chahal, 1986b; Chattopadhyay & Bagchi, 1994; Gupta *et al.* 1985; Kaushik *et al.* 1984; Tripathi *et al.* 1987). Post-flowering application of fungicides on pods is most important. It protects them from infection, increases seed yields and improves germination of harvested seeds (Chahal & Kang, 1979a; Humpherson-Jones & Maude, 1982; Ogilvy, 1984).

Integrated control of Alternaria blight and aphid (*Lipaphis erysimi*), the most serious insect pest of rapeseed and mustard, was achieved by treating the crop with fungicide (dithane M-45, difolatan, deconil 2787 and blitox) and insecticide (metasystox, rogor and dimecrone) mixture. A slight reduction in toxicity of metasystox against the insect pest took place when mixed with fungicides. Three applications of dithane M-45 (0-2 per cent) + metasystox (0.03 per cent) mixture on Indian mustard cv. Pusa Bold starting from 15th January at fortnightly intervals gave a very low intensity of both disease and aphid infestation, and the highest seed yield amongst the various spray treatments tried (Munde, 1983; Munde & Bhowmik, 1984; Tripathi *et al.* 1987).

2.2.2 White Rust

White rust, often called white blister is caused by the fungal pathogen, *Albugo candida* (Per.ex. Lev.) Kuntze. It is an important disease of cruciferous plants, both cultivated and wild, besides being found on members of Capparidaceae and Cleomaceae families (Walker, 1957). Parisi (1924) recorded it on *Onobrychis crista*, a member of the sub-family Papilionaceae. In India, it is found on turnip, cabbage, cauliflower, radish, horse radish, cress, *Brassica juncea*, *B. campestris*, *B. campestris* var. *glauca*, *B. napus*, *B. nigra*, *Capsella bursa-pastoris*, *Cleome viscosa*, *(Polanisia icosandra*), *Coronopus didyma, Eruca sativa, Merremia marginata, Nasturtium palustra, Sauss-urea lappu, Symbrium irio, Cardamine subumbelata*, (Butler, 1918; Damle, 1944; Singh *et al.* 1993), *B. tournefortii* and *B. carinata*. Singh (1989) reported it on *Amaranthus viridis*.

From India, white rust was first reported by Butler (1918) and then by Mitter and Tandon (1930), and others from different parts of the country. It was considered to be of little economic importance in the past (Choudhary, 1944; Chupp, 1925; Klemm, 1938; Loof, 1959; Mitter & Tandon, 1930) but in recent years it has gained the notoriety of being the most widespread and destructive disease of rapeseed and mustard in the country particularly in the north and north-western regions as compared to the eastern states of Bihar, Orissa, West Bengal and Assam, and other north-eastern states where Alternaria blight predominates.

2.2.2.1 Symptoms

The disease is first seen on lower leaves of plants towards the beginning of January in the field, shortly after the appearance of Alternaria blight. It rapidly spreads to upper leaves and other aerial parts of the plant. Two types of infection are seen, local and systemic.

Fig. 2.5. (a) White rust pustules on the under surface of a leaf of *B. juncea*

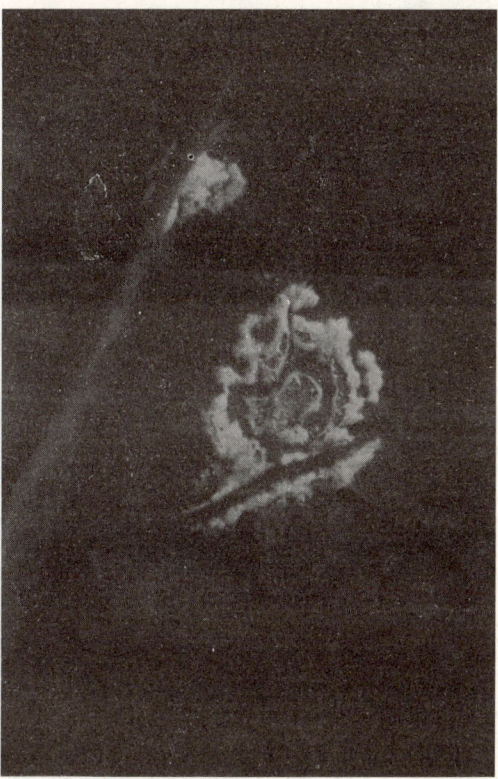

Fig. 2.5. (b) A single white rust sporangial pustule

Local infection is characterized by the formation of isolated raised creamy white sporangial pustules on leaves, tender shoots and on green siliquae, and these often coalesce into patches (Fig. 2.5a, b). Generally, the pustules are first formed on the undersurface of leaves, while the corresponding areas on upper surface become tan-yellow, constituting one of the chief diagnostic symptom of the disease. Later, pustules appear on the upper leaf surface. In resistant hosts, more pustules first appear on the upper leaf surface than on the lower surface, a distinctive trait of such plants (Verma, 1987). When the pustule matures, the host epidermis ruptures exposing the white powdery spore mass, which are carried away by air currents to cause fresh infection. Several crop of these spores may be formed from a single pustule. As the pustule ages and the affected leaves are about to beome senescent, necrosis sets-in around and in the pustule.

Systemic infection of white rust is mostly seen in tender shoots and young inflorescence. The pathogen stimulates hypertrophy and hyperplasia resulting in abnormal swelling and malformation of affected organs. Affected stem may become swollen up to a considerable length and show conspicuous bending due to unequal expansion in one side. When the inflorescence is affected, it turns into what is called as staghead. Floral organs turn green, become greatly enlarged and distorted, and seed formation is prevented (Butler, 1918). Pods, if formed, become curved or twisted, and contain fewer but bolder seeds (Fig. 2.6a, b). According to Bisht and co-workers (1994), staghead incidence and severity are highly correlated with days to flowering and maturity, and are greater on late-flowering and late-maturity genotypes. Maximum staghead formation was obtained in 26d old *B. juncea* plants by inoculating differentiating flower buds with a zoospore suspension of *A. candida* race 2V; exposing apical meristem tissues to inoculum by opening the flower buds proved more conducive to staghead formation. Inoculation of 35- and 45d old plants produced fewer stagheads while inoculation of 7- and 13d old plants produced only hypertrophied branches at the

Fig. 2.6. (a) White rust-induced hypertrophied inflorescence of *B. juncea* (left) and its healthy counterpart (right)

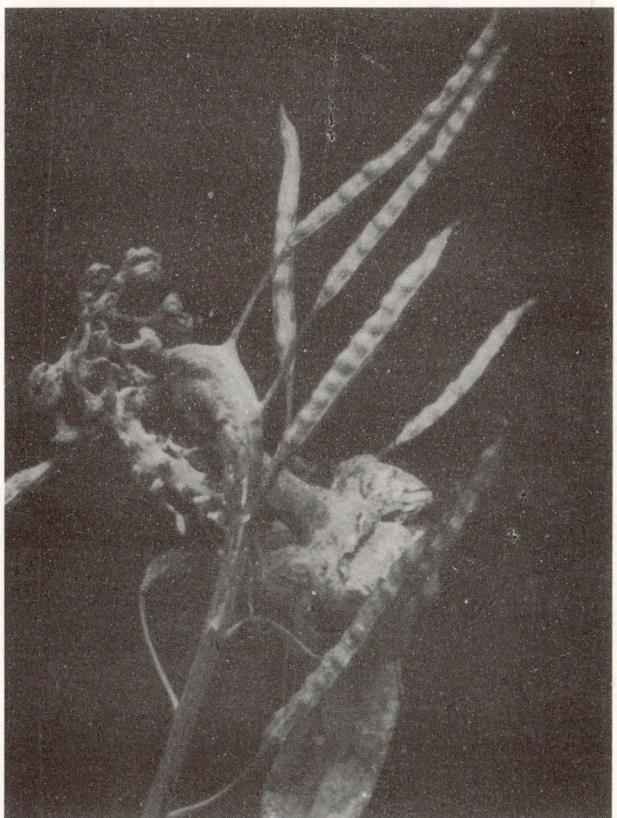

Fig. 2.6. (b) A hypertrophied inflorescence with reduced number of seed-pods

first node on the main stem but not hypertrophied flowers (Goyal *et al*. 1996b). Oospores of the rust pathogen are formed in plenty in infected leaves and hypertrophied organs. Downy mildew (*Peronospora parasitica*) frequently co-exists with white rust on cruciferous hosts in the field forming a "disease complex" (Butler, 1918). Heavily infected plants lose vigour and dry-up pre-maturely.

Leaves and flowers of Brassica species differ in their reaction to *A. candida*. Both leaves and flowers of *B. juncea* (Indian mustard) become readily infected with white rust, but flowers are more susceptible in case of *B. napus*, *B. carinata* and *B. juncea* × *B. napus* cross (Bains, 1993). The incidence and severity of stagheads vary on different genotypes despite similar levels of leaf infection (Bisht *et al*. 1994). Mustard leaves, during early growth phase of plants show only localized infection but later, the terminal ones become somewhat thickened, dwarf and in-rolled due to systemic infection (Lahiri & Bhowmik, 1993).

White rust causes considerable reduction in crop yield. Although critical appraisal of losses due to this disease is wanting, the incidence of staghead infection may be directly correlated with loss in yield (Harper & Pittman, 1974). In Canada, the systemic infection of white rust caused an average loss of 60 per cent in seed yield (Petrie & Vanterpol, 1974), and 6 per cent average yield reduction in turnip rape (*B. campestris*) during 1970-72 seasons (Petrie, 1973). In India, 23.0 to 54.5 per cent of inflorescences of mustard (*B. juncea*) turned into stagheads and the loss in seed yield varied between 2.0 to 20.0 per cent (Bisht *et al.* 1994; Saharan *et al.* 1984; Verma & Bhowmik, 1989a).

2.2.2.2 The pathogen

Albugo candida, (Pers. ex. Lev.) Kuntze, also called *Cystopus candida* (Pers. Lev.) or *Albugo cruciferarum S.F. Gray* is an obligate parasite, the mycelium is intercellular and produces globular or knob-like haustoria inside the host cells. It ramifies within the host tissues and finally forms sporangial beds or sori beneath the epidermis. The sporangiophores, borne in close proximity to one another, are hyaline, short, clavate, thickened at the base and measure 35-40 × 15-17 μm. They form sporangia whose development is blastic (Khan, 1977). Sporangia are joined by coloured disjunctors in basipetal succession into chains, all hyaline, globose, thin walled and measure 12-18 μm in diameter (Butler, 1918). They are multinucleate (Alexopoulos, 1962). Both the growth of the fungus and the production of numerous sporangia exert a pressure from below on the host epidermis, causing it to burst and release the sporangial mass to disseminate the fungus.

Sporangia germinate when they are completely immersed in water while fresh or within about 6 weeks of their formation. Germination is usually by the formation of zoospores and very rarely by germ-tubes (Butler, 1918; deBary, 1860; Walker, 1957). Freshly formed sporangia germinate most readily, and chilling induces them to produce zoospores (Melhus, 1911). Their germination is also dependent on temperature, the maximum is 25°C and the optimum is 10°C. The zoospores are

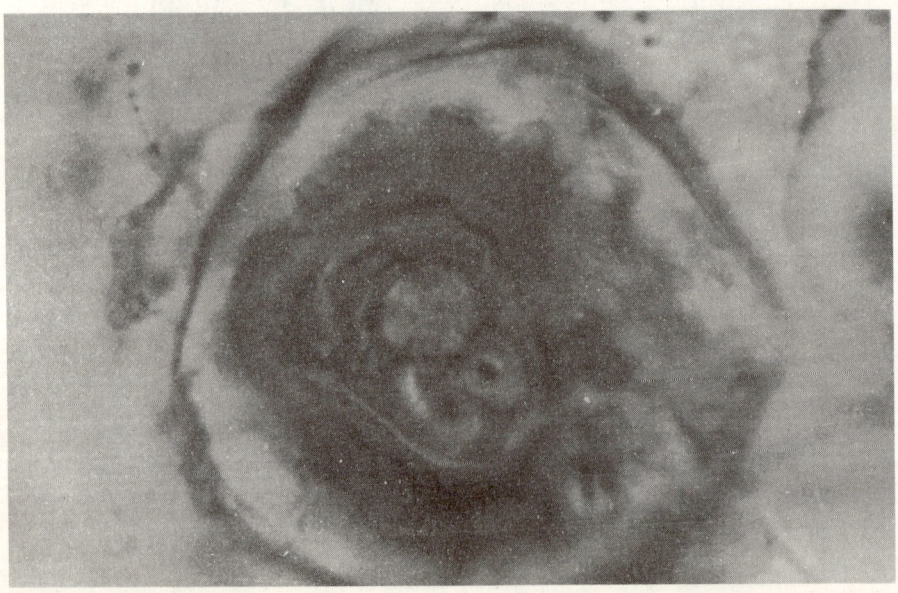

Fig. 2.7. Oospore of *A. candida.* Note the tuberculate epispore

flattened ovate to kidney-shaped, and biflagellate with one long and one short flagella. They swim for a while, settle down and germinate by a germ-tube which enters through the stomata of cotyledons, leaves and possibly young inflorescence and develops into a parasitic intercellular mycelium within the host plant (Butler, 1918).

Albugo candida, is heterothallic (Sansome & Sansome, 1974) and forms sexual spores (oospores) in infected tissues. Oogonia globose and are borne singly on short terminal or lateral branches; antheridia club shaped and arise near the oogonia (Wagger, 1986). Oospore production in detached leaves of Indian mustard infected with *A. candida* race 2V occurred at the incubation temperature range of 10-27°C with optimum production at 23°C. The earliest development of oogonia occurred at 25°C, 6d after inoculation and incubation, and mature oospores were observed at 12d (Goyal *et al.* 1996a). Oospores are globose, dark brown and 40-45 µm in diameter with highly differentiated 5-layered cell wall, epispore tuberculate with flattened branched ridges (Fig. 2.7). Oospores have long periods of viability, about 20 years in dry storage in the laboratory (Verma & Petrie, 1975).

2.2.2.3 Germination of oospores

Oospores of *A. candida* are difficult to germinate. deBary (1866) first noticed oospores of *A. candida* to germinate by the production of sessile vesicle from which zoospores were released. Venterpool (1959) described the second method of germination, the discharge tube with terminal vesicle type but the germination was irregular and poor (< 4 per cent). Later, Petrie and Verma (1974), and Verma and Petrie (1975) reported a third type of germination in which oospores germinated by the production of one or two simple or branched germ tube giving rise directly to mycelium, though germination by the production of sessile vescicle was the most common type. These workers used three methods to induce high percentage of oospore germination: the first was that of Hiura (1930) in which oospores were incubated on moist filter paper for about 21 days at 10 and 15°C, and this gave maximum germination of 65 and 88 per cent, respectively at the two temperatures. High germination also resulted from slow leaching of oospores for 15 days or more on sintered glass filter at 13°C. In the third method, oospores were subjected to washing in sterile water on a rotary shaker at 200 rpm for 3-4 days at 18-20°C, followed by a day in still-culture at 13°C. This was the most rapid method of securing high germination. Dormancy is not a factor since oospores germinated two weeks after their collection (Petrie & Verma, 1974). In India, germination of oospores was obtained by subjecting them to continuous leaching with water for 15 days at 15°C. Germination was poor (av. 21.36 per cent), and took place by both sessile vesicle and germ-tube, the latter type being rare (Verma & Bhowmik, 1988).

A further improvement in percentage (≥ 80 per cent) germination of oospores was obtained by agitating them for upto 24 h in sterile distilled water containing a mixture of B-glucuronidase and aryl sulfatase followed by 3 days of washings on a rotary shaker at room temeprature and 15 h of chilling at 13°C. Effectiveness of the enzymes on stimulation of germination depended on the stage of oospore maturity. Both aging and chilling of oospores stimulated their germination (Liu & Rimmer, 1993).

2.2.2.4 Growth of A. candida in host-tissue culture

Lahiri and Bhowmik (1993) established dual culture of *A. candida*, and its host on MS medium (Murashige & Skoog, 1962) at 18°C using explants of systemically infected tissue of *B juncea* cv. Pusa Bold. Pieces of hypertrophied young peduncles and thickened terminal leaves proved most suitable explants for the production of dual culture, the success with the former being better than with the latter. Leaf and stem explants with white rust pustules did not form callus.

Infected callus grows faster than its healthy counterpart, after about two weeks, its growth rate gradually declines and only a marginal increase in its size is observed on the 25th day, while the healthy callus grows into a large callus mass during the same period (Fig. 2.8). In both the cases, the callus gradually turns brown and dies unless subcultured into fresh medium.

Infected callus contains large thin-walled cells with few intercellular spaces and abundant coenocytic intercellular mycelium with spherical haustoria within host cells. Such callus

Fig. 2.8. Comparative growth of callus tissues derived from systemically infected (left) and healthy (right) inflorescence axis (peduncle) of *B. juncea* on Murashige and Skoog medium after 3 weeks

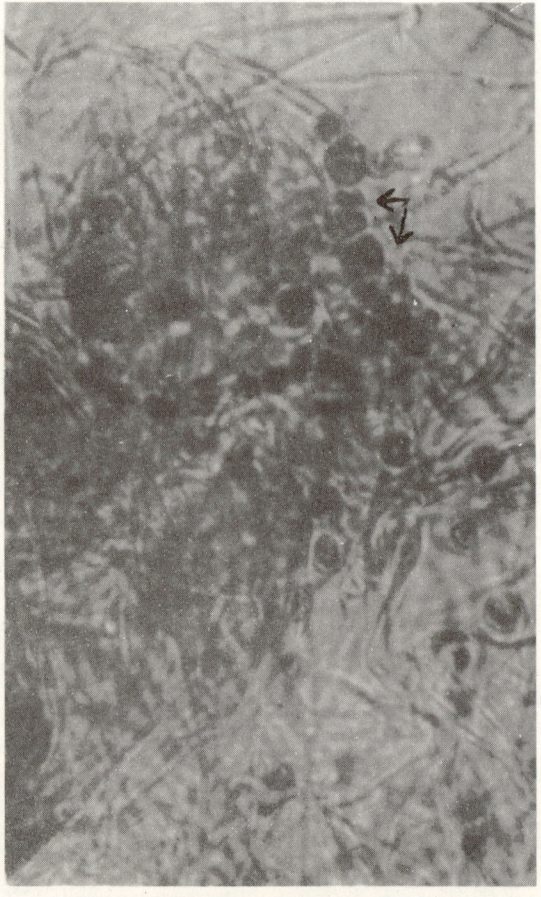

Fig. 2.9. Sporangial chains of *A. candida* in callus tissue. Magnification 10X, 100X in oil immersion

maintained at 15 and 20°C for 15 to 30 days forms only sporangial chains (Fig. 2.9) that remain confined within the callus tissue, while those maintained at 25 and 30°C contain both sporangia and oospores. Oospores are intercellular (Fig. 2.10). The pathogen can be maintained in infected callus tissue for prolonged periods by periodic subculturing and it keeps pace with the growth of the callus tissue. Placement of an infected callus in close contact with a healthy one does not result in infection of the latter (Lahiri & Bhowmik, 1993). Similar findings were reported by Goyal *et al.* (1995). Pathogenicity test carried out by these workers with callus culture contianing *A. candida* sporangia, produced typical rust pustules on leaves and cotyledons of *B. juncea* cv. Varuna after six days of inoculation.

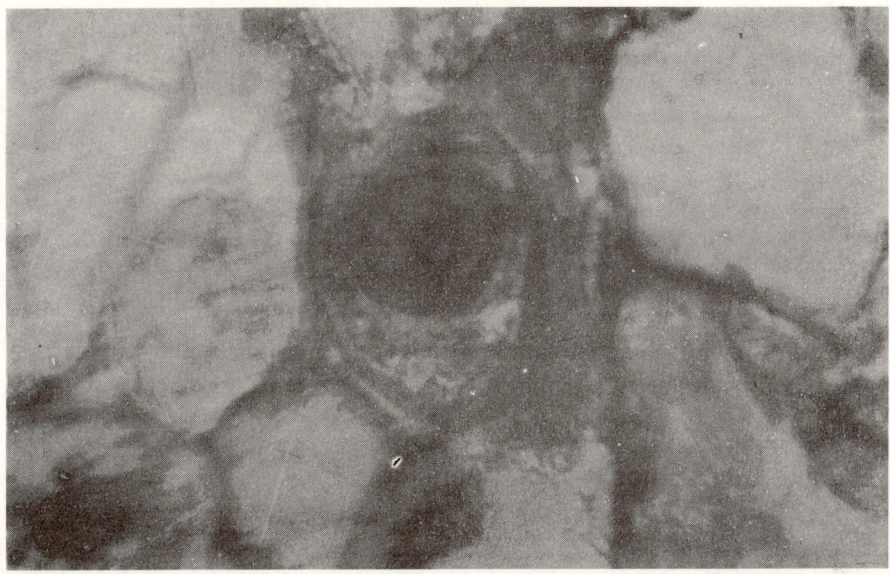

Fig. 2.10. *A. candida* oospore in the intercellular space of callus tissue. Magnification 10X, 40X in oil immersion

2.2.2.5 Perpetuation

One of the chief means of survival of *A. candida* is through oospores. During crop harvest, they enter the soil along with infected plant debris. According to Butler (1918), early disease attacks in annual plants are due to infection by zoospores arising from germinating oospores left in the soil. Other workers like Chupp (1925), and Takeshita and Linn (1953) also considered survival of the pathogen through soil borne oospores. While zoospores from germinating oospores of *A. candida*, may act as primary inoculum for the young host plant (Verma & Petrie, 1980), no experimental evidence is available about the direct role of soil-borne oospores in initiating infection to the next season crop especially under our sub-tropical climate. Interestingly, report from Verma and Bhowmik (1988) shows that oospores of *A. candida* do not remain viable in field soil through summer months under north Indian conditions. They could not detect oospores in washings from soil samples collected from white rust infested mustard fields (cv. Pusa Bold) in the following season nor could they recover viable oospores from hypertrophied host organs buried 6-inch below the soil surface after six months. This aspect needs confirmation.

However, the most important means of perpetuation of the pathogen is through oospores carried with seeds, and sowing of such contaminated seeds results in both locally and systemically infected plants in the field (Barbetti, 1981; Verma & Petrie, 1980). In India, seed samples from six cultivars of *B. juncea* and one from *B. campestris* showed heavy contamination with *A. candida* oospores whose number per gramme of seeds ranged from 12.0 to 81.0 (Verma & Bhowmik, 1988).

Possibly, the pathogen also survives in cooler places on various host species listed earlier, and its sporangiospores from these hosts act as primary inoculum to initiate the disease in rapeseed and mustard during the crop season.

2.2.2.6 Epidemiology

The incidence and severity of white rust on Brassica species are profoundly influenced by the prevailing weather conditions of the region. Prevalence of low temperature coinciding with high humidity — the effect of the latter being more dominant, cloudiness, and less of sunshine hours during flowering stage of the crop, are the conducive conditions for epidemic development of white rust disease. According to Sempio (1940), temperature most favourable for *A. candida* infection to Red radish was 16-18°C, though the disease developed most readily at 12-21°C, relative humidity at 60-80 per cent produced more severe infection than at 98-100 per cent, and 1-3 days darkness following infection stimulated the disease but continued darkness reduced it.

Field experiments carried out at the IARI, New Delhi during 1983-86 seasons on the epidemiology of white rust on Indian mustard (cv. Pusa Bold) indicated that mean temperature (MT) less than 16°C and mean relative humidity (MRH) more than 60 per cent are essential for development of the disease. Infection rate was highest (0.574) when MT and MRH was 14.7°C and 73.25 per cent, respectively and rainfall was around 230 mm. Infection rate declined with the increase in MT and decrease in MRH. Long sunshine hours for prolonged periods coincided with poor rust development (Verma and Bhowmik, 1989b). At Hissar, Haryana, dew fall more than 100 mm, MT of 10-18°C, MRH more than 65 per cent, potential evapotranspiration less than 60 per cent, cloudy weather and wind velocity of 2.7-3.4 km/h favoured faster increase in the number and size of rust pustules and epidemic development of the disease (Lakra & Saharan, 1991; Saharan *et al.* 1988). At Pantnagar, UP, high incidence of stagheads due to white rust and downy mildew (*Peronospora parasitica*) infection, was obtained with only 2-6 h sunshine per day concomitant with mean maximum and minimum temperature of 21-25°C and 6-10°C respectively, MRH of 68-73 per cent and rainfall upto 161 mm (Kolte *et al.* 1985).

In South India at Dharwad, Karnataka, prevalence of moderate MT (23-24°C), high MRH (83.8-86.3 per cent) and high mean rainfall (3.1-9.3 mm) invited heavy incidence of both leaf infection (75-86 per cent) and floral malformation (41.8-86.3 per cent) on mustard crops (cv. Varadhan) sown from the first week of June to the third week of August 1988. On the other hand, crops sown during the first to third week of either September or October 1988, showed considerable reduction in both leaf infection and floral malformation. This was mainly attributed to the prevalence of low

MRH (73.2-76.9 per cent) and low rainfall (0.0-0.6 mm) during the period, though there was not much change in MT (22.8-23.9°C) (Hegde & Anahosur, 1994).

Host age also influences disease development. Older leaves are more susceptible than younger ones (Kumar *et al*. 1995). Susceptibility of mustard plants (cv. Pusa Bold) to white rust increases with age till they are about 60 days old and then declines (Verma, 1987). Medium aged turnip rape (*B. campestris*) show maximum infection than younger and older ones. Leaves develop more rust pustules, when detached from plants at the end of a dark period than at the end of a light period (Verma et al. 1983).

Incubation period was longer but rust intensity higher on inoculated mustard plants maintianed at 8-26°C than at 10-31°C (Verma & Bhowmik, 1986).

2.2.2.7 *Brassica–Albugo candida interaction*

Albugo candida enters the resistant host through stomata as readily as in susceptible host. But in resistant host, the growth of the pathogen usually ceases in the substomatal chamber unlike the development of its intercellular mycelium and production of haustorium in a susceptible host (Napper, 1933). Verma *et al*. (1975) compared the infection process of *A. candida,* in susceptible (*B. juncea, B. campestris*), moderately susceptible (*B. hirta*) and resistant (*B. napus*) hosts by inoculating their cotyledons with zoospores of the pathogen. They observed similar sequence of events from encystment to the formation of first haustorium in all hosts, resistance came into effect only after contact between hyphal tip and host mesophyll was established, and upto this point there was apparently no morphological barrier to zoospore encystment and subsequent penetration through stomata. According to Verma (1987), morphological traits of leaf namely, the number and size of stomata, thickness of cuticle-epidermis, palisade and spongy layers, of susceptible *B. juncea* (cv. Pusa Bold), moderately resistant (cv. NA 38) and immune (cv. NA 38 Sel) *B. napus* plants, bear no relationship to their reaction to *A. candida*. In susceptible host-parasite combination, the hyphal growth rate of the pathogen increases rapidly after the formation of first haustorium, the hyphae develop around palisade mesophyll cells, penetrating individual cells with a variable number of haustoria. In resistant host (*B. napus*), the process is much slower and usually one haustorium is formed after which the hyphae ceases to elongate and at 2-3 days after inoculation, a marked encapsulation is formed around each single haustorium. On the other hand, in susceptible hosts at about 3-4 days after inoculation, the first sign of a developing pustule is observed and their cells contain massive amount of fungus thallus emphasizing highly specialized type of parasitism evolved by the pathogen (Verma *et al*. 1975).

Resistant reaction is characterized by long incubation period, small discrete, chlorotic or necrotic lesions (Fig. 2.11a, b), low disease intensity and low sporulaion in contrast to short incubaiotn period, large spreading lesions, higher disease intensity and higher sporulation exhibited by susceptible reaction (Bhardwaj & Sud, 1989; Verma, 1987).

Rust resistance in plants has been also associated with higher concentration of anthocyanins, total phenols, and sugars but lower concentration of chlorophyll a,b, total chlorophylls and carotenoids, total nitrogen and soluble proteins, and free amino acids compared to that in susceptible hosts (Verma, 1987). Gupta *et al*. (1977b), on the other hand, reported positive role of chlorophyll for

Fig. 2.11. (a) Large, white rust pustules on a leaf of susceptible *B. juncea* (cv. Pusa Bold) plant. Note the spreading nature of pustules

Fig. 2.11. (b) Small, discrete white rust pustules on a leaf of resistant *B. napus* (str. ISN. 65) plant. Note the necrosis around the pustules

resistance to *A. candida* in Indian mustard. Existence of negative correlation between white rust severity and reducing sugars was reported by Yadava *et al.* (1994).

Significant decrease in the levels of IAA (Khangura & Sokhi, 1995; Saxena, 1983; Srivastava *et al.* 1962), reducing- and nonreducing sugars, total amino acids, free proline, total proteins, anthocyanins and total phenolic compounds but increase in the levels of gibberellic acid, zeatin and abscisic acid and, chlorophyll a,b, total chlorophylls and carotinoids were also noted in rust infected floral organs of susceptible Brassica plants (Dhingra et al. 1982; Khangura & Sokhi, 1995; Kumari *et al.* 1970; Verma & Bhowmik, 1997).

The role of these compounds in conferring resistance to white rust needs confirmation.

2.2.2.8 Biological races

Biological specialization in *A. candida*, was first reported by Eberhardt (1904). He recognized two specialized groupings of the fungus viz., one attacking Capsella, Lepidium and Arabis, and the other attacking Brassica, Sinapis and Diplotaxis. Host-specificity of *A. candida* was also reported by other workers (Hiura, 1930; Melhus, 1911; Napper, 1933) but none of their specialized grouping or race was based on distinct positive or negative sporulation responses of their hosts (Pound & Williams, 1963).

Pound and Williams (1963) collected *A. candida* from 6 different cruciferous hosts and cross-inoculated them on a number of wild and cultivated crucifer species. Each collection exhibited a distinct host range and constituted a distinct biological race of the pathogen. In every case, the original host species from which the isolate was taken, supported uniformly heavy sporulation constituting the best differential host for that race. Six races were identified: race 1 on *Raphanus sativus*, race 2 on *Brassica juncea* var. Southern Giant Curled, race 3 on *Armoracia rusticana* var. Common, race 4 on *Capsella bursa-pastoris,* race 5 on *Sisymbrium officinale,* race 6 on *Rorippa islandica. Albugo candida* race 7 was identified on *B. campestris* (Pidskalny & Rimmer, 1985; Verma *et al.* 1975) and race 8 on *B. nigra* (Delwiche & Williams, 1977). Later, Petrie (1994) reported two "new" races 2V and 7V, respectively on *B. juncea* and *B. rapa* (*B. campestris*) cultivars.

The situation regarding the prevalence of *A. candida* race(s) on rapeseed and mustard in India is not very clear. Existence of 9 biologic races of *A. candida* designated as new races/forms based on their reaction on a number of wild and cultivated cruciferous hosts was reported from Himachal Pradesh (Bhardwaj & Sud, 1988; Singh & Bhardwaj, 1984). Lakra and Saharan (1988a) identified 5 races on cruciferous hosts at Hissar, Haryana, using a set of 16 differentials. But the nomenclature of all these races of *A. candida* and the set of differentials used to distinguish them are different from those used by early workers (Pound & Williams, 1963; Verma *et al.* 1975). Out of the 5 races identified by Lakra and Saharan (1988a), two were found on *B. juncea*: one (race 2) infected *B. juncea, B. campestris* var. Brown sarson and *B. nigra*, and the other (race 3) attacked only *B. juncea* and *B. campestris* var. Toria. These authors, however, did not specify the degree of affinity of the two races (race 2 and 3) for the host species inoculated and the particulars of the cultivars used in the study. Generally, the host range of race extends especially to Brassica species which share genomes with the homologus hosts from which it was originally collected (Liu *et al.* 1996).

Verma and Bhowmik (1989a) reported an isolate of *A. candida* (presumably race 2) from *B. juncea* (cv. Pusa Bold) that attacked the genotype BN-38 Sel of *B. napus*. According to Verma (1990) both *B. juncea* and *B. campestris* (var. Toria) isolates of *A. candida* from India, infected a series of cruciferous hosts of both Canadian and Indian origin. In addition to cultivars of *B. juncea*, they infected Yellow sarson, Brown sarson, Toria, *B. nigra* and *B. alba*. Both the isolates gave highest disease severity ratings on *B. juncea* although there were some differences in their virulence on other hosts, implying their similarity to *A. candida* race 2. Similar view was expressed by Lahiri and Bhowmik (1995), when three isolates of *A. candida* obtained from *B. juncea, B. campestris* and *B. nigra* were tested on a set of host differentials (Pound & Williams, 1963). These isolates, though showed some variations in their reaction to different hosts, readily cross-infected the three host species of their origin and consistently produced high disease severity on cultivars of *B. juncea*, the host differential of *A. candida* race 2. The identity of *A. candida* race(s) parasitizing oilseed brassicas in India should be established on a standard set of internationally recognized host differentials to avoid ambiguous nomenclature.

The AICRP (R&M). (1998) has suggested a set of differential hosts for identification of races/pathotypes of *A. candida* in India (Table 2.3).

Table 2.3. List of differntial hosts proposed for identification of races/pathotypes of *A. candida* in India.

Host species	Cultivars
Brassica juncea	Varuna, Pusa Bold, Kranti
B. rapa	Torch, Topin, Parkland (Canadian)
B. rapa var. Brown sarson	BSH-1
B. rapa var. Yellow sarson	YST-151, NC-1, NDYS-2
B. rapa var. Toria	T-9, Bhawani, PT-303
B. carinata	HC-9605, HC-9606
B. napus	GSL-1
B. nigra	Any variety
B. tournefortii	Any variety
Sinapis alba	Kirby (Canadian)
Raphanus sativus	Pusa Rashni
Eruca sativa	TM-27, RTM-314
Sisymbriumn officinale	Any cultivar
Rorippa islandica	Any cultivar
Capsella bursa-pastoris	Any cultivar

Source: AICRP (R&M). 1998, p 71

2.2.2.9 Resistance

Resistance to *A. candida* is race specific. *Albugo candida* race 2 is predominantly restricted to *B. juncea* although it attacks cultivars of closely related species, *B. campestris, B. nigra, B. napus* and

B. carinata (Petrie, 1988; Pidskalny & Rimmer, 1985; Pound & Williams, 1963; Verma & Bhowmik, 1989a). According to Tiwari *et al.* (1988), resistance to *A. candida* race 2 in the Russian accession Vniimk 405 of *B. juncea* is controlled by a single dominant gene and this could be transferred to adopted genotypes through back crossing. Selection within a rapid-cycling population of *B. campestris* with variable resistance to *A. candida* race-2 showed absence of major resistance genes, and the resistance is polygenic in nature (Edward & Williams, 1987).

A single dominant gene confers resistance to *A. candida* race 2 in *B. nigra* and *B. carinata* (Delwiche & Williams, 1974, 1976, 1977).

According to Verma and Bhowmik (1989a), resistance in *B. napus* to *B. juncea* pathotype of *A. candida* (race-2) is controlled by dominant duplicate genes. Resistance to Indian collection of *A. candida* race 2 in Canadian cvs. Domo and Cutlass of *B. juncea* is controlled by a single dominant gene (Sachan *et al.* 2000). Inheritance of resistance to *A. candida* (race unspecified) in F_1-, F_2- and BC_1- progenies of crosses between resistant *B. napus* (Indian synthetic Napus) and susceptible *B. juncea* was studied by Rao and Raut (1994), and Subudhi and Raut (1994). All hybrids were resistant. F_2- progenies segregated into 13 resistant : 3 susceptible ratio. Progenies of back crossing to susceptible parents segregated into 1 susceptible : 1 resistant while those from back crossing to resistant parents were resistant. All these ratios indicated digenic inheritance with dominant and recessive gene interaction.

In Canada, the *B. campestris* cv. Tobin is resistant to *A. candida* race 7 and the resistance is controlled by a single dominant gene. Resistance to the western Canada pathotype of race 7 (race 7V) was also detected in the populations of cv. Tobin at low frequency (Downey & Rimmer, 1993). Genetic control of resistance to white rust in the populations derived from *B. napus* cv. Major × Steller cross is governed by a dominant allele at a single locus. The locus has been mapped. Other loci might also be involved in the control of intensity of sporulation of the fungus in the plant (Ferreira *et al.* 1995).

Good sources of resistance to the white rust pathogen exist in *B. tournefortii* and *Diplotaxis* spp. (Gupta *et al.* 1995a; Yadav *et al.* 1991). All wild and cultivated accessions of *Eruca vesicaria* (*E. sativa*) have been found resistant to *A. candida* race-2 and all the wild accessions resistant to race 7 (Bansal *et al.* 1997).

Yashpal *et al.* (1991) suggested improvement in both seed yield and resistance to white rust by resorting to simple pedigree selection in the *B. juncea* progeny of Indian exotic origin. Sharma and Singh (1995) established callus culture from explants of young seedlings obtained from 40 Kr gamma-ray irradiated seeds of Indian mustard cv. Varuna on MS medium supplemented with growth hormones. Out of 42 somaclones obtained from these calli, 6 were resistant to *A. candida* and 7 were very resistant to *A. brassicae*. Resistance to *A.candida* and *A. brassicae* in some of the somaclones was stable and heritable in the R_2 generation under field conditions.

2.2.2.10 *Evaluation of germplasm*

Evaluation of germplasm lines for resistance to white rust is done both under artificial conditions of inoculation and natural incidence of the disease in the field as in the case of Alternaria blight.

a. Disease rating scale

Fox and Williams (1984) suggested a visual white rust interaction phenotype (IP) rating scale to correlate spore production by *A. candida* on its host. Plants are rated 0-9 according to the amount of leaf necrosis or area covered by white rust pustules (Fig. 2.12).

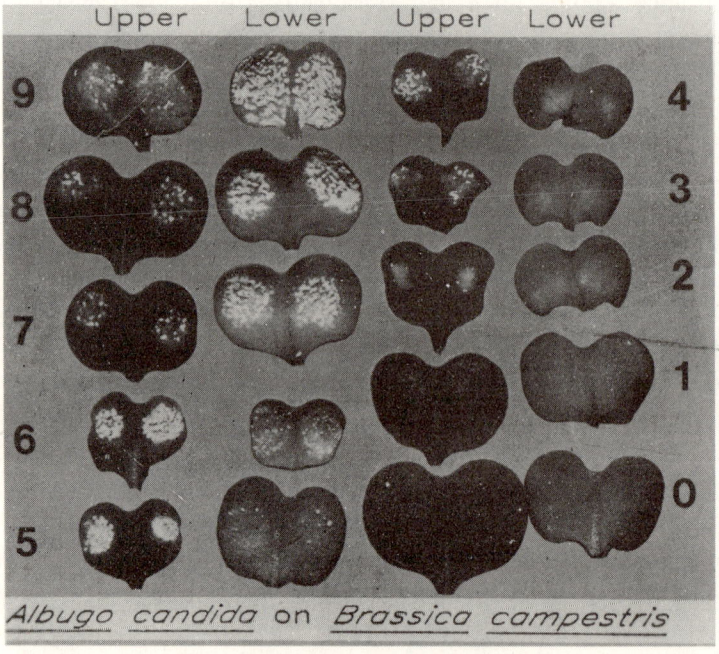

Fig. 2.12. White rust 0-9 rating scale
(*Courtesy*: P.H. Williams)

Seedlings are raised in small plastic pots at the rate of one in each. They are watered daily with 0.5 strength Hoagland's solution, and maintained at 24°C and 250 μ Em^{-2} S^{-1} continual illumination. Inoculation is done by placing a 10 μ ml drop-let of zoospore suspension of *A. candida* to each half of the adaxial cotyledon surface of 4d old seedlings. The inoculated plants are incubated at 100% RH and 20°C for 16 h and then returned to the growth chamber. Un-inoculated sub-samples of IP populations are used as controls. One week after inoculation, the plants are visually evaluated according to the 0-9 rating scale. Symptoms and signs for IP ratings on the adaxial/abaxial cotyledon surface used are:

0 = No symptoms/no symptoms,
1 = Small necrotic flecks/nothing to occassional necrotic flecks,
3 = Very sparse, one to few minute pustules/none to very few pustules,
5 = Few to many small pustules/none to few postules,
7 = Many to few pustules/many small to large pustules, and
9 = Very few to no pustules/many large coalescing pustules.

b. Disease Index

$$DI = \frac{\sum_{i=0}^{9}(i \times j)}{n}$$

where, n = Total plants, i = IP class,
         j = Number of plants/class.

Selection =
   Susceptible controls, IP = 7-9 by 7 days following inoculation;
   Partial resistance, IP = 3-5;
   Resistant plants, IP = 0-1.   (Williams, 1981, 1985)

In India, germplasm lines are evaluated by using an arbitrary visual 0-5 rating scale similar to that used for Alternaria blight disease (AICORPO. 1984; Bhowmik & Munde, 1987; Parui & Bandopadhyay, 1973). Bhardwaj and Sud (1995) suggested the use of 0-9 visual rating scale for assessment of white rust on crucifers at 2 vegetative and reproductive stages. The scale may also be used to determine the yield losses of crops.

Verma (1987) studied the impact of floral malformation on per plant seed yield in seven Brassica cultivars and reported a strong positive correlation (r = + 0.944) between per cent floral malformation and reduction in seed yield of plants, and having relationship as:

$$Y = -3.5738 + 0.9828 X$$

where, Y = Per cent reduction in yield
         X = Per cent floral malformation

2.2.2.11 Screening for resistance

a. Inoculation

Plants are inoculated with zoospore suspension of *A. candida* to induce white rust infection. Sporangia are collected in number # 00 gelatin capsules using a small mouth operated cyclone separator. These are preserved at –20 to –10°C and they remain viable for over a year (Fox & Williams, 1984; Pound & Williams, 1963). Sporangia stored at 0°C in ordinary butter paper packets also showed high germinability after 9 months (Verma & Bhowmik, 1991). For inoculation, stored or freshly collected sporangia are suspended in water, incubated at 10-16°C for 3-6h for germination and release of zoospores, and then sprayed on to plants (Fan *et al*. 1983; Pound & Williams, 1963; Singh & Singh, 1983; Verma *et al*. 1975).

Verma and Bhowmik (1986) used freshly collected sporangial suspension (15-20 sporangia/microscopic field) to inoculate white rust on 45d old Indian mustard plants (cv. Pusa Bold). Inoculated plants were incubated at 8-26°C for 24 h in a moist-chamber and then removed to the glasshouse for rust development. This is a simpler but equally efficient method like the use of zoospore suspension and can be employed with ease for rapid screening of germplasm.

b. Screening techniques

i. Screening at the cotyledonary stage   Plants are raised in growth chamber under proper conditions of temperature, humidity and light, and their apical meristems are removed. After 10-days following sowing, cotyledons of these plants are drop-inoculated with zoospore suspension of *A. candida*. Inoculated plants are kept over night in moist-chamber and then removed to the growth chamber.

At different intervals after inoculation, whole cotyledons are fixed in 95% ethanol-acetic acid (1:1), cleared in 70% lactic acid at 40ºC for 2-4 days, and stained with aniline blue in lactophenol. The preparations are then examined for infection, hyphal ingress and progress under a compound microscope (Verma *et al*. 1975).

ii. Screening with detached leaves   Medium aged leaves from 12 to 14d old seedlings of Brassica species are harvested at the end of a dark period and transferred to Petri dishes containing 20-25 ml sterile 0.8% agar medium mixed with 0.5% benzyladinine. Leaves are placed in dishes with their lower surface on the medium within 15 minutes of detachment and then drop- inoculated with zoospore suspension (10^4–15^4 spores/ml) of *A. candida*. Inoculated leaves are incubated at 100% humidity for 22 h at 21 and 16ºC during day and night, respectively. Plant reactions are rated 10-17 days after inoculation (Verma *et al*. 1983; Verma & Petrie, 1978).

iii. Screening with flower buds   Verma and Petrie (1980) inoculated young flower buds of 26d old plants of Torch (*Brassica campestris*) with a zoospore suspension (10^4–15^4 spores/ml) derived from sporangia of *A. candida* race 7. After inoculation, plants were kept in mist chamber for 72-h with day-night temperatures of 21 and 16ºC, respectively. Following an initial 24-h dark period, an 18-h day was maintained for the duration of the experiment, and 3 weeks after inoculation, 55% of the flower-bud-inoculated plants developed stagheads. The method is useful in assessing the resistance of various Brassica cultivars and lines to systemic infection.

iv. Screening of adult plants   Sowing of Brassica seeds infested with oospores of *A. candida* results in white rust infected plants. Verma and Petrie (1980) mixed oospores of *A. candida* race 7 with seeds of turnip rape (*B. campestris* L. cv. Torch) prior to their sowing in the field and obtained both local and systemic infection.

2.2.2.12 *Sources of resistance*

To date, no commercial variety of rapeseed and mustard resistant to white rust pathogen, *A. candida* has been developed in India (Verma & Bhowmik, 1989a). However, a large number of germplasm lines/genotypes of Brassica species has been screened for resistance to white rust at different research centres and institutes. Screening has been done mostly under field conditions using heavy disease pressure created by sowing seeds mixed with oospores and/or spray inoculating the plants and flower buds with sporangial suspension of the pathogen isolate prevalent in the area [AICORPO. 1981-1993; AICRP (R&M). 1994-1997; Lakra & Saharan, 1989]. Materials reported highly tolerant or resistant to white rust (race unspecified) are:

Brassica alba (Saharan *et al.* 1988); *B. carinata* lines HC-1 to -5, BC-2, HPC-1, PC-3, PCC-5 and -7, PPSC-1, Pusa Gaurav [AICORPO. 1988; AICRP (R&M). 1996, 1997; Lakra & Saharan, 1989; Saharan *et al.* 1988; S.C. Gulati, per. commun.]; *B. napus* lines Tower-1 to -4, Midas-24 and -54, Gullivar-1 and -2, GS-7005, -7027 and -7029, GSL-441, -449 and -491, Norin, Regent, HNS-1 to -9, H-715 and -2019, HPN-1 and -3 (AICORPO. 1981, 1986-1988; Saharan, 1993; Saharan *et al.* 1988); *B. juncea* lines T-4 (Parui & Bandopadhyay, 1973), DIRA-313-6 and -313-7, Pusa Agrani, Domo, Domo-4, YRT-3, Lethbridge, Metapolka, Zem-1 and -2, Newton, Stoke, Blaze, Purbiraya, Chamba-3, Heera, JGM-868, -9588, R-908, -8802 and -8803, RW-81-59 and -2351-B2, RH-8515 B, -8537 to -8547, RC-781, -1001, -1401, -1405, -1408, -1424, -1425 and -1449, BEC-108, -109, -111, -115, -131, -132, -135 and -142 to 144, EC-126126, -126126-1, -126721, -126741, -126743, -126743-1, -126743-2, -126745, -126745-1, -126746, -126746-2, -126746-3, -126747, -129121-1 and 129126-1, GN-4, -5 and -7, CSR-343, PR-86-23, -101 and PYSR-8, -13 and -14, PWR-17, PWR-9541, JMMR 941-1-2, JMMWR 93-37, 38-39 and KMY 95-5 [AICORPO. 1981, 1986-1988, 1990; AICRP (R&M). 1995-98; Lakra & Saharan, 1989; Saharan, 1984; Saharan *et al.* 1988; S.C. Gulati Per. Commun.]; *B. campestris* lines Tobin, Canoli, Candle, Cutlass, Span, Bele, Bhabani, KBS-3, BS-15, BSH-1, PYS-6 and -16, PT-77 and Type-6 (AICORPO. 1988, 1990; Gangopadhyay *et al.* 1994; Kolte, 1987; Kolte & Tewari, 1980; S.C. Gulati, per. commun.).

2.2.2.13 Control

a. Cultural practices

Clean cultivation and sowing of tolerant/resistant cultivars free from contamination with *A. candida* oospores are important disease management practices. Sowing date, being dependent upon the weather conditions, affects crop growth as well as the incidence and severity of the rust disease. In northern region of the country, the most favourable time for sowing rapeseed and mustard is around the middle of October, when the mean daily temperature ranges between 25-26°C (Gangasaran & Giri, 1985). Early sown crops maturing by the third week of March, generally escape the severity of both white rust and Alternaria blight attack (Bhowmik, 1985b). Late sown crops, on the other hand, suffer most from white rust infection (Kumar *et al.* 1995). At Pantnagar, UP, Indian mustard had the least incidence (0-20%) and severity (0-9%) of the staghead phase of white rust when sown in the first week of October whereas, sowing in late October or in November invited high incidence (10-30%) and severity (23-43%) of rust infecton (Kolte *et al.* 1986).

As in the case of Alternaria blight disease mentioned earlier, closely planted crops produce higher seed yields than sparsely planted ones even though the incidence of white rust disease becomes higher and yield per plant lower. In a micro-plot experiment during 1985-86, the effect of three inter-row (20,30 and 40 cm) × three intra-row (10, 15 and 20 cm) spacing combinations on the intensity of white rust infection and seed yield in Indian mustard cv. Pusa Bold was examined at the IARI, New Delhi. Both highest rust intensity (26.75%) and total per plot seed yield (2.26 kg) were obtained from 20 × 10 cm spacing plots although this resulted in lowest per plant yield (12.63 g). On the other hand, the lowest disease intensity (20.20%) and the highest per plant seed yield (29.16 g) were obtained from 40 × 20 cm spacing plots but this gave the lowest per plot yield (1.05 kg)

(Verma & Bhowmik, 1996). Both total yield and net profit should be higher if appropriate disease control measure is incorporated.

b. Chemical control

In the absence of resistance to white rust in commercial cultivars of rapeseed and mustard in India, the use of chemicals constitutes the most effective means of its control. At least, two to three spray applications of protectant fungicides like mancozeb (dithane M-45), zineb (dithane Z-78), polyram, copper oxychloride (miltox, blitox-50), thiram, captan, captafol (difolatan), benomyl, thiovit (sulphur), cuman, thiophenate-methyl (topsin-M) and chlorothalonil, etc., starting from the first appearance of the disease and then followed by one or two applications during the flowering stage of the crop provide effective control of both foliar and floral infection, and increase crop yield (Bhowmik, 1985b; Dubey & Misra, 1994; Gupta *et al*. 1977a; Gupta & Sharma, 1978; Kapoor & Sugha, 1995; Lakra & Saharan, 1988b; Perwaiz *et al*. 1969; Verma, 1987). In Sikkim, India, blitox-50 was found to be the most effective amongst 9 fungicides, both in controlling the rust disease and in increasing the yield of mustard (Srivastava & Verma, 1989). Similarly, minimum rust intensity and floral infection, and highest seed yield of Indian mustard were obtained following mixed application of topsin-M (0.025%) + blitox-50 (0.10%) in a field trial at Bihar (Dubey, 1996). Both blitox and zineb are effective against mixed infection of white rust and downy mildew (*Peronospora parasitica*) on Indian mustard (Bains & Jhooty, 1979).

Among the systemic chemicals, metalaxyl (ridomil) is an excellent product possessing both protective and eradicative activity against *A. candida* (Dueck & Stone, 1979; Stone *et al*. 1987). Pre-sowing treatment of seeds with metalaxyl-35 (apron SD-35) at 5-8 g a.i./kg provides protection to seedlings against primary infection from germinating oospores (Mathur *et al*. 1991; Saharan, 1984; Sharma & Kolte, 1985; Stone *et al*. 1987), but it was ineffective in providing protection to plants against white rust which appeared after 70 days of sowing in the field (Bhowmik & Singh, 1984). As soil drench, metalaxyl (@ 0.25-1.0 kg a.i./ha) prevents foliar infection of seedlings though it may show slight phytotoxic effect (Stone *et al*. 1987).

Spray application of metalaxyl at 0.2% conc. controls both foliage infection and staghead formation, reduction in the latter type of infection becomes more evident when plants are sprayed at the flowering stage (Lakra & Saharan, 1988; Stone *et al*. 1987). Both metalaxyl (ridomil) and readymix (ridomil + mancozeb 75 WP) at 0.1% conc. provide effective control of white rust, the two are highly persistent on Indian mustard (cv. Pusa Bold) and show both upward and downward movement in plants including their absorption through roots. Out of two other systemic chemicals namely, aliette (fosetyl) and pervicur (promocarb), the former is comparatively less effective than metalaxyl, shows only upward movement and absorption through roots while the latter is ineffective (Saharan *et al*. 1984; Verma, 1987).

At the IARI, New Delhi, two spray applications with either 0.2% dithane M-45 or 0.1% readymix on mustard cv. Pusa Bold at fortnightly intervals starting from mid-January onwards were highly effective against white rust and in improving seed yield/plant, and readymix performed better in respect to both disease control and plant yield (Verma, 1987). In the rainy season at Karnataka under high pressure of rust disease, seed treatment plus two sprays with metalaxyl MZ at 2 g a.i., gave maximum disease control (94% reduction of leaf infection and 96% reduction of floral systemic infection) and contributed to a 81.3% increase in seed yield of mustard (Hegde & Anahosur, 1993).

Metalaxyl-25 (ridomil-25) shows complete compatibility with captafol and metasystox, the chemicals respectively effective against Alternaria blight and aphid pest (*Lipaphis erysimi*) of rape-seed and mustard. Applications of metalaxyl-25 either alone or in conjunction with captafol or with captafol plus metasystox provided significant reduction in intensity, respectively of white rust, white rust + Alternaria blight, and of these two diseases and aphid infestation beside increased seed yield. Mixed applications of these three chemicals proved most effective in achieving not only an excellent control of these two diseases and aphid infestation but also in getting the highest seed yield per plot, which was 123 per cent higher than that from control (Bhowmik & Singh, 1984).

2.2.3 Downy Mildew

Downy mildew, *Peronospora parasitica* (Pers. ex.Fr.) Fr. occurs on a wide range of cruciferous hosts, including the cultivated Brassicas in various countries throughout the world (Channon, 1981). In India, it attacks Sarson, Toria, Rai, Black mustard, cauliflower, cabbage, radish, turnip, Taramira (Rocket) and others (Butler, 1918). Thind (1942) found it on *Malcomia africana*. The disease is minor in importance and causes little damage under normal conditions but if the weather is favourable, it may attack all the aerial parts of the plant causing serious injury. Severe outbreaks of downy mildew damaging cabbage and cauliflower seedlings have been recorded in India and abroad (Butler, 1918; Lebeau, 1945). Effect of the disease on the yield of oilseed rape is not known (Davies, 1986) but mixed infection of downy mildew and white rust caused 17-34 per cent loss in yield of rapeseed and mustard in India (Bains & Jhooty, 1973; Kolte *et al.* 1981).

2.2.3.1 *Symptoms*

Downy mildew is seen twice on the crop, first in the early season and then again in the late season. Early season infection of young seedlings is most damaging than infection to adult plants (Kluczewski & Lucas, 1982). Infection is first seen in the form of small discoloured lesions on the cotyledonary and lower leaves of young emerging seedlings. At Hissar, Haryana its attack starts from the end of October and continues upto the end of November, before the appearance of white rust in the field (Mehta & Saharan, 1993). At Berhampur, West Bengal it appears on Toria in November when the day and night temperature is about 25-30°C and 15-18°C, respectively (A.K. Chattopadhyay, Per. commun.). The under surface of the infected cotyledons becomes covered with fine downy growth of conidiophores and conidia of the pathogen, especially in the morning when they remain moist with dew. Affected cotyledons turn brownish-grey, shrivel and shed, weakening or killing the seedlings. On the foliage, the disease is seen as small, discrete, angular brownish-white lesions with patchy growth of mycelium on the undersurface corresponding to pale yellow-brown spots on the upper surface (Fig. 2.13). In severe attacks, the lesions turn into irregular patches, the leaf dries up, shrivels and cracks (Butler, 1918). The disease disappears with the gradual fall in diurnal temperature and the seedlings that grow appear normal without any distortion of stem or floral organs. Downy mildew re-appears, occasionally in and around the white rust pustules of leaf and stem in the mid-season (February) but almost invariably on hypertrophied

Fig. 2.13. Downy mildew lesions on a leaf of *B. juncea* caused by *P. parasitica*

Fig. 2.14. Mealy growth of *P. parasitica* on a hypertrophied floral axis of *B. juncea*

floral organs (Fig. 2.14) and siliquae, in the end-season (March-April) when the weather gets little warmer and humid.

2.2.3.2 Albugo–Peronospora disease complex

Butler (1918) reported that in nature, *P. parasitica* frequently co-exists with *Cystopus* (*Albugo*) *candida* on cruciferous hosts in the form of a single disease complex in which the former produces the greatest deformations in the stem and the latter in the flowers. In inflorescence infested with Peronospora, the flowers are not swollen except the young ovary. Flower buds get atrophied. Petrie and Vanterpool (1974) found that out of the association of over 20 species of fungi with hypertrophied inflorescences (stagheads), stem and pod blisters produced on various species by *A. cruciferarum* (*A. candida*), *P. parasitica* is one of the most prevalent associate of Albugo. Colonization of *A. cruciferarum* induced galls of mustard (*B. campestris*) by the downy mildew pathogen has also been reported by Chaurasia *et al.* (1982). In Albugo induced swellings, the epidermal and cortical cells are thin-walled (Butler, 1918) and this may facilitate the entry of the downy mildew pathogen in them.

Young *B. juncea* (cv. Pusa Bold) plants on inoculation with *P. parasitica*, develop mildew lesions on leaves, stem and floral organs without inducing hypertrophy but those inoculated with either *A. candida* or a mixture of *A. candida* and *P. parasitica*, produce floral hypertrophies, *P. parasitica* in the latter case covers the hypertrophied organs with powdery growth of its conidiophores and conidia (Bhowmik, 1988; Lahiri *et al.* 1997). Likewise, radish separately inoculated with *P. parasitica* and *A. candida* develops respectively, mildew lesions, and rust pustules and floral hypertrophy. Inoculation with these two pathogens together results in extreme hypertrophy of inflorescences. The auxin level in the hypertrophied tissues becomes higher than in healthy tissues and the highest levels are obtained in tissues infected by both the pathogens (Achar, 1993).

Ingram (1969) established *P. parasitica* on Brassica callus tissue culture but the dual culture instead of making stimulated growth, degenerated rapidly. Leaf explants of Brassica (cv. Pusa Bold) with fresh incipient lesion of *P. parasitica* or explants taken from margins of such lesion yield only *P. parasitica* but not the dual culture of the biotrop and its host on callusing medium. They shrivell and die. On the other hand, explants with fresh (unruptured) white rust pustule, occasionally yield *P. parasitica* in culture plates indicating that Albugo infected tissues provide the favourable medium for its invasion and growth (Lahiri *et al.* 1997).

Rust pustule infested with *P. parasitica* does not grow or mature in *in vitro* unlike the non-infested one. However, placement of young hypertrophied peduncle pieces with incipient growth of downy mildew, produces callus tissue with mixed infection of *A. candida* and *P. parasitica* which exhibits poorer growth rate compared to that of both healthy and Albugo infected callus, the growth rate of the latter being the highest. *Albugo-Peronospora* infected callus shows rapid degeneration and can not be maintained by sub-culturing, whereas the dual culture of *A. candida* and its host, shows much faster growth rate and can be sub-cultured (Lahiri & Bhowmik, 1993; Lahiri *et al.* 1997). These accounts indicate that in *Albugo-Peronaspora* disease complex, *P. parasitica* is the secondary invader with little or no stimulatory effect on the host.

2.2.3.3 The pathogen

Peronospora parasitica, like *A. candida*, is also an obligate parasite. The mycelium is intercellular which ramify extensively between the host cells. Haustoria arise as branches of hyphae within the host cells, and often vary in size and shape within the same host species (Channon, 1981). They are large, elongated club shaped, often branched and nearly fill the host cells. The conidiophores arise directly from the mycelium either singly or in groups through stomata or between the epidermal cells. The conidiophores measure 200-500 μm in height, bifurcate 6-8 times towards the top to form pairs of finely pointed and incurved sterigmata, bearing single terminal conidium. The conidia are broad, oval, colourless and measure 24-27 × 10-20 μm in diameter, fall off readily and germinate by a germ-tube (Butler, 1918; Channon, 1981). At 8°C, the whole process from emergence to spore formation by conidiophores takes about 4-6 h (Davison, 1968). The optimum temperature for sporulation is 8-10°C, for conidial germination is 8-12°C, and penetration of the host (cabbage) occurs most readily at 16°C (Felton & Walker, 1946). Penetration is usually direct and occasionally through the stomata (Butler, 1918; Chou, 1970; Shiraishi *et al.* 1975).

Conidia of the pathogen can be preserved in a freezer at –21°C for a period of one year using glycerine, polyethylene glycol (PEG) 400 or PEG 1000 as cryoprotective agents. Glycerine at a conc. of 20% is the most suitable additive with germination rates of 21% after storage for one year (Klodt-Bussmann & Paul, 1995).

During sexual reproduction, the fungus forms oogonia and antheridia, respectively the female and male organs. Fertilization is accomplished by the discharge of nuclear material from the antheridium into the oogonium leading to the formation of oospores. Oospores are globose, yellowish-brown, irregularly thick walled with crest-like folds, measure 30-40 µm in diameter and germinate by germ-tube (Butler, 1918). Conditions of light, temperature and age, and deficiency of nutrition to the host that promote senescence of the leaf, generally favour oospore formation (McMeekin, 1960). They are found abundently in necrotic or chlorotic leaves but more frequently in cotyledons than in leaves since the former senesce more rapidly (Channon, 1981).

In nature, *P. parasitica* exists in both heterothallic and homothallic forms (deBruyn, 1937; Sheriff & Lucas, 1989a). Heterothallic forms are self-sterile, belong to one of two sexual compatibility types, designated as P_1 and P_2 by Sheriff and Lucas (1989a). Oospore formation was induced when heterothallic isolates differently virulent on different host species were inoculated together on a host capable of supporting growth of both the forms (Sheriff & Lucas, 1989a). Moss *et al.* (1994) recovered sexual progenies from oospore populations produced in vitro from pairing between isolates specialized, both to the same host species (homologous pairings) as well as to different host species (heterogenous pairings), and obtained evidence that they are hybrid in nature.

Homothallic isolates are self-fertile. Sheriff and Lucas (1989a) examined 33 laboratory isolates of *P. parasitica* obtained from different Brassica host species and various geographical locations for their ability to produce oospores in monoculture in susceptible seedlings. Oospores were produced in host tissue infected by all the *B. napus* isolates, and by only a few of the isolates from *B. campestris* and *B. oleracea* but not by the sole *B. juncea* isolate. Self-fertility in *B. napus* isolates was found to be a highly stable character (Sheriff & Lucas, 1989a,b).

From India, Chaurasia *et al.* (1982) reported that cross-section of mustard (*B. campestris*) galls and galls infected with *P. parasitica* showed oospores of only the white rust pathogen, *A. cruciferarum* (*A. candida*). The present author was also unable to detect oospore of *P. parasitica* in leaves and hypertrophied floral organs of *B. juncea* (cv. Pusa Bold), both artificially inoculated and naturally infected with downy mildew, presumably the pathogen-isolate involved belonged to either one of the two sexual compatibility types. Vishunavat and Kolte (1993), however, reported the presence of oospores of the pathogen on the seed surface and in hypodermis of seed coat tissue in Sarson, Toria and Indian mustard. Clearly, this aspect needs further study.

2.2.3.4 Physiological specialization and resistance

Peronospora parasitica exhibits physiological specialization. Pathogen isolates differ in their ability to infect different cruciferous hosts. Specialization of parasitism in *P. parasitica* may be exhibited at the generic, specific and lower taxonomic levels of the host (Channon, 1981).

Gaumann (1926) recognized three formae speciales infecting cruciferous hosts viz., *P. parasitica* f.sp. *brassicae* infecting different Brassica species like *B. oleracea*, *B. napus* and *B.*

rapa, etc.; *P. parasitica* f.sp *sinapidis* infecting *Sinapis arvensis* and *S. alba*; and *P. parasitica* f.sp. *raphani* infecting *Raphanus sativus* and *R. raphanistrum*. Wang (1944) named the *P. parasitica* isolates found on different host genera as separate varieties viz., *P. parasitica* var. *brassicae* on Brassica; *P. parasitica* var. *raphani* on *Raphanus*; and *P. parasitica* var. *capsellae* on Capsella. Chang *et al*. (1964), on the other hand, called the pathogen isolates on different host genera as separate formae speciales of the fungus.

Wang (1944) further subdivided the pathogen variety viz., *P. parasitica* var. *brassicae* into separate specialized forms on the basis of their ability to infect different Brassica species namely, cabbage, Chinese cabbage, *B. juncea* and swede, etc. Chang *et al*. (1964), likewise, subdivided *P. parasitica* f.sp. *brassicae* into three subforms: pekinensis, oleracea and juncea.

Natti *et al*. (1967) indicated the existence of separate physiologic races within a pathogenic variety/formae speciales since host genotypes respond differently to different pathogen isolates. Normally, isolates of *P. parasitica* are most virulent on host species from which they were originally derived, although restricted growth and sporulation can occur on some genotypes of other species at least at the seedling stage (Dickinson & Greenhalgh, 1977; McMeekin, 1969; Sheriff & Lucas, 1990). Within this wide host range, however, there exists a continuous gradation of reaction types, from hypersensitive collapse of the first few cells penetrated in highly resistant hosts (Wong, 1949), to systemic growth of the fungus without host-cell necrosis in fully suscpetible hosts (Kluczewski & Lucas, 1982).

Nine isolates of *P. parasitica* derived from six Brassica species in India, were found to be of two distinct pathotypes when tested on a set of host differentials, one pathotype was from cauliflower and the other from oil yielding Brassicas (Mehta & Saharan, 1994).

According to Nashaat and Awasthi (1995), the UK rape cultivar Ariana, susceptible to isolates of *P. parasitica* from rape in the UK, was resistant to pathogen isolates from Indian mustard in India, whereas all Indian msutard accessions, with few exceptions, were resistant to isolates derived from rape in the UK. The rape cultivar, Cresor was highly resistant to all the field isolates of *P. parasitica* from *B. napus* as well as to those from *B. oleracea*, the resistance in Cresor to oilseed rape isolates of the pathogen was controlled by a single dominant gene and is race-specific (Lucas *et al*. 1988; Moss *et al*. 1988). Screening of rape germplasm collected from different countries for resistance against 4 isolates of *P. parasitica*, yielded two groups of new sources of resistance. One group of materials carried resistance equivalent to that in Cresor. The second group was resistant to all the 4 isolates, indicating new major genes for resistance different from that expressed in Cresor (Nashaat & Rawlinson, 1991). Rape accessions with high glucosinolate and high erucic acid contents were less susceptible to *P. parasitica* isolates than those with high glucosinolate but low erucic acid or low glucosinolate and low erucic acid contents. Similar inconsistency in the expression of resistance to pathogen isolates at 3 different growth stages was also observed among some rape accessions with seeds low in erucic acid but differing in glucosinolate contents (Nishaat & Rawlinson, 1994).

2.2.3.5 *Perpetuation and epidemiology*

Perpetuation and epidemiology of the downymildew pathogen, *P. parasitica* has not been well studied in India. The pathogen possibly survives on alternative hosts and through oospores. The pathogen isolates are also capable of infecting species other than their original host, including a number of cruciferous weeds (Chang *et al.* 1964; Dickinson & Greenhalgh, 1977; McMeekin, 1969). Oospores are probably the primary source of infection. Limited systemic infection was noted in Chinese cabbage seedlings in which the pathogen penetrated the hypocotyl and reached the first pair of leaves but did not spread further to the stem. Such infection may initiate epiphytotics of the disease (Chang *et al.* 1963; Lebeau, 1945).

Prevalence of temperature between 8-16°C, moist weather conditions and low light intensity favours infection of oilseed rape (*B. napus*) by *P. parasitica* (Jonsson, 1966). According to Mehta *et al.* (1995), temperature regimes of 15-22°C are most favourable for infection and development of the pathogen on *B. juncea* seedlings, infection takes place within 24 h of inoculation. Infection is low at 25°C and does not occur at 30°C. Leaf wetness duration of 4-6 h at 20° and 6-8 h at 15°C are necessary for significant infection and development of downy mildew. Increasing the duration of leaf wetness over the range of 2-10 h favours the disease. High intensity of mixed infections of *A. candida* and *P. parasitica* on ·*B. juncea* inflorescence, was favoured by the prevalence of low temperature and high moisture conditions. Mixed infection was high (29.06%) when the average temperature was low (14.30°C) and total rainfall was high (151.90 mm) in one season, compared to low infection (0.52%) obtained under high temperature (17.0°C) and low total rainfall (50.80 mm) in another season (Bains & Jhooty, 1979).

2.2.3.6 Evaluation of germplasm

Germplasm lines are evaluated both at the seedling and adult stages for their reaction to downy mildew disease.

Seedlings are inoculated at the cotyledonary stage with zoospore suspension of *P. parasiticia* and then rated for their disease reaction according to either 0-5 or 0-9 rating scale as described for white rust disease. Grontoff (1993) used a rapid screening method for testing large number of breeding lines of Brassica. Several hundred breeding lines of Brassica species were sown on greenhouse tables filled with soil. A week later, the cotyledons were artificially inoculated and covered with a plastic tunnel. About two weeks later, the average percentage of wilted leaf area was estimated and the disease response of the lines evaluated.

In India, the adult plants are rated for their reaction to mixed infeciton of white rust and downy mildew as they occur together under field conditions according to the method described for white rust disease.

2.2.3.7 Sources of resistance

Brassica genotypes reproted resistant (tolerant) to downy mildew or white rust-downy mildew disease complex under field conditions in India are: *B. tournefortii* lines SPS 1-1 and -9-4 (Rajpurohit & Chowdhary, 1995); *B. alba*; *B. carinata* lines HC-1, -2 and BC-2; *B. napus* lines Tower, Tower-4, Regent, Midas-24 and -54, Gulivar-1 and -3, GS-7005 and -7027, GSL-1, -441 and -491, HNS-1 to 9, H-2019 and RK-8605; *B. juncea* lines Pusa Kranti, Seeta and RW-351 (Patil *et al.* 1991; Rai, 1991), Blaze, Chamba-3, Domo, Lethbridge, Metapolka, PHR-1, RC-781, Zem-1 and -2, BEC-111, -115, -135, -142, -143, -145 and -149-2, CSR-43, -73 and -343, RH-8515B,

-8537 to -8547, EC-1267121, -126741, -126743, -126743-2, -126745, -126746-2, -126746-3 and -129126-1; and *B. campestris* lines Canoli, Candle, Cutlas, Bele and Span (AICORPO. 1986-1988; Saharan, 1984; S.C. Gulati, Per. Commun.).

Resistant cultivars reproted from the UK and other countries include *B. napus* cultivars Eurora, Janetski, Primor (Dixon, 1975), Cresor (Lucas *et al.* 1988) and Synra (Klodt-Bussmann & Paul, 1995).

2.2.3.8 Control

Measures recommended against white rust are also effective against downy mildew disease. Both seed treatment with apron SD-35 (@ 4-6 g/kg seeds) or seed treatment followed by two sprays with ridomil MZ (@ 0.2-0.6% conc.) provide effective control of the disease (Mathur *et al.* 1991; Mehta *et al.* 1996; Puzari & Saikia, 1997).

2.2.4 Powdery Mildew

Powdery mildew (*Erysiphe polygoni* DC and *E. cruciferarum* Opiz ex.Junell) can be seen on oilseed brassicas throughout the world. In India, Butler (1918) was probably the first to notice a severe out break of the disease in 1907 over large irrigated areas in Chenab canal colony of Punjab. He noted the pathogen as *Erysihe polygoni* which also attacked pea. This is a regular menace to rapeseed and mustard crops in India (Bhander *et al.* 1963; Shankhla *et al.* 1967; Singh *et al.* 1984; Vasudeva, 1958). *Erysiphe cruciferarum* is the other incitant of the powdery mildew disease of these crops in India (Sharma, 1979; Saharan & Kaushik, 1981). Both have wide host range (Salmon, 1900; Alexopoulos, 1972).

Powdery mildew is usually a minor disease and causes little damage but in regions such as in Rajasthan, Haryana and Punjab, its occasional outbreaks in epidemic form cause considerable losses in crop yield (Saharan & Kaushik, 1981; Singh *et al.* 1984; Shankhla *et al.* 1967; Sharma, 1979). In Delhi region, the damage is negligible as the disease severity normally reaches its height when the crop is almost mature. In Gujarat and in some non-traditional areas of the south, the disease is emerging as a serious threat to the crop in recent years [AICORPO. 1990; AICRP (R&M). 1996; Patel *et al.* 1992] while in eastern states of the country, it is only sporadic in nature and economically unimportant. No loss estimate is available.

2.2.4.1 Symptoms

Symptoms caused by the two pathogens are almost similar. In the beginning small, white circular powdery patches consisting mainly of conidiophores and conidia of the fungus appear on both surfaces of lower leaves and stem of the plant (Sharma, 1979). As the day temperature rises, the powdery patches increase in size, coalesce and rapidly spread to green stem, branches, leaves and pods giving the entire plant a dirty white appearance. Leaves turn yellow and shed (Singh & Solanki, 1974), flowers abort and pods remain empty or produce few seeds at base with twisted sterile tips. Later, towards the end of March, cleistothecia of *E. cruciferarum* in the form of small black bodies, scattered and in small groups, appear on the infected host surface (Saharan &

Kaushik, 1981). The cleistothecial stage of *E. polygoni* on *B. campestris* and *B. juncea* was noted by Shankhla *et al.* (1967).

2.2.4.2 The pathogens

These are obligate parasites and their mycelium is entirely superficial. It consists of a net work of hyphae present on the epidermis of the infected parts of the host and securely anchored thereon by numerous haustoria which penetrate into the epidermal cells to obtain nutrition (Alexopoulus, 1972). The conidia are borne on short and erect conidiophores. The conidia of *E. cruciferarum* are nearly cylindrical with rounded ends and measure 12.0–15.0 × 31.0–37.0 μm in diameter. Cleistothecia are brown to dark-brown, globose or sub-globose, with brownish septate mycelioid appendages. Cleistothecia measure 104.0-119.0 μm in diameter and contain 3-8 asci with 2-6 asco-spores per asci. Asci are sub-globose to broadly ovate, stalked, brown to yellowish and measure 32.0-35.0 × 52.0-62.0 μm on average (Saharan & Kaushik, 1981).

2.2.4.3 Perpetuation and epidemiology

The mode of perpetuation of the powdery mildew disease has not been worked out in India. These pathogens probably survive on other plant species which they are known to infect. Cleistothecial bodies also help in their perpetuation from one season to the other.

Powdery mildew is a late season disease, usually seen during early to mid-February when the plants are in end-flowering or pod formation stage. Dry weather is favourable and rainfall is injuri-ous for the development of the disease (Yarwood, 1957). Prevalence of moderate temperature (maximum 25.01°C and minimum 7.1°C), low relative humidity (65 per cent) and dry weather con-ditions (rainfall 0.6 mm) during February and March favour the initiation and epidemic develop-ment of powdery mildew of Brassica. The disease development is hindered under conditions of low mean temperature (13.7-14.6°C) and high rainfall (33.3-66.3 mm) during February. Rainfall during these months suppresses the disease due to its washing out effects on conidial forms, thereby reduc-ing the inoculum potential of the pathogen. Cleistothecia formation is favoured by alternating low and moderate tempeature (maximum 27.5°C and minimum 11.2°C), heavy sporulation, low host nutrition, low relative humidity, dry soil and aging of the host (Saharan & Kaushik, 1981).

Plants grown in soils of high pH have higher powdery mildew infection because of less manga-nese content of their leaves compared to plants grown in soils of low pH. Mildew infection becomes progressively less on plants supplied with increasing quantities of manganese (Brain & Whittington, 1981; Denton & Whittington, 1975).

2.2.4.4 Control

Control measure is not required against powdery mildew under normal conditions. Early sown crop escapes the severity of attack. Before deciding on control measures, plants should be assessed for severity of infection by sampling leaves taken from all stem positions, as top leaves tend to be much less infected (Jong & Hasper, 1996). In case of heavy infection, 3 sprays with 0.1-0.2 per cent Karathane at 10-20 days intervals starting from the first appearance of the disease provide most effective control and significant increase in yield [AICRP (R&M). 1998; Chahal, 1982; Singh &

Chauhan, 1996; Singh & Solanki, 1974)]. Sulphur dust (Butler, 1918), elosal and thiovit (Singh & Solanki, 1974), biloxazole (baycor) and triadimefon (bayleton) (Singh *et al.* 1984), calixin, wet sulphur, bavistin, blitox-50 and topsin-M (Singh & Chauhan, 1996) are among the other highly effective fungicides.

A few genotypes of *B. napus, B. carinata, B. juncea, B. alba, B. oleracea* var. *alboglabra, B. japonica* and *Eruca sativa* possess some degree of resistance to powdery mildew (Narain & Siddiqui, 1965; Gupta & Singh, 1994). According to Dang *et al.* (1997), *B. alba,* the genotypes HC-1 (*B. carinata*), DIR 1522 and Tower (*B. juncea*) and, GS 7027 and Midas (*B. napus*) have stable multiple resistance against Alternaria leaf blight, white rust, downy mildew and powdery mildew diseases.

2.2.5 Blackleg

Black leg or stem canker is caused by the pathogen *Leptosphaeria maculans* (Desm.) Ces. & De Not. (anamorph = *Phoma lingam* (Tode: Fr.) Desm.). It occurs on a wide range of plants, mostly of the Cruciferae, and also of the Compositae, Onagraceae and Gentiaceae. It is particularly common on Brassica species (Gabrielson, 1983; Johnson & Lewis, 1994; Petrie & Vanterpool, 1968). Black leg is endemic in most of the rapeseed producing countries because of world wide seed transmission (Gabrielson, 1983). Severe outbreaks of black leg devastated rapeseed crop in many countries since 1966. In Australia, rapeseed was introduced in 1968, black leg appeared in 1971, and a serious epidemic of the disease in 1972 virtually eliminated the crop. The area under rapeseed in Western Australia declined 96% by 1974 (Bokor *et al.* 1975; Roy & Reeves, 1975). In England, black leg was little known on winter rapeseed before 1977, but increased intensity of its cultivation led to serious outbreak of the disease in 1977 and 1978. During 1977, the disease incidence and yield loss were estimated at 100% and 50%, respectively in some fields (Cook & Evans, 1978; Evans & Gladders, 1981; Rawlinson & Muthyalu, 1979). Similarly in France, rapid expansion of winter oilseed rape cultivars was followed by serious outbreak of the disease in 1966 (Alabouvetti & Brunin, 1970), and then again in central and western France in autumn 1993 (Page & Penaud, 1995). In Manitoba, Canada, the disease caused an overall yield reduction of 9.6% (Platford, 1988). In 1990, black leg epidemic caused upto 80% yield loss in south east of Russell vile, Kentucky, USA (Mengistu *et al.* 1990). Fortunately, black leg is not found on rapeseed and mustard (*B. campestris* and B. *juncea*) in India, probably because of uncongenial drier climate of the crop season, short growth period of these crops. and mustard, which is resistant, occupies the major area.

2.2.5.1 *Symptoms*

The pathogen may attack any part of the plant. In the seedling stage, the disease appears on cotyledons as small, round to irregular, greyish white lesions bearing numerous black tiny fruiting bodies or pycnidia. On leaves, lesions appear as pale to fawn coloured, circular spots which gradually turn grey-white and become studded with pycnidia (Fig. 2.15). Pink masses of pycnidiospores in mucilage oozing out of pycnidia are dispersed to incite further leaf spots and stem lesions or cankers. Susceptibility of leaf increases with age (Hammond & Lewis, 1987). On susceptible cultivars of oilseed rape *(B. napus* ssp. *oleifera),* leaf infection initiates systemic infection of the leaf lamina

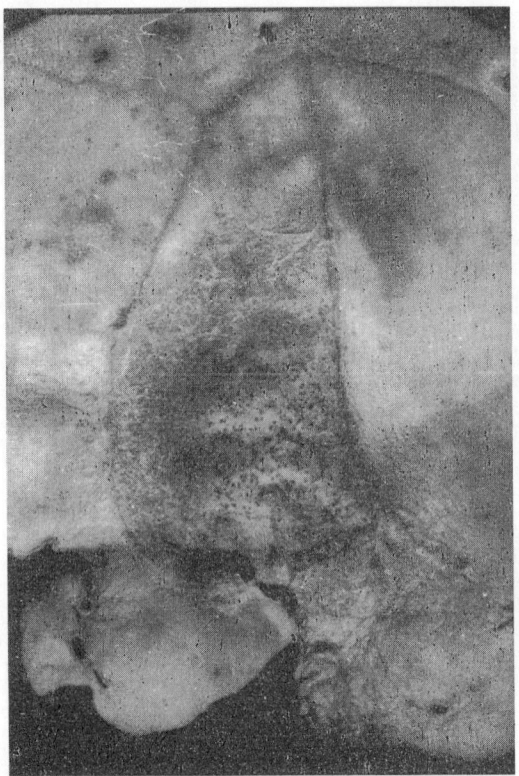 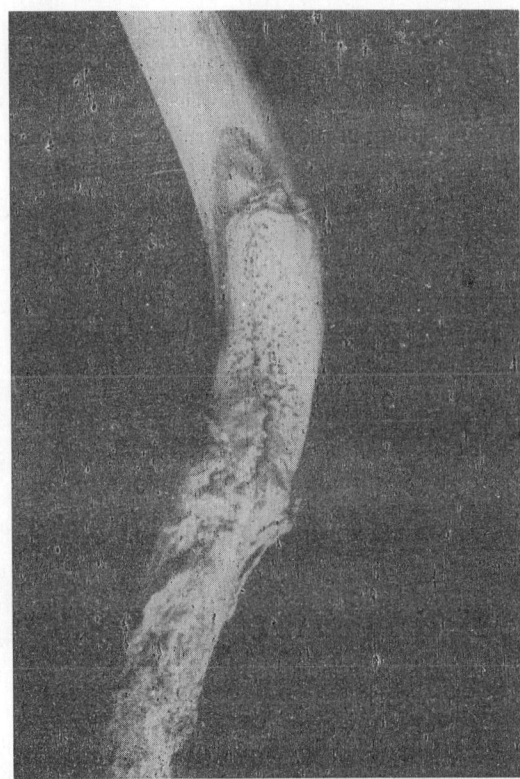

Fig. 2.15. Lesions of *L. maculans* on a leaf of *Brassica* sp. in Canada. Note the lesion surface studded with tiny pycnidial bodies. (*Courtesy*: P.R. Verma)

Fig. 2.16. Stem canker of *Brassica* sp. caused by *L. maculans* in Canada. Note the pycnidial bodies on stem surface (*Courtesy*: P.R. Verma)

and petiole resulting in a lesion in the stem cortex near the petiole base (Hammond *et al.* 1985; Hammond & Lewis, 1986). On old plants, stem cankers occur at the base of the stem (Fig. 2.16) close to the attachment of the lower leaves (Gladders & Musa, 1980).

Stem cankers are similar in appearance to leaf lesions except that they are sunken in the plant tissue and have a black or purple border. In case of severe infection, the canker expands girdling the stem base and restricting the flow of nutrients and water, and this results in pre-mature ripening of plants. The basal lesions sometimes sever the plant completely from the root system and cause it to lodge.

Pods from infected plants produce seeds that are light, shrivelled and infected. The crop yield is greatly reduced. Most losses in yield are caused by crown cankers, which develop mainly by infection of young plants from the cotyledons to 8th-leaf stages (Davis, 1986; Hall, 1992; Petrie, 1975).

2.2.5.2 *The pathogen*

The mycelium of *L. maculans* is septate, first hyaline but later turns black. Pycnidia variable in size and shape, dark tan or black, remain sunken in the substratum or erumpent, ostiolate and papillate. Conidiophores are very short, pycnidiospores are hyaline, one celled, oval to cylindrical, meausre 3-5 × 1.5-2.0 μm, and are produced in abundance within the pycnidium in pinkish masses in gelatinous matrix. Perithecia (Pseudothecia) dark or black coloured, polyascal with pseudoparaphyses; ascospores first hyaline but later turn tan coloured, 5-septate with constriction at the central septum, and measure 30-70 × 4-9 μm (Petrie & Vanterpool, 1968; Smith & Sutton, 1964). *Leptosphaeria maculans* is a heterothallic fungus (Gabrielson, 1983).

2.2.5.3 *Perpetuation and epidemiology*

Leptosphaeria maculans survives as perithecia and pycnidia on cruciferous seeds, crop residues and weeds. Infected seeds introduce the disease or more virulent strains to new areas (Alabouvette & Brunin, 1970; Davies, 1986; Hall, 1992; Williams, 1992).

Ascospores are the principal primary source of inoculum for the next crop. Ascospores released from perithecia in stubble residues of winter rape were seen blown over 8 km to infect autumn plantings in Germany (Steinbach *et al*. 1989).

Ascospores and pycnidiospores from weeds may also initiate the disease (Hall, 1992). Plant residues that are left on the soil surface or those brought to the surface by ploughing 2-4 years later, may contain perithecia of the fungus. Release of ascospores from perithecia is governed by rainfall (> 1 mm), relative humidity and temperature (optimum 15°C), the release follows a seasonal pattern coinciding usually with susceptible growth stage (sixth leaf stage) of the crop (Alabouvette & Brunin, 1970; McGee, 1977; Sudarmadi & Wallace, 1982). In Germany, perithecia develop on old rapeseed plants in autumn but in dry weather, their development is delayed upto November. Release of ascospores is followed by the development of leaf spots. Pycnidiospores produced after harvest also cause infection in autumn at the collar of late sown crop. From leaf spots in autumn, further inoculum develops and infects the spring crop. In France, autumn sown crops become severely infected by ascospores originating from fields with old stalks lying on soil surface (Kruger, 1988; Kruger & Wittern, 1985). In Cambridgeshire, UK, greatest number of ascospores were seen between October and April, although they were detected throughout the year. The degree of leaf spot infection correlated well with stem canker infection at the end of the flowering season and with severe stem canker at harvest (Gladders & Musa, 1980).

Secondary cycles are initiated by pycnidiospores produced on the crop and on stubble debris after harvest. They are spread by rain splash and wind within and between the neighbourhood fields where rape has been lately sown. If conditions are not suitable, the fungus remains latent on epidermal peels (Kruger, 1988; Sudarmadi & Wallace, 1984). It can survive in vegetable crucifer seeds upto 10 years (Gabrielson, 1983). In a study on the pathogenicity of *L. maculans* isolates on Brassica species and cruciferous hosts, Gugel *et al*. (1990) obtained basal stem lesion and internal blackening of stem and root tissue with many combinations of host and isolate.

Incidence of black leg is positively correlated with insect larvae damage (Broschewitz *et al* 1993). Resistance mechanism in cultivars does not operate where stem tissue is damaged by insect

(Newman & Plumridge, 1983). Grazing of sheep on rapeseed stubble does not spread the disease as propagules of the pathogen do not survive through their digestive system (MacNish, 1979a).

2.2.5.4 Physiological specialization

Isolates of *L. maculans* existing in different geographical regions comprise atleast two distinct virulence groups (Humpherson-Jones, 1983; Humpherson-Jones & Ainsworth, 1983; McGee & Petrie, 1978), the non-aggressive and the aggressive (Johnson & Lewis, 1990; Williams, 1992). They can be further categorized into 4 pathogenicity groups (PG) based on their differential reactions on the cotyledons of *B. napus* cvs. Westar, Quinta and Glacier. The non-aggressive isolates are designated PGl and are distinguished by their lack of virulence on the 3 cultivars. The isolates of the aggressive groups are of 3 pathotypes, PG2, PG3 and PG4 based on their differences in virulence on the cotyledons of the test cultivars (Koch *et al* 1991; Mengistu *et al*. 1990, 1991a,b). In culture, non-aggressive isolates produce a yellow or brown pigment, whereas the aggressive isolates do not (Hanacziwsky & Drysdale, 1984; Humpherson-Jones, 1983). Only the aggressive isolates produce the phytotoxins, sirodesmins *in vitro* (Koch *et al*. 1989). In culture filtrates of aggressive strains, the main components of sirodesmins identified were: sirodesmin PL, sirodesmin C, deacetyl sirodesmin PL and deacetyl sirodesmin C. They are systemically transported to and produce symptoms of phytotoxicity on leaves of rape seedlings when applied to their roots (Badawy & Hoppe, 1989). Production of sirodesmins depends on temperature, highest amount was obtained at 18 and 22°C, and production greatly decreased when the temperature was increased from 22 to 27°C. At different temperatures, sirodesmins production was incompatible with different host-parasite interactions of the aggressive isolates (Badawy, 1995).

Non-aggressive and aggressive isolates differ widely genetically (Johnson & Lewis, 1990; Taylor *et al*. 1991). Both groups infect wide range of cruciferous hosts including *B. napus, B. campestris, B. oleracea, B. juncea, B. carinata, B. nigra, Thlaspi arvense* and *Raphanus sativus*. Non-aggressive isolates are generally more aggressive on cotyledons than aggressive isolates in causing local lesions with subsequent systemic invasion of the majority of test species. In a susceptible *B. napus* line CrGC 5, both groups caused systemic infections of the leaf and petiole but non-aggressive isolates rarely entered the stem to form cortical lesions or cankers. Aggressive group of isolates is mainly associated with infection of the cortex near the stem base and development of typical canker lesion, whereas the non-aggressive group damages the pith tissue beside causing superficial chlorotic lesions on stem and inflorescences. Non-aggressive isolates are important in the epidemiology of black leg disease (Johnson & Lewis, 1990).

2.2.5.5 Resistance

Brassica nigra and *Sinapis arvensis* are more resistant to *L. maculans* than *B. juncea, S. alba* and *B. carinata* (Zhu & Spainer, 1991). Generally, *B. nigra, B. juncea* and *B. carinata* having the B genome, are very resistant and exhibit a hypersensitive type of reaction to black leg except for a few accessions which are susceptible, whereas *B. campestris* (*B. rapa*) and *B. napus* with C genome are susceptible (Downey & Rimmer, 1993; Helms & Cruickshank, 1979; Roy, 1978a; Sacristan and Gerdemann, 1986; Sjodin & Glimelius, 1988). *Brassica nigra* and *B. juncea* are commonly used in resistance breeding though resistance is also available in some cultivars of *B. napus*. The *B. napus* cultivars Jet Neuf, Rafal and Bienvenu are resistant to black leg in England (Davies, 1986). In France, the *B. carinata* cv. Awassa and *B. nigra* cv. Junius are completely resistant, and among the *B. napus cvs*, Darmor is most resistant (Brun *et al*. 1989) while Vivol is least susceptible to *L. maculans* (Page & Penaud, 1995).

Black leg resistance was readily transferred from the French rapeseed cultivar Major into the Australian cultivar Wesro (Roy, 1978b). Several lines derivd from spring rape (*B. napus*) cultivars Nosovsky, Ceska and Zollerngold were resistant to black leg. Lines that were highly resistant in the seedling stage were also the most resistant in the field (Cargeeg & Thurling, 1979).

Cotyledon resistance of a French winter breeding line to black leg is controlled by a single gene, Lml. A second dominant gene (Lm2) confers resistance in another line (Delwiche, 1980). Tests for independent inheritance of these two genes indicated linkage, whereas inheritance of cotyledon resistance in two lines of spring oilseed rape is controlled by a single recessive gene (Sawatsky, 1989).

Adult plant resistance to black leg in the two spring rape lines, R 83-14 and R 83-17 is governed by two genes with dominant alleles, designated Bl-1 and Bl-2. The presence of both dominant alleles (Bl-1, Bl-2) confers a high level of resistance whereas a single dominant allele (either Bl-1 bl-1, bl-2 bl-2) or (bl-1 bl-1, Bl-2 bl-2) confers intermediate levels of resistance (Sawatsky, 1989). The genetic control of black leg resistance in *B. napes* line R-13 (579 N048-109-DG-1589) possessing *B. juncea* like resistance (JR) was elucidated by analysing the segregation ratios in F_2 and F_3 populations derived from a cross between R-13 and the susceptible cv. Tower. The bimodal segregation ratios obtained in the F_2 population indicated that resistance in R-13 is controlled by major genes. Segregation ratios for F_3 families revealed that their resistance is controlled by 3 nuclear genes, which exhibited a complex interaction. All F_3 progeny plants had normal diploid somatic chromosome number for *B. napus* (Pang & Halloran, 1996).

The seedling resistance seen in *B. juncea* or *B. carinata* lines is controlled by genes located on the B genome. This is considered to be more effective than seedling resistane in *B. napus* (Roy 1984; Sacristan & Gerdemann, 1986).

The *B. juncea* cultivar Bj 168 exhibits both seedling and adult plant resistance, the resistance is heritable and can be transferred to susceptible *B. napus* (Roy, 1978a). The line Onap[JR] with complete resistance to black leg was developed from a cross between the *B. juncea* cv. Bj 168 and the *B. napus* swede rape cv. Cresus-O-Precose. Segregation for resistance in later generations of Onap[JR] indicated that resistance is governed by at least one major gene (Roy, 1984). The virulence of Australian isolates of *L. maculans* pathogenic to *B. juncea* cvs. Stoke and Zaria was found to be controlled by an allele at a single locus, when crossed with isolates avirulent on *B. juncea* (Chen *et al*. 1996).

Resistance in *B. nigra* to blackleg is considered to be polygenic and governed by at least 3 *B. nigra* chromosomes (Zhu *et al*. 1993).

A novel intergeneric somatic hybrid, the *Brassica naponigra* was synthesized by combining *B. napus* and *B. nigra* through protoplast fusion. The hybrid plants contianed chromosomes of both the plants and all had *B. napus* type of chloroplast. The resistance to *L. maculans* found in the *B. nigra* cultivar used in the development of the somatic hybrid, was expressed in 26 of the 30 somatic hybrid plants studied. The hybrids contained all of the 3 Brassica genomes (A, B and C) and most of the plants were fertile and resistant to *L. maculans* (Sjodin & Glimelius, 1989).

Leptosphaeria maculans stimulates accumulation of phytoalexins in leaf and stem tissue of Brassica species (Dahiya & Rimmer, 1988). A phytoalexin ($C_9H_6N_2S$) was isolated from the leaves of *B. juncea* cv. Aura (hypersensitive to *L. maculans)* following inoculation with the pathogen (Rouxel *et al.* 1989). Non-specific elicitation also induces phytoalexin accumulation in plants. All highly susceptible *B. napus* cultivars weakly accumulate the phytoalexin, 'brassilexin' whereas *B. juncea, B. carinata* and *B. nigra* displaying a hyper sensitive response to the pathogen, accumulate more brassilexin than *B. napus*. Similarly, interspecific hybrid progeny also display same correlation between resistance to *L. maculans* and phytoalexin accumulation (Rouxel *et al.* 1990).

In black leg resistant rape varieties, there is early differentiation of xylem which inhibits the growth of the fungus (Brunin, 1972). Resistance in *B. napus* is also associated with lignification of walls, and rapid and specific accumulation of calcium (Hammond & Lewis, 1980).

2.2.5.6 *Screening for resistance*

Plants may be screened for resistance to black leg by raising them in contaminated nursery beds or field. But screening carried out in green-house or growth-chamber under controlled conditions ensures reduction in the number of disease escapes generally associated with field nurseries and also accelerates the development of cultivars because two or three generations of plants can be grown in a year (Rimmer & Van den Berg, 1992).

Plants may be also screened at various growth stages using different methods of inoculation. Cotyledons or leaves are inoculated with ascospore or pycnidiospore suspension (Alabouvette *et al.* 1974; McGee & Petrie, 1978; Mithen *et al.* 1987), ascospores are more effective inoculum than pycnidiospores (Wood & Berbetti, 1977; Wittern & Kruger, 1985), and wounding the cotyledons and leaves at the time of application of inoculum increases the number of infected plants (Brunin & Lacoste, 1970). Stems are infected directly by injecting them with a pycnidiospore suspension or indirectly by inoculating cotyledons, leaves or petioles with a pycnidiospore suspension (Brunin & Lacoste, 1970; McGee & Petrie, 1978; Newman & Bailey, 1987).

Disease reaction of individual plant is determined by using a variety of rating scales. Cotyledon reactions are classified according to lesion size, the occurrence of necrosis or chlorosis and the presence of pycnidia (Williams, 1985). Similarly, reaction of leaves may be based on lesion type and its size (McGee & Petrie, 1978; Mithen & Lewis, 1988). Stem reaction is assessed using internal and external symptoms such as percentage of the stem girdled by the lesion, penetration of the lesion into the stem or length of the lesion or a combination of these observations (Newman & Bailey, 1987; Kutcher, 1990).

2.2.5.7 *Control*

Maintenance of proper sanitary conditions such as removal and destruction by burning of cruciferous weeds and infected plant debris or burying them into the soil by deep ploughing, locating new rape plantings at maximum distance away from old crop stubbles, timely sowing with proper seed rate, avoidance of injury to plants during tillage operations and observance of sufficiently long rotations to reduce the inoculum in the field, are the important measures that keep down the incidence of black leg disease (Cook & Evans, 1978; Dacbclcr *et al*. 1980; Gugel & Petrie, 1992; Seidal *et al*. 1984). Maintenance of about 5 to 8 km distance of new plantings from the previous rape stubbles was helpful in keeping rapeseed crops reasonably free from black leg infection in Australia (Bokor *et al*. 1975). In France, delaying sowing from late August or early September to middle or late September resulted in lower infection rate in rape during, 1995 (Page and Penaud, 1995). In Germany, crop density of more than 80 plants/m^2 favoured black leg infestation (George *et al*. 1985). Growing the crop in rotation with non-susceptible crop such as cereals after at least 4 years also ensured good control of the disease (George *et al*. 1985; Gladders & Gould, 1983; MacNish, 1979b).

Development and use of resistant cultivars with desirable agronomic traits is the most reliable measure to prevent yield reduction due to black leg (Kruger, 1982). Sources of resistance and cultivars found resistant to black leg have been mentioned in the preceding paragraphs.

Sowing seeds certified to be free of *L. maculans* and treated with recommended fungicide is essential to prevent introduction of the pathogen or its virulent strains to new cropping area. The use of chemicals against black leg is not very popular because the results are often varied, inconsistent and not cost effective (Davies, 1986; Garbe, 1993; Gugel & Petrie, 1992). Chemical treatments to be effective should be timed according to the dynamics of ascospore release (Gugel & Petrie, 1992). Seed treatment with benomyl or Procloraz is effective against only seedling infection by *L. maculans* but not against adult plant infection in the field (Brown *et al*. 1976; Kharbanda, 1992). In Australia, application of benomyl, 8 weeks after sowing, significantly reduced the occurrence of stem lesions but a second application, after 11 weeks had no additional effect (Nuzum & Kaldor, 1988). However, application of flutriafol at sowing as fungicide treated superphosphate at 50-200g a.i./ha reduced black leg disease in rapeseed and increased the seed yield (Ballinger *et al*. 1988). In England, seed treatment with benomyl (5 g/kg seeds) followed by one or more additional spray application (1.12 a.i kg/ha) before stem elongation phase of the crop resulted in significant control of canker (Rawlinson & Mathyalu, 1979). The fungicide procloraz reduced black leg infection in oilseed rape following its application in late autumn and spring in England, but it did not result in significant yield increase (Evans *et al*. 1984).

In Germany, combined spring and autumn application of benzimidazol and triazole fixngicides coinciding, respectively with the time of ascospore release in autumn and to disease progress in winter and early spring, and to pest damage resulted in effective control of *L. maculans* (Steinbach *et al*. 1991). According to Page and Penaud (1995), fungicidal seed treatment provided protection against infection for only 4-6 weeks, after which fungicide treatment at growth stage B3 gave best control in France. This growth stage coincided with first peak of ascospore discharge. No difference in efficacy was found between several fungicides tested.

An integrated approach combing all the measures is required for effective, efficient and longer-lasting control of black leg (Gugel & Petrie, 1992).

2.2.6 Sclerotinia Stem Rot

Stem rot is caused by *Sclerotinia sclerotiorum* (Lib.) de-Bary. The disease is also called stalk break (Kirchner & Pluschkell, 1973), white blight (Roy & Saikia, 1976), white stalk or rape canker

(Kruger, 1983), etc. based on symptoms produced on the host. *Sclerotinia sclerotiorum* is one of the most serious, non-specific, omnivorous and successful plant pathogenic fungus with a host range encompassing about 400 species, mostly among dicotyledonous plants (Willetts & Wong, 1980). The pathogen flourishes well in relatively cool and moist area of the world, is found in both hot and dry localities and has been reported from many countries located in all continents (Purdy, 1979).

Stem rot is a major disease of oilseed brassicas in many parts of the world, including Canada (Morrall & Dueck, 1982), Germany (Kruger & Stoltenberg, 1983), Sweden (Nordin & Svensson, 1987a) and China (Liu *et al.* 1990). Severe yield losses, decreases in fat content and erucic acid of seeds, have been reported in oilseed rape (*B. napus* ssp. *oleifera*) due to stem rot (Kruger *et al.* 1980; Regnault *et al.* 1987). Seed and oil yield per plant are significantly negatively correlated with the severity of sclerotinia infection in all *Brassica* spp. (Chen *et al.* 1993).

The disease was first reported from Pusa (Bihar), India in 1915 on *Brassica campestris* var. *glauca* (Shaw & Ajrekar, 1915) and thereafter on *Eruca sativa* (Mehta *et al.* 1946), *B. campestris* var. Sarson, *Raphanus sativus* (Chona *et al.* 1958), *B. juncea*, *B. rogosa*, *B. oleracea* var. *botrytis*, *B. oleracea* var. *capitata*, *B. oleracea* var. *gemmifera*, *B. oleracea* var. *gongyloides* (Roy, 1973), *Alyssum* spp., *B. campestris* var. Toria, *B. nigra* and *Cheiranthus cheiri*, etc. (Rai *et al.* 1974; Saxena, 1972) and many other hosts. In Assam, mustard crop failed due to stem rot attack (Roy & Saikia, 1976). During 1986, the disease incidence on *B. campestris* var. Yellow sarson and *B. campestris* var. Toria ranged from 50-60% and 35-40%, respectively in Darbhanga, Bihar (Saxena & Rai, 1986).

Stem rot is also prevalent in Punjab, Haryana, Rajasthan, Delhi, Uttar Pradesh, Bihar, West Bengal, Orissa, N.E. Hill States, and Anadaman and Nicobar islands [AICRP (R&M). 1996]. It affected about 5-10 per cent of rapeseed and mustard crops in Bharatpur district of Rajasthan during 1995-96 season (Shukla & Sharma, 1997). However, no estimate of yield losses due to stem rot is available nor it is considered to be a major production constraint for rapeseed and mustard in India at present.

2.2.6.1 Symptoms

Sclerotinia sclerotiorum attacks all the above ground parts of the plant. Even roots may be infected (Saxena & Rai, 1986). Infection at the plant base leads to collar rot. Usually, the first symptoms are seen on leaves or stem as light brown water soaked spots which rot very quickly in moist weather. In case of stem infection which is most important and common, infection usually starts at a leaf node (Fig. 2.17a, b) and spreads in both directions in the stem (Kruger, 1988), infection occurring on other parts of a leaf has less effect on stem (Chen & Zhang, 1991). The rotted areas become covered with white frosty growth of mycelium, lesions expand longitudinally, often show distinct concentric zonations and gradually girdle the stem. The leaves arising from the infected patches droop down and shed. Numerous sclerotia appear embedded in the external mycelium and within the rotted stem. Infected pods become similarly covered with superficial mycelium, show no seed formation but often contain mycelium and sclerotia. The severely affected parts rot and shred into fibres, the stem may break at the point of infection or the entire plant collapses and becomes covered with mycelium and sclerotia. The sclerotia fall on the ground and persist in the soil or get

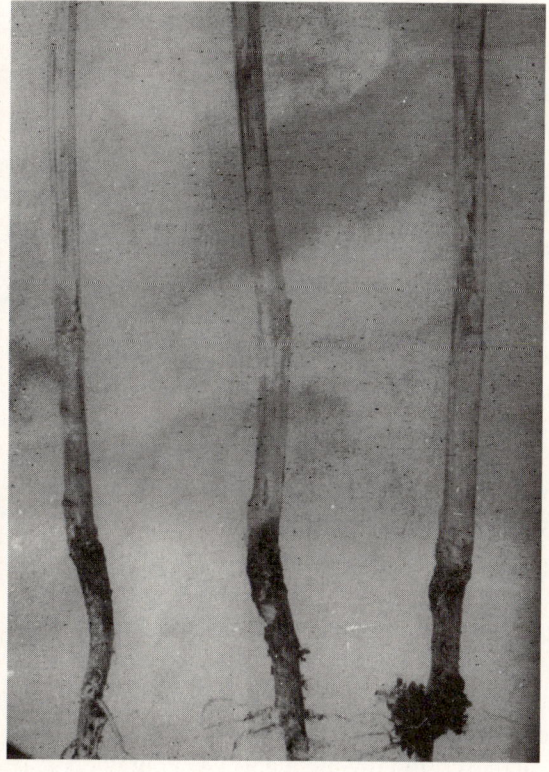 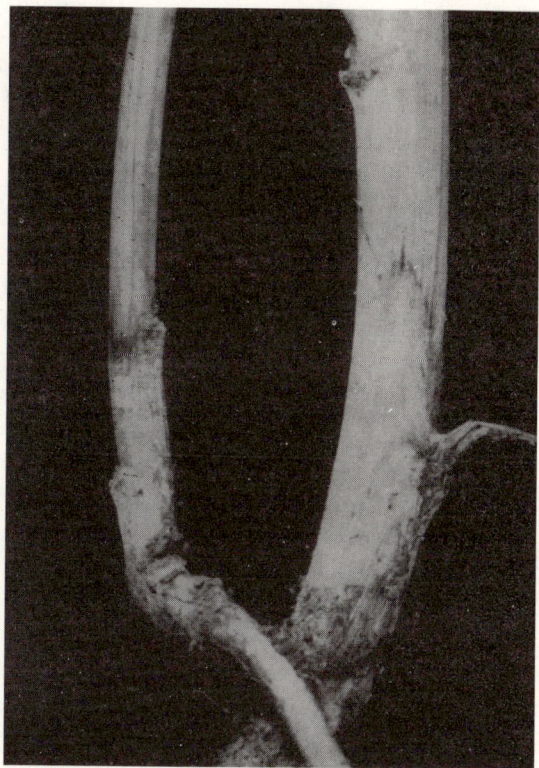

Fig. 2.17. (a) Collar rot of *Brassica* sp. caused by *S. sclerotiorum* in Canada (*Courtesy*: P.R. Verma)

Fig. 2.17. (b) Stem rot of *Brassica* sp. caused by *S. sclerotiorum* in Canada (*Courtesy*: P.R. Verma)

harvested with seeds. In dry weather, infections remain restricted as necrotic spots (Davies, 1986; Mehta *et al.* 1946; Roy, 1973).

2.2.6.2 *The pathogen*

The fungus mycelium is both inter- and intracellular. The fungus produces micro-conidia and sclerotia, the latter show both myceliogenic or carpogenic germination (Willetts & Wong, 1980). It can grow between the temeprature of 0-30°C, but 18-25°C is considered optimum for both growth and formation of sclerotia. In Germany, sclerotia lying in the upper soil layer germinated under moist conditions with soil temperature of 6-10°C (Kruger, 1975). According to Mehta and co-workers (1946), the fungus sclerotia formed on *Eruca sativa* were variable in size and shape, and measured 2-12 mm (av. 6mm). Sclerotia lying buried in moist soil germinate giving rise to apothecia. Usually 1-5 cylindrical and flexuous fruiting stipes are produced from each buried sclerotium. The stipes are often dichotomously branched and each of them supports a shallow, flat or concave apothecium at its tip, which when mature measures 6-9 mm in diameter. The asci measure 122.9 × 5.9 μm in size and the ascospores are 8.9 × 3.9 μm. Kruger (1975) observed the ascospores to germinate at 20°C in the presence of free water with high relative humidity of 94% or relative humidity alone greater than 94%. No germination occurred at or below 84% relative humidity even when free water was present.

2.2.6.3 Perpetuation and epidemiology

Sclerotinia sclerotiorum can remain viable both as mycelium and ascospores. The fungus sclerotia may remain viable in the soil for atleast eight years (Davies, 1986; Williams & Stelfox, 1980a,b).

Infection of suscpetible host plants in the field is caused by mycelium that originates from eruptive germination of sclerotia. Direct mycelial infection of rape plants from soil-borne sclerotia can occur but it is relatively unimportant compared with ascospsore infection (Kruger, 1975; Morrall & Dueck, 1982). Sclerotia develop apothecia and eject ascospores which become air-borne (Purdy, 1979; Saxena & Rai, 1986) and land on plants (Kruger, 1988). They were detected at a height of 147 cm above the soil surface and were also intercepted at a distance of 150 m from the nearest source indicating the feasibility of air borne spores being carried to rape fields not previously infested with *S. sclerotiorum* (Williams & Stelfox, 1979). Ascospores may also adhere on pollen grains, and honey bees spread the fungal propagules between rape plants while collecting the contaminated pollens (Stelfox *et al.* 1978).

The development of stem rot is most rapid during flowering period of the crop under cool temperature and moist soil conditions (Roy & Saikia, 1976; Teo *et al.* 1989). Soils with high organic carbon, P and electrical conductivity were associated with lower disease incidence. When soil was deficient in these characteristics, the disease incidence became more (Sharma & Singh, 1998). In humid conditions, infected plant parts show high degree of rotting while plants growing wide apart and in fields with low moisture contents, show whitish localized spots and restricted infection (Saxena & Rai, 1986). Disease incidence is not consistently correlated with apothecia formation or agronomic practices (Morrall & Dueck, 1982), nor seeding date, seeding rate and Brassica cultivars influence either apothecia formation or disease development. More apothecia were produced in high nitrogen plots than in normal nitrogen plots but disease development was unaffected (Nordin *et al.* 1992; Teo *et al.* 1989). The amount of rain during the full flowering period of rapeseed crop is a major influencing factor on the development of apothecia. If apothecia are present during such a period, then the risk of disease is considerable, both at normal and high humidities in the field (Nordin *et al.* 1992). There is, however, no correlation between total rainfall and ascospore production. Ascospore release is reduced during wet, overcast and calm conditions, with the greatest reduction occurring in rainy, calm weather. Changing weather conditions with some rains, slight wind and moist fields are most favourable for ascospore production (Kruger, 1974, 1975, 1988).

Ascospores require exogenous nutrient source such as dead flowers, injured leaves or organic matter (Abawi & Grogan, 1975; Huang & Kokko, 1992; Natti, 1971; Newton & Sequeria, 1972; Purdy & Bardin, 1953) for germination and infection of host tissue. They also infect the petals on intact flowers. When infected petals fall, they adhere to lower leaves, leaf axils or stem (Lamarque, 1983). They are the primary unit of disease dissemination, and infection of rape plants occurs via infected petals (Jamaux *et al.* 1995).

Ascospores landing on rapeseed petals adhere, germinate and there is rapid collapse of petal tissues in advance of fungal growth due to the production of extracellular lytic enzymes (Dhawan,

1980; Dhawan *et al.* 1987; Lumsden, 1976; Marciano *et al.* 1982; Rai & Dhawan, 1976a) and oxalic acid. Oxalic acid minus mutants are non-pathogenic (Godoy *et al.* 1990; Marciano *et al.* 1982; Rai & Dhawan, 1976b). Penetration occurs on petals without appressoria formation and mycelium is both inter- and intracellular in its endophytic colonization. Mycelium emerging from the petal penetrates the leaf cuticle directly via infection cushions. Ascospores landing directly on leaf surfaces do not adhere, and die (Jamaux *et al.* 1995; Lamarque, 1983; Tarique & Jeffries, 1984). Disease incidence is positively correlated with petal infestation under favourable conditions for infection (Turkington & Morrall, 1993) and this relationship may be exploited and used as a quantitative method of forecasting stem rot epidemics (Gugel & Morrall, 1986). The distribution of ascospores of *S. sclerotiorum* on petals of *Brassica* spp. can be determined by the immunofluorescence staining technique (Lefol & Morrall, 1996).

Kohli *et al.* (1992) determined clonal variability within and among field populations of *S. sclerotiorum* isolated from canola (rape) petals in Western Canada using mycelial compatibility and DNA finger prints as two independent criterion. *Sclerotinia sclerotiorum* clones may be distributed over long geographical distances and field populations of the pathogen may be composed of more than one clone. Intact clonal genotypes also may be dispersed as ascospores.

2.2.6.4 *Resistance*

Progress in breeding for resistance to *S. sclerotiorum* has been rather slow because of wide host range of the pathogen, lack of host specificity of its isolates and the availability of effective chemicals for its control. In places where high level of infection is consistently obtained, large scale screening of cultivars may be done under field conditions but in drier regions, where the disease appears sporadically, testing and selection should be done under controlled conditions in the green-house.

Plants may be inoculated by placing young mycelial blocks of the pathogen on the leaf stalk or by inserting tooth picks impregnated with mycelium (Brun *et al.* 1987b; Hu & Rimmer, 1989). Plants can be also inoculated by placing Sclerotinia- infected kernels of rye in leaf axil, 10-15 cm above the soil line. The rate of stem lesion expansion is considered to be a reliable index of resistance of Brassica stem tissue to invasion and colonization by *S. sclerotiorum*. The highest average rate of stem lesion expansion is observed in *B. campestris* followed in decreasing order of susceptibility by *B. juncea* and *B. nigra*, whereas both *B. carinata* and *B. napus* with lowest stem lesion expansion are resistant. In resistant *B. carinata* cultivars, all inoculated leaves absci before the fungus can infect the stem, signifying this to be an additional trait for resistance. The occurrence of leaf abscission reaction is weak to moderate in *B. napus*, *B. juncea* and *B. nigra*, but is absent in the highly susceptible *B. campestris* (Sedun *et al.*1989).

Tolerance to stem rot in *B. napus* is controlled by nuclear genes and is unlinked to the low-erucic acid trait (Liu *et al.* 1990). The genes for Sclerotinia stem rot resistance are located in genomes B and C of Brassica genus (Chen *et al.* 1993). Mullins and co-workers (1995) developed a near-isogenic line, HH1 of *B. napus* cv. Linetta using induced mutagenesis. The line HH1 expressed significantly higher levels of resistance to stem rot than the common commercial oilseed germplasm. Partial resistance in HH1 was typified by a distinct reduction in lesion girdling and presence of much less amount of pathogen mycelium in inoculated stems, which also remained closer to the site of inoculation than in cv. Linetta.

Apetalous cultivars show less incidence of stem rot as compared to their normal petalous counterparts (Downy & Rimmer, 1993). Fu (1990), and Lu and Fu (1990) developed one apetalous line, APL 0256 of *B. napus* and studied the inheritance of apetalous character in plants derived from crosses between APL 0256 and normal petalous cultivars. Apetalous trait was found to be controlled by 4 pairs of recessive genes, p1p1p2p2p3p3p4p4. Apetalous cultivars require less energy because of having to produce fewer floral parts, get more light energy for crop canopy and show reduced incidence of *S. sclerotiorum* because of the absence of petals as disease spreading units.

2.2.6.5 Control

Incidence of stem rot can be greatly minimized by soil treatment with chemicals like calcium cyanamide, fentin acetate and quintozene to inhibit the germination of soil-borne sclerotia (Kruger, 1973; Winter *et al.* 1993). Field application of calcium cyanamide at 10-12 cwt/ha reduces the disease incidence by 40 to 90 per cent. It has long persistence and high efficacy, and should be applied when the plants are dry to avoid phytotoxicity (Kruger, 1973, 1980, 1988). Among the substances formed in the soil during transformation from calcium cyanamide to ammonium salts, dicyandiamide (DCD) and guanylurea sulphate persist long periods and cause strong inhibition of sclerotial germination and apothecial formation (Finck, 1989; Kruger, 1980).

Spray application of fungicides during flowering period of the crop to prevent infection by air borne ascospores is a highly effective measure but this should be done when the expected yield increase is economically rewarding (Davies, 1986; Morrall *et al.* 1985, 1989; Thomson *et al.* 1984). Roy and Saikia (1976) obtained good control of the disease and increase is seed yield of mustard by spraying the crop with 0.025% benomyl. Singh *et al.* (1994) recommended seed treatment followed by spraying with benomyl or carbendazim for its effective control in Indian mustard. Iprodione, vinclozolin and metalaxyl also provide effective control of stem rot of rapeseed and mustard (Singh, 1988).

A single application of benomyl or vinclozolin at 25% bloom stage controls the stem rot in rapeseed according to Dueck *et al.* (1983). Efficacy of vinclozolin against *S. sclerotiorum* has been also confirmed by other workers (Nordin *et al.* 1992; Nordin & Svensson, 1987b; Saur, 1983). Two applications of benomyl, vinclozolin or iprodione at 0.3 kg a.i/ha at early and full bloom provided good control under both low and high disease pressure (Morrall *et al.* 1985).

Removal of all leaves under 1 m of the main stem of oilseed rape controlled the disease and increased the yield by 6.4-15.4% (Fu & Tang, 1994). Seed treatment, rotations between vegetable and cereal crops, optimum fertilizer dose, rational close planting, pruning of old and infected leaves, and spray application of 50% carbendazole are the integrated disease control measures found effective against sclerotinia rot of oilseed rape in Shanxi, China (Yu *et al.* 1995)

2.2.7 Collar Rot

Collar rot of mustard is caused by *Sclerotium rolfsii* Sacc. [*Athelia rolfsii* (Curzi.) Tu & Kimbrough]. It is a plant pathogen with more than 500 plant species as host (Aycock, 1966). In

India, it was seen first time on Toria and mustard at Banaras, UP by Upadhyay and Pavgi (1967) and then studied by Khan (1985). Collar rot affected about 10 per cent mustard seedlings after 30-40 days of sowing at Pantnagar. Disease development was more severe in sandy soil than in heavy soil in greenhouse test (Khan & Kolte, 1989). In Himachal Pradesh, highest incidence of the disease was seen in sarson (*B. campestris*) followed by Indian mustard and *B. carinata* in 5th October sown crops (Kumar & Thakur, 1997).

The disease is characterized by rotting of tissues of the collar region of affected seed-lings. The rotted area turns brown, which later develops profuse white mycelial growth interpersed with light brown or tan coloured mustard seed-like sclerotial bodies. Infected plants wilt and die.

Collar rot of rapeseed and mustard is infrequent in appearance and economically unimportant in India.

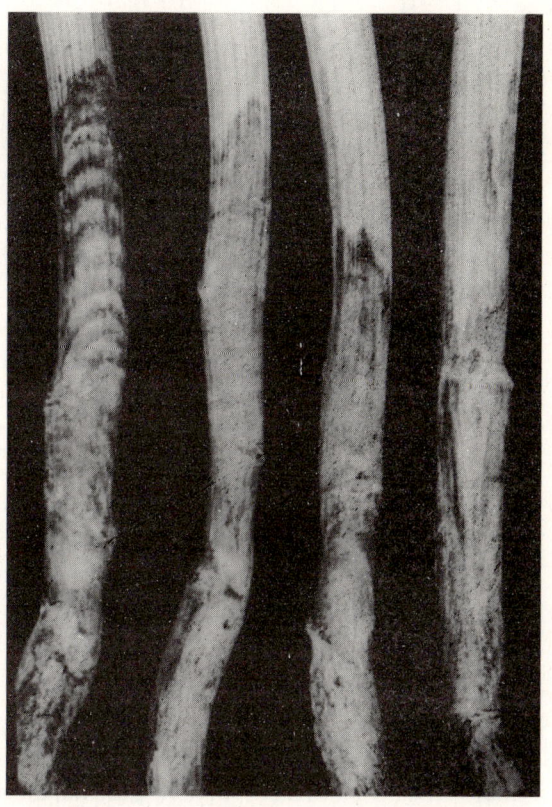

Fig. 2.18. Stem canker of *Brassica* sp. caused by *R. solani* in Canada. Note the concentric rings on stem surface and the damaged tap root. (*Courtesy*: P.R. Verma)

2.2.8 Rhizoctonia Rot

Rhizoctonia solani Kuhn (Telemorph: *Thanatephorus cucumeris* (Frank) Donk.), and *R. bataticola* (Taub.) Butler (Pycnidial state: *Macrophomina phaseolina* (Tassi) Goid) are important soil borne pathogens of oilseed brassicas. They have wide host range, geographical distribution and environmental adaptability (Anderson, 1982; Dhingra & Sinclair, 1978; Parmeter & Whitney, 1970).

2.2.8.1 Symptoms

Rhizoctonia solani causes pre- and postemergence seedling damping-off and stem canker, root rot or aerial blight of adult rape and canola plants in large areas. Root rots are prevalent in varying severity in the different provinces across the Canadian prairie (Kataria & Verma, 1992). The disease is seen as light brown lesions on the tap root and lateral roots, usually at or following the onset of flowering. Lesions become sunken, darker and may enlarge to girdle the basal stem (Fig. 2.18) and tap root resulting in premature death of plants. Dessication and lodging of plants are common. Losses are greatest when high temperature and dry wind follow the root damage. Root rot affected plants show poor pod formation, pod sterility, loss of seed weight, shrivelled seeds, premature senescence of the pods, lodging and uneven ripening. The disease reduced the yield by 30% in the Peace River region of Alberta, Canada both in the year 1983 and 1984 (Kataria & Verma, 1992; Sippell *et al*. 1985).

In India, *R. solani* causing root and collar rot of rapeseed and mustard has been reported from UP (Srivastava, 1968) and Sikkim (Gupta, 1985). *Brassica campestris* var. Toria, *B. campestris* var. Sarson and *B. juncea* were severely infected in the Gangtok area of Sikkim during January 1984. The yellow sarson cvs. YS-51, YSIK-711, YS-9 and YS-5516 suffered most. Affected plants developed typical reddish brown lesions on the collar region which extended to the roots leading to premature death of plants and serious loss in yield (Gupta, 1985).

The pathogen also incites serious leaf blight. Leaf blight appears as small, water-soaked greyish spots which gradually turn straw to light brown patches and the affected leaves shed prematurely. Fungal hyphae bearing sclerotia appear first on the infected leaf area and then spread to all other affected plant parts. The sclerotia measure 217-66 × 178-443 μm in size. The disease spreads in the field through physical contact of affected plants with the healthy ones. Leaf blight becomes most severe under warm and humid conditions with heavy dew formation during the night, and the disease spreads rapidly to larger plant populations (Chauhan & Saxena, 1974).

2.2.8.2 The pathogens

The Rhizoctonia mycelium shows constriction of hyphal branches at their point of origin, and the septum is placed close to the point of branching. The lateral growth of branches is given out almost at right angles. The mycelium is both intra- and intercellular in the host tissue and form sclerotia both in the host and on organic residues in the soil. The sclerotia produced by *R. solani* are spherical to oval, dark brown or black whereas the sclerotia (called microsclerotia) produced by *R. bataticola* are small, round to irregular and black. They are released in the soil upon decay of their organic substrate and host tissue to constitute the chief source of inoculum. *Rhizoctonia bataticola* in its Macrophomina stage produces numerous small, black, ostiolate pycnidia sunk in the host tissue, which give out hyaline, spherical to oval pycnidiospores to disseminate the pathogen (Alexopoulos, 1972).

The taxonomic relations among isolates of *R. solani* are usually determined on the basis of hyphal anastomosis. The anastomosis group (AG) of a field isolate is determined by pairing it with a known tester isolate, say on 2% water agar and examined under a compound microscope. If no fushion occurs at the junction of hyphae of the two isolates, the field isolate is considered to be in a different AG than the tester isolate. However, if fushion occurs between hyphae of the two isolates as evident by vaculation and death of 5-6 cells on either side of the fushion point, they are considered to be of the same AG (Parmeter *et al*. 1969). Each group of isolates has distinctive morphological, pathological and physiological characteristics with a few overlapping ones (Sherwood, 1969), and each is regarded genetically isolated and non-inter breeding population (Anderson, 1982; Bolkan & Ribeiro, 1985). Parmeter *et al*. (1969) recognized four distinct AG's of *R. solani* (AG 1, AG 2, AG 3 and AG 4). Kuninaga *et al*. (1979) expanded the concept to include six AGs, and Ogoshi (1972) have proposed two subgroups within both AG 1 and AG 2.

These groups display distinct specificity in infecting particular host plants. Besides, the pathogenicity and virulence of *R. solani* in different hosts are also influenced by the source of the isolates (Anderson, 1982; Grisham & Anderson, 1983; Herr & Robert, 1980; Ichielevich-Auster *et al*. 1985; Ruppel, 1972; Stephens *et al*. 1982). Isolates from soils are less virulent than those from seedlings and adult plants in causing seed and seedling infections (Yitbarek *et al*. 1987). The populations of *R. solani* that infect oilseed rape and canola (*B. napus* and *B. campestris*) are mainly composed of the anastomosis groups AG 2-1 and AG 4 (Kataria & Verma, 1992).

The isolates of AG 2-1 grow at temperature of 2°C but not at 36°C whereas reverse is the case with isolates of AG 4 (Kaminski & Verma, 1985). AG 2-1 isolates are more virulent than AG 4 isolates at low temperatures (Yitbarek *et al*. 1988). Seedling damping-off and root rot caused by AG 2-1 isolates are favoured by cool weather and high soil moisture at the time of sowing during spring, whereas subsequent warm weather and drier soils in summer is more favourable to severe root rot by AG 4 isolates in maturing crop (Kataria & Verma, 1992).

2.2.8.3 Brassica–Rhizoctonia solani interaction

Rhizoctonia solani infects hypocotyls and roots of susceptible rape seedlings by forming specialized infection cushions. The hyphae grow on the host surface, branch repeatedly and ultimately form short and stout branches. These branches finally form compact dome-shaped cushions on the surface of hypocotyl and roots. Infection pegs arise from the underside of an infection cushion and penetrate the hypocotyl directly through the cuticle and junction of the anticlinal walls of epidermal cells. Once inside the cortex, the hyphae grow both inter- and intracellularly (Yang *et al*. 1992b).

The sequence of events in the infection process are similar in both resistant mustard (*Sinapis alba*) and susceptible rape (*B. napus*) hypocotyls but the progress of infection is slower in the resistant than in the susceptible host. Infection cushions are appreciably less frequent on the resistant host. Lobate appressoria and penetration through stomata are not seen. In the early stages of infection, the hyphae invade the vascular tissue of the susceptible host while they are limited to the cortical tissue in the resistant host. The infected plants undergo cytological changes like the formation of reaction zones, swelling and degradation of cell wall, retraction of plasmalemma, and plasmolysis and collapsing of cytoplasm (Kataria & Verma, 1992; Yang *et al*. 1992b).

2.2.8.4 Resistance

Among Brassica species, *S. alba* shows greater resistance to *R. solani*. *Brassica nigra* and *B. juncea* also show some resistance whereas *B. napus*, *B. campestris*, *B. carinata* and *B. oleracea* (kale) are highly susceptible. The disease is less severe on mature plants than seedlings, and resistance in seedlings is manifested in adult plants as well. The resistance of *S. alba* and old plants of *B. napus* is due to thickness of their cuticle layer (Gugel *et al*. 1987; Kataria & Verma, 1992; Yang *et al*. 1989, 1992a; Yang & Verma, 1992).

2.2.8.5 Control

Incorporation of resistance in commercial cultivars is the best method of protection against damping-off and root rot of oilseed rape. Seed treatment with chemicals provides protection against damping-off and root rot of seedlings though it is not effective against root rot in adult plants. Benodanil, benomyl, carboxin (Vitavax), cyproconazole, flutolanil and tolclofos-methyl showed strong activity against *R. solani* isolates of both AG 2-1 and AG 4 in laboratory tests. Iprodione and tolclofos-methyl provide maximum protection against post-emergence root rot. Disease control is better when a fungicide is used in combination with the insecticide counter (terbufos) or lindane (gamma-HCH). They have additive effects (Kataria & Verma, 1989, 1990, 1992).

Some bioagents are also effective against *R. solani* damping-off and root rot of oilseeds. Amendments of soil with *Trichoderma harzianum* provide good control of damping-off in mustard (Akhtar, 1969). Dahiya and Woods (1987) isolated a strain of *Pseudomonas fluorescence* antagonistic to *R. solani* and treatment of canola seeds with the bacterium controlled damping-off in infested soil. Fiddaman and Rossall (1995) isolated one *Bacillus subtilis* 205 antagonistic to *R. solani* from oilseed rape. A simple slurry coat formulation of *B. subtilis* 205 provided excellent control of pre-emergence damping-off and best result was obtained under autum sowing field conditions.

2.2.8a Macrophomina Wilt

Macrophomina phaseolina causes pre-mature death of oilseed rape in Indiana and Kentucky, USA (Baird *et al.* 1994) and severe wilt disease of mustard in India (Singh & Pavgi, 1980). In India, the wilt disease of mustard was noticed mostly in the sandy loam soils of Varanasi, UP. Infection is seen at the seedling stage in early November and later, on maturing plants during December to mid-January. In case of early infection, plants become stunted in growth, lower leaves shrivel and wither, and the plant is killed. In late infections, yellowing and gradual drying of mature leaves is followed by premature death of plants. Plants stand out as defoliated dry stem in the field. Partial wilting of plants may also occur (Singh & Pavgi, 1980).

Stray incidence of the disease can be seen throughout north India, mostly in fields with moisture-stressed soil. The disease incidence in Chinese mustard was positively correlated with maximum temperature and the disease intensity had a highly significant negative correlation with relative humidity, soil moisture and soil pH (Srivastava & Dhawan, 1979). Severely affected plants easily come out of the soil with their tap root showing only a few secondary and tertiary roots. The stem base of such plants becomes ash-grey, shrivelled and shredded, and bears numerous microsclerotia on the rind and in the discoloured pith.

All these diseases are sporadic in appearance and economically not very important.

2.2.9 Fusarium Wilt

The Fusarium wilt of mustard (*Brassica juncea*) caused by *Fusarium oxysporum* fsp. *conglutinans* (Wr.) Snyder & Hansen was first reported by Rai and Singh (1973). The disease was observed on crops near Lucknow in December 1965 and thereafter, at several places in UP with incidence varying from 5 to 10 per cent. Later, Fusarium wilt affecting Indian mustard was reported by Gupta (1990) from Rajasthan. The pathogen was also responsible for severe wilt in *B. nigra* at Faizabad, UP (Kanaujia & Kishore, 1981). Another record of wilt disease of *B. juncea* caused by an unidentified species of Fusarium is from the USA (Index of plant diseases in the United States, No. 65,

1960, U.S.D.A., Washington, D.C.). In Canada, Calman *et al.* (1986) found *F. avenaceum* as one of the causal agents of seedling blight of canola (*Brassica campestris* and *B. napus*).

2.2.9.1 Symptoms

Plants of all ages are affected by the disease. The leaves of affected plants show drooping, vein clearing and chlorosis followed by wilting and drying, and then death of plants. In the early stage of development, affected plants do not show all the typical symptoms. Plants affected in the pre-flowering and early flowering stages show defoliation and their stem externally develops ridges and furrows, which are not generally observed in the later stage of attack. Plants become stunted and this becomes more pronounced when they are infected in the pre-flowering stages. Roots of diseased plants dot not exhibit external abnormality but show the presence of fungal hyphae in all their tissues. Sometimes, their vascular tissues become completely plugged with the hyphae. In the stem, the hyphae are observed in the vascular tissues only. Vascular tissues of both root and stem show marked swelling, browning of cell walls and their plugging with dark brown gummy substances (Rai & Singh, 1973).

2.2.9.2 The pathogen

The fungus on potato-dextrose agar produces cottony growth of white or pansy-violet mycelium, hyphae septate and branch profusely. Micro-conidia are borne on simple and short conidiophores. They are 1-2 celled, ovoid, fusoid or ellipsoid in shape, straight or curved, and are produced in abundance. Macro- conidia are often scanty, 2-4 celled, curved or sickle shaped and attenuate. Chlamydospores are smooth walled or slightly to highly warted. Two types of isolates of the fungus, designated as group A and group B, differing in both cultural and morphological characters were obtained from the diseased plants and both were pathogenic to *B. juncea*, the isolates of group B were more virulent than those of group A. Isolates of both the groups are pathogenic to *B. campestris* var.Toria, *B.campestris* var. Yellow sarson, *B.oleracea* var. botrytis, *B. oleracea* var. *capitata*, *Eruca sativa*, *Raphanus sativus* and *Mathiola incana*. Disease incidence is favoured by warm weather, and sand or sandy-loam and dry soil conditions (Rai & Singh, 1973).

Fusarium wilt is rarely seen in the field and is not economically important.

2.2.10 Club Root

Clubroot is caused by the fungus *Plasmodiophora brassicae* Worn. It was known in Europe since the thirteenth century as a destructive disease of cruciferous crops (Sherf & MacNab, 1986). McRae (1928) first noted its occurrence on *Brassica oleracea* (cabbage and cauliflower) in India. Clubroot is a serious menace to these crops in the Kalimpong hills, West Bengal. It is an important disease of oilseed brassicas in France (Maltais & Bouchard, 1978), Germany (Daebeler *et al.* 1980), Sweden (Engqvist, 1994), Canada (Vigier *et al.* 1989), UK (Williamson, 1989), New Zealand (Lammerink & Hart, 1985) and other countries.

The incidence of clubroot attack on mustard (*B. campestris* var. Yellow sarson) was first reported from West Bengal in 1985 (Laha *et al.* 1985). The disease was observed in irrigated areas of several districts of the state during 1983-85 on the mustard cv. Benoy (*B. campestris*). Das *et al.*

(1987) observed the disease at Bhubaneswar, Orissa first in 1979 and then again in 1983 on the Toria cv. M-27. According to Chattopadhyay and Bagchi (1989), the incidence of clubroot is rare in the Gangetic alluvial region, the major mustard (*B. campestris*) growing areas of West Bengal but quite severe in laterite soil. During survey in 1985 and 1986 seasons, the mustard crop (cv. Benoy) in large patches in low lying tracts of Birbhum and Burdwan districts of West Bengal, showed 70-80 per cent clubroot infection where the soil was moist and acidic in reaction (pH 5.7 to 6.2) (Bhowmik, 1986). The disease incidence increased rapidly with repeated growing of the crop in infected fields, and about 70 per cent infection was obtained after three years of successive cultivation (Chattopadhyay, 1991).

The disease reduces the seed and oil yield. In West Bengal, the loss in yield of mustard cv. Benoy ranged between 32.5 to 52.5 per cent (Chattopadhyay, 1991; Laha *et al.* 1985). In Sweden, clubroot reduced the yield and oil content but increased the chlorophyll content of susceptible spring rape (*B. napus*) cultivars. The reduction in raw oil yield was 10 to 20 per cent (Engqvist, 1994).

2.2.10.1 Symptoms

The disease symptom is noticeable after about 60 days of sowing. The aerial parts of the affected plant turn pale or yellow and the plant remains stunted in growth. Affected plants bear lesser number of pods, their size is reduced, become thick and curved. In sunny days, plants show signs of wilting as if suffering from chronic water deficiency. The tap root as well as the lateral roots become malformed into small or large club-like bodies or galls, about 8 to 12 per plant (Chattopadhyay & Bagchi, 1989). The clubs are spindle shaped, thickened at the middle and tapering towards the ends (Fig. 2.19). With age, these malformed bodies, turn black, rot and spread secondary infections.

2.2.10.2 The pathogen

The life-cycle of *Plasmodiophora brassicae* has been described by Woronin (1878) and detailed cytological observations on the fungus was made by Ingram and Tommerup (1972). The fungus produces numerous haploid resting spores within the

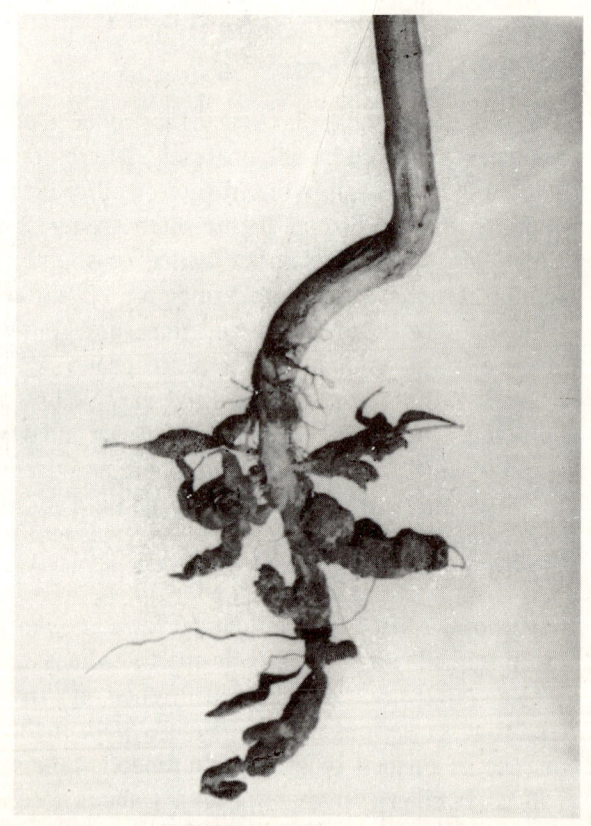

Fig. 2.19. Club root of *B. campestris* var. Yellow sarson (cv. Benoy) caused by *P. brassicae*. Note the club/ spindle shaped roots

host cells. They are hyaline and spherical, and each germinates to produce a single biflagellate zoo-spore. The zoospores infect the root hairs of the host and form multinucleate primary plasmodia which in turn cleave into zoosporangia in the affected host cell. Secondary zoospores are released from the zoosporangia, fuse, and re-infect the root producing the multinucleate secondary plasmodia which invade the host cortical cells and cause characteristic club like structures. Karyogamy occurs within secondary plasmodium, followed by meiosis and cleavage of the plasmodium into haploid resting spores. If the fungus does not become a pathogen until it develops into the secondary plasmodial stage, it may be possible to control the disease by arresting the fungus in its non-pathogenic root hair phase (Campbell & Greathead, 1989). According to Arnold *et al.* (1996), *P. brassicae*, though an obligate biotroph, is capable of having atleast a short lived period of saprotrophic amoebal growth.

Soil acidity and lack of soil aeration are the two important factors that predispose cruciferous crops to clubroot attack. In acid soils, more spores of *P. brassicae* are released and plants are more susceptible than in alkaline soils. The fungus may be present in soils of pH 5.0 to 7.8, but germination and infection do not occur at pH 7.1 to 7.4. As the fungus requires moisture for its germination, low-lying, badly drained soils harbour the disease, but infection may occur in well drained soil saturated by heavy rain. Soil aeration rather than absence of moisture is inhibiting (Whiteheads, 1946). A daily temperature range of 2-12°C or a mean daily temperature of 7°C favours gall formation (Williamson, 1989).

Plasmodiophora brassicae exhibits physiological specialization (Honing, 1931; Lammerink, 1965; Williams, 1966) and classification of races is based on the reaction of pathogen isolates on a standard set of 15 differentials, called the European Clubroot Differentials (ECD) set (Buczacki *et al.* 1975). Information on the existence of physiologic races of the clubroot pathogen in India is lacking.

2.2.10.3 Germplasm screening techniques

A number of techniques are available for inoculating crucifer germplasm for resistance to clubroot. The inoculum is prepared by separating resting spores of *P. brassicae* from the host by comminuting the infected roots or clubs in a liquidizer, followed by either repeated centrifugation of the resulting suspension or filtering it through layers of muslin till relatively free from bacterial contamination, and finally the spore concentration is adjusted to the desired level (Castlebury & Glawe, 1993; Williamson, 1987). Inoculation techniques followed are:

The first method consists in coating roots of seedlings with a mixture of resting spores and soil (Williams, 1966). The second method consists of dipping roots of young seedlings (1 or 2 week old) in the suspension of resting spores (Johnston, 1968). The third method involves planting of young seedlings in non-infested soil and then injection of spore suspension into a hole close to each plant-let so that the roots of the plant-let are contaminated with the spore suspension (Schoeller & Grunewaldt, 1987). In the fourth method, a slice of infected cabbage root (containing approximately 5×10^6 resting spores) is placed next to the seedling roots. This is considered to be a much faster and more effective technique compared to other procedures described, and it ensures larger number of resting spores to be in close proximity to plant roots (Castlebury & Glawe, 1993).

Recently, a simple technique of inoculation using a single resting spore of *P. brassicae* has been developed. The single resting spore is obtained by placing a 0.5 μl drop spore suspension (conc. 2000 spores/ml) on a sterilized coverglass with a micropipette. The drop is checked under a microscope to ensure that it carries only one spore. The cover glass is placed on the surface of autoclaved soil in a pot. One, 1 or 2 d old seedling of the test cultivar is then inoculated by placing it over the spore drop, covered it with a small amount of soil, and grown in a growth chamber. This ensures efficient infection (Kageyama *et al.* 1995). Narisawa *et al.* (1996) has described another simpler method of obtaining single resting spore of *P. brassicae*. The spore suspension is purified through step-wise density gradient centrifugation yielding about 80% viable spores as may be evident by staining with calcofluor white and ethidium bromide. Approximately 90% of these resting spores contain 1 nucleus, the remainders are larger with 2 nuclei. Single resting spores which are small and viable, are then isolated under a microscope and inoculated into 1-d old seedling using automatic system transferring single cells.

Per cent incidence of clubroot disease is determined by counting the number of plants bearing malformed roots after 60 days of sowing and the disease severity of cultivars is assessed on a 0-3 scale. A test cultivar with no club formation is rated 0, a few small clubs on the secondary roots is rated 1, considerable clubbing on the lateral roots is rated 2 and large number of clubs with bigger size on primary and secondary roots is rated 3 (Chattopadhyay, 1996; Chattopadhyay *et al.* 1991; Seaman *et al.* 1963).

2.2.10.4 *Sources of resistance*

Existence of resistance to *P. brassicae* in Brassica spp. has been reported but it should be ensured that the resistance obtained is also operative against all the races of the pathogen prevalent in the region. Materials reported resistant to club root include: *B. nigra* or black mustard (Walker *et al.* 1937); turnip rape (*B. campestris*) cultivar Wasslander (Johnston, 1974); the swede (*B. napus* ssp. *rapifera*) cultivar Tina (Lammerink & Hart, 1985), swede seed lines SV 8525952 and SV 8525953, Svalof, Sweden and the Canadian cv. OAC Triton (Vigier *et al.* 1989).

In India, the cultivars Tower, Midas (*B. napus*); HC-1, HC-4, HC-5 (*B. carinata*) and ACC BN-479 (*B. nigra*) were either free of or resistant to *P. brassicae* infection under sick-plot screening test (Chattopadhyay *et al.* 1991), and Toria (*B. campestris* var. Toria) varieties B-54, PT-83, Raute 17 and TK 101 were resistant in pot culture test at Bhubaneswar, Orissa (Das *et al.* 1987).

2.2.10.5 *Control*

Prompt destruction by burning of all diseased plant debris, elimination of cruciferous weeds and long rotation of crops, are important preventive measures because, the resistant spores persist in host tissues for long periods. Liming the soil to bring the pH to atleast 7.2 is also very effective (Duggar, 1989; Whiteheads, 1946). Use of smaller particle size lime and its thorough mixing with soil give better results (Dobson *et al.* 1983). Avoidance of all acid-reacting fertilizers, improvement of soil aeration by attending to drainage, and application of liberal doses of well-rotted organic matter are the other recommended control measures (Whiteheads, 1946).

In West Bengal, soil amendment with lime ($CaCO_3$) 3 mt/ha 30 days before sowing increased the soil pH to 7.2 and 7.4 from initial pH level of 5.7 and 6.2, respectively in 1987-88 and 1988-89 and the number of clubs per plant was reduced from 13.8 to 3.2 and from 7.8 to 3.6, respectively during the corresponding period. Most plants in lime treated plots formed clubs in lateral roots whereas those in control plots formed clubs in primary roots (Chattopadhyay, 1991). The seed yield of mustard cv. Benoy was 532.4 kg/ha in clubroot infested soil compared to 1000 kg/ha in soil amended with lime at 3t/ha (Chattopadhyay & Bagchi, 1991). Amendment of soil with Margosa cake 1.5 mt/ha either alone or in combination with lime also reduced the severitiy of clubroot incidence but had adverse effect on crop yield (Chattopadhyay, 1996).

2.2.11 Root Gall Smut

Root gall smut affecting mustard (*Brassica campestris* var. Sarson) was observed for the first time in India in 1921 at Pusa, Bihar (Shaw, 1921) and was thought to be caused by *Urocystis coralloides* Rostrup (McRae, 1922, 1926). Later, Mundkur (1938) identified the pathogen as *Urocystis brassicae* n. sp.

According to Mitra (1928), the disease is characterized by the formation of gall like bodies on all parts of the root system. At first the galls are small, light grey to whitish but later they become greyish-black and measure upto 1.5 inch in diameter. Young galls are full of inter- and intracellular mycelium, composed of thin walled, septate hyphae with binucleate cells. Infected plants become stunted in growth and branch poorly (McRae, 1922). The mustard plants grown in the infested soil flowered 5 days earlier than those in smut free soil and showed poor seed formation (Mundkur, 1938). The disease continued to appear year after year in the same infested plot and did not spread to any other adjacent plot in the vicinity. The spores of the fungus are extremely difficult to germinate and are apparently incapable of infecting mustard seeds (McRae, 1926). Mitra (1928), however, obtained infection through infested soil.

The spore balls of *U. brassicae* measure 25-58 × 20-45 μm (mean 38 × 32 μm), with 1-5 but mostly 2-3 fertile cells. The fertile spores are deep brown, measure 13-25 × 9-20 μm (mean 20 × 16 μm) and are surrounded by numerous bright brown, elongated sterile spores, measuring 5 to 15 × 3 to 10 μm (mean 9.9 × 6.1 μm) and forming a continuous layer. With the decay of infected roots, the spores are released in the soil to infect the surrounding crop. The pathogen is incapable of infecting *Turritis glabra* and *Mathiola sinuta* to which *U. coralloides* is pathogenic (Mundkur, 1938). The disease is extremely rare in occurrence and has not been seen in recent years.

2.3 BACTERIAL DISEASES

2.3.1 Black Rot

Black rot of cruciferous crops is caused by *Xanthomonas campestris* pv. *campestris* (Pommel) Dowson. The disease is present throughout the world. The occurrence of black rot on cabbage (*Brassica oleracea* var. *capitata*) in India was first reported by Patwardhan (1928). It was probably introduced into the country along with imported cabbage seeds. Besides cabbage, the bacterium was noted on *B. oleracea* var. *botrytis*, *Raphanus sativus*, *R. sativus* var. *caudatus*, *B. rapa*,

B. caulorapa, Lepidium sativum, B. juncea, B. campestris var. Brown sarson, *B. campestris* var. Yellow sarson, *B. nigra, B. alba, B. carinata, B. tournefortii* and *B. chinensis*. It does not infect *Eruca sativa* and *Camelina sativa* (Gandhi & Parashar, 1978; Patel *et al.* 1949). Vir *et al.* (1973) found the pathogen responsible for severe stem and leaf rot of Raya (*B. juncea*) during 1971-72 at Hissar, Haryana. The disease incidence in some of the commonly cultivated varieties ranged between 20 to 60 per cent while some other strains remained free from infection. Black rot is present on all crucifers in Sikkim, India and was detected on seeds of radish, rayosag (*B. juncea*) and cauliflower (Gupta & Chaudhary, 1995). Loss in yield is not known. It is a minor disease of rapeseed and mustard.

2.3.1.1 Symptoms

The disease is first seen on plants when they are about 2 months old in the form of black streaks of varying length on the stem near the base or a few inches above the soil level. The streaks enlarge and girdle the stem. Affected stem becomes soft and hollow due to rotting of internal tissues, shows cracking and the plant topples over. Rotting of leaves may start from the mid rib and then spreads to the entire leaf area. Sometimes, necrosis starts from the leaf margin and then progresses inwards. Infected stem and leaves show profuse exudation of yellowish fluid containing bacteria.

2.3.1.2 The bacterium

The bacterium isolate from *B. juncea* makes best growth on Nutrient Dextrose Agar (NDA). The colonies are dark yellow, circular, non-fluidic, convex, entire and opaque. The optimum temperature for growth is 20 to 25°C and pH 6.6. The bacterium is rod-shaped, motile with a single polar flagellum, gram-negative, non-acid fast, encapsulated, aerobic, hydrolyses starch and gelatin. It is positive for H_2S production, catalase test, lipolytic activity and potato soft-rot test but negative for nitrate reduction, indole production, Voges Pras Kauer and methyl red tests. Reaction on milk is alkaline accompanied by peptonization. Produces acid but no gas from glucose, fructose, lactose, sucrose, ribose, raffinose, xylose, cellobiose, manitol and starch. Thermal death point is 58°C. It causes no blackening of veins and is weakly aggressive on cauliflower (Gandhi & Parashar, 1977).

2.3.1.3 Epidemiology

Xanthomonas campestris pv. *campestris* is a vascular pathogen. It is both seed and soil borne. Infected plants and plant debris in soil from previous crop harbour the pathogen. The mode of penetration of the bacterium and development of infection in rapeseed and mustard have not been studied. But the bacterium is known to enter the host through the hydathodes, stomata and wound. In case of cabbage leaf, the lesions start along the margin as the bacterium gains entry through the hydathodes. Infection spreads and progresses downwards in the petiole and stem. Lesions resulting from stomatal invasion remain localized as the bacterium cannot reach the vascular elements in the leaves (Bhide, 1949). The disease is disseminated through infected seeds, rain and irrigation water. Dispersal of bacteria from leaf surfaces occurs through water-splash (Butterworth & McCartney, 1991). Shelton and Hunter (1985) showed that insects like flea bettle *Phyllotreta cruciferae* also transmists *X. campestris* pv. *campestris* from infected broccoli plants to healthy plants.

2.3.1.4 Control

Clean cultivation and use of healthy seeds for sowing are good preventive measures. Spraying with captafol (0.2%) at 20 days intervals and a total of 4 sprays starting from one month old crops give good results against bacterial rot of Raya (Vir *et al.* 1973). Gandhi and Parashar (1978) reported aureomycin (@ 200 µg/ml) among antibiotics, and carboxin (@ 250 µg/ml) among fungicides as most effective both in reducing the disease and in increasing the yield of Raya. In case of Swede, treatment of seeds with 500 µg/ml streptomycin followed by 30 min in 0.5 W/V sodium hypochlorite eliminates the bacterium without causing any reduction in plant stand or phytotoxicity (McKeen, 1981). The Bacillus str. (Hsb-19) isolated from the phylloplane of rapeseed and mustard cultivars provides better control than streptocycline (64.21%) when sprayed on to inoculated plants (Jalali & Parashar, 1995).

2.3.2 Stalk Rot

Stalk rot of rapeseed and mustard caused by *Erwinia carotovora* (Jones) Holland (*E. carotovora* pv. *carotovora*) was first noticed in the Pali district of Rajasthan in 1979 (Bhowmik & Trivedi, 1980). The disease appeared in epiphytotic form on the popular *Brassica juncea* cv. Varuna during mid-October in Roopawas and Mandi areas of Pali where on average about 40 per cent of the crop was affected, although in isolated areas more than 60 per cent of the plants were lost. The incidence was relatively more in crops sown during the first week of September than those planted later. Vigorously growing succulent plants, due to an extra dose of nitrogen as well as those grown on poorly drained moist soil suffered most. The disease was also noticed in fodder crops of Brassica spp. at the IARI, New Delhi.

Subsequent observations in Swaimadhupur and Alwar districts of Rajasthan, and Ballavgarh area of Haryana during 1984 and 1985 showed considerable mortality of plants due to stalk rot. At Ballavgarh, 10 to 15 per cent mustard crops (cv. Varuna) were damaged during 1984 (Bhowmik, 1984, 1985). The loss in grian yield in partially and completely diseased *B. juncea* plants was estimated at 92 and 96 per cent and that in *B. campestris* plants at 87 and 89 per cent, respectively (Sobti, 1983). During February, 1991, hundreds of hectare of Brassica crop at the flowering and pod formation stage were seriously affected by the disease in and around Naujheel block, Mathura, UP (Y. Singh, Plant Prot. Officer, Per.commun.). More recently, a similar soft rot and wilt of rape (*B. campestris*) cv. TH-68 due to Erwinia has been reported from Hissar, Haryana (Pal *et al.* 1997).

2.3.2.1 Symptoms

The disease is characterised by the appearance of water-soaked lesions at the collar region of plants which is usually accompanied by a white frothing. The lesions advance rapidly upwards affecting the tender branches. The foliage shows signs of water stress and withering. The pith tissues of the affected stem and branches become soft, pulpy and often produce dirty white ooze with foul smell. The infected collar region becomes sunken, turns buff white to pale brown in colour (Fig. 2.20a, b). Badly affected plants topple over at the basal region within a few days.

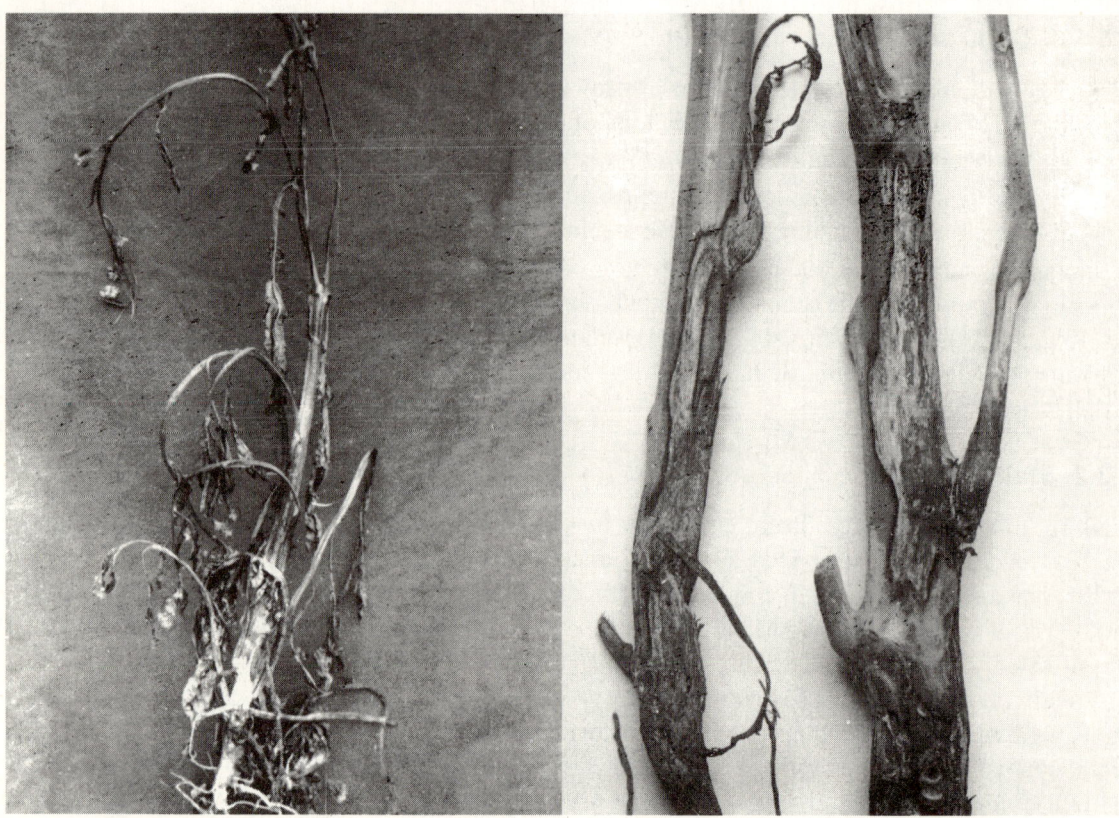

Fig. 2.20. (a) A wilted plant of *B. juncea* (cv. Varuna) caused by *E. carotovora* pv. *carotovora*

Fig. 2.20. (b) Stalk rot of *B. juncea* (cv. Varuna) caused by *E. carotovora* pv. *carotovora*

2.3.2.2 *The bacterium*

The bacterium grows on Nutrient Agar (NA) producing colonies which are greyish, circular, translucent, shining, smooth, with raised centre and wavy margin. The slopes of YGCA, PDA and NA supplemented with dextrose support better growth. Nutrient broth becomes uniformly turbid within 24 hours without formation of pellicle even on prolonged incubation.

The bacterium is Gram negative, rod shaped with blunt ends, capsulated, motile with peritrichous flagella. Acid but no gas is produced from glucose, arabinose, sucrose, lactose, cellobiose, meso-inositol, salicin, raffinose and galactose. Neither acid nor gas is produced with inulin on Dye's medium C. It shows fermentative metabolism of glucose with Hugh and Leifson's medium; aesculin, gelatin and sodium polypectate are hydrolysed but not starch; produces ammonia and hydrogen sulphide from peptone water; Voges Proskeur test is negative while methyl red and catalase tests are positive; nitrate is reduced to nitrite and asparagine is utilized as a sole source of carbon and nitrogen. The bacterium does not produce fluorescence or green pigment on King's medium B.

2.3.2.3 *Host range*

It infects *Nicotiana tabaccum, Lycopersicon esculentum, Daucus carota, Brassica oleracea* var. *botrytis*. It rots potato and radish discs at 28°C and 100% RH. According to Mathur and Swarup (1965), *E. carotovora* was reported on *B. chinensis* only from Germany.

2.3.2.4 *Control*

Control measures have not been worked out. Maintenance of proper moisture condition of the soil and use of balanced fertilizer dose will reduce the susceptibility of the crop to the disease. Application of bleaching powder in contaminated soil will have beneficial effect.

2.3.3 Bacterial Wilt

A wilt disease of cruciferous crops caused by *Pseudomonas solanacearum* Smith was reported by Singh (1992) from Nagaland. It affected the rapeseed (*Brassica campestris* var. Toria), mustard (*B. juncea*) and cabbage (*B. oleracea* var. *capitata*) crops at the ICAR Research Complex, Jharnapani, Nagaland during rabi 1988-89 season. The severity of the disease varied from 0.75 to 13.97 per cent in rapeseed-mustard and 20 to 30 per cent in cabbage.

2.3.4 Slimy Bacteriosis

Pseudomonas syringae as the cause of slimy bacteriosis of rapeseed and mustard in Pakistan was reproted by Akhtar and Mirza (1987). Earlier, the bacterium was found to cause pod spot of rape in Canada (Henry, 1974). It incites soft rot in stagheads of *Brassica rapa* and *B. juncea* caused by *Albugo candida*, the rotting is more pronounced in young fleshy stagheads than in matured ones. Rotted stagheads contain aborted oogonia and antheridia of *A. candida*, and thus the bacterium reduces the natural spread of *A. candida* (Tiwari *et al.* 1998).

2.4 VIRUS AND PHYTOPLASMA DISEASES

Virus and phytoplasma diseases of rapeseed and mustard have not been studied well in India although they are known to cause considerable damage to oilseed rape crops in other countries. Generally, plants suffering from these maladies are not very common in the plains of India where only a few isolated cases may be seen occassionally in some fields but virus diseases in *Brassica* spp., radish•and turnip are quite common in the hills.

2.4.1 Sarson Mosaic

The earliest record on the occurrence of a mosaic virus in Indian mustard was made by Vasudeva (1957, 1959). The disease was transmitted by the vector *Macrosiphum granarium*. Azad and Sehgal (1959) also observed a severe mosaic disease on chinese sarson (*Brassica juncea* var. *rugosa* Roxb.). The distinguishing features of this virus disease are vein clearing, green vein banding, mottling and severe puckering of leaves. Affected plants become stunted in growth and they either do not produce any flower or produce only a few. Pods, if formed, are poorly filled and shrivelled.

Azad and Sehgal (1959) transmitted the disease by both sap and aphid vectors, *Aphis gossypii* Glov., *Brevicoryne brassicae* Lin. and *Myzus persicae* Sulz. Later, Azad *et al.* (1963) reported *A. rumicis* to be an additional vector and the virus is transmissible in a nonpersistent way. The disease is transmissible to a variety of hosts in Cruciferae including important oleiferous brassicas viz. *B. juncea, B. nigra, B., campestris* var. Toria, *B. hitra* (*B. alba*) and *B. napus*, etc. but not to any of the cabbages or coles (Vasudeva, 1958). Etiology of the disease is not known.

2.4.2 Rai Mosaic

Rai mosaic affecting about 30 to 43 per cent Rai (Indian mustard) was reported by Sharma (1973) from Kalimpong (Darjeeling), West Bengal. Affected plants become stunted in growth, their leaves show characteristic mosaic symptoms and prominent deformation of lamina. There is no masking of disease symptoms during winter.

Rai mosaic is a sap transmissible virus. It produces typical mosaic symptoms on *B. juncea* and *B. rugosa*, and chlorotic local lesions on *Chenopodium quinoa*. The virus is transmitted by aphid vectors, *Myzus persicae* Sulz. and *Lipaphis erysimi* Kalt. in a non-persistent manner. It is not seed borne but perpetuates on semrai (*B. rugosa*), a local weed in Kalimpong. The physical properties are: thermal death point, 68°C; dilution end point, 1/5000-1/7000; and longevity in vitro, 12 days at 22°C. Etiology of the disease is not known.

2.4.3 Radish Mosaic

The occurrence of mosaic disease of radish (*Raphanus sativus* L.) in India was first reported by Raychaudhuri and Pathanian (1955). The virus had thermal death point at 90°C, dilution end point 10^7 and longevity *in vitro* 101 days at 6-8°C and 17 days at 17-22°C. Later, a strain of radish mosaic affecting 40 to 60 per cent plants of Taramira (*Eruca sativa* Mill) and causing considerable damage to certain oil yielding crucifers was reported from Lucknow, UP by Verma *et al.* (1969). The virus is sap transmissible to the members of Cruciferae.

Another mosaic disease of radish caused by turnip mosaic virus, and widely prevalent in Sikkim, West Bengal, UP and the union Territory of Delhi, was observed in 1973 (Ahlawat & Chenulu, 1982a). This also affects rapeseed and mustard. Mosaic affected plants become stunted in growth with reduced leaf lamina and roots. Diseased leaves show interveinal necrosis, vein banding and dark green patches on light green background, curling and puckering. Stem, petioles and pods display mosaic pattern. Mosaic incidence ranged between 7 to 63 per cent in radish and 5 to 51 per cent in *Brassica juncea*. The disease is readily transmitted by mechanical inoculants and through seed in *B. rugosa* and *Cardamine impatiens*. It is not transmitted by soil or radish seed (Ahlawat & Chenulu, 1984).

Radish mosaic was transmitted by 10 species of aphids out of which *Lipaphis erysimi* Kalt. is the most efficient vector. The virus infects members of the Cruciferae, Chenopodiaceae, Solanaceae, Papaveraceae, Caryophyllaceae, Leguminosae and Compositae. Plants that act as symptomless hosts of the virus are: *Bidens pilosa, Cosmos bipinnatus, Nasturtium officinarum, Phaseolus vulgaris, Schizanthus wisetonensis* and *Stellaria media*. The virus has a thermal death point of 57°C, dilution end point of 1:4000 and longevity *in vitro* of 6 days at room temperature

Fig. 2.21. Radish mosiac on a leaf of *B. juncea*. Note the reduced size of the affected leaf

Fig. 2.22. Radish mosaic with ring spot lesions on a leaf of *B. napus* (str. Na 38)

(22-25°C), 90 days at 80°C and upto 120 days at 0°C. The virus particle is a long flexuous rod having a modal length of 760 nm and width of 12 nm. The virus is considered to be a strain of turnip mosaic virus and belongs to the poty-virus group (Ahlawat & Chenulu, 1982b, 1984).

During 1983-84, the Brassica genotypes, No.38 (*B. napus*), and RC 781, YRT-3, PHR-1, PR-5 and cv. Pusa Bold (*B. juncea*) growing at the IARI farm, New Delhi showed symptoms of typical Turnip mosaic virus (Radish mosaic) although such cases were very few. The line B.na-sel (*B. napus*) showed no symptoms. All these materials and one Na-129 (*B. napus*) when test inoculated with Radish mosaic (courtesy: Y.S. Ahlawat) developed symptoms identical to those seen in the field (Fig. 2.21) except the lines No. 38 and Na-129 which developed mosaic, interpersed with ring spots on older leaves (Fig. 2.22). The line B.na-sel showed no symptom (Bhowmik, 1984).

2.4.4 Phyllody

Phyllody is caused by a phytoplasma. Affected plants of *Brassica campestris* var. Toria and *B. campestris* var. Yellow sarson show symptoms somewhat similar to the phyllody disease of sesamum (Vasudeva, 1958). Bindra and Bakhetia (1967) also observed this disease on Toria, Yellow sarson, sunhemp and gram at Ludhiana, Punjab. They found that in Toria, the average seed

Fig. 2.23. Phyllody of *B. campestris* var. Yellow sarson. Note the stunted and bushy growth of the affected plant

yield is only 0.63 g per diseased plant compared to 5.62 g per healthy plant. The effect of phyllody on seed yield and oil percentage in the Toria variety ITSA was estimated by Kaushik *et al.* (1978). The seed yield was 47.0 and 10.0 g, and the percentage of oil was 39.5 and 28.6, respectively in 10 healthy and 10 infected plants. Reduction in plant height, pod length, seed yield and seed oil content in Toria due to phyllody was also observed at Hissar, Haryana during 1980-81 (AICORPO. 1981). Although these observations show that the losses to individual plants due to phyllody are considerable, the total loss to the crop is likely to be negligible since the incidence of affected plants in the field is usually very low (Vasudeva, 1958).

2.4.4.1 Symptoms

The characteristic symptoms of phyllody are the transformation of floral parts into green leafy structures, resulting in sterility. The corolla becomes green and sepaloid, the stamens turn green and become indehiscent, gynoecium is borne on a distinct gynophore and there are no ovules in the ovary. Leafy structures become attached to the false septum (Vasudeva, 1958). Affected plants remain stunted in growth. Besides, proliferation of axillary buds results in the development of a large number of side shoots giving the plant a bushy and broom-like appearance (Fig. 2.23).

2.4.4.2 The causal agent

The disease was earlier considered to be of virus in nature and transmitted by the jassid, *Orosius albicinctus* Distant *(Deltocephalus burmeisler)*. The pathogen-vector relationship was studied on sesamum, and the phyllody of Toria and Yellow sarson was shown to be due to phyllody of sesamum (Sahambi, 1958; Vasudeva & Sahambi, 1957). Later, Klein (1977) showed that sesamum phyllady is caused by a Mycoplasma-like organism (MLO), now designated as phytoplasma. The pathogen survives on several dicotyledonous plants in the field and attacks the succeeding crop.

2.4.4.3 Control

Cultural practices like date of sowing and planting distance greatly influence the disease incidence. Crops sown in the last week of August to early September show high incidence of phyllody whereas those sown later have low incidence (Sandhu *et al.* 1969), probably because of lower diurnal temperature variation which may be unfavourable for the jassid vector (Bindra & Bhakhetia, 1967). Delayed sowing from the normal date (30th August) to the middle of September (17th September), minimized the incidence of phyllody. Sowing the crop at closer spacing (30.0 × 7.5 cm) gave lower incidence (8 per cent) compared to higher incidence (12.5 per cent) of phyllody in wider spaced (45 × 7.75 cm) crop (Kaushik *et al.* 1978).

REFERENCES

Abawi, G.S. and Grogan, R.G. 1975. Source of primary inoculum and effects of temperature and moisture on infection of beans by *Whetzelinia sclerotiorum. Phytopathology* 65: 300-309.

Achar, P.N. 1993. Hypertrophy in tissues of radish due to mixed infection by *Peronospora parasitica* and *Albugo candida. Phyton* (Buenos Aires) 54(1): 45-49.

Agarwal, A., Garg, G.K., Singh, U.S. and Misra, D.P. 1994. Detection and role of chlorotic toxin and phytohormones in the pathogenesis of Alternaria blight in *Brassica napus. Curr. Sci.* 66(6): 442-443.

Ahlawat, Y.S. and Chenulu, V.V. 1982a. Losses due to radish mosaic caused by a strain of turnip mosaic virus and its control. *Indian Phytopath.* 35: 255-260.

Ahlawat, Y.S. and Chenulu, V.V. 1982b. Studies on the transmission of radish mosaic virus by the aphid, *Lipaphis erysimi. Indian Phytopath.* 35: 633-638.

Ahlawat, Y.S. and Chenulu, V.V. 1984. Radish mosaic: A new disease caused by turnip mosaic virus in India. *Trop. Agric.* (Trinidad). 61(3): 188-192.

AICORPO. 1979-93. Annu. Prog. Rept. 1979 to 93. *All India Coord. Res. Proj. Oilseeds*, Direct. Oilseeds Res., *ICAR*, Hyderabad, India.

AICRP (R&M). 1994-98. Annu. Prog. Rept. 1994 to 98. *All India Coord. Res. Proj. Rapeseed & Mustard*, Natn. Res. Centr. Rapeseed and Mustard, ICAR, Bharatpur, Rajasthan, India.

Akhtar, M.A. 1969. Biological control of *Rhizoctonia solani* causing seed decay and damping-off of mustard. *West Pakistan. J. Agric. Res.* 7: 29-52.

Akhtar, M.A. and Mirza, M.S. 1987. Slimy bacteriosis of rape and mustard—a new record in Pakistan. *Pakistan J. Agric. Res.* 8(4): 485.

Alabouvette, C. and Brunin, B. 1970. Researches on disease of rape caused by *Leptosphaeria maculans* (Desm.) Ces. et de Not. I. The role of plant residues in the survival and spread of the pathogen. *Ann. Phytopath.* 2: 463-475.

Alabouvette, C., Brunin, B. and Louvet, J. 1974. Researches on a disease of rape caused by *Leptosphaeria maculans* (Desm.) Ces. et de Not. IV. Infectivity of pycnidiospores and varietal susceptibility. *Ann. Phytopath.* 6(3): 625-675.

Alexopoulos, C.J. 1972. *Introductory Mycology. Second Edition.* pp. 613, Wiley Eastern (P) Limited, New Delhi.

Anderson, N.A. 1982. The genetics and pathology of *Rhizoctonia solani. Annu. Rev. Phytopathol.* 20: 329-347.

Ansari, N.A., Khan, M.W. and Muheet, A. 1988a. Effect of Alternaria blight on oil content of rapeseed and mustard. *Curr. Sci.* 57(18): 1023-1024.

Ansari, N.A., Khan, M.W. and Muheet, A. 1988b. Effect of temperature and relative humidity on spore germination of *Alternaria brassicae* and development of Alternaria blight on oilseed crucifers. *Rev. Trop. Plant Pathol.* 5: 79-84.

Ansari, N.A., Khan, M.W. and Muheet, A. 1989. Effect of some factors on growth and sporulation of *Alternaria brassicae* causing Alternaria blight of rapeseed and mustard. *Acta Bot. Indica.* 17(1): 49-93.

Arnold, D.L., Blakesley, D.B. and Clarkson, J.M. 1996. Evidence for the growth of *Plasmodiophora brassicae* in vitro. *Mycol. Res.* 100(5): 535-540.

Aulakh, K.S. 1971. Damping-off of Toria seedlings due to *Pythium butleri. Indian Phytopath.* 24: 611-612.

Awasthi, R.P. and Kolte, S.J. 1989. Variability in *Alternaria brassicae* affecting rapeseed and mustard. *Indian Phytopath.* 42(2): 275 (Abstr.).

Awasthi, R.P. and Kolte, S.J. 1994. Epidemiological factors in relation to development and prediction of Alternaria blight of rapeseed and mustard. *Indian Phytopath.* 47(4): 395-399.

Aycock, R. 1966. Stem rot and other diseases caused by *Sclerotium rolfsii* Sacc. *N.C. Agri. Exp. Tech. Bull.* 174: 202.

Ayer, W.A. and Pena-Rodriguez, L.M. 1987. Metabolites produced by *Alternaria brassicae*, the black spot pathogen of Canola. Part I. The Phytotoxic components. *J. Natur. Prod.* 50(3): 400-407.

Azad, R.N., Nagaich, B.B. and Sehgal, O.P. 1963. Chinese sarson mosaic virus-vector relationship. *Indian Phytopath.* 16: 21-30.

Azad, R.N. and Sehgal, O.P. 1959. A mosaic disease of Chinese sarson (*Brassica juncea* (L.) Coss. Var. *rugosa* Roxb.) *Indian Phytopath.* 12(1): 45-52.

Badawy, H.M.A. 1995. Effect of temperature on phytotoxic sirodesmin production by different aggressive isolates of *Leptosphaeria maculans. Bull. Facult. Agric. Univ. Cairo.* 46(1): 149-159.

Badawy, H.M.A. and Hoppe, H.H. 1989. Production of phytotoxic sirodesmins by aggressive strains of *Leptosphaeria maculans* differing in interactions with oilseed rape genotypes. *J. Phytopath.* 127(2): 146-157.

Bains, P.S. and Tewari, J.P. 1987. Purification, chemical characterization and host specificity of toxin produced by *Alternaria brassicae. Physiol. Mol. Plant Pathol.* 30: 259-271.

Bains, P.S., Tewari, J.P. and Ayer, W.A. 1993. A note on phytotoxicity of homodestruxin B—a compound produced by *Alternaria brassicae. Phytoprotection* 74(3): 157-160.

Bains, S.S. 1993. Differential reaction of leaves and young flowers of different cruciferous crops to *Albugo candida. Plant Dis. Res.* 8(1): 70-72.

Bains, S.S. and Jhooty, J.S. 1979. Mixed infection of *Albugo candida* and *Peronospora parasitica* on *Brassica juncea* inflorescence and their control. *Indian Phytopath.* 32: 268-271.

Baird, R.E., Harshman, D.E. and Christmass, E.P. 1994. Occurrence of *Macrophomina phaseolina* on canola in Indiana and Kentucky. *Plant Dis.* 78(3): 316.

Ballinger, D.J., Salisbury, P.A., Kollmorgen, J.F., Potter, T.D. and Coventry, D.P. 1988. Evaluation rates of flutriafol and control of black leg of rapeseed. *Aust. J. Exptl. Agric.* 28(4): 517-519.

Bandhopadhyay, D.C., Saha, G.N. and Mukherjee, D. 1974. Note on the variation in qualitative composition of seeds of B-9 variety of Yellow sarson caused by Alternaria blight. *Indian J. Agric. Sci.* 44: 406.

Banga, S.S., Labana, K.S. and Medhi, B.N. 1984. Alternaria incidence in some alloplasmic lines of Indian mustard (*Brassica juncea* (L.) Coss.). *Theor. Appl. Genet.* 67: 195-196.

Bansal, V.K., Senguin-Swartz, G., Rakow, G.F.W. and Petrie, G.A. 1990. Reaction of Brassica species to infection by *Alternaria brassicae. Can. J. Plant Sci.* 70(4): 1159-1162.

Bansal, V.K., Tewari, J.P., Tewari, I., Gomez-Campo, C. and Stringam, G.R. 1997. Genus Eruca: a potential source of white rust resistance in cultivated brassicas. *Plant Genet. Resour. Newsl.* 109: 25-26.

Barbetti, M.J. 1981. Effect of sowing date and oospore seed contamination upon subsequent crop incidence of white rust (*Albugo candida*) in rapeseed. *Aust. Plant Pathol.* 10: 44-46.

Begum, H.A., Meah, M.B., Howlider, M.A.R. and Kashem, M.A. 1993. Effect of Alternaria infection on husk constituents in mustard. *Bangladesh J. Plant Pathol.* 9(1-2): 31-34.

Berry, L.A. and Lennard, J.H. 1988. Foliar infection of Brassica plants by *Alternaria brassicae* in relation to leaf surface characteristics. *Cruciferae Newsl.* 13: 104-105.

Bhander, D.S. and Maini, N.S. 1965. Studies on the resistance of oleiferous Brassica to Alternaria blight. *Indian Oilseeds J.* 9: 58.

Bhander, D.S., Thakur, R.N. and Hussain, A. 1963. A new disease of rapeseed and mustard in India. *Plant Dis. Reptr.* 47: 1039.

Bhardwaj, C.L. and Sud, A.K. 1988. A study on the variability of *Albugo candida* from Himachal Pradesh. *Indian J. Mycol. Plant Pathol.* 18(3): 287-291.

Bhardwaj, C.L. and Sud, A.K. 1989. Reaction of Brassica cultivars against *Albugo candida* isolates from Kangra valley. *Indian Phytopath.* 42(2): 293 (Abstr.).

Bhardwaj, C.L. and Sud, A.K. 1995. A visual rating scale for white rust disease assessment of cruciferous crops. *Indian J. Mycol. Plant Pathol.* 25(3): 181-183.

Bhide, V.P. 1949. Stomatal invasion of cabbage by *Xanthomonas campestris* (Pammel) Dowson. *Indian Phytopath.* 2: 132-133.

Bhowmik, T.P. 1980. Annu. Prog. Rept. 1980. *AR.14. Diseases of oilseed crops and their management with special reference to root rot of groundnut and foliar diseases of Brassica spp.* Div. Mycol. & Plant Pathol., IARI, New Delhi.

Bhowmik, T.P. 1984. Annu. Prog. Rept. 1984. *AR.14. Diseases of oilseed crops and their management with special reference to root rot of groundnut and foliar diseases of Brassica spp.* Div. Mycol. & Plant Pathol., IARI, New Delhi.

Bhowmik, T.P. 1985a. Annu. Prog. Rept. 1985. *AR.14. Diseases of oilseed crops and their management with special reference to root rot of groundnut and foliar diseases of Brassica spp.* Div. Mycol. & Plant Pathol., IARI, New Delhi.

Bhowmik, T.P. 1985b. Disease management for stabilizing productivity of oilseed crops, pp. 433-445. In: H.C. Srivastava, S. Bhaskaran, B. Vatsya and K.K.G. Menon. Eds., *Oilseed Production: Constraints and Opportunities.* Oxford and IBM Publishing Co., New Delhi.

Bhowmik, T.P. 1986. Annu. Prog. Rept. 1986. *AR.14. Diseases of oilseed crops and their management with special reference to root rot of groundnut and foliar diseases of Brassica spp.* Div. Mycol. & Plant Pathol., IARI, New Delhi.

Bhowmik, T.P. 1988. Annu. Prog. Rept. 1988. *AR.14. Diseases of oilseed crops and their management with special reference to root rot of groundnut and foliar diseases of Brassica spp.* Div. Mycol. & Plant Pathol., IARI, New Delhi.

Bhowmik, T.P. and Munde, P.N. 1987. Identification of resistance in rapeseed and mustard against *Alternaria brassicae* (Berk.) Sacc. and some resistant sources. *Beitrage trop. Landwirtsch. Veterinarmed.* 25: 49-53.

Bhowmik, T.P. and Singh, A. 1984. Efficacy of metalaxyl against white rust (*Albugo candida*) of rapeseed and mustard and its compatibility with captafol and metasystox. *Symp. Chemical Control of Plant Diseases,* Feb. 16-18, 1984. Indian Phytopath. Soc., New Delhi (Abstr.).

Bhowmik, T.P. and Trivedi, B.M. 1980. A new bacterial stalk rot of Brassica. *Curr. Sci.* 49 (17): 674-675.

Bijral, J.S., Sharma, T.R., Gupta, B.B. and Singh, K. 1995. Interspecific hybrids of *Brassica maurorum* with Brassica crops and their cytology. *Eucarpia Cruciferae Newsl.*(France) 17: 18-19.

Bindra, O.S. and Bakhetia, D.R.C. 1967. A note on natural incidence of sesamum phyllody virus disease in Brassica spp. at Ludhiana. *J. Res.* 4: 406-408.

Bisht, I.S., Agarwal, R.C., Singh, R. 1994. White rust (*Albugo candida*) severity in mustard (*Brassica juncea*) varieties and its effect on seed yields. *Plant Varieties and Seeds* 7(2): 85-89 (NBPGR, IARI, New Delhi).

Bokor, A., Barbetti, M.J., Brown, G.P., MacNish, G.C. and Wood, P.M. 1975. Blackleg of rapeseed. *J. Agric. West Aust.* 16: 7-10.

Bolkan, H.A,. and Ribeiro, W.R.C. 1985. Anastomosis groups and pathogenicity of *Rhizoctonia solani* isolates from Brazil. *Plant Dis.* 69: 599-601.

Brain, P.J. and Whittington, W.J. 1981. The influence of soil pH on the severity of swede powdery mildew infection. *Plant Path.* 30: 105-109.

Brar, J.S. and Chahal, A.S. 1993. Chemical control of foliar diseases of Raya under Punjab conditions. *Plant Dis. Res.* 8(2): 156.

Broschewitz, B., Steinbach, P. and Gottermann, S. 1993. The effect of insect larvae damage on the attack of winter oilseed rape by *Phoma lingam* and *Botrytis cineria. Gesunde Pflanzen* 45(3): 106-110.

Brown, A.G.P., Barbetti, M.J. and Wood, P.H. 1976. Effect of benomyl on "black leg" disease of rape in western Australia. *Aust. J. Exp. Agric. Anim. Husb.* 16: 276-279.

Browne, L.M., Conn, K.L., Ayer, W.A. and Tewari, J.P. 1991. The Camalexins: new phytoalexins produced in the leaves of *Camelina sativa* (Cruciferae). *Tetrahedron* 47(24): 3909-3914.

Brun, H., Plessis, J. and Renard, M. 1987a. Resistance of some crucifers to *Alternaria brassicae* (Berk.) Sacc. pp. 1222-1227. *Proc. 7th Int. Rapeseed Conf.*, Paris.

Brun, H., Renard, M., Tribodet, M., Plessis, J. and Tanguy, X. 1989. Contribution to the genetic control of rapeseed diseases. *Phytoma* 404 (36-37): 40-41.

Brun, H., Tribodet, M., Renard, M., Plessis, J. and Tanguy, X. 1987b. A field study of rapeseed (*Brassica napus*) resistance to *Sclerotinia sclerotiorum*. pp. 1216-1221. *Proc. 7th Int. Rapeseed Conf.*, Paris.

Brunin, B. 1972. Research on diseases of rape caused by *Leptosphaeria maculans* (Desm.) Ces. et.de Not. III. Anatomical aspects of collar necrosis. *Ann. Phytopathol.* 4: 87.

Brunin, B. and Lacoste, L. 1970. Recherches sur la maladie du Colza due a *Leptosphaeria maculans* (Desm.) Ces. et de Not.II. Pouvoir pathogene des ascospores. *Ann. Phytopathol.* 2: 447-488.

Buchwaldt, L. and Green, H. 1992. Phytotoxicity of destruxin B and its possible role in pathogenesis of *Alternaria brassicae*. *Plant Pathol.* 41: 55-63.

Buchwaldt, L. and Jensen, J.S. 1991. HPLC purification of destruxins produced by *Alternaria brassicae* in culture and in leaves of *Brassica napus*. *Phytochem.* 30: 2311-2316.

Buczacki, S.T., Toxopeus, H., Mattusch, P., Johnston, T.D., Dixon, G.R. and Hobolth, L.A. 1975. Study of physiologic specialization in *Plasmodiophora brassicae*: Proposal for attempted rationalization through an international approach. *Trans. Br. Mycol. Soc.* 65: 295-303.

Butler, E.J. 1918. *Fungi and diseases in plants*. Thacker Spink & Co., Calcutta, pp. 547.

Butterworth, J. and McCartney, H.A. 1991. The dispersal of bacteria from leaf surface by water splash. *J. Appl. Bacteriol.* 71(6): 484-496.

Calman, A.I., Tewari, J.P. and Gugala, M. 1986. *Fusarium avenaceum* as one of the causal agents of seedling blight of Canola in Alberta. *Plant Dis.* 70(7): 964.

Campbell, R.N. and Greathead, A.S. 1989. Control of club root of Crucifers by liming. p. 217. In: A.W. Engelhard ed., *Soil borne plant pathogens: Management of diseases with Macro- and Microelements*. The Am. Phytopath. Soc., Scientific Publishers, 5A, New Pali Road, Jodhpur, India.

Cargeeg, L.A. and Thurling, N. 1979. Seedling and adult plant resistance to black leg (*Leptosphaeria maculans* (Desm.) Ces et de Not.) in spring rape (*Brassica napus* L.). *Aust. J. Agric. Res.* 30: 37-46.

Castlebury, L.A. and Glawe, D.A. 1993. A comparison of three techniques for inoculating Chinese cabbage with *Plasmodiophora brassicae*. *Mycologia* 85(5): 866-867.

Chahal, A.S. 1981. Seed borne infection of *Alternaria brassicae* in Indian mustard and its elimination during storage. *Curr. Sci.* 50(14): 621-623.

Chahal, A.S. 1982. Diseases of rapeseed and mustard. *Indian Fmg.* 32(6): 27-36.

Chahal, A.S. 1986a. Relationship of Alternaria blight with age of Brown sarson. *Indian J. Mycol. Plant Pathol.* 16: 166-167.

Chahal, A.S. 1986b. Losses and chemical control of Alternaria blight in rapeseed-mustard in Punjab. *Plant Dis. Res.* 1 (1-2): 46-50.

Chahal, A.S. and Jaura, N.S. 1994. Sources for Alternaria resistance in Brassicas. *Indian Phytopath.* 47(3): 306 (Abstr.).

Chahal, A.S. and Kang, M.S. 1979a. Different levels of Alternaria blight in relation to grain yield of Brown sarson. *Indian J. Mycol. Plant Pathol.* 9: 260-261.

Chahal, A.S. and Kang, M.S. 1979b. Influence of meteorological factors on the development of Alternaria blight of rapeseed and mustard in the Punjab. *Indian Phytopath.* 32(1): 171 (Abstr.).

Chahal, A.S. and Kang, M.S. 1979c. Some aspects of seed borne infection of *Alternaria brassicae* in rape and mustard cultivars in the Punjab. *Indian J. Mycol. Plant Pathol.* 9: 51-56.

Chahal, A.S. and Sekhon, J.S. 1980. How to control Alternaria blight of rapeseed and mustard? *Prog. Fmg.* 17(3): 15.

Chang, I.H., Shih, N.L. and Chiu, W.F. 1964. A preliminary study on the physiological differentiation of the downy mildew (*Personospora parasitica* (Pers.) Fr.) of Chinese cabbage and other cruciferous vegetables in the vicinity of Peking and Tientsin. *Acta Phytopath. Sin.* 7: 33-44.

Chang, I.H., Xu, R.F. and Chiu, W. 1963. On the primary sources of infection of the downy mildew of Chinese cabbage caused by *Peronospora brassicae* (Pers.) Fr. and the limited systemic infection of seedlings. *Acta Phytopath. Sin.* 6: 153-162.

Changstri, W. and Weber, G.F. 1963. Three Alternaria species pathogenic on certain cultivated crucifers. *Phytopathology* 53: 643-648.

Channon, A.G. 1981. Downy mildew of Brassicas. pp. 77-86. In: D.M. Spencer ed., *The Downy Mildews*. Academic Press, London.

Chatterjee, S.C., Gopal, M. and Mukherjee, I. 1997. Bio efficacy of Iprodione against Alternaria blight and its residue in mustard. p. 354 *Golden Jubilee Int. Conf., Integrated Plant Disease Management for Sustainable Agriculture,* Nov.10-15, 1997, Indian Phytopath. *Soc.*, New Delhi.

Chattopadhyay, A.K. 1989. Relationship of phenols and sugars in Alternaria blight resistance of rapeseed-mustard. *Indian J. Mycol. Res.* 27(2): 195-199.

Chattopadhyay, A.K. 1991. Studies on the control of club root disease of rapeseed-mustard in West Bengal. *Indian Phytopath.* 44: 397-398.

Chattopadhyay, A.K. 1996. Soil amendment with lime and organic matter on the control of club root disease of rapeseed-mustard. *Indian Phytopath.* 49(3): 283-285.

Chattopadhyay, A.K. and Bagchi, B.N. 1989. Occurrence of club root disease on rapeseed-mustard in West Bengal. *Indian J. Mycol. Res.* 27(1): 83-84.

Chattopadhyay, A.K. and Bagchi, B.N. 1991. Curbing the club root disease of rapeseed. *Indian Fmg.* 40(12): 24.

Chattopadhyay, A.K. and Bagchi, B.N. 1994. Relationship of disease severity and yield due to leaf blight of mustard and spray schedule of mancozeb for higher yield. *J. Mycopath. Res.* 32(2): 83-87.

Chattopadhyay, A.K., Bagchi, B.N. and Roy Choudhury, U.K. 1991. Reaction of some cultures of rapeseed-mustard against club root disease. *Indian Phytopath.* 44: 238-239.

Chauhan, L.S. and Saxena, H.K. 1974. A new Rhizoctonia leaf blight of rapeseed and mustard. *Indian J. Farm Sci.* 2: 98-99.

Chaurasia, S.N.P., Singh, V.P. and Singh, H.B. 1982. Preferential parasitism of *Peronospora parasitica* on galls of *Brassica campestris* caused by *Albugo cruciferarum*. *Trans. Br. Mycol. Soc.* 78: 379-381.

Chen, C.Y., Plummer, K.M. and Howlett, B.J. 1996. Ability of a *Leptosphaeria maculans* isolate to form stem cankers on Indian mustard (*Brassica juncea*) segregates as a single locus. *European J. Plant Path.* 102: 349-352.

Chen, Y.Q. and Zhang, J.F. 1994. Distribution of fallen floral organs and diseased leaves on rapeseed plants in relation to the incidence of Sclerotinia blight. *Jiangsu J. Agri. Sci.* 10(4): 54-56.

Chen, Y.Q., Zhang, J.F., Wu, Y.M., Hou, Q.S., Zhou, Y.J. and Han, H. 1993. Studies on Sclerotinia blight and virus disease resistance (tolerance) of rapeseed germplasms in the Brassica genus. *Oil Crops of China* 2: 4-7.

Chevre, A.M., Eber, F., Brun, H., Plessis, J., Primard, C. and Renard, M. 1991. Cytogenetic studies of *Brassica napus-Sinapis alba* hybrids from ovary culture and protoplast fushion. Attempts to introduce Alternaria resistance into rapeseed. pp. 346-351. *Proc. 8ᵗʰ Int. Rapeseed Cong.*, Saskatoon, Canada.

Chona, B.L., Lall, G. and Kakria, N.C. 1958. *ICAR, Bull. No.81*, New Delhi.

Chou, C.K. 1970. An electron-microscope study of host-penetration and early stages of haustorium formation of *Peronospora parasitica* (Fr.) Tul. on cabbage cotyledons. *Ann. Bot.* 34: 189-204.

Choudhary, S. 1944. Some fungi from Assam. *Indian J. Agric. Sci.* 19: 230-235.

Chup, C. 1925. *Manual of Vegetable Garden Diseases*. MacMillan, New York, pp. 530.

Conn, K.L. and Tewari, J.P. 1989. Interactions of *Alternaria brassicae* conidia with epicuticular wax of canola. *Mycological Res.* 93(2): 240-242.

Conn, K.L., Tewari, J.P. and Awasthi, R.P. 1990. A disease assessment key for Alternaria black spot in rapeseed and mustard. *Can. Plant Dis. Surv.* 70: 19-22.

Conn, K.L., Tewari, J.P. and Dahiya, J.S. 1988. Resistance of *Alternaria brassicae* and phytoalexin-elicitation in rapeseed and other crucifers. *Plant Sci.* (Limerik, Irel.) 55(1): 21-25.

Cook, R.J. and Evans, E.J. 1978. Build up of diseases with intensification of oilseed rape in England. *Proc. 5ᵗʰ Int. Rapeseed Conf.*, Malmo, Sweden, 1: 333-337.

Daebeler, F., Amelung, D., Pluschkell, H.J. and Legde, G. 1980. Occurrence and importance of fungus diseases in winter rape in the northern part of GDR. *Nachrichtenbl. den Pflanzenschutz DDR.* 34: 17-20.

Dahiya, J.S. and Rimmer, S.R. 1988. Phytoalixm accumulation in tissues of *Brassica napus* inoculated with *Leptosphaeria maculans*. *Phytochem*. 27(10): 3105-3107.

Dahiya, J.S. and Tewari, J.P. 1991. Plant growth factors produced by the fungus *Alternaria brassicae*. *Phytochem*. 30: 2825-2828.

Dahiya, J.S., Tewari, J.P. and Woods, D.L. 1988. Abscisic acid from *Alternaria brassicae*. *Phytochem*. 27: 2983-2984.

Dahiya, J.S. and Woods, D.L. 1987. Control of *Rhizoctonia solani*, casual agent of crown girdling root rot of canola/rapeseed by *Pseudomonas fluorescens*. *Can. J. Plant Pathol*. 9: 275-276.

Damle, V.P. 1944. A new species found on *Cardamine subumbelata*. *J. Univ. Bombay* 12: 42-45.

Dang, J.K., Kaushik, C.D. and Sangwan, M.S. 1995. Quantitative relationship between Alternaria leaf blight of rapeseed-mustard and weather variables. *Indian J. Mycol. Plant Pathol*. 25(3): 184-185.

Dang, J.K., Sangwan, M.S., Kaushik, C.D. and Mehta, N. 1997. Multiple disease resistance in Brassica. p. 393. *Golden Jubilee Int. Conf., Integrated Plant Disease Management for Sustainable Agriculture*, Nov. 10-15, 1997, Indian Phytopath. Soc., New Delhi.

Das, S.N., Mishra, S.K. and Swain, P.K. 1987. Reaction of some Toria varieties to *Plasmodiophora brassicae*. *Indian Phytopath*. 40: 120.

Dasgupta, B. 1991. Effect of fungicidal sprays on the incidence of Alternaria blight and yield of mustard. *Natn. Bot. Soc.* 45: 53-57.

Davies, J.M.L. 1986. Diseases of oilseed rape. pp. 195-236. In: D.H. Scarisbrick and R.W. Daniels, eds., *Oilseed rape*. Collins, London.

Davison, E.M. 1968. Development of sporangiophores of *Peronospora parasitica* (Pers. ex Fr.) Fr. *Ann. Bot*. 32: 623-631.

deBary, A. 1860. Surla formation de zoospores chez qualques champi gnons. *Ann. Sci. nat., Ser.* 13: 236-251.

deBary, A. 1866. *Morphologie und physiologia der Pilze, Flechten und Myxomyceten*. Wilhelm Engelmann, Leipzig.

deBruyn, H.L.G. 1937. Heterothallism in *Peronospora parasitica*. *Genetica* 19: 553-558.

Degenhardt, K.J. 1978. Alternaria black spot of rapeseed and mustard: Phytotoxins and other aspects of the host-parasite interaction. Ph.D. thesis, Univ. Saskatchewan, Canada (cited from P.S. Bains and J.P. Tewari 1987. *Physiol. Mol. PlantPathol*.30: 259-271),

Degenhardt, K.J., Petrie, G.A. and Morrall, R.A.A. 1982. Effects of temperature on spore germination and infection of rapeseed by *Alternaria brassicae, A. brassicicola* and *A. raphani*. *Can. J. Plant Pathol*. 4(2): 115-118.

Degenhardt, K.J., Skoropod, W.P. and Konda, Z.P. 1974. Effect of Alternaria black spot on yield, oil content and protein content of rapeseed. *Can. J. Plant Sci*. 54: 795-799.

Delwiche, P.A. 1980. Genetic aspects of black leg (*Leptosphaeria maculans*) resistance in rapeseed (*Brassica napus*). Ph.D. Thesis, Univ. Wisconsin, Madison, Wisconsin (cited from S.R. Rimmer and C.G.J. vanden Berg, 1992. *Can. J. Plant Pathol*. 14: 56-66).

Delwiche, P.A. and Williams, P.H. 1974. Resistance to *Albugo candida* race 2 in Brassica species. *Proc. Am. Phytopathol. Soc.* 1: 66 (Abstr.).

Delwiche, P.A. and Williams, P.H. 1976. Identification of marker genes in *Brassica nigra*. *Proc. Am. Phytopathol. Soc.* 3: 324 (Abstr.).

Delwiche, P.A. and Williams, P.H. 1977. Genetic studies in *Brassica nigra* (L.) Koch. *Cruciferae Newsl*. No.2: 39.

Denton, O.A. and Whittington, W.J. 1975. The response of swede varieties and their hybrids to soil pH. *J. Agric. Sci.* (Cambridge) 85: 395-401.

Dey, P.K. 1948. Plant Pathology. *Adm. Rep. Agric. Dept.*, UP, 1946-47: 39-42.

Dhawan, S. 1980. Protease activity in *Brassica juncea* plants infected with *Sclerotinia sclerotiorum*. *Curr. Sci.* 49(7): 291-292.

Dhawan, Shashi., Srivastava, S.K. and Dharwan, S. 1987. Trans-eliminative (lytic) pectic enzymes in Sclerotinia infection of *Brassica juncea*. *Indian J. Mycol. Plant Pathol*. 17(3): 325-327.

Dhingra, O.D. and Sinclair, J.B. 1978. Biology and pathology of *Macrophomina phaseolina*. *Universidade Federal De Vicosa*, pp. 166.

Dhingra, R.K., Chauhan, N. and Chauhan, S.V.S. 1982. Biochemical changes in the floral parts of *Brassica campestris* infected by *Albugo candida*. *Indian Phytopath.* 36(1): 177-179.

Dickinson, C.H. and Greenhalgh, J.R. 1977. Host range and taxonomy of Peronospora on crucifers. *Trans. Br. Mycol. Soc.* 69: 111-116.

Dikshit, R.K. and Srivastava, A.N. 1991. "Vardan" mustard is suited to late planting on irrigated lands. *Indian Fmg.* 40(12): 19.

Dixon, G.R. 1975. The reaction of some oilseed rape cultivars to some fungal pathogens. pp. 503-506. *Proc. 8th Br. Insecticide & Fungicide Conf.*, 1975, England.

Dobson, R.L., Gabrielson, R.L., Baker, A.S. and Bennett, L. 1983. Effects of lime particle size and distribution and fertilizer formulation on club root disease caused by *Plasmodiophora brassicae*. *Plant Dis.* 67: 50-52.

Doughty, K.J., Blight, M.M., Bock, C.H., Fieldsend, J.K. and Pickett, J.A. 1996. Release of alkenyl isothiocyanates and other volatiles from *Brassica rapa* seedlings during infection by *Alternaria brassicae*. *Phytochem.* 43(2): 371-374.

Doughty, K.J., Porter, A.J.R., Morton, A.M., Kiddle, G., Bock, C.H. and Walls Grove, R. 1991. Variation in the glucosinolate content of oilseed rape (*Brassica napus* L.) leaves. II. Response to infection by *Alternaria brassicae* (Berk.) Sacc. *Ann. Appl.Biol.* 118(2): 469-477.

Downey, R.K. and Rimmer,S.R. 1993. Agronomic improvement in oilseed Brassicas. *Adv. Agron.* 50: 1-66.

Dube, V.P., Charaya, M.U., Tyagi, S. and Devi, S. 1980. Effect of *Alternaria brassicae* (Berk.) Sacc. and its culture fillrates on the permeability of cauliflower leaves. *Acta Bot. Indica* 8: 265-267.

Dubey, S.C. 1996. Chemical control of white rust of mustard. *Plant Dis. Res.* 11(2): 155-158.

Dubey, S.C. and Misra, B. 1994. Evaluation of fungicides against white rust of mustard. *Indian J. Mycol. Plant Pathol.* 24(2): 150.

Dueck, J., Morrall, R.A.A. and McKenzie, D.L. 1983. Control of *Sclerotinia sclerotiorum* in rapeseed with fungicides. *Can. J. Plant Pathol.* 5(4): 289-293.

Dueck, J. and Stone, J.R. 1979. Evaluation of fungicides for control of *Albugo candida* in turnip rape. *Can. J. Plant Sci.*59: 423.

Duggar, B.M. 1989. *Fungous Diseases of Plants*. Agro Botanical Publishers (India). IV E 176, J.N. Vyas Nagar, Bikaner, India, pp. 508.

Eberhardt, A. 1904. Contribution a' l'etude de *Cystopus candidus*. *Lev Zentr Bakteriol Parasitenk* 12: 235-249; 426-439.

Ebrahimi, A.G., Delwiche, P.A. and Williams, P.H. 1976. Resistance in *Brassica juncea* to *Peronospora parasitica* and *Albugo candida* race 2. *Proc. Am. Phytopathol. Soc.* 3: 273 (Abstr.)

Edwards, M.D. and Williams, P.H. 1987. Selection for minor gene resistance to *Albugo candida* in a rapid-cycling population of *Brassica campestris*. *Phytopathology* 77: 527-532.

Engqvist, G. 1994. Look out for club root. *Svensk Frotidning*. 63(10): 13-16.

Evans, E.J. and Gladders, P. 1981. Diseases of winter oilseed rape and their control, east- and south-east England, 1977-81. *Proc. 1981 Br. Crop Prot. Conf., Pest and Diseases*, 2: 505-512.

Evans, E.J., Gladders, P., Davies, J.M.L., Ellerton, D.R., Hardwick, N.V., Hawkins, J.H., Jones, D.R. and Simkin, M.B. 1984. Current status of diseases and disease control of winter oilseed rape in England. *Aspects Appl. Biol.* (6): *Agronomy, Physiology, Plant Breeding and Crop Protection of Oilseed rape.* pp. 323-334.

Fan, Z., Rimmer, S.R. and Stefansson, B.R. 1983. Inheritance of resistance to *Albugo candida* in rape (*Brassica napus* L.). *Can. J. Genet. Cytol.* 25: 420-424.

Felton, M.W. and Walker, J.C. 1946. Environmental factors affecting downy mildew of cabbage. *J. Agri. Res.* 72: 69-81.

Ferreira, M.E., Williams, P.H. and Osborn, T.C. 1995. Mapping of a locus controlling resistance to *Albugo candida* in *Brassica napus* using molecular markers. *Phytopathology* 85: 218-220.

Fiddaman, P.J. and Rossall, S. 1995. Selection of bacterial antagonists for the biological control of *Rhizoctonia solani* in oilseed rape (*Brassica napus*). *Plant Pathol.* 44(4): 695-705.

Finck, G. 1989. Application of transformation products of calcium cyanamide in field for inhibition of sclerotial germination of *Sclerotinia sclerotiorum*, casual agent of stem rot of rape. *Z. Pflanzenkrankh. Pflanzensch.* 96(5): 508-520.

Fox, D.T. and Williams, P.H.1984. Correlation of spore production by *Albugo candida* on *Brassica campestris* and a visual white rust rating scale. *Can. J. Plant Pathol.* 6: 175-178.

Fu, S.Z. 1990. New thinking on rape breeding for high yield and disease resistance-breeding a petal less genotype. *Acta. Agri.* (Shanghai) 6(3): 76-77.

Fu, Y.L. and Tang, J.X. 1994. A new technique to control Sclerotinia rot of rape (*Sclerotinia sclerotiorum*). *Bull. Agri. Sci. Tech.* 3: 30.

Gabrielson, R.L. 1983. Black leg disease of crucifers caused by *Leptosphaeria maculans* (*Phoma lingam*) and its control. *Seed Sci. Technol.* 11: 749-780.

Gandhi, S.K. and Parashar, R.D. 1977. Bacterial rot of Raya (*Brassica juncea*). *Indian Phytopath.* 30(1): 24-27.

Gandhi, S.K. and Parashar, R.D. 1978. Evaluation of some fungicides and antibiotics against *Xanthomonas campestris* causing bacterial rot of Raya. *Indian Phytopath.* 31: 210-213.

Gangasaran and Giri, G. 1984. Agronomic manipulations for increasing yields of edible oilseeds, pp. 285-292. In: H.C. Srivastava, S. Bhaskaran, B. Vatsya and K.K.G. Menon eds., *Oilseed production: Constraints and Opportunities.* Oxford and IBH Publishing Co., New Delhi.

Gangopadhyay, S., Bhatia, J.N., Godara, S.L. and Pundhir, P. 1994. Identification of sources of resistance against white rust (*Albugo cruciferarum*) and mixed infection of mustard. *Indian Phytopath.* 47(3): 306 (Abstr.).

Garbe, V. 1993. Effects of fungicide treatment in different varieties of winter rape. *Bull. OILB/SROP.* 16(9): 116-123.

Garg, S., Dhawan, K., Chawla, H.K.L. and Nainawatee, H.S. 1999. Leakage of solutes from *Brassica juncea* leaves during *Alternaria brassicae* pathogenesis. *Cruciferae Newsl.* No.21: 121-122.

Gauman, E. 1926. On the specialization of downy mildew *Peronospora brassicae* Gm. on cabbage and related species. *Landw. Jbr. der. Schweiz.* 40: 463-468.

George, W., Heidel, W. and Metzner, V. 1985. On the occurrence of root collar necrosis of rape in Neubrandenburg county with particular regard to crop rotation. *Nachrichtenbl. den. Pflanzenschutz. DDR* 39(12): 237-239.

Gladders, P. and Gould, H.J. 1983. Pests and diseases of oilseed rape, brassica seed crops and field beans. In: N. Scopes and M. Ledieu eds., *Pest and Disease Handbook. Br. Crop Prot. Council Publications*, England.

Gladders, P. and Musa, T.M. 1980. Observations on the epidemiology of *Leptosphaeria maculans* stem canker in winter oilseed rape. *Plant Pathol.* 29(1): 28-37.

Godoy, G., Steadman, J.R., Dickman, M.B. and Dam, R. 1990. Use of mutants to demonstrate the role of oxalic acid in pathogenicity of *Sclerotinia sclerotiorum* on *Phaseolus vulgaries*. *Physiol. Mol. Plant Pathol.* 37: 179-191.

Gong, Z.H., He, Y. and Wang, M. 1944. Studies on the resistance of intergeneric hybrids of Chinese cabbage × white mustard to Alternaria leaf spot. *Acta Horticul. Sin.* 21(4): 401-403.

Goyal, B.K., Kant, U. and Verma, P.R. 1995. Growth of *Albugo candida* (race unidentified) on *Brassica juncea* callus cultures. *Plant and Soil* 172: 331-337.

Goyal, B.K., Verma, P.R. and Spurr, D.T. 1996a. Temperature effects on oospore development of *Albugo candida* race 2V in detached *Brassica juncea* leaves. *Indian J. Mycol. Plant Pathol.* 26(2): 224-228.

Goyal, B.K., Verma, P.R., Spurr, D.T. and Reddy, M.S. 1996b. *Albugo candida* staghead formation in *Brassica juncea* in relation to plant age, inoculation sites, and incubation conditions. *Plant Pathol.*45(4): 784-794.

Govindu, H.C. and Thirumalachar, M.J. 1955. Notes on Indian Cercospora. VI. *Sydowia* 9: 221-228.

Grisham, M.P. and Anderson, N.A. 1983. Pathogenicity and host specificity of *Rhizoctonia solani* isolated from carrot. *Phytopathology* 73: 1564-1569.

Grontoft, M. 1986. Resistance to Alternaria spp. in oil crops. *Sver. Utsadesfor. Tidsk.,* 96 (13): 263.

Grontoft, M. 1993. A rapid screening method for testing the resistance of cotyledons to downy mildew in *Brassica napus* and *B. campestris*. *Plant Breed.*.110 (3): 207-211..

Grontoft, M. and O'Connor, D. 1990. Green house method of testing resistance of young Brassica plants to *Alternaria brassicae*. *Plant Breed.* 105(2): 160-165.

Gugel, R.K. and Morrall, R.A.A. 1986. Inoculum-disease relationships in Sclerotinia stem rot of rapeseed in Saskatchewan. *Can. J. Plant Pathol.* 8: 89-96.

Gugel, R.K. and Petrie, G.A. 1992. History, occurrence, impact and control of black leg of rapeseed. *Can. J. Plant Pathol.* 14(1): 36-45.

Gugel, R.K., Seguin-Swartz, G. and Petrie, G.A. 1990. Pathogenicity of three isolates of *Leptosphaeria maculans* (Tode ex Fr.) Desm. on Brassica species and other crucifers. *Can. J. Plant Pathol.* 12: 75-82.

Gugel, R.K., Yitbarek, S.M., Verma, P.R., Morrall, R.A.A. and Sadasivaiah, R.S. 1987. Etiology of Rhizoctonia root rot complex of canola in Peace River region of Alberta. *Can. J. Plant Pathol.* 9: 119-128.

Gupta, A.K. 1990. Occurrence of Fusarium wilt of mustard in Rajasthan. *Indian Bot. Reptr.* 9(1): 22.

Gupta, D.K. 1985. Root and collar rot of mustard in Sikkim. *Indian J. Mycol. Plant Pathol.* 15(2): 225.

Gupta, D.K. and Chaudhary, K.C.B. 1995. Infection of radish and rayosag seeds by *Xanthomonas campestris* pv. *campestris. Indian J. Mycol. Plant Pathol.* 25(3): 332.

Gupta, I.J. and Sharma, B.S. 1978. Chemical control of white rust of mustard. *Pesticides* 12(12): 45-46.

Gupta, J.F., Sharma, B.S. and Delela, D.G. 1977a. Control of white rust and Alternaria leaf spot of mustard. *Indian J. Mycol. Plant Pathol.* 7(2): 163-164.

Gupta, M.L., Singh, G., Raheja, R.K., Ahuja, K.L. and Banga, S.K. 1977b. Chlorophyll content in relation to white rust (*Albugo candida*) resistance in Indian mustard. *Cruciferae Newsl.* No.19: 105-106.

Gupta, R.B.L. and Singh, Mahabeer 1994. Sources of resistance to white rust and powdery mildew of mustard. *Int. J. Tropical Plant Diseases* 12(2): 225-227.

Gupta, R.P., Sinha, J.N. and Gufran, S.N. 1985. Field evaluation of fungicides for the control of Alternaria blight of Indian mustard. *Pesticides* 19(8): 47-50.

Gupta, S., Sharma, T.R. and Chib, H.S. 1995a. Evaluation of wild allies of Brassica under natural conditions. *Cruciferae Newsl.* No.17: 10-11.

Gupta, S.K., Gupta, P.P. and Kaushik, C.D. 1995b. Changes in leaf peroxidase, polyphenol oxidase, catalase and total phenol due to Alternaria leaf blight in Brassica species. *Indian J. Mycol. Plant Pathol.* 25(3): 175-180.

Gupta, S.K., Kaushik, C.D. and Yadava, T.P. 1998a. Alternaria blight induced changes in fatty acid composition of siliquae wall and seeds of mustard (*Brassica juncea* L.). *Cruciferae Newsl.* No.20: 81-82.

Gupta, S.K., Kumar, P., Yadava, T.P. and Saharan, G.S. 1984. Changes in phenolic compounds, sugars and total nitrogen in relation to Alternaria leaf blight in Indian mustard. *Haryana Agric. Univ. J. Res.* 14: 535-537.

Gupta, S.P., Singh, B.R. and Tripathi, D.P. 1997. Management of blight disease of mustard. p. 346. *Golden Jubilee Int. Conf., Integrated Plant Disease Management for Sustainable Agriculture,* Nov.10-15, 1997, Indian Phytopath. Soc., New Delhi.

Gupta, V., Chawla, H.K.L., Dhawan, K. and Mehta, N. 1998b. Alterations in total phenols and glucosinolates in *Brassica juncea* leaves during interaction with *Alternaria brassicae. Cruciferae Newsl.* No.20: 83-84.

Hall, R. 1992. Epidemiology of black leg of oilseed rape. *Can. J. Plant Pathol.* 14(1): 46-55.

Hammond, K.E. and Lewis, B.G. 1980. Ultrastructural studies on the limitation of lesions caused by *Leptosphaeria maculans* in stems of *Brassica napus. Physiol. Mol. Plant Pathol.* 20: 251-265.

Hammond, K.E. and Lewis, B.G. 1986. The timing and sequence of events leading to stem canker disease in populations of *Brassica napus* var. *oleifera* in the field. *Plant Pathol.* 35: 551-564.

Hammond, K.E. and Lewis, B.G. 1987. Differential responses of oilseed rape leaves to *Leptosphaeria maculans. Trans. Br. Mycol. Soc.* 88(3): 329-333.

Hammond, K.E., Lewis, B.G. and Musta, T.M. 1985. A systemic pathway in the infection of oilseed rape plants by *Leptosphaeria maculans. Plant Pathol.* 34(4): 557-565.

Hanacziwskyj, P. and Drysdale, R.B. 1984. Variation in the pathogenicity of *Leptosphaeria maculans* to oilseed rape and other brassicas. *Aspects Appl. Biol.* 6: 343-353.

Harper, F.R. and Pittman, U.J. 1974. Yield loss by *Brassica campestris* and *B. napus* from systemic stem infection by *Albugo cruciferarum. Phytopathology* 54: 408-410.

Hegde, V.M. and Anahosur, K.H. 1993. Chemical control of white rust of mustard. *Karnataka J. Agri. Sci.* 6(3): 263-267.

Hegde, V.M. and Anahosur, K.H. 1994. Influence of sowing date of mustard on the epidemiology of white rust. *Indian Phytopath.* 47(4): 391-394.

Helms, K. and Cruickshank, I.A.M. 1979. Germination-inoculation technique for screening cultivars of oilseed rape and mustard for resistance to *Leptosphaeria maculans*. *Phytopath. Z.* 95(1): 77-86.

Henry, A.W. 1974. Bacterial pod spot of rape in Alberta. *Can. Plant Dis. Surv.* 54: 91-94.

Herr, I.J. and Robert, D.L. 1980. Characterization of Rhizoctonia population obtained from sugarbeet fields with differing soil texture. *Phytopathology* 70: 476-480.

Hiura, M. 1930. A simple method for the germination of oospores of *Sclerospora graminicola*. *Science* (Wash.) 72: 95.

Holiday, Paul 1981. *Fungal diseases of Tropical Crops,* pp. 8-9. Cambridge University Press, Cambridge.

Hong, C.X. and Fitt, B.D.L. 1995. Effects of inoculum concentration, leaf age and wetness period on the development of dark leaf spot and pod spot (*Alternaria brassicae*) on oilseed rape (*Brassica napus*). *Ann. Appl. Biol.* 127(2): 283-295.

Hong, C.X. and Fitt, B.D.L. 1996. Factors affecting the incubation period of dark leaf and pod spot (*Alternaria brassicae*) on oilseed rape (*Brassica napus*). *European J. Plant Pathol.* 102(6): 545-553.

Honing, F. 1931. The causal organism of finger-toe disease (*Plasmodiophora brassicae* Wor.). A monograph. *Gartenbauwissensch.* 5(2-3): 116-125.

Howlider, M.A.R., Meah, M.B., Jalaluddin, M. and Rahman, M.A. 1985. Effect of fungicides in reducing the intensity of Alternaria blight of mustard. *Bangladesh J. Agri.* 10(4): 41-46.

Hu, B. and Rimmer, S.R. 1989. Preliminary study of artificial inoculation for resistance (tolerance) to *Sclerotinia sclerotiorum* in rapeseed using detached leaves. *Anhui Agric. Sci.* 11: 56-58.

Huang, H.C. and Kokko, E.G. 1992. Pod rot of dry peas due to infection by ascospores of *Sclerotinia sclerotiorum*. *Plant Dis.* 76: 597-600.

Huang, J.W. and Chung, W.C. 1993. Characteristics of black spot pathogens, *Alternaria brassicicola* and *A. brassicae*. *Plant Pathol. Bull.* 2(3): 141-148.

Humpherson-Jones, F.M. 1983. Pathogenicity studies on isolates of *Leptosphaeria maculans* from brassica seed production crops in south-east England. *Ann. Appl. Biol.* 103: 37-44.

Humpherson-Jones, F.M. 1989. Survival of *Alternaria brassicae* and *Alternaria brassicicola* on crop debris of oilseed rape and cabbage. *Ann. Appl. Biol.* 115(1): 45-50.

Humpherson-Jones, F.M. 1992. Epidemiology and control of dark leaf spot of brassicas. pp. 267-288. In: J. Chelkowski and A. Visconti eds. *Alternaria-Biology, Plant Diseases and Metabolites—Topics in Secondary Metabolism.* Vol.III, Elsevier Science Publishers, Amsterdam.

Humpherson-Jones, F.M. and Ainsworth, L.F. 1983. Canker of brassicas. pp. 62-63. In: *33rd Annu. Rept.* 1982, *Natn. Veg. Res. Stn.* Warwick, U.K. 1983,

Humpherson-Jones, F.M., Hocart, M.J. and Ainsworth, L.F. 1983. Alternaria disease of brassica seed crops. pp. 63-64. In: *33rd Annu. Rept.* 1982, *Natn. Veg. Res. Stn.* Warwick, U.K. 1983.

Humpherson-Jones, F.M. and Maude, R.B. 1982. Control of dark leaf spot (*Alternaria brassicae*) of *Brassica oleracea* seed production crops with foliar sprays of iprodione. *Ann. Appl. Biol.* 100: 99-104.

Humpherson-Jones, F.M. and Maude, R.B. 1983. The seed-borne source of *Alternaria brassicae* and *Leptosphaeria maculans* in oilseed rape in the United Kingdom. Prospects for control. *Sixth Int. Rapeseed Conf.,* 2: 916-921.

Humpehrson-Jones, F.M. and Phelps, K. 1989. Climatic factors influencing spore production in *Alternaria brassicae* and *Alternaria brassicicola*. *Ann. Appl. Biol.* 114(3): 449-458.

Hussain, A. and Thakur, R.N. 1963. Some sources of resistance to Alternaria blight of rapeseed and mustard. *Indian Oilseeds J.* 7: 259-264.

Hussain, A. and Thakur, R.N. 1966. Production of a toxin by *Alternaria brassicae* (Berk.) Sacc. *in vitro*. *Labdev. J. Sci. Tech.* 4(2): 144-145.

Ichielevich-Auster, M., Sneh, B., Koltin, Y. and Barash, I. 1985. Pathogenicity, host specificity and anastomosis groups of Rhizoctonia spp. isolated from soils in Israel. *Phytoparasitica* 13: 103-112.

Ingram, D.S. 1969. The susceptibility of Brassica callus to infection by *Peronospora parasitica. J. Gen. Microbiol.* 58: 391-401.

Ingram, D.S. and Tommercup, I.C. 1972. The life history of *Plasmodium brassicae* Woron. *Proc. R. Soc. Lond. B.* 180: 103-112.

Jalali, I. and Parashar, R.D. 1995. Biocontrol of *Xanthomonas campestris* pv. *campestris* in *Brassica juncea* with phylloplane antagonist. *Plant Dis. Res.* 10(2): 145-147.

Jamaux, I., Gelie, B. and Lamarque, C. 1995. Early stages of infection of rapeseed petals and leaves by *Sclerotinia sclerotiorum* revealed by scannign electron microscope. *Plant Pathol.* 44: 22-30.

Jejelowo, O.A., Conn, K.L. and Tewari, J.P. 1991. Relationship between conidial concentration, germling growth and phytoalexin production by *Camelina sativa* leaves inoculated with *Alternaria brassicae. Mycol. Res.* 95(8): 928-934.

Jimenez, L.D., Ayer, W.A. and Tewari, J.P. 1997. Phytoalexins produced in leaves of *Capsella bursa-pastoris* (Shepherd's Purse). *Phytoprotection.* 78: 99-103.

Johnson, R.D. and Lewis, B.G. 1990. DNA polymorphism in *Leptosphaeria maculans. Physiol. Mol. Plant Pathol.* 37: 417-424.

Johnson, R.D. and Lewis, B.G. 1994. Variation in host range, systemic infection and epidemiology of *Leptosphaeria maculans. Plant Pathol.* 43: 269-277.

Johnston, T.D. 1968. Club root in Brassica: a standard inoculation technique and the specification of races. *Plant Pathol.* 17: 184-187.

Johnston, T.D. 1974. Transfer of disease resistance from *Brassica campestris* L. to rape (*B. napus*). *Euphytica* 23: 681-683

Jong, P.D.DE. and Hasper, G.A. 1996. Threshold value for chemical control of powdery mildew (*Erysiphe cruciferarum*) on Brussels sprouts. *European J. Plant Pathol.* 102(2): 205-208.

Jonsson, R. 1966. *Peronospora parasitica* on oil-yielding Brassicas: methods of testing resistance in winter rape and their results. *Sver. Utsadesfor Tidsk.,* 76: 56.

Kadian, A.K. and Saharan, G.S. 1984. Studies on spore germination and infection of *Alternaria brassicae* of rapeseed and mustard. *J. Oilseeds Res.* 1: 183-188.

Kageyama, K., Kamimura, Y. and Hyakumachi, M. 1995. A simple inoculation method with a single resting spore of *Plasmodiophora brassicae. Ann. Phytopath. Soc. Japan.* 61(5): 415-418.

Kaminski, D.A. and Verma, P.R. 1985. Cultural characteristics, virulence, and *in vitro* temperature effect on mycelial growth of Rhizoctonia isolates from rapeseed. *Can. J. Plant Pathol.* 7: 256-261.

Kanaujia, R.S. and Kishore, R. 1981. A new wilt disease of *Brassica nigra* caused by *Fusarium oxysporium* f. *conglutinans. Indian Phytopath.* 34: 84-85.

Kapoor, A.S. and Sugha, S.K. 1995. Efficacy of some fungicides in controlling white rust of mustard. *Indian J. Mycol. Plant Pathol.* 25(3): 285-286.

Kataria, H.R. and Verma, P.R. 1989. Activity of fungicides against damping-off and root rot of rapeseed/canola cultivars caused by *Rhizoctonia solani. Can. J. Plant Pathol.* 11: 192.

Kataria, H.R. and Verma, P.R. 1990. Efficacy of fungicidal seed treatments against pre-emergence damping-off and post-emergence seedling root rot of growth-chamber grown canola caused by *Rhizoctonia solani* AG 2-1 and AG-4. *Can. J. Plant Pathol.* 12(4): 409-416.

Kataria, H.R. and Verma, P.R. 1992. Rhizoctonia damping-off and root rot in oilseed rape and canola. *Crop Prot.* 11: 8-13.

Katiyar, R.K. and Chamola, R. 1994. A note on incorporation of resistance to Alternaria leaf spot into *Brassica juncea* from *B. carinata. New Botanist* 21(1-4): 131-134.

Kaushik, C.D., Kaushik, J.C. and Saharan, G.S. 1983. Field evaluation of fungicides for control of Alternaria blight of *Brassica juncea. Indian J. Mycol. Plant Pathol.* 13(3): 262-264.

Kaushik, C.D., Saharan, G.S. and Kaushik, J.C. 1984. Magnitude of losses in yield and management of Alternaria blight in rapeseed-mustard. *Indian Phytopath.* 37(2): 398 (Abstr.).

Kaushik, C.D., Tripathi, N.N. and Vir, S. 1978. Effect of date of sowing of Toria on phyllody incidence and estimation of losses. *Haryana Agric. Univ. J. Res.* 8: 28-30.

Khan, R.U. 1985. Studies on seedling diseases of rapeseed and mustard, M.Sc. (Ag.) Thesis. G.B. Pant Univ. Agric. & Tech. Pantnagar, UP, pp. 109.

Khan, R.U. and Kolte, S.J. 1989. Influence of different factors on the incidence of collar-rot of mustard caused by *Sclerotium rolfsii* Sacc. *Indian J. Mycol. Plant Pathol.* 19(1): 234-236.

Khan, S.R. 1977. Light and electron microscopic observations on sporangium formation in *Albugo candida* (Peronosporales, Oomycetes). *Can. J. Bot.* 55(6): 730-739.

Khangura, R.K. and Sokhi, S.S. 1995. Hormonal make up of stagheads of Brassica infected by *Albugo candida*. *Indian Phytopath.* 48(1): 32-34.

Kharbanda, P.D. 1992. Performance of fungicide to control black leg of canola. *Can. J. Plant Pathol.* 14(2): 169-176.

Kirchner, H.A. and Pluschkell, H.J. 1973. On the occurrence of rape stalk break (*Sclerotinia sclerotiorum* (Lib) deBary) in the Rostock district. *Nachrichtenbl den Pflanzenschutz. DDR* 27(2): 38-40.

Klein, M. 1977. Sesamum phyllody in Israel. *Phytopath. Z.* 88: 165-171.

Klemm, M. 1938. The most important diseases and pests of colza and rape. *Rev. Appl. Mycol.* 17: 717, 1938 (Abstr.).

Klodt-Bussmann, E. and Paul, V.H. 1995. Studies on the preservation and aggressiveness of *Peronospora parasitica* and results with regard to the disease resistance of winter oilseed rape to the pathogen. *J. Phytopathol.* 143(10): 613-617.

Kluczewski, S.M. and Lucas, J.A. 1982. Development and physiology of infection by the downy mildew fungus *Peronospora parasitica* (Pers. ex Fr.) Fr. in susceptible and resistant Brassica species. *Plant Pathol.* 31: 373-389.

Kohle, H. and Hoffman, G.H. 1989. Studies on the physiology of Alternaria infection of rape. *Z. Pflanzenkrankh. Pflanzensch.* 96(3): 225-238 (Abstr.).

Kohli, Y., Morrall, R.A.A., Anderson, J.B. and Kohn, L.M. 1992. Local and trans-Canadian clonal distribution of *Sclerotinia sclerotiorum* from canola. *Phytopathology* 82(8): 875-880.

Kolte, S.J. 1980. Seed production of rapeseed and mustard with special reference to certification standards for Alternaria blight. *Discussion on Recommendation and Finalization of Certain Disputed Seed Certification Standards. Annu. Group Meeting, Rapeseed and Mustard, ICAR,* Orissa Univ. Agric. & Tech., Bhubaneswar, August 28-30, 1980.

Kolte, S.J. 1987. Important diseases of rapeseed and mustard in India—Present research progress and future research needs. pp. 91-106. *Proc 3rd Oil Crops Network Workshop.* Ethiopia.

Kolte, S.J., Awasthi, R.P.and Vishwanath. 1986. Effect of planting dates and associated weather factors on staghead phase of white rust and downy mildew of rapeseed and mustard. *Indian J. Mycol. Plant Pathol.* 16(2): 94-102.

Kolte, S.J., Awasthi, R.P. and Vishwanath. 1987. Assessment of yield losses due to Alternaria blight in rapeseed and mustard. *Indian Phytopath.* 40(2): 209-211.

Kolte, S.J., Awasthi, R.P., Vishwanath., Sawant, S.D. and Thakur, R. 1985. Plant Pathology. In: *Oilseed Research at Pantnagar.* Direct. Expt. Stn., G.B. Pant Univ. Agric. Tech., Pantnagar, *Tech. Bull.* 111: 36-62.

Kolte, S.J., Sharma, K.D. and Awasthi, R.P. 1981. Yield losses and control of downy mildew and white rust of rapeseed and mustard. p. 70. *Third Int. Symp. Plant Pathology,* New Delhi, Dec.14-18, 1981.

Kolte, S.J. and Tewari, A.N. 1980. Note on the susceptibility of certain oleiferous Brassicaceae to downy mildew and white blister diseases. *Indian J. Mycol. Plant Pathol.* 10: 191-192.

Kotch, E., Badawy, H.M.A. and Hoppe, H.H. 1989. Differences between aggressive and non-aggressive single spore lines of *Leptosphaeria maculans* in cultural characteristics and phytoalexin production. *J. Phytopathol.* 124: 52-62.

Kotch, E., Song, K., Osborn, T.C. and Williams, P.H. 1991. Relationship between pathogenecity and phylogeny based on restriction fragment length polymorphism in *Leptosphaeria maculans. Mol. Plant-Microbe Interact.* 4: 341-349.

Kruger, W. 1973. Measures for controlling *Sclerotinia sclerotiorum* (Lib.) deBary on rape. *Phytopath. Z.* 77(2): 125-127.

Kruger, W. 1974. Untersuchungen uber die Epidemiologie des Rapskrebses, verursacht durch *Sclerotinia sclerotiorum* (Lib.) deBary. pp. 595-596. *Proc. Int. Raps Konggress. Giessen,* West Germany.

Kruger, W. 1975. The effect of environmental factors on the development of apothecia and ascospores of rape stalk break pathogen, *Sclerotinia sclerotiorum* (Lib.) deBary. *Z. Pflanzenkrankh. Pflanzensch.* 82(2): 101-108.

Kruger, W. 1980. On the effect of calcium cyanamide on the development of apothecia of *Whetzelinia sclerotiorum* (Lib.) Krof. and Dumont, the causal agent of stalk rot of rape. *Nachrichtenbl. Deut. Pflanzenschutz.* 32(2): 17-21.

Kruger, W. 1982. The root collar and stem rot of rape by *Phoma lingam,* a disease difficult to control. *Z. Pflanzenkrankh. Pflanzensch.* 89(9/9): 498-507.

Kruger, W. 1983. White stalk rot (rape canker). Information on integrated plant protection. *Nachrichtenbl. Deut. Pflanzenschutz.* 35(10): 159-160.

Kruger, W. 1988. Diseases of oilseed rape and control measures. *Rev. Trop. Plant Path.* 5: 193-206.

Kruger, W., Marquard, R. and Schlosser, E. 1980. Plant disease-product quality II. Influence of the stem canker (*Sclerotiana sclerotiorum* (Lib.) deBary) on the quality of rapeseed. *Med. Fac. Landbouww. Gent.*45(2): 113-443.

Kruger, W. and Stoltenberg, J. 1983. Control fo rape diseases. II. Measures for disease reduction of *Sclerotinia sclerotiorum* with regard to economic factors. *Phytopath. Z.* 108(2): 114-126.

Kruger, W. and Wittern, I. 1985. Epidemiologische untersuchungen bei der Wurzelhals und Stengelfaule des Rapses, verursacht durch *Phoma lingam. Phytopath. Z.* 113: 125-140.

Kumar, A. 1996. Efficacy of different fungicides against Alternaria blight, white rust and stag head infection of mustard. *Plant Dis. Res.* 11(2): 174-177.

Kumar, A. and Thakur, K.S. 1997. Incidence and occurrence of root rot of Brassicas in Himachal Pradesh. *Cruciferae Newsl.*No.19: 107-108.

Kumar, K. and Singh, D.P. 1986. Control of *Alternaria brassicae* infection in mustard and rapeseeds. *Pesticides* 20(6): 22-23.

Kumar, V., Kaushik, C.D. and Gupta, P.P. 1995. Role of various factors in the development of white rust disease of rape-seed-mustard. *Indian J. Mycol. Plant Pathol.* 25(3): 145-148.

Kumari, K., Varghese, T.M. and Suryanarayana, D. 1970. Qualitative changes in the amino acid contents of hypertro-phied organs in mustard due to *Albugo candida. Curr. Sci.* 39: 240-241.

Kuninaga, S., Yokosawa, R. and Ogoshi, A. 1979. Some properties of anastomosis Group 6 and B1 in *Rhizoctonia solani* Kuhn. *Ann. Phytopath. Soc.,* Japan 45: 207-214.

Kutcher, H.R. 1990. Studies on black leg disease of oilseed rapes: germplasm evaluation, variation for virulence and crop loss/disease relationships. M.Sc. Thesis, Univ. Manitoba, Winnipeg, Manitoba, pp. 101. (Cited from S.R. Rimmer and C.G.J. Vanden Berg 1992. *Can. J. Plant Pathol.* 14: 56-66).

Laha, J.N., Naskar, I. and Sharma, B.D. 1985. A new record of club root disease on mustard. *Curr. Sci.* 54(23): 1247.

Lahiri, I. and Bhowmik, T.P. 1993. Growth of the white rust fungus *Albugo candida* in callus tissue of *Brassica juncea. J. Gen. Microbiol.* 139: 2875-2878.

Lahiri, I. and Bhowmik, T.P. 1995. Occurrence of white rust race 2 in India. p. 72. *Natn. Symp. Perspectives in eco-friendly approaches to plant protection,* Sept. 7-8, 1995. *Souvenir and abstracts.* Soc. Plant Prot. Sci., IARI, New Delhi.

Lahiri, I., Verma, Uma and Bhowmik, T.P. 1997. Role of *Peronospora parasitica* in Albugo-Peronospora disease complex of Brassicas. p. 53. *Natn. Symp. Integrated Pest Management in India — Constraints and Opportunities,* Oct.23-24, 1997. Soc. Plant Prot. Sci., IARI, New Delhi.

Lakra, B.S. and Saharan, G.S. 1988a. Mycological and pathological variations in *Albugo candida. Indian J. Mycol. Plant Pathol.* 18 (2): 149-156.

Lakra, B.S. and Saharan, G.S. 1988b. Efficacy of fungicides in controlling white rust of mustard through foliar sprays. *Indian J. Mycol. Plant Pathol.* 18(2): 157-163.

Lakra, B.S. and Saharan, G.S. 1989. Sources of resistance and effective screening techniques in Brassica-Albugo system. *Indian Phytopath.* 42(2): 293 (Abstr.).

Lakra, B.S. and Saharan, G.S. 1991. Influence of thermo-hydro and potential evapotranspiration on white rust epidemic of mustard. *Cruciferae Newsl.* No.14-15: 150-151.

Lamarque, C. 1983. Conditions climatiques qui favorisent le processus naturel de la contamination du colza par le *Sclerotinia sclerotiorum. Proc. 6th Int. Rapeseed Conf.* 2: 903-907.

Lamarque, C., Leconte, M., Berrier, J. and Jaunet, A.M. 1985. Recherche des sites de contaminations du capitule de tournesol par les ascospores de *Sclerotinia sclerotiorum* (Lib.) deBary. CETION. *Informations Techniques* 92: 27-35 (cited from I. Jamaux *et al.* 1995. *Plant Pathol.* 44: 22-30).

Lammerink, J. 1965. Six pathogenic races of *Plasmodiophora brassicae* Wor. in New Zealand. *N. Z.J. Agric. Res.* 8(1): 156-164.

Lammerink, J. and Hart, R.W. 1985. "Tina" a new swede cultivar with resistance to dry rot and club root. *N. Z.J. Agric. Res.* 13(4): 417-420.

Lebeau, F.J. 1945. Systemic invasion of cabbage seedlings by the downy mildew fungus. *J. Agric. Res.* 70(10): 453-463.

Lefol, C. and Morrall, R.A.A. 1996. Immunoflorescent staining of sclerotinia ascospores on canola petals. *Can. J. Plant Path.* 18: 237-241.

Liu, C.Q., Du, D.Z., Zou, C.S. and Huang, Y.J. 1990. Initial studies on tolerance to *Sclerotinia sclerotiorum* (Lib.) de Bary in *Brassica napus* L. *Proc. Symp. China Int. Rapeseed Sci.*, 70-71. (cited from R.K. Downey and S.R. Rimmer 1993. *Adv. Agron.* 50: 1-66).

Liu, J.Q., Parks, P. and Rimmer, S.R. 1996. Development of monogenic lines for resistance to *Albugo candida* from a Canadian *Brassica napus* cultivar. *Phytopathology* 86: 1000-1004.

Liu, J.Q. and Rimmer, S.R. 1993. Production and germination of oospores of *Albugo candida. Can. J. Plant Pathol.* 15: 265-271.

Loof, B. 1959. Economically important diseases of cruciferous oil crops and possibilities of their control especially by breeding for resistance. *Rev. Appl. Mycol.* 39: 334, 1960 (Abstr.).

Louvet, J. 1958. The black spot disease of colza, *Alternaria brassicae. C.R. Acad. Agric. Fr.*, 44: 694.

Lu, Z.J. and Fu, S.Z. 1990. Inheritance of apetalous character in rape (*Brassica napus* L.) and its implications in breeding. *Jiangsu J. Agric. Sci.* 6(4): 30-36.

Lucas, J.A., Crute, I.R., Sherriff, C. and Gordon, P.L. 1988. The identification of a gene for race-specific resistance to *Peronospora parasitica* (downy mildew) in *Brassica napus* var. *oleifera* (oilseed rape). *Plant Pathol.* 37: 538-545.

Lumsden, R.D. 1976. Pectolytic enzymes of *Sclerotinia sclerotiorum* and their localization in infected bean. *Can. J. Bot.* 54: 2630-2641.

MacNish, G.C. 1979a. Role of sheep in the spread of black leg of rapeseed. *Aust. Plant Pathol.* 8(2): 22-23.

MacNish, G.C. 1979b. Survival of *Leptosphaeria maculans* in rapeseed root tissue. *Aust. Plant Pathol.* 8(2): 23-24.

Mahmud, K.A. 1950. Damping-off of *Brassica juncea* Coss. caused by *Pythium aphanidermatum* (Eds.) Fitz. *Sci. & Cult.* 16(5): 208-209.

Maltais, B. and Bouchard, C.J. 1978. Une moutard des oiseaux (*Brassica rapa* L.) resistante a l'atrizine. *Phytoprotection* 59: 117-119.

Marciano, P., Di Lenna, P. and Magro, P. 1982. Polygalacturonase isoenzymes produced by *Sclerotinia sclerotiorum* in *vivo* and *in vitro. Physiol. Plant Pathol.* 20: 201-212.

Mathur, R.S. and Swarup, J.S. 1965. Bacterial diseases of oilseed crops. *Indian Oilseeds J.* 9: 254-256.

Mathur, Sneh., Bhatnagar, M.K. and Mathur, S. 1991. Comparative tolerance of *Albugo candida* and *Peronospora parasitica* to metalaxyl. *Int. J. Tropical Plant Diseases.* 9(2): 195-199.

Maude, R.G. and Humpherson-Jones, F.M. 1980. Studies on the seed-borne phases of dark leaf spot (*Alternaria brassicicola*) and grey leaf spot (*Alternaria brassicae*) of brassicas. *Ann. Appl. Biol.* 95: 311-319.

McDonald, W.C. 1959. Grey leaf spot of rape in Manitoba. *Can. J. Plant Sci.* 39: 409.

McGee, D.C. 1977. Black leg (*Leptosphaeria maculans* (Desm.) Ces et de Not.) of rapeseed in Victoria. Sources of infection and relationships between inoculum, environmental factors and disease severity. *Aust. J. Agric. Res.* 28: 53-62.

McGee, D.C. and Petrie, G.A. 1978. Variability of *Leptosphaeria maculans* in relation to black leg of oilseed rape. *Phytopathology* 68: 625-630.

McKeen, W.E. 1981. Black rot of rutabaga in Ontario and its control. *Can. J. Plant Pathol.* 3(4): 244-246.

McMeekin, Dorothy 1960. The role of oospores of *Peronospora parasitica* in downy mildew of crucifers. *Phyto-pathology* 50(2): 93-97.

McMeekin, Dorothy 1969. Other hosts for *Peronospora parasitica* from cabbage and radish. *Phytopathology* 59: 693-696.

McNabb, W.M., Van den Berg, C.G.J. and Rimmer, S.R. 1993. Comparison of inoculation methods for selection of plants resistant to *Leptosphaeria maculans* in *Brassica napus. Can. J. Plant Sci.* 73: 1199-1207.

McRae, W. 1922. Report of the Imperial Mycologist, *Sci. Rept. Agric. Res. Inst.*, Pusa, 1921-22: 44-50.

McRae, W. 1926. Report of the Imperial Mycologist, *Sci. Rept. Agric. Res. Inst.,* Pusa, 1925-26: 54-69.

McRae, W. 1928. Report of the Imperial Mycologist, *Sci. Rept. Agric. Res. Inst.,* Pusa, 1927-28: 56-70.

McRoberts, N. and Lennard, J.H. 1991. The behaviour of three Alternaria species in relation to leaf penetration of hosts and non-hosts. *Cruciferae Newsl.* No.14-15: 156-157.

Mehta, N. and Saharan, G.S. 1993. Effect of planting time on the infection and development of white rust and downy mildew disease complex in mustard. *Plant Dis. Res.* 8(2): 158.

Mehta, N. and Saharan, G.S. 1994. Morphological and pathological variations in *Peronospora parasitica* infecting Brassica species. *Indian Phytopath.* 47(2): 153-158.

Mehta, N., Saharan, G.S. and Kaushik, C.D. 1996. Efficacy and economics of fungicidal management of white rust and downy mildew complex in mustard. *Plant Pathol.* 26(3): 243-247.

Mehta, N., Saharan, G.S. and Sharma, O.P. 1995. Influence of temperature and free moisture on the infection and development of downy mildew on mustard. *Plant Dis. Res.* 10(2): 114-121.

Mehta, P.R., Singh, Babu and Bose, S.K. 1946. Some new hosts of *Sclerotinia sclerotiorum* (Lib.) deBary. *Curr. Sci.* 15(6): 171-172.

Melhus, I.E. 1911. Experiments on spore germination and infection in certain species of oomycetes. *Wis. Agric. Expt. Stn. Res. Bull.* 15: 25-30.

Mengistu, A., Rimmer, S.R., Koch, E. and Williams, P.H. 1991a. Pathogenecity grouping of isolates of *Leptosphaeria maculans* on *Brassica napus* cultivars and their disease reaction profile. *Plant Dis.* 75(12): 1279-1282.

Mengistu, A., Rimmer, S.R., Koch, E. and Williams, P.H. 1991b. Pathogenecity grouping of *Leptosphaeria maculans* isolates based on three cultivars of *Brassica napus. Cruciferae Newsl.* No.4-5: 152-153.

Mengistu, A., Williams, P.H., Hershmann, D.E. and Sippell, D.W. 1990. Black leg of canola (*Brassica napus* var. *oleifera*) in Kentucky. *Plant Dis.* 74(11): 938.

Mithen, R.F. and Lewis, B.G. 1988. Resistance to *Leptosphaeria maculans* in hybrids of *Brassica oleracea* and *B. insularis. J. Phytopathol.* 123: 253-258.

Mithen, R.F., Lewis, B.G., Heaney, R.K. and Fenwick, G.R. 1987. Resistance of leaves of Brassica species to *Leptosphaeria maculans. Trans. Br. Mycol. Soc.* 88: 525-531.

Mitra, M. 1928. Gall formation on the roots of mustard due to a smut (*Urocystis coralloides* Rostrup.). *Agric. J. India* 23: 104-106.

Mitter, J.H. and Tandon, R.N. 1930. Fungus flora of Allahabad. *J. Indian Bot. Soc.* 9: 190.

Morrall, R.A.A. and Dueck, J. 1982. Epidemiology of *Sclerotinia* stem rot of rapeseed in Saskatchewan. *Can. J. Plant Pathol.* 4: 161-168.

Morrall, R.A.A., Rogers, R.B. and Rude, S.V. 1989. Improved techniques of controlling *Sclerotium* stem rot of canola (rapeseed) with fungicides in Westen Canada. *Med. Fac. Landbouww. Rijksuniv. Gent.* 54: 643-649.

Morrall, R.A.A., Verma, P.R. and Dueck, J. 1985. Recent progress in chemical control of *Sclerotinia* stem rot of rape in Western Canada. *Med. Fac. Landbouww Rijksuniv. Gent.* 50: 1189-1194.

Moss, N.A., Crute, I.R. and Lucas, J.A. 1994. Laboratory production of oospores of *Peronospora parasitica* (crucifer downy mildew) and the recovery and characterization of sexual progeny from crosses between isolates with different host specificity. *Plant Pathol.* 43: 713-725.

Moss, N.A., Crute, I.R., Lucas, J.A. and Gorden, P.L. 1988. Requirements for analysis of host-species specificity in *Peronospora parasitica* (downy mildew). *Cruciferae Newsl.* No.13: 114-116.

Mridha, M.A.U. 1983. Virulence of different isolates of *Alternaria brassicae* on witner oilseed rape cultivars. p. 194. *6th Int. Rapeseed Conf.*, Paris, May 17-19, 1983.

Mridha, M.A.U. and Wheeler, B.E.J. 1993. In vitro effects of temperature and wet periods on infection of oilseed rape by *Alternaria brassicae*. *Plant Pathol.* 42(5): 671-675.

Mridula, K., Mohanty, A.K., Acharya, N.N. and Sethi, P.N. 1994. Efficacy of some selected fungicides against *Alternaria brassicae* causing leaf blight of mustard. *Orissa J. Agric. Res.* 7 Suppl.: 90-91.

Mukherjee, P., Singh, G.P. and Singh, B.B. 1983. Cercospora spot on *Brassica campestris* var. *Sarson* in India. *Indian J. Mycol. Plant Pathol.* 13(1): 87.

Mullins, E., Quinlan, C. and Jones, P. 1995. Analysis of mechanisms of partial physiological resistance to *Sclerotinia sclerotiorum* using induced mutants of *Brassica napus*. *Aspects Appl. Biol.* 42: 307-314.

Munde, P.N. 1983. Studies on the leaf spot of rapeseed and mustard caused by *Alternaria brassicae* (Berk.) Sacc. Ph.D. Thesis, IARI, New Delhi, pp. 122.

Munde, P.N. and Bhowmik, T.P. 1984. A spray schedule of fungicides and insecticide mixture for the control of Alternaria leaf blight and aphid pest of rapeseed and mustard. *Indian Phytopath.* 37(2): 398 (Abstr.).

Munde, P.N. and Bhowmik, T.P. 1985. A source of morphological resistance to leaf blight disease of rapeseed and mustard caused by *Alternaria brassicae* (Berk.) Sacc. *Curr. Sci.* 54(11): 514-515.

Mundkur, B.B. 1938. Host range and identity of the smut causing root galls in the genus Brassica. *Phytopathology* 28: 134-142.

Murashige, T. and Skoog, F. 1962. A revised medium for rapid growth and bioassays with tobacco tissue cultures. *Physiol. Plantarum.* 15: 473-497.

Napper, M.E. 1933. Observations on spore germination and specialization of parasitism in *Cystopus candidus*. *J. Pomol. Hort. Sci.* 11: 81-100.

Narain, A. and Siddiqui, J.A. 1965. Field reaction of species of Brassica to *Erysiphe polygoni*. *Indian Oilseeds J.* 9(2): 153-154.

Narisawa, K., Kageyama, K. and Hashiba, T. 1996. Effect of root infection with single resting spores of *Plasmodiophora brassicae*. *Mycol. Res.* 100(7): 855-858.

Nashaat, N.I. and Awasthi, R.P. 1995. Evidence for differential resistance to *Peronospora parasitica* (downy mildew) in accessions of *Brassica juncea* (mustard) at the cotyledon stage. *J. Phytopathol.* 143(3): 157-159.

Nashaat, N.I. and Rawlinson, C.J. 1991. New sources of resistance to downy mildew in *Brassica napus* ssp. *oleifera*. *Cruciferae Newsl.* No.4-5: 146-147.

Nashaat, N.I. and Rawlinson, C.J. 1994. The response of oilseed rape (*Brassica napus* ssp. *oleifera*) accessions with different glucosinolate and erucic acid contents to four isolates of *Peronospora parasitica* (downy mildew) and the identification of new sources of resistance. *Plant Pathol.* 43: 278-285.

Natti, J.J. 1971. Epidemiology and control of bean white mold. *Phytopathology* 61: 669-674.

Natti, J.J., Dickson, M.K. and Atkin, D.D. 1967. Resistance of *Brassica oleracea* varieties to downy mildew. *Phytopathology* 57: 144-147.

Neergaard, P. 1945. *Danish species of Alternaria and Stemphylium.* Copenhegan Einar Munksgaard, London, Oxford Univ. Press, pp. 560.

Newman, P.L. and Bailey, D.J. 1987. Screening for resistance to canker (*Leptosphaeria maculans*) in winter oilseed rape (*Brassica napus* ssp. *oleifera*). *Plant Pathol.* 36: 346-354.

Newman, P.L. and Plumridge, H. 1983. The effect of insect damage on the incidence of infection by *Phoma lingam* in winter oilseed rape. *Cruciferae Newsl.* No. 8: 30-31.

Newton, H.C. and Sequeria, L. 1972. Ascospores of *Sclerotinia sclerotiorum* in Wisconsin. *Plant Dis. Reptr.* 56: 798-802.

Nijhawan, H.L. and Hussain, A. 1964. Effect of Alternaria blight on the chemical composition of yellow sarson. *Indian Oilseeds J.* 8: 44.

Nordin, K., Sigvald, R. and Svensson, C. 1992. Forecasting the incidence of Sclerotinia stem rot on spring-sown rape-seed. *Z. Pflanzenkrankh. Pflanzensch.* 99(3): 245-255.

Nordin, K. and Svensson, C. 1987a. Sclerotinia stem rot on oilseed crops in Sweden. *Bull. SROP* 10(4): 13-16.

Nordin, K. and Svensson, C. 1987b. Current research on *Sclerotinia sclerotiorum* in Sweden. *Bull. SROP* 10(4): 17-20.

Nuzum, C. and Kaldor, C.J. 1988. Assessment and control of latent infection of rape, *Brassica napus* by *Leptosphaeria maculans*. *Aust. Plant Pathol.* 17(3): 74-78.

Ogilvy, S.E. 1984. Disease control in oilseed rape, with particular reference to *Alternaria brassicae*. In: *Crop Protection in Northern Britain* 1984. Scottish Crop Res. Inst. 6: 210-215.

Ogoshi, A. 1972. Some characters of hyphal anastomosis group in *Rhizoctonia solani* Kuhn. *Ann. Phytopath. Soc.*, Japan, 38: 123-129.

Page, R. Le. and Penaud, A. 1995. Phoma on rape. Everything depends on the first ascopores peak. *Oleoscope* No.28: 23, 25-27 (Fr.).

Pal, V., Jalali, I. and Kaushik, C.D. 1997. Bacterial soft rot and wilt of oilseed-rape in Haryana—a new report. p. 343. *Golden Jubilee Int. Conf., Integrated Plant Disease Management for Sustainable Agriculture,* Nov.10-15, 1997, Indian Phytopath. Soc., New Delhi.

Pang, E.C.K. and Halloran, G.M. 1996. The genetics of adult plant black leg (*Leptosphaeria maculans*) resistance from *Brassica juncea* in *B. napus. Theor. Appl. Genet.* 92(3/4): 382-387.

Parisi, R. 1924. A Cystopus of *Onobrychis crusta-galli* Lam. from Cyrenaica. *Riv. Patol. Veg.* 14: 165-171.

Parmeter, J.R. Jr., Sherwood, R.T. and Platt, W.D. 1969. Anastomosis grouping among isolates of *Thanatephorus cucumeris. Phytopathology* 59: 1270-1278.

Parmeter, J.R. Jr. and Whitney 1970. Taxonomy and nomenclature of the imperfect-state. pp. 7-19. In: J.R. Parmeter, Jr. ed., *Rhizoctonia solani: Biology and Pathology.* Univ. Calif., Press. pp. 255.

Parui, N.R. and Bandopadhyay, D. 1973. A note on screening of rai (*Brassica juncea* L. Coss.) against white rust (*Albugo candida* Pers. Kuntze.). *Curr. Sci.* 42: 798-799.

Patel, M.K., Abhyankar, S.G. and Kulkarni, Y.S. 1949. Black rot of cabbage. *Indian Phytopath.* 2(1): 58-61.

Patel, A.O., Khemalas, M.B. and Boramanikar, P.K. 1991. Reaction of mustard cultivars to downy mildew caused by *Peronospora parasitica. Indian Phytopath.* (Suppl.) 45: 111.

Patwardhan, G.B. 1928. Field, Garden and Orchard crops of the Bombay Presidency. *Bull. Dept. Agric. Bombay*: 30.

Paul, V.H. and Rawlinson, C.J. 1992. *Diseases and pests of rape.* Verlag Th. Mann., Gelsenkirchen-Buer. pp. 132.

Pedras, M.S. and Smith, K.C. 1997. Sinalexin, a phytoalexin from white mustard elicited by destruxin B and *Alternaria brassicae. Phytochem..* 46(5): 833-837.

Pena-Rodriguez, L.M. 1985. Bioactive metabolites of *Alternaria brassicae* and *Monocillium nordinni*. Ph.D. Thesis, Univ. Alberta, Edmonton. (Cited from P.S. Bains and J.P. Tewari 1987. *Physiol. Mol. Plant Pathol.* 30: 259-271).

Perwaiz, M.S., Moghal, S.M. and Kamal, M. 1969. Studies on the chemical control of white rust and downy mildew of rape (Sarson). *West Pakistan J. Agric. Res.* 7: 71-75.

Petrie, G.A. 1973. Diseases of Brassica species in Saskatchewan, 1970-72. I. Staghead and Aster yellows. *Can. Plant Dis. Surv.* 53: 19-25.

Petrie, G.A. 1975. Diseases of rapeseed and mustard. In: J.T. Harapiak ed., *Oilseeds and Pulse Crops in Western Canada.* Modern Press, Saskatoon, Saskatchewan.

Petrie, G.A. 1978. Occurrence of a highly virulent strain of black leg (*Leptosphaeria maculans*) on rape in Saskatchewan (1975-77). *Can. Plant Dis. Sur.* 58(2): 21-25.

Petrie, G.A. 1988. Races of *Albugo candida* (white rust and staghead) on cultivated Cruciferae in Saskatchewan. *Can. J. Plant Pathol.* 10: 142-150.

Petrie, G.A. 1994. "New" races of *Albugo candida* (white rust) in Saskatchewan and Alberta. *Cand. J. Plant Path.* 16: 251-252.

Petrie, G.A. and Vanterpool, T.C. 1968. The occurrence of *Leptosphaeria maculans* on *Thlapsi arvense.* Can. J. Bot. 46: 869-871.

Petrie, G.A. and Vanterpool, T.C. 1974. Fungi associated with hypertrophies caused by infection of Cruciferae by *Albugo cruciferarum. Can. Plant Dis. Surv.* 54: 37-42.

Petrie, G.A. and Verma, P.R. 1974. A simple method for germinating oospores of *Albugo candida. Can. J. Plant Sci.* 54: 595-596.

Pidskalny, R.S. and Rimmer, S.R. 1985. Virulence of *Albugo candida* from turnip rape (*Brassica campestris*) and mustard (*Brassica juncea*) on various crucifers. *Can. J. Plant Pathol.* 7: 283-286.

Platford, R.G. 1988. Survey of plant diseases of canola in Manitoba in 1987. *Can. Plant Dis. Surv.* 68: 117-118.

Prakash, S. and Raut, R.N. 1983a. Artificial synthesis of *Brassica napus* and its prospects as an oilseed crop in India. *Indian J. Genet.* 43: 283-291.

Prakash, S. and Raut, R.N. 1983b. Genetic recombination of *B. napus* and its adoption as a new oleiferous crop in India. pp. 227-232. *Proc. 6th Int. Rapeseed Conf.*, Paris.

Prasanna, K.P.R. 1988. Studies on oilseed rapeseed and seedling infection by *Alternaria brassicae* and *Alternaria brassicicola*. pp. 624-631. In: P.K. Agrawal, A. Gaur, M. Dadlani and A. Varier, eds., *Seed Research Spl. Vol.I*, 1993. Indian Soc. Seed Tech., IARI, New Delhi.

Purkayastha, R.P. and Mallik, F. 1976. Two new species of Hypomyces from India. *Nova Hedwigia* 27: 781.

Pound, G.S. and Williams, P.H. 1963. Biological races of *Albugo candida. Phytopathology* 53: 1146-1149.

Purdy, L.H. 1979. *Sclerotinia sclerotiorum*: History, diseases and symptomatology, host range, geographic distribution and impact. *Phytopathology* 69(8): 875-880.

Purdy, L.H. and Bardin, R. 1953. Mode of infection of tomato plants by the ascospores of *Sclerotinia sclerotiorum. Plant Dis. Reptr.* 37: 361-362.

Puzari, K.C. and Saikia, U.N. 1997. Efficacy of fungicides for controlling downy mildew of rapeseed. *Indian Phytopath.* 50(4): 520-523.

Rai, B. 1991. "Kranti" would boost mustard production. *Indian Fmg.* 40(11): 14-15.

Rai, B., Kolte, S.J. and Tewari, A.N. 1976. Evaluation of oleiferous Brassica germplasm for resistance to Alternaria leaf blight. *Indian J. Mycol. Plant Pathol.* 6: 76-77.

Rai, J.N. and Dhawan, S. 1976a. Production of polymethyl galacturonase and cellulase and its relationship with virulence in isolates of *Sclerotinia sclerotiorum* (Lib.) deBary. *Indian J. Expt. Biol.* 14(2): 197-198.

Rai, J.N. and Dhawan, S. 1976b. Studies on purification and identification of toxic metabolite produced by *Sclerotinia sclerotiorum* causing white rot disease of crucifers. *Indian Phytopath.* 29(4): 407-411.

Rai, J.N. and Singh, R.P. 1973. Fusarial wilt of *Brassica juncea. Indian Phytopath.* 26(2): 225-232.

Rai, J.N., Tewari, J.P., Singh, R.P. and Saxena, V.C. 1974. Fungal diseases of Indian Crucifers. *Nova Hedwigia* 47(Suppl.): 477-486.

Rajpurohit, T.S. and Chowdhary, B.R, 1995. Downy mildew (*Peronospora parasitica*) of wild turnip (*Brassica tournefortii*), a new record in Rajasthan. *Indian J. Agric. Sci.* 65(5): 377.

Rao, B.R. 1977. Species of Alternaria on some Cruciferae. *Geobios* 4: 163.

Rao, M.V.B. and Raut, R.N. 1994. Inheritance of resistance to white rust (*Albugo candida*) in an interspecific cross between Indian mustard (*Brassica juncea*) and rapeseed (*B. napus*). *Indian J. Agric. Sci.* 64(4): 249-251.

Rawlinson, C.J. and Muthyalu, G. 1979. Diseases of winter oilseed rape: occurrence, effects and control. *J. Agric. Sci. Camb.,* 93: 593-606.

Raychaudhuri, S.P. and Pathanian, R.S. 1955. A mosaic disease of radish (*Raphanus sativus* L.). *Indian Phytopath.* 8: 99-104.

Regnault, Y., Laville, J. and Penaud, A. 1987. Colza maladies. CETION, Cahier Technique, Mars, 19-24 (cited from I. Jamaux *et al.* 1995. *Plant Pathol.* 44: 22-30).

Ridgeway, R. 1912. *Color standard and color nomenclature*, Washington.

Rimmer, S.R. and Van den Berg, C.G.J. 1992. Resistance of oilseed Brassica spp. to black leg caused by *Leptosphaeria maculans. Can. J. Plant Pathol.* 14: 56-66.

Roy, A.K. 1973. Host range of *Sclerotinia sclerotiorum* and *Sclerotium rolfsii* in Jorhat, Assam. *Sci. & Cult.* 39(7): 319-320.

Roy, A.K. and Saikia, U.N. 1976. White-blight of mustard and its control. *Indian J. Agric. Sci.* 46(6): 274-277.

Roy, N.N. 1978a. A study on disease variation in the populations of an interspecific cross of *Brassica juncea* × *Brassica napus* L. *Euphytica* 27: 145-149.

Roy, N.N. 1978b. Wesreo-a black leg resistant rapeseed. *J. Agri. West. Aust.* 19: 42.

Roy, N.N. 1984. Interspecific transfer of *Brassica juncea* type high black leg resistance to *Brassica napus*. *Euphytica* 33(2): 295-303.

Roy, N.N. and Reeves, J. 1975. Breeding better rape and linseed in western Australia. *J. Agric. West Aust.* 16: 93-97.

Rouxel, T., Renard, M., Kollman, A. and Bousquet, J.F. 1990. Brassilexin accumulation and resistance to *Leptosphaeria maculans* in Brassica spp. and progeny of interspecific cross *Brassica juncea* × *B. napus*. *Euphytica* 46(2): 175-181.

Rouxel, T., Sarniguet, A., Kollman, A. and Bousquet, J.F. 1989. Accumulation of a phytoalexin in Brassica spp. in relation to hypersensitive reaction to *Leptosphaeria maculans*. *Physiol. Mol. Plant Pathol.* 34(6): 507-517.

Rozej, A. 1974. The susceptibility of different varieties of winter rape (*Brassica napus* var. *oleifera*) to infection by *Alternaria brassicae* (Berk.) Sacc. *Rev. Plant Pathol.* 55: 860, 1976 (Abstr.).

Ruppel, E.G. 1972. Correlation of cultural characters and source of isolates with pathogenecity of *Rhizoctonia solani* from sugarbeet. *Phytopathology* 62: 202-205.

Sachan, J.N., Kolte, S.J. and Singh, Basudeo. 2000. Inheritance of resistance of white rust (*Albugo candida* race 2) in *Brassica juncea*. *Indian Phytopath.* 53(2): 206-209.

Sacristan, M.D. and Gerdemann, M. 1986. Different behaviour of *Brassica juncea* and *B. carinata* as sources of *Phoma lingam* resistance in experiments of interspecific transfer to *B. napus*. *Z. Pflanzenzuecht.* 97: 304-314.

Sahambi, H.S. 1958. Virus diseases of sesamum and their control. *Mycological Research Workers' Conference, ICAR, Simla, India*, pp. 81-85.

Saharan, G.S. 1984. A review of research on rapeseed and mustard pathology in India. *Annu. Workshop. All India Coord. Res. Proj. Oilseeds, ICAR.*, Jaipur, Aug. 6-10, 1984.

Saharan, G.S. 1993. Disease resistance. In: K.S. Labana, S.S. Banga, S.K. Banga, eds., *Monographs on Theoratical and Applied Genetics Vol.19, Breeding Oilseed Brassicas*, pp. 251.

Saharan, G.S. and Chand, J.N. 1988. Diseases of oilseed crops. *Haryana Agric. Univ., Hisar*, pp. 268.

Saharan, G.S. and Kadian, A.K. 1983a. Physiologic specialization in *Alternaria brassicae*. *Cruciferae Newsl.* No.8: 32-33.

Saharan, G.S. and Kadian, A.K. 1983b. Analysis of components of horizontal resistance in rapeseed and mustard cultivars against *Alternaria brassicae*. *Indian Phytopath.* 36: 503-507.

Saharan, G.S., Kaushik, C.D., Gupta, P.P. and Tripathi, N.N. 1984. Assessment of losses and control of white rust of mustard. *Indian Phytopath.* 37(2): 397 (Abstr.).

Saharan, G.S., Kaushik, C.D. and Kaushik, J.C. 1988. Sources of resistance and epidemiology of white rust of mustard. *Indian Phytopath.* 41(1): 96-99.

Saharan, G.S. and Kaushik, J.C. 1981. Occurrence and epidemiology of Powdery mildew of Brassica. *Indian Phytopath.* 34(1): 54-57.

Saharan, G.S., Kaushik, J.C. and Kaushik, C.D. 1981. Progress of Alternaria blight on Raya cultivars in relation to environmental conditions. p. 136. *Third Int. Symp. Plant Pathol.*, New Delhi, Dec. 14-18, 1981.

Saharan, G.S., Kaushik, J.C. and Kaushik, C.D. 1982. Two new host records of *Alternaria brassicae*. *Indian Phytopath.* 35(1): 172.

Saini, J.S. 1982. Production technology for mustard. *Indian Fmg.* 32(5): 7-10.

Salmon, E.S. 1900. *A monograph of the 'Erysiphaceae', Mem. Torrey Bot. Club.* 91: 1-292.

Sandhu, R.S., Singh, G. and Bhatia, N.L. 1969. Studies on the effect of sowing dates and spacing on the incidence of phyllody in Indian rape (*Brassica campestris* L. var. Toria Duth. and Full.). *Indian J. Agric. Sci.* 39: 959-961.

Sansome, E. and Sansome, F.W. 1974. Cytology and life history of *Peronospora parasitica* on *Capsella bursa-pestoris* and of *Albugo candida* on *C. bursa-pestoris* and on *Lunaria annua. Trans. Br. Mycol.Soc.* 62(2): 323-332.

Sarkar, B. and Sengupta, P.K.1978. Studies on some aspects of the epidemiology of Alternaria blight of mustard (*Brassica* sp.). *Beitr. Trop. Landwirtsch. Veterinaermed.* 16: 91-96.

Saur, R. 1983. Experiments with spore traps for timing the control of *Sclerotinia sclerotiorum* on winter rape. *Z. Pflanzenkrankh. Pflanzensch.* 90(3): 225-231,

Sawatsky, W. 1989. Evaluation of screening techniques for resistance to *Leptosphaeria maculans* and genetic studies of resistance to the disease in *Brassica napus.* M.Sc. Thesis, Univ. Manitoba, Winnipeg, Manitoba, Canada.(Cited from R.K. Rimmer and C.G.J. van den Berg 1992. *Can. J. Plant Pathol.* 14: 56-66).

Saxena, V.C. 1972. Physiopathological studies on fungal diseases of Crucifers with special reference to Albugo-Peronospora complex. Ph.D. Thesis, Univ. Lucknow, UP.

Saxena, V.C. 1983. *Albugo* and *Albugo-Peronospora* complex infection of Eruca- changes in indole acetic acid content and IAA oxidase activity. *Indian J. Plant Pathol.* 3: 94-99.

Saxena, V.C. and Rai, J.N. 1986. Survey of occurrence of white rot of Crucifers caused by *Sclerotinia sclerotiorum* in Uttar Pradesh and Bihar. *Indian J. Mycol. Plant Pathol.* 17(1): 89-91.

Schoeller, M.and Grunewaldt, J. 1987. Comparison of inoculation techniques for testing Brassica seedling resistance against *Plasmodiophora brassicae* Wor. *Cruciferae Newsl. No.*12: 86-87.

Seaman, W.L., Walker, J.C. and Larson, R.H. 1963. A new race of *Plasmodiophora brassicae* affecting badgershipper cabbage. *Phytopathology* 53: 1426-1429.

Sedum, F.S., Seguin-Swartz, G. and RaKow, G.F.W. 1989. Genetic variation in reaction to *Sclerotinia sclerotiorum* in Brassica species. *Can. J. Plant Sci.* 69: 229-232.

Seidel, D., Daebeler, F., Amelung, D., Engel, K.H. and Luke, W. 1984. Occurrence, damage and control of *Phoma lingam* in winter rape. *Nachrichtenbl. den Pflanzenschutz DDR.* 38: 120-123.

Seidel, E., Rude, S. and Petrie, A. 1995. The effect of Alternaria black spot of canola on seed quality and seed yield, and studies on disease control. Final Rept. Saskatoon Dev. Fund, *Agriculture and Agri. Food, Canada*, 1995 p. 41.

Sempio, C. 1940. Contributo alla Conosceaza dele azione esercitata de vari fattori anbientali su al cune malattie parasitarie di piante colbivate. *Riv. Patol. Veg.* 30: 29-64.

Shankhla, H.C., Singh, H.G., Dalela, G.G. and Mathur, R.L. 1967. Occurrence of perithecial stage of *Erysiphe polygoni* on *Brassica campestris* var. Sarson and *Brassica juncea. Plant Dis. Reptr.* 51: 800.

Sharma, A.K. 1979. Powdery mildew diseases of some crucifers from J.&K. state. *Indian J. Mycol. Plant Path.* 9: 29-32.

Sharma, D.C. 1973. Rai mosaic virus. *Indian Phytopath.* 26(2): 346-348.

Sharma, J., Agrawal, K. and Singh, D. 1997. Pathological effects of seed borne infection of *Alternaria brassicicola* in Indian mustard. p. 423. *Golden Jubilee Int. Conf., Integrated Plant Disease Management for Sustainable Agriculture*, Nov. 10-15, 1997, Indian Phytopath. Soc., New Delhi.

Sharma, K.D. and Kolte, S.J. 1985. Metalaxyl in the control of downy mildew and white rust of rapeseed and mustard. *Pestology* 9(1): 31-35.

Sharma, Sushil and Singh, Sultan. 1998. Influence of soil and water characteristics on the incidence of white rot in Indian mustard. *Cruciferae Newsl.* No.20: 85-86.

Sharma, S.K. and Gupta, J.S. 1978. Seasonal and diurnal variation in the air spora over a field of Brown sarson. *Indian Phytopath.* 31(3): 389.

Sharma, S.R. and Kolte, S.J. 1994. Effect of soil-applied NPK fertilizers on severity of black spot disease (*Alternaria brassicae*) and yield of oilseed rape. *Plant and Soil.* 67(3): 313-320.

Sharma, T.R. 1990. Induction and transfer of resistance to Alternaria blight of mustard caused by *Alternaria brassicae* and *A. brassicicola*. Ph.D. Thesis. Himachal Pradesh Krishi Vishwavidyalaya, Palampur, India.

Sharma, T.R. and Singh, B.M. 1992a. Parameters of resistance to *Alternaria brassicae* in some Brassica species. *Indian Phytopath.* 45(Suppl.) P.LIX (Abstr.).

Sharma, T.R. and Singh, B.M. 1992b. Transfer of resistance to *Alternaria brassicae* in *Brassica juncea* through interspecific hybridization among Brassicas. *J. Genet. Breed.* 46(4): 373-378.

Sharma, T,R. and Singh, B.M. 1994. Induction of sporulation in non-sporulating isolate of *Alternaria brassicae* (Berk.) Sacc. *Plant Dis. Res.* 9(1): 84-86.

Sharma, T.R. and Singh, B.M. 1995. Generation and evaluation of somaclones of *Brassica juncea* for resistance to *Albugo candida* and *Alternaria brassicae*. *Proc. Indian Natn. Sci. Acad. Part B, Biol. Sci.* 61(2): 155-161.

Shaw, F.J.P. 1921. Report of the Imperial Mycologist. *Sci. Rept. Agric. Res. Inst., Pusa,* 1920-21: 34-40.

Shaw, F.J.P. and Agrekar, S.L. 1915. The genus Rhizoctonia in India. *Mem. Dept. Agric. India., Bot. Surv.* 7: 177-194.

Shelton, A.M. and Hunter, J.E. 1985. Evaluation of the potential of the flea beetle *Phyllotreta cruciferae* to transmit *Xanthomonas campestris* pv. *campestris*, causal agent of black rot of crucifers. *Can. J. Plant Pathol.* 7(3): 308-310.

Sherf, A.F. and MacNab, A.A. 1986. *Vegetable diseases and their control.* John Willey and Sons, NY, USA, pp. 728.

Sheriff, C. and Lucas, J.A. 1989a. Heterothallism and homothallism in *Peronospora parasitica. Mycol. Res.* 92: 311-316.

Sheriff, C. and Lucas, J.A. 1989b. Cytogenetic study on heterothallic and homothallic isolates of *Peronospora parasitica. Mycol. Res.* 92: 302-310.

Sheriff, C. and Lucas, J.A. 1990. The host range of isolates of downy mildew *Peronospora parasitica* from Brassica crop species. *Plant Pathol.* 39: 77-91.

Sherwood, R.T. 1969. Morphology and physiology in four anastomosis groups of *Thanatephorus cucumeris. Phytopathology* 59: 1924-1959.

Shiraishi, M., Sokomoto, K., Asada, Y., Nagatoni, T. and Hadaka, H. 1975. A scanning electron microsopic observation on the surface of Japanese radish leaves infected by *Peronospora parasitica* (Fr.) Fr. *Ann. Phytopath. Soc. Japan.* 41: 24-32.

Shivanna, K.P. and Sawhney, V.K. 1993. Pollen selection of Alternaria resistance in oilseed brassicas: responses of pollen grains and leaves to a toxin of *Alternaria brassicae. Theor Appl. Genet.* 86: 339-344.

Shivpuri, A. and Siradhana, B.S. 1989. Seed borne infection of *Alternaria brassicae* on Indian mustard and its elimination during storage. *Indian Phytopath.* 42(2): 275 (Abstr.).

Shivpuri, A., Siradhana, B.S. and Bansal, R.K. 1988. Management of Alternaria blight of mustard with fungicides. *Indian Phytopath.* 41(4): 644-646.

Shukla, A.K. and Sharma, R.C. 1997. Progressive spread of Sclerotinia stem rot of rapeseed and mustard in Bharatpur district of Rajasthan. p. 457. *Golden Jubilee Int. Conf., Integrated Plant Disease Management for Sustainable Agriculture*, Nov.10-15, 1997, Indian Phytopath. Soc., New Delhi.

Simmons, E.G. 1992. Alternaria taxonomy: current status, view point, challenge. pp. 1-35. In: J. Chelkowski and A. Visconti eds. *Alternaria-Biology, Plant Diseases and Metabolites—Topics in Secondary Metabolism.* Vol.III, Elsevier Science Publishers, Amsterdam.

Singh, A. and Bhowmik, T.P. 1985. Persistance and efficacy of some common fungicides against *Alternaria brassicae*, the causal agent of leaf blight of rapeseed and mustard. *Indian Phytopath.* 38: 35-38.

Singh, B. 1992. Rapeseed, mustard and cabbage, new hosts for *Pseudomonas solanacearum. Indian Phytopath.* 45(2): 277.

Singh, B.M. and Bhardwaj, C.L. 1984. Physiologic races of *Albugo candida* on Crucifers in Himachal Pradesh. *Indian J. Mycol. Plant Pathol.* 14: 25 (Abstr.).

Singh, D.V. and Singh, J. 1983. A technique for inoculating *Albugo candida* on Lahi. *Indian Phytopath.* 36: 139-140.

Singh, H.V. 1997. Effect of temperature on sporangial germination of *Peronospora parasitica* and *Albugo candida* from *Brassica juncea* cv. Varuna. *Plant Dis. Res.* 12(2): 192-194.

Singh, N.I. 1989. *Amaranthus viridis*: host of white rust caused by *Albugo candida* (Liv.). *Indian J. Hill Fmg.* 2(1): 93.

Singh, R., Tripathi, N.N. and Kaushik, C.D. 1994. Management of Sclerotinia rot of Indian mustard (*Brassica juncea* (L.) Czern. & Coss.) by fungicides. *Crop Res.* (Hissar) 7(2): 276-281.

Singh, R.B. and Chauhan, Y.S. 1997. Integrated management of Alternaria blight of mustard. p. 358. *Golden Jubilee Int. Conf., Integrated Plant Disease Management for Sustainable Agriculture*, Nov.10-15, 1997, Indian Phytopath Soc., New Delhi.

Singh, R.B., Lal, B.B., Thakore, R.B.L. and Mathur, Sneh 1984. Field evaluation of fungicides for the control of powdery mildew of *Brassica juncea. Agri. Sci. Digest*, 4(1): 51-53.

Singh, R.M., Agarwal, D.K. and Sarbhoy, A.K. 1993. *HCIO descriptions of plant pathogenic fungi, Set 11*, Nos.61-66, IARI, New Delhi.

Singh, R.R. and Solanki, J.S. 1974. Fungicidal control of powdery mildew of *Brassica juncea. Indian J. Mycol. Plant Path.* 4(2): 210-211.

Singh, S.L. and Pavgi, M.S. 1980. Diseases of cruciferous crops in Varanasi. *Indian Phytopath.* 33(2): 321-324.

Singh, S.R., Ravi, N.S. and Singh, N.I. 1990. Yield loss on Indian mustard in Manipur caused by *Albugo candida. New Agriculturist.* 1: 39-42.

Singh, V.K. and Chauhan, V.B. 1996. Management of powdery mildew of mustard. *Ann. Plant Prot. Sci.* 4(2): 184-185.

Singh, Yogendra 1998. Management of Sclerotinia rot of rapeseed and mustard through chemicals. *Plant Dis. Res.* 13(2): 149-150.

Sinha, R.K.P., Rai, B. and Sinha, B.B.P. 1992. Epidemiology of leaf spot of rapeseed-mustard caused by *Alternaria brassicae. J. Appl. Biol.* 2(1/2): 70-75.

Sippell, D.W., Davidson, J.G.N. and Sadasivaiah, R.S. 1985. Rhizoctonia root rot of rapeseed in the Peace River region of Alberta. *Can. J. Plant Pathol.* 7: 184-186.

Sjodin, C. and Glimelius, K. 1988. Screening of resistance to black leg, *Phoma lingam* (Tode ex.Fr.) Desm. within Brassicaceae. *J. Phytopath.* 123(4): 322-332.

Sjodin, C. and Glimelius, K. 1989. *Brassica naponigra*, a somatic hybrid resistant to *Phoma lingam. Theor. Appl. Genet.* 77(5): 651-656.

Skoropod, W.P. and Tewari, J.P. 1977. Field evaluation of the role of epicuticular wax in rapeseed and mustard in resistance to Alternaria black spot. *Can. J. Plant Sci.* 57: 1001.

Smith, H.C. and Sutton, B.C. 1964. *Leptosphaeria maculans*, the ascogenous state of *Phoma lingam. Trans. Br. Mycol. Soc.* 47: 159-165.

Sobti, A.K. 1983. Assessment of losses due to *Erwinia carotovora* on *Brassica juncea* and *Brassica campestris. Indian J. Mycol. Plant Pathol.* 13(3): 378.

Srivastava, B.I.S., Shaw, M. and Vanterpool, T.C. 1962. Effect of *Albugo candida* (Pers. ex.Chev.) Kuntz. on growth substances in *Brassica napus* L. *Can. J. Bot.* 40: 53-59.

Srivastava, L.S. and Verma, R.N. 1989. Fungicidal control of white rust of mustard in Sikkim. *Indian Phytopath.* 42(1): 84-86.

Srivastava, O.P. 1968. Dry rot and bottom rot of mustard caused by *Rhizoctonia solani. Indian J. Mycol. Plant Pathol.* 8: 277-278.

Srivastava, S.K. and Dhawan, S. 1979. Epidemiology of Macrophomina stem and root rot of *Brassica juncea* (L.) Czern. & Coss. in Northern India. *Proc. Indian Natn. Sci. Acad. B.* 45(6): 617-622.

Stankova, J. 1972. Varietal variability of winter rape in its susceptibility to dark leaf spot and the factors influencing the development of the disease. *Rostlinna Vyroba* 18(6): 625-630.

Steinbach, P., Daebeler, F. and Seidel, D. 1989. Investigations into the pathogenesis of root collar rot and black leg in winter rape due to *Phoma lingam. Nachrichtenbl. den Pflanzenschutz DDR.* 43(10): 212-215.

Steinbach, P., Daebeler, F. and Seidel, D. 1991. Some problems of chemical control of black leg (*Phoma lingam*) in winter oilseed rape. *Bull. SROP* 14(6): 282-285.

Stelfox, D., Williams, J.R., Sochngen, U. and Topping, R.C. 1978. Transport of *Sclerotinia sclerotiorum* ascospores by the rapeseed pollen in Alberta. *Plant Dis. Reptr.* 62(7): 576-579.

Stephens, C.T., Herr, L.J., Schmitthenner, A.F. and Powell, C.C. 1982. Characterization of Rhizoctonia isolates associated with damping-off of bedding plants. *Plant Dis.* 66: 700-703.

Stone, J.R., Verma, P.R., Dueck, J. and Spurr, D.T. 1987. Control of *Albugo candida* race 7 in *Brassica campestris* cv. Torch by foliar, seed and soil application of metalaxyl. *Can. J. Plant Pathol.* 9: 137-145.

Stovold, G.E., Mailer, R.J. and Francis, A. 1987. Seed borne levels, chemical seed-treatment and effects on seed quality following a severe outbreak of *Alternaria brassicae* on rapeseed in New South Wales. *Plant Prot. Quart.* 2(3): 128-131.

Subudhi, P.K. and Raut, R.N. 1994. White rust resistance and its association with parental species type and leaf waxiness in *Brassica juncea* L. Czern. & Coss. X *Brassica napus* L. crosses under the action of EDTA and gamma-ray. *Euphytica* 74(1-2): 1-7.

Sudarmadi and Wallace, H.R. 1982. Rape diseases. p. 143. In *Bienn. Rept. Waite Agric. Res. Inst.*, 1980-81. South Aust. Univ., Adelaide.

Sudarmadi and Wallace, H.R. 1984. Black leg disease of rapeseed. p. 146. In: *Bienn. Rept. Waite Agric. Res. Inst.*, 1982-83. South Aust. Univ., Adelaide.

Takeshita, R.M. and Linn, M.B. 1953. Possible means of over wintering of the horse radish white rust fungus, *Albugo candida*. *Dis. Abstr.* 13: 483-487.

Tarique, V.N. and Jeffries, P. 1984. Appresorium formation by *Sclerotinia sclerotiorum*: Scannign electron microscopy. *Trans. Br. Mycol. Soc.* 82: 645-651.

Taylor, J.L., Borgmann, I. and Seguin-Swartz, G. 1991. Electrophoratic Karyotyping of *Leptosphaeria maculans* differentiates highly virulent from weakly virulent isolates. *Curr. Genet.* 19: 273-277.

Teo, B.K., Morrall, R.A.A. and Verma, P.R. 1989. Influence of soil moisture, seeding date and canola cultivars (Tobin and Westar) on the germination and rotting of sclerotia of *Sclerotinia sclerotiorum*. *Can. J. Plant Pathol.* 11(4): 393-399.

Tewari, J.P. 1986. Subcuticular growth of *Alternaria brassicae* in rapeseed. *Can. J. Bot.* 64(6): 1227-1231.

Tewari, J.P. 1991. Resistance to *Alternaria brassicae* in crucifers. *IOBC/WPRS Bull.* 14: 154-161.

Tewari, J.P. and Conn, K.L. 1993. Reactions of some wild crucifers to *Alternaria brassicae*. *IOBC/WPRS Bull.* 16: 53-58.

Tewari, J.P., Conn, K.L. and Dahiya, J.S. 1987. Resistance to *Alternaria brassicae* in crucifers. pp. 1085-1090. *Proc. 7th Int. Rapeseed Conf.*, Paris.

Tewari, J.P. and Skoropad, W.P. 1976. Relationship between epicuticular wax and black spot caused by *Alternaria brassicae* in three lines of rapeseed. *Can. J. Plant Sci.* 56: 781.

Tewari, J.P., Tewari, I. and Chatterjee, S.C. 1998. Natural biological control of *Albugo candida* by a bacterium. *Phytopathology* 88(9): S 89. Publication No. P.1998-0642-AMA.

Thind, K.S. 1942. The genus Peronospora in the Punjab. *J. Indian Bot. Soc.* 21: 197-215.

Thomson, J.R., Thomas, P.M. and Evans, I.R. 1984. Efficacy of aerial application of benomyl and iprodione for the control of *Sclerotinia sclerotiorum* stem rot of canola (rapeseed) in central Alberta. *Can. J. Plant Pathol.* 6(1): 75-77.

Tiwari, A.S. Petrie, G.A. and Downey, R.K. 1988. Inheritance of resistance to *Albugo candida* race 2 in mustard (*Brassica juncea* (L.) Czern.). *Can. J. Plant Sci.* 68: 297-300.

Tripathi, N.N.and Kaushik, C.D. 1984. Studies on the survival of *Alternaria brassicae*, the causal organism of leaf spot of rapeseed and mustard. *Madras Agric. J.* 71(4): 237-241.

Tripathi, N.N., Kaushik, C.D., Yadava, T.P. and Yadava, A.K. 1980. Alternaria leaf spot resistance in Raya. *Haryana Agri. Univ. J. Res.* 10(2): 166-168.

Tripathi, N.N., Saharan, G.S., Kaushik, C.D., Kaushik, J.C. and Gupta, P.P. 1987. Magnitude of losses in yield and management of Alternaria blight of rapeseed and mustard. *Haryana Agri. Univ. J. Res.* 17(1): 14-18.

Tsuneda, A. and Skoropad, W.P. 1977. Formation of microsclerotia and chlamydospores from conida of *Alternaria brassicae*. *Can. J. Bot.* 55: 1276.

Townsend, G.R. and Heuberger, J.W. 1943. Methods for estimating losses caused by disease in fungicidal treatments. *Plant Dis. Reptr.* 27: 340-342.

Turkington, T.K. and Morrall, R.A,.A. 1993. Use of petal infestation to forecast Sclerotinia stem rot of canola: the influence of inoculum variation over the flowering period and canopy density. *Phytopathology* 83(6): 682-689.

Upadhyay, R. and Pavgi, M.S. 1967. Some new hosts for *Pellicularia rolfsii* (Sacc.) West. from India. *Sci. & Cult.* 33(2): 71-73.

Vaartnou, H. and Tewari, I. 1972. *Alternaria alternata* parasitc on rape in Alberta. *Plant Dis. Reptr.* 56: 676-677..

Vanterpool, T.C. 1959. Oospore germination in *Albugo candida. Can. J. Bot.* 37: 169-172.

Vasudeva, R.S. 1957. *Report of the Division of Mycology and Plant Pathology,* p. 87. *Sci. Rept.* 1954-56. Indian Agric. Res. Inst., New Delhi.

Vasudeva, R.S. 1958. Diseases of rapeseed and mustard, pp. 77-86. In: D.P. Singh ed., *Rape and Mustard.* Indian Central Oilseeds Committee, Hyderabad.

Vasudeva, R.S. 1959. Plant virus research in India. *Indian Phytopath.* 12: 1-7.

Vasudeva, R.S. and Sahambi, H.S. 1957. Phyllody disease transmitted by a species of *Deltocephalous burmeisler.* p. 359. *Proc. 4th Int. Crop Prot. Conf.,* Hamburg.

Verma, G.S., Verma, H.N. and Hajela, O.P. 1969. A severe mosaic disease of rocket salad, *Eruca sativa* Mill. *Indian J. Agric. Sci.* 39: 865-869.

Verma, P.R. 1990. *Report of the post-doctoral transfer of work on white rust (Albugo candida),* Nov. 1989-Mar. 1990, *JNKVV Regional Agric. Res. Stn., Morena, MP, India. Inter-institutional Collaborative Research Programme between India (ICAR) and Canada (IDRC) for Rapeseed-Mustard Improvement.*

Verma, P.R., Harding, H., Petrie, G.A. and Williams, P.H.1975. Infection and temporal development of mycelium of *Albugo candida* in cotyledons of four Brassica species. *Can. J. Bot.* 53: 1016-1020.

Verma, P.R. and Petrie, G.A. 1975. Germination of oospores of *Albugo candida. Can. J. Bot.* 53: 836-842.

Verma, P.R. and Petrie, G.A. 1978. A detached leaf culture technique for the study of white rust disease of Brassica species. *Can. J. Plant Sci.* 58: 69-73.

Verma, P.R. and Petrie, G.A. 1980. Effect of seed infestation and flower bud inoculation on systemic infection of turnip rape by *Albugo candida. Can. J. Plant Sci.* 60: 267-271.

Verma, P.R., Spurr, D.T. and Petrie, G.A. 1983. Influence of age and time of detachment on development of white rust on detached *Brassica campestris* leaves at different temperatures. *Can. J. Plant Pathol.* 5: 200-205.

Verma, Uma 1987. Studies on the white rust of Brassica caused by *Albugo candida* (Pers. ex. Lev.) Kunze. Ph.D. Thesis, IARI, New Delhi, pp. 115.

Verma, Uma and Bhowmik, T.P. 1986. A simple method of inoculating white rust on rapeseed and mustard. *Int. J. Tropical Plant Diseases.* 4: 41-43.

Verma, Uma and Bhowmik, T.P. 1988. Oospores of *Albugo candida* (Pers. ex. Lev.) Kunze.—its germination and role as the primary source of inoculum for whtie rust disease of rapeseed and mustard. *Int. J. Tropical Plant Diseases.* 6: 265-269.

Verma, Uma and Bhowmik, T.P. 1989a. Inheritance of resistance to a *Brassica juncea* pathotype of *Albugo candida* in *Brassica napus. Can. J. Plant Pathol.* 11: 443-444.

Verma, Uma and Bhowmik, T.P. 1989b. Epidemiology of white rust disease of mustard, *Brassica juncea. Indian Phytopath.* 42(2): 274-275, (Abstr.).

Verma, Uma and Bhowmik, T.P. 1991. A simple technique for the preservation of white rust (*Albugo candida*) inoculum. *Int. J. Tropical Plant Diseases.* 9: 87-89.

Verma, Uma and Bhomik, T.P. 1996. Effect of crop density on the incidence of white rust and seed yield in Indian mustard. *Ann. Plant Prot. Sci.* 4(2): 185-187.

Verma, Uma and Bhowmik, T.P. 1997. Biochemical changes in mustard (*Brassica juncea*) leaf and inflorescence due to white rust (*Albugo candida*) infection. p. 96. *Natn. Symp. Integrated Pest Management in India—Constraints and Opportunities,* Oct. 23-24, 1997, Soc. Plant Prot. Sci., IARI, New Delhi.

Verma, V.D. and Rai, B. 1980. Note on induced mutagenesis for spotting out the source of resistance to Alternaria spot in Indian mustard. *Indian J. Agric. Sci.* 50(3): 278-280.

Vigier, B., Chiang, M.S. and Hume, D.J. 1989. Source of resistance to club root (*Plasmodiophora brassicae* Wor.) in triazine-resistant spring canola (rapeseed). *Can. Plant Dis. Surv.* 69: 113-115.

Vir, S., Kaushik C.D. and Chand, J.N. 1973. The occurrence of bacterial rot of raya (*Brassica juncea*. Coss.) in Haryana. *PANS.* 19(1): 40.

Vishnuavat, K., Agarwal, V.K. and Singh, R.S. 1985. Relationship of discolouration of mustard (*Brassica campestris* var. Sarson) seed to infection by *Alternaria brassicae* and its longevity on seed. *Seed Res.* 13(1): 53-56.

Vishnuavat, K. and Kolte, S.J. 1993. Brassica seed infection with *Peronospora parasitica* (Pers. ex. Fr.) Fr. and its transmission through seed. *Indian J. Mycol. Plant Pathol.* 23(3): 247-249.

Wadhwani, K. and Dudeja, S.K. 1982. The primary source of inoculum of leaf spot disease of *Brassica juncea* due to Alternaria. *Indian Bot. Reptr.* 1(2): 162-163.

Wagger, H. 1986. On the structure and reproduction of *Cystopus candida* Lev. *Ann. Bot.* 10: 295-297.

Walker, J.C. 1957. *Plant Pathology*, Mc. Graw Hill, New York, pp. 242.

Walker, J.C., Morell, S. and Foster, H.H. 1937. Toxicity of mustard oil and related sulphur compounds to certain fungi. *Am. J. Bot.* 24: 536-541.

Wang, C.M. 1944. Physiological specialization in *Peronospora parasitica* and reaction of hosts. *Chin. J. Sci. Agric.* 1: 249-257.

Whiteheads, S.B. 1946. Control of club root. pp. 9-10. *Gdnrs' Chron., Ser.3.* CXIX, 3080.

Willetts, H.S. and Wong, J.A.L. 1980. The biology of *Sclerotinia sclerotiorum, S. trifoliarum* and *S. minor* with emphasis on specific nomenclature. *Bot. Rev.* 46: 101-165.

Williams, J.R. and Stelfox, D. 1979. Dispersal of ascospores of *Sclerotinia sclerotiorum* in relation to Sclerotinia stem rot of rapeseed. *Plant Dis. Reptr.* 63: 395-399.

Williams, J.R. and Stelfox, D. 1980a. Occurrence of ascospores of *Sclerotinia sclerotiorum* in areas of central Alberta. *Can. Plant Dis. Surv.* 60(4): 51-53.

Williams, J.R. and Stelfox, D. 1980b. Influence of farming practices in Alberta on germination and apothecium production of sclerotia of *Sclerotinia sclerotiorum*. *Can. J. Plant Pathol.* 2(3): 169-172.

Williams, P.H. 1966. A system for the determination of races of *Plasmodiophora brassicae* that infect cabbage and rutabaga. *Phytopathology* 56: 624-626.

Williams, P.H. 1981. *Screening Crucifers for multiple disease resistance.* Univ. Wis., Madison, Dept. Plant Pathol., pp. 168.

Williams, P.H. 1985. *Resource Book. Crucifer Genet. Coop.,* Univ.Wis., Madison, WI 53706 (608-262-6496).

Williams, P.H. 1992. Biology of *Leptosphaeria maculans. Can. J. Plant Pathol.* 14: 30-35.

Williamson, C.J. 1987. Assessment of resistance to *Plasmodiophora brassicae* in swedes. *Plant Pathol.* 36: 264-275.

Williamson, C.J. 1989. An assessment of the importance of club root in oilseed rape. *Aspects Appl. Biol.* 12: 439-449.

Wiltshire, S.P. 1947. *Species of Alternaria on Brassicae. Mycological Paper No.12.* C.M.I., Kew, England.

Winter, W., Burkhard, L., Banziger, I. and Krebs, H. 1993. Rape diseases: occurrence on rape varieties, effect of fungicides and preventive control measures. *Revue-Suisse-d'Agriculture:* 25(5): 287-294.

Wittern, L. and Kruger, W. 1985. Sporen Keimung Von *Phoma lingam* (Tode ex. Fr.) Desm. und Resistenzprufung bei Raps im Gewachshus. *Phytopath. Z.*113: 113-124.

Wong, T.M. 1949. Studies on the mechanism of resistance of cruciferous plants to *Peronospora parasitica. Phytopathology* 39: 541-547.

Wood, P. McR. and Barbetti, M.J. 1977. A study on the inoculation of rape seedlings with ascospores and pycnidiospores of the black leg disease causal agent, *Leptosphaeria maculans. J. Aust. Inst. Agric. Sci.* 43(1/2): 79-80.

Woronin, M.S. 1878. *Plasmodium brassicae: The cause of cabbage hernia. Phytopathol. Classic No.4.,* Am. Phytopath. Soc., St. Paul, MN, pp. 32.

Yadav, R.C., Sareen, P.K. and Chowdhury, J.B. 1991. Interspecific hybridization in *Brassica juncea × B. tournefortii* using ovary culture. *Cruciferae Newsl.* No.14-15: 84.

Yadava, O.P., Yadava, T.P., Kumár, P. and Gupta, S.K. 1994. Inheritance of reducing sugars in relation to white rust resistance in Indian mustard. *Indian Phytopath.* 47(1): 56-59.

Yang, J. and Verma, P.R. 1992. Screening genotypes for resistance to pre-emergence damping-off and post-emergence seedling root rot of oilseed rape and canola caused by *Rhizoctonia solani* AG2-1, *Crop Prot.* 11: 443-448.

Yang, J., Verma, P.R., Rakow, G.F.W. and Downey, R.K. 1989. Screening for resistance to *Rhizoctonia solani* AG2-1 in rapeseed and mustard. *Can. J. Plant Pathol.* 11: 200.

Yang, J., Verma, P.R. and Lees, G.L. 1992a. The role of cuticle and epidermal cell wall in resistance of rapeseed and mustard to *Rhioctonia solani. Plant and Soil.* 142(3): 315-321.

Yang, J., Verma, P.R. and Tewari, J.P. 1992b. Histopathology of resistant mustard and susceptible canola hypocotyls infected by *Rhizocotnia solani. Mycol. Res.* 96(3): 171-179.

Yarwood, C.E. 1957. *'Powdery mildews'. Bot. Rev.* 23: 235-312.

Yashpal, H.S. and Singh, H. 1991. Genetic components of white rust resistance and seed yield in Indian mustard (*Brassica juncea*). *J. Oilseeds Res.* 8(2): 259-262.

Yitbarek, S.M., Verma, P.R., Gugel, R.K. and Morrall, R.A.A. 1988. Effect of soil temperature and inoculum density on pre-emergence damping-off of canola caused by *Rhizoctonia solani. Can. J. Plant Pathol.* 10: 93-98.

Yitbarek, S.M., Verma, P.R. and Morrall, R.A.A. 1987. Anastomosis groups, pathogenecity, and specificity of *Rhizoctonia solani* isolates from seedling and adult rapeseed/canola plants and soils in Saskatchewan. *Can. J. Plant Pathol.* 9: 6-13.

Yu, W.D., He, J. and Miao, G.F. 1995. Effective control method of rape Sclerotia rot (*Sclerotinia sclerotiorum*) in the south area of Shonxi. *Bull. Agri. Sci. Tech.* 1: 31.

Zhu, J.S., Spanier, A. 1991. Resistance sources to *Phoma lingam* and *Alternaria brassicae. Cruciferae Newsl.* No.4-5: 143.

Zhu, J.S., Struss, D. and Robbelen, G. 1993. Studies on resistance to *Phoma lingam* in *Brassica napus—Brassica nigra* addition lines. *Plant Breed.* 111(3): 192-197.

Chapter 3

Insect Pests

3.1 INTRODUCTION

Damage caused by insect pests is a major constraint in the growth and productivity of oilseed brassicas (predominantly *Brassica campestris* L. and *B. juncea* L.) in India. These crops have been under cultivation in this sub-continent since time immemorial and it is only during the last three decades or so, that radical changes in their cropping patterns and cropping intensity have been brought about by various production thrusts to meet their growing demands. Changes in ecology of the biotic complex resulted in aggravation of insect pest problems due to enhanced notoreity of the traditional crucifer specialists and the appearance of some polyphagous species as pests of these crops. The growing list of pests will be evident from a brief survey of the literature.

In 1976, 24 insects were listed as pests of rapeseed and mustard of which the mustard aphid (*Lipaphis erysimi* Kalt.), the mustard sawfly (*Athalia proxima* Klug.), and the painted bug (*Bagrada hilaris* Burm.) were referred as the major pests of all-India importance while those with regional importance included the flea beetles (*Phyllotreta cruciferae* Goeze and *P. chotanica* Duvivier), the surface grass hoppers (*Chrotogonus* sp. and *C. trachypterus* Blanchard), the cabbage butterfly (*Pieris brassicae* L.), and the *Gujhia* weevil (*Tanymecus indicus* Faust.) (Rai, 1976). In 1977-78, 4 new insect pests of mustard were reported from Andhra Pradesh (Nagalingam & Punnaiah, 1980). At Haryana State, *Myzus persicae* Sulzer and *Plutella xylostella* Lin., till then considered as minor, appeared as key pests in 1982 (Singh & Singh, 1983) while 3 more insects infesting rapeseed and mustard were identified as new pests during oilseed crop survey in 1982-83 (Kalra, 1987). The total number of insect pests reported on oilseed brassicas in India stood at 38 during 1984 (Bakhetia & Sekhon, 1984), of which 15 are considered economically important (Table 3.1).

Regular country-wide crop surveys are, therefore, necessary to determine the insect species that attack oilseed brassicas in India, their distribution and economic status in relation to crop growth.

Mustard aphids inflict most serious injury to the crop and have accordingly received the maximum attention of Indian workers especially in regard to their effect on crop yield, population dynamics and management. As regards other insect pests, little is known on their life-history,

Table 3.1. Status of insects attacking rapeseed and mustard in India.

Pest status	Pest name	Activity period
Key	1.Mustard aphid, *Lipaphis erysimi* Kalt.	Oct.-April
	2. Sawfly, *Athalia lugens proxima* Klug.	Aug.-March
Major but sporadic	3. Painted bug, *Bagrada hilaris* Burm.	Aug.-April
	4. Pea leaf miner, *Chromatomyia horticola* Goureau	Jan.-May
	5. Bihar hairy caterpillar, *Diacrisia obliqua* Walker	Aug.-Oct.
	6. Cabbage butter fly, *Pieris brassicae* Linn.	Feb.-April
	7. Flea beetle, *Phyllotreta cruciferae* Goeze.	Feb.-Oct.
	8. Green peach aphid, *Myzus persicae* Sulzer	Oct.-Dec.
	9. Diamond back moth, *Plutella xylostella* Linn.	Oct.-Feb.
New	10. Large moth, *Crocidolomia binotalis* Zeller	Jan.-March
	11. Cabbage top borer, *Hellula undalis* Fab.	Oct.-March
	12. Cabbage aphid, *Brevicoryne brassicae* Linn.	Oct.-April
	13. White fly, *Bemisia tabaci* Gen.	March-April
	14. Cabbage semi-looper, *Plusia orichalcia* Fab.	Oct.-Dec.
	15.Turnip moth, *Agrotis segetum* Dennis and Schiff.	Oct.-Nov.

Source: Bakhetia and Singh 1992.

bioecology and management, etc. besides other aspects. Further, the correct identities of parasites and predators found associated with insect pests in India and their efficacy in suppressing them under field conditions as alternative/supplement to chemical control are yet to be determined.

The present review furnishes updated information on economically important insect pests of oilseed brassicas cultivated in India besides a brief account on rape sawfly (*Athalia rosae* L.), pollen beetles (*Meligethes aeneus* Fab.), seed weevil (*Ceutorhynchus assimilis* Payk.), pod midge (*Dasineura brassicae* Winn.), and stem weevil (*Ceutorhynchus quadridens* Panz.) which in continental Europe cause serious damage to seed rape (*B. napus* L.) (Williams, 1980), a host species that has been recently introduced in India for commercial exploitation.

3.2 PAINTED BUG

3.2.1 Painted Bug, *Bagrada hilaris* Burm.

(Hemiptera: Pentatomidae)

Syn: *Bagrada cruciferarum* Kirkaldy

3.2.1.1 Damage

Bagrada hilaris Burm., popularly known as the painted bug because of its black and grey body with orange spots (Fig.3.1), is a major pest of rapeseed and mustard in India (Narayana & Phadke, 1988). Both the nymphs and adults damage the cruciferous crops by sucking away the cell sap.

Stray populations of the painted bug may be encountered in the field almost the year round but in certain years the crops may suffer severe damage when its population reaches an epidemic level. Plants become completely devitalized if the infestation occurs in the early growth stage. The young plants wilt and die and re-sowing of the crop becomes a necessity. The green foliage, on which the pest feeds, show silvery or pale grey spots or patches as a typical symptom of attack (Batra, 1958). Normally, the older plants are more seriously damaged later in the season when huge populations of the bug cluster over leaves and pods, and thus adversely affect both the quantity and quality of seeds (Narayanan, 1954b). The pest feeds and breeds on the mustard seeds whether on the ground or within the pods (Batra, 1958) causing, for example, a reduction of 30.1 and 2.75 per cent in seed weight and oil content, respectively of Indian mustard (*Brassica juncea* L.) (Singh *et al.* 1980a).

Fig. 3.1. Adult Painted bug.
Bagrada hilaris

3.2.1.2 Life history

Adults mate in the field within 2-6 days after emergence (Narayanan, 1954b). Under Punjab conditions, the average duration of pre-copulation period was 1-2 days in April and 3-4 days in December; pre-oviposition period was 4-6 days in June and 22-25 days in December. On average, a single female laid from a minimum of 31-43 to a maximum of 95-110 eggs during different months of the year (Bhai & Singh, 1961). Eggs are laid singly or in clusters of 12 or more, and when laid in loose soil, as many as 75 eggs may be found from one laying (Narayanan, 1954b). They are also laid in debris composed of dry leaves and seed pods, on green leaves, stems and inflorescence of plants, in which case the eggs are firmly glued on the plant surface by a sticky secretion (Atwal, 1959).

Freshly laid eggs of *B. hilaris* are pale yellow in colour but turn pinkish before hatching. They are oval in shape and measure 1.0×0.5 mm (Narayanan, 1954b). Weather condition greatly influences the duration of egg stage. The egg stage occupied 3 days in June, 5-12 days in November and 20-21 days in December. Their viability varied from 17-92 per cent, the highest viability was seen in June and lowest in December (Bhai & Singh, 1961). Incubation temperature and not the relative humidity, influences the duration of egg stage (Atwal, 1959).

Young nymphs are bright orange in colour with bright red eyes and measure about 1.2 mm $\times$ 0.9 mm in size. A nymph passes through 5 successive moults in about 3-3.5 weeks before developing into a winged adult (Narayanan, 1954b). An average of 21 per cent of the nymphs develop into adults in a year. The males and females differ in their longevity, the former lives a little longer (18-31 days) than the latter (17-28 days). The females slightly out number their male counterpart (Bhai & Singh, 1961).

Bagrada hilaris is primarily a pest of cruciferous plants, though it is polyphagous in nature. It feeds on rape, mustard, other cruciferous vegetables and particularly the radish seed pods. From

September onwards to the entire winter season, a very large number of these bugs in all stages is found infesting these plants. The bug is most active during April and May when it multiplies rapidly. It is seen on cabbage in April, and on late-sown cabbage, cowpea, sorghum and maize during May-June. By the end of May, a large number of adults die due to high atmospheric temprature. They escape the summer heat by congregating under the heaps of harvested mustard, radish or other dry vegetables in the threshing floor or nearby compost heaps. A few even takes shelter in crevices in bunds near irrigation channels. Thereafter, the pest moves on to cauliflower and cabbage seedlings in nursery beds in June-July when it also feeds on *Quisqualis, Euphorbia geniculata*, some flower plants and grass. It then thrives on transplanted cauliflower, knol kohl, cabbage, early-sown turnip and radish in August and thus completes its life-cycle (Atwal, 1959; Batra, 1958; Narayanan, 1954b).

3.2.1.3 Natural enemies

Natural enemies keep the population of painted bug under check by parasitizing both the egg mass and the adult pest. Two chalcids, *Trissoleus samueli* Mani (*Lisphanurus samueli* Mani) (Mani, 1942) and *Typhodytes* sp. parasitize the egg masses (Samuel, 1942). The adult bug is parasitized by a tachinid fly, *Alophora* sp. (Rakshpal, 1949).

3.2.1.4 Control

Bagrada hilaris, because of its high prolificacy, must be controlled in the early stages when its population is small. Clean cultivation, removal of weeds and other cruciferous plants from the crop field and its vicinity are essential for its effective control. A number of insecticides are effective. Application of aldicarb and phorate to the soil as granules at sowing caused 100 per cent mortality after 8 and 4 days respectively, while carbofuran granules caused 97 per cent mortality after 4 days of application and their LT_{50} value was 35, 29 and 26 days, respectively. Seed treatment with 2.5% monocrotophos and phosphamidon provided protection for 39 days, and with 1.0% lindane and carbosulphan for 28 days against this pentatomid bug (Jagdish & Dhingra, 1990). Seed treatment with carbofuran resulted in 88.7 and 100 per cent bug mortality after 4 and 20 days of treatment, respectively with LT_{50} of 11.7 days. The LT_{50s} of foliar sprays with monocrotophos, fenvalerate, oxydemeton-methyl, phosphamidon, quinalphos and lindane were 7.9, 7.3, 6.8, 6.5, 4.4 and 3.2 days, respectively. Application of quinalphos and malathion as dust was also quite effective and resulted in 86.7 and 73.3 per cent mortality, respectively with corresponding LT_{50s} of 3.2 and 2.0 days (Narayana & Phadke, 1988).

3.2.2 Painted Bug, *Bagrada trilobata* Ahmad and Kamaluddin

(Hemiptera: Pentatomidae)

This bug, originally reported from Pakistan (Ahmad & Kamaluddin 1981), was seen feeding along with *B. hilaris* over the dried pods of Indian mustard and rapeseed (*B. napus* L.) in May 1989 at Hissar (Haryana), India, though their number was extremely low. The females of *B. trilobata* maintained at 28 ± 2°C, laid 9 and 12 eggs on the first and second day, respectively and then died on the third day. The freshly laid eggs were creamy white but changed to crimson red before hatching. The average incubation period was 7.8 days. The nymphs were dirty cream in colour, they passed through 5 instars which were completed in 34.60 days. The average longevity of adult *B. trilobata* was 11.50 days. The colour of their fore-wings and abdomen was dirty cream, and the length of *B. trilobata* females was 3.25 mm as compared to 6.5 mm of *B. hilaris* (Singh, 1992).

3.3 APHID

Aphids (Homoptera: Aphididae) comprise a small but extremely fascinating group of small, soft bodied homopterous insects and stand out probably as the most notorious group of crop pests on a global scale. They cause appreciable damage by sucking plant sap and more so by transmitting a larger number of plant viruses. The biology of aphids is as intricate as their taxonomy which includes polymorphism, and usually a succession of taxonomically remote plant hosts. Besides winged and wingless forms, intermediate morphs between the two, and that between oviparous and viviparous forms are not uncommon in this group. There may be also physiological forms due to weather and nutritional factors. Such wide range of intraspecific variations make aphid taxonomy highly complicated.

Unlike the aphids under temperate conditions, which prevail only in the hills at higher altitudes, the problem of the aphids inhabiting the Indian plains is not to over winter but to tide over the summer. Records of sexual forms of a number of Indian aphids in recent years are restricted to morphological descriptions without any information on the overall biology of the species. Under Indian conditions, their reproduction is almost entirely parthenogenetic, the females being viviparous, giving birth to females only (Basu & Handa, 1987).

Three species of aphid are important pests of cruciferous oilseed crops, viz., *Lipaphis erysimi* Kaltenbach, *Bravicoryne brassicae* Linnaeus and *Myzus persicae* Sulzer.

3.3.1 Mustard Aphid, *Lipaphis erysimi* Kalt.

(Homoptera: Aphididae)

Syn. *Rhopalosiphum erysimi* Kalt.

R. pseudobrassicae Davis

Siphocoryne indobrassicae Das

Hyadapis erysimi Kalt.

Lipaphis erysimi Kalt., with its world-wide distribution including temperate as well as subtropical regions (Blackman & Eastop, 1984), exists in at least two different, geographically separated forms (Muller, 1986) viz., *L.e. erysimi* Kalt., the European specimen and *L.e. pseudobrassicae* Davis (Muller, 1986; Srinivaschar & Malik, 1972), the form prevalent in India and North America. The European form is darker in colour and also differs with the other in its host plant preference. Nevertheless, since the aphid form prevalent in India is still being designated as *L. erysimi* Kalt., the same nomenclature is retained in the present text.

The mustard aphid is by far the most serious insect pest of *Brassica* spp. in India. Local cultivators call it *Tela, Mahun* or *Chepa* (Narayanan, 1954a). In USA, it is known as turnip aphid or false cabbage aphid. The nymphs of *L. erysimi* are minute and very delicate. The apterous adults are about 2 mm long, globular and whitish cream or pale green in colour. The wings of alate adults are transparent and their abdomen yellowish. Both the nymphs and adult aphids devitalize the crop by sucking the cell sap (Bakhetia, 1991).

3.3.1.1 Damage

All growth stages of the crop including the roots may be attacked by the pest but the greatest damage is done during the flowering and pod formation stages. They are attracted more towards yellow colour of inflorescence (Bakhetia & Sandhu, 1973; Kundu & Pant, 1968; Singh & Singh, 1988). The infested leaves become yellow, curled or crinkled and young plants wilt and dry up. During severe infestation, all aerial parts of the plant, especially the inflorescence become thickly covered with aphids and most of the flower buds are destroyed (Fig.3.2). Partially affected flowers

Fig. 3.2. Heavy infestation of mustard aphids, *Lipaphis erysimi* on the inflorescence of *B. juncea*

produce under-developed and deformed pods containing fewer seeds which are also smaller, shrivelled, discoloured and poor in quality. The aphids secrete a sweet sticky fluid called the "honey dew", on which shooty molds develop giving the plants a dirty look besides interfering with their photosynthetic activity (Narayanan, 1954a; Rai, 1976).

    Lipaphis erysimi transmists many virus diseases. Kennedy *et al.* (1962) provided a break-up of the viruses transmitted by *L. erysimi* Kalt. and *L. erysimi pseudobrassicae* Davis. While *L. erysimi* transmits beet yellows, cabbage black ring spot, cucumber mosaic, potato virus Y and Tropaeolum mosaic, *L. erysimi pseudobrassicae* transmits bean common mosaic, beet mosaic, cabbage black ring spot, cauliflower mosaic, celery mosaic, onion yellow dwarf, pea mosaic, poison hemlock ring spot, radish mosaic and stock mosaic.

3.3.1.2 Host range

Though the pest is commonly known as mustard aphid, both mustard and rape are its preferred hosts. It is also a serious feeder of all other cruciferous plants grown under cold weather, viz., radish, spinach, lettuce, turnip, knol-khol, tobacco, potato (Narayanan, 1954a), besides being known to feed on beans, peas, beet, celery, onion, cucumber, *Chenopodium album, Tropaeolum* (Bakhetia, 1991) and aswagandha (*Withania somnifera*) (Chandra & Kushwaha, 1986).

A group of toxic secondary substances, glucosinolates, exists in the parenchyma of crucifers in intact as well as in aglycone forms, including some volatiles. Mustard aphid has not only overcome this barrier by feeding on phloem, but also sequesters these compounds and retains them in the body. Some are metabolized, while others are concentrated in the body for further use. Additionally, an endogenous myrosinase enzyme present in aphids (different from that of host plants) improves the utilization and detoxification of glucosinolates. The presence of such an enzyme-substrate system is indication of exploitation of glucosinolates by the mustard aphid (Dilawari *et al.* 1998).

3.3.1.3 Losses in yield

Losses in yield of oilseed brassicas due to attack by *L. erysimi* have been reported by several workers from India (Brar *et al.* 1987; Nath & Saha, 1974; Prasad & Phadke, 1984; Rawat & Singh 1983; Singh *et al.* 1983 a,b; Singhvi *et al.* 1973; Suri *et al.* 1988). The mean loss in yield of rapeseed and mustard due to aphid infestation has been estimated to vary from 35.4 to 73.3 per cent under different agro-climatic conditions and is about 54.2 per cent on all India basis (Bakhetia, 1983). Magnitude of yield reduction is influenced by the growth stage of the crop variety during aphid infestation, duration and intensity of attack, soil and environmental conditions, etc.

In Punjab, *L. erysimi* reduced the yield of sarson and Indian mustard by 80.6 and 31.4 per cent, respectively. Loss in yield was maximum when the pest appeared at the early growth stage of the crop and there was an overall reduction of 45 per cent in seed yield (Singh *et al.* 1983 a,b). In Haryana, the aphid caused 65 and 28 per cent losses in seed yield, and 67 and 32 per cent losses in oil yield of Toria and Indian mustard, respectively (Singhvi *et al.* 1973).

In case of Brown sarson, the age of plant at aphid infestation was inversely related to its seed yield, and the number of siliquae per plant. A delay by one day in the initiation of aphid infestation beyond 60 days of plant age resulted in an increase of 2.75 siliquae and 0.077 g seed yield per plant. Avoidable losses in yield were estimated at 42.1 per cent in Kangra valley (Himachal Pradesh), India. Under natural aphid infestation, an increase of 200 aphids resulted in the corresponding decrease of 4 cm in plant height, 0.46 primary branches, 23.6 siliquae and 0.702 seed per plant (Suri *et al.* 1988). This type of negative correlation between infestation level of *L. erysimi* and plant growth characters was also demonstrated in Indian mustard by Malik and Deen (1998). They confirmed that an increase in aphid numbers causes reduction in plant height, branches per plant, siliquae per plant, grains per siliquae, test weight, oil content and oil yield.

Crop varieties also differ in their response to aphid attack. Nine varieties of Brassica crop suffered yield reduction ranging from 11.6 to 77.5 per cent due to infestation by *L. erysimi* in a field trial during 1977-78 season (Prasad & Phadke, 1979). According to Singh and Pandey (1996), the mean loss in seed yield/plant, oil content and grain yield/ha of *Brassica compestris* cultivars due to infestation by *L. erysimi* were higher than the mean loss of *B. juncea* cultivars, implying higher susceptibility of the former Brassica species to aphid attack than the latter. Aphid infestation also affects the quality of oilseeds. Seeds from *L. erysimi* infested Indian mustard plants showed reduced weight, viability and oil content, but contained higher isothiocynate, moisture, ash and sugar content (Nath & Saha, 1974).

3.3.1.4 Life history

The biology and rate of reproduction of the pest are highly influenced by the prevailing climatic conditions of the place of its occurrence. In the plains of India, the weather conditions during October-March are very congenial not only for the luxuriant growth of cruciferous crops but also for the intense activity of the pest. Under Punjab conditions, the pre-reproduction period of *L. erysimi* lasts for 8 to 18 days and 6 to 8 days, and the reproduction period lasts for 13 to 30 days and 4 to 9 days during October-March and April-September, respectively. The post-reproduction period varies between 5 to 18 days during February-March and upto 4 days during the remaining months of the year. The life cycle is completed in 23 to 60 days during October-March, and in 11 to 17 days during April-October. A female aphid produces 5 to 9 young ones in a day, and 26 to 32 off-springs in her life time (Narayanan, 1954a; Sidhu & Singh, 1964). It has 4 nymphal instars, each of 2 to 4 days duration (Srivastava & Srivastava, 1961).

3.3.1.5 Population dynamics

The initial infestation starts with the appearance of winged migrants of *L. erysimi* on the young seedlings of oilseed brassica during October-November/early December (Bakhetia, 1991; Narayanan, 1954a) under north Indian conditions. They settle down on the crops more during the evening than in noon or morning hours of the day (Sachan *et al*. 1985). The quantum of initial adult alate alighters on the crop determines the extent and intensity of aphid population. Thereafter, the growth of aphid population and its structure become related to the crop phenology, independent of the influence of the migrant aphids (Bhattacharya *et al*. 1995).

In the plains of West Bengal, the establishment of colonies and subsequent spread of infestation were accomplished by the immigrant alate viviparous females of *L. erysimi*. Infestation spread to almost throughout the crop area of the locality within three weeks due to quick population build up owing to their short pre-reproductive stage, high fecundity, viviparous reproduction and overlapping of generations. Intra-plot dispersal was mainly due to adult alates that developed in the plot. Proportion of alatoid morphs was relatively higher in the colonies at basal part or older stem of the plant, older leaves and fruits compared to younger plant parts (Ghosh, 1980). The greatest number of aphids was found on the upper third of plants, and sampling of aphids from this stratum provided the most reasonable and reliable estimation of aphid density (Chander & Phadke, 1995). Wingless or apteroid females contribute to the population build up. Rich nutrients in the vegetative and flowering stages of the crop support growing aphid populations with corresponding increase in the proportion of the nymphs and the alatae. Maximum fecundity and faster rate of development take place when individual nymph feed on young leaves. Average adult life span and rate of increase are the maximum in aphids that feed on young leaves. Aphid population attain the highest growth rate in the later part of the vegetative stage, reaches its peak at flowering and pod initiation stages of plants and then gradually declines. The flowering behaviour and maturity periods of different varieties also play a crucial role in influencing the population build up (Bhattacharya *et al.* 1995; Brar *et al.* 1976; Kundu & Pant, 1968; Prasad & Phadke, 1980). Late sown crops receive more aphid infestation than early sown ones because of their acquisition by the alate viviparous females generated in the adjacent earlier sown crops (Ghosh, 1980; Phadke & Prasad, 1987a; Singh *et al.* 1984b; Tripathi & Singh, 1964). Longevity and life cycle periods of aphids are shortest and longest on flowering shoot and stem, respectively (Singh *et al.* 1983c).

Cloudy and moist weather are conducive to the rapid multiplication of the pest in the plains of north India (Narayanan, 1954a). Temperature and humidity play significant role among the ecological factors that influence the incidence of *L. erysimi* on its hosts. The important meteorological factors that govern the aphid population in the field are: mean minimum temeprature 4-12°C, mean maximum temperature 16-30°C and mean relative humidity 50-78 per cent (Bakhetia et al. 1986). The population of *L. erysimi* and *M. persicae*, both in the initial rising and final declining phases is negatively correlated with maximum and mean temperature, and positively correlated with humidity (Chandra & Kushwaha, 1986). At Sabour (Bihar), the build up of aphid population on Indian mustard took place in January-February with infestation reaching its peak in mid-February when the ambient maximum and minimum temperatures were about 22-23° and 7-9°C, respectively and the minimum humidity ranged between 56-69 per cent. High humidity had little impact on population build up but aphid activity ceased at or below 51 per cent humidity. Frequent rains during population rise phase (January-February) adversely affected their population (Sinha et al. 1989). In Himachal Pradesh, the maximum abundance of *L. erysimi* on *B. campestris* var. Sarson was seen in the last week of February during the years 1989, 1990 and 1991. During the peak population period in these years, the mean maximum and minimum temperature, and the mean relative humidity ranged between 15.0-19.0°C, 5.5-8.0°C and 32-65 per cent, respectively. Low rainfall, 1.3-3.3 mm during the third week of February favoured high multiplication of aphids (Devi *et al.* 1995). Rainfall along with high wind velocity limit the population build up. Rainfall of 1 cm or above reduces aphid population through washing out and killing effect (Atwal *et al.* 1971; Bakhetia & Sidhu, 1983; Singh *et al.* 1984c; Singh & Singh, 1982).

Generally, the population build up and peak period of aphid infestation on rapeseed and mustard occur from the middle of December to the end of February depending upon the climatic conditions of the region (Table 3.2).

A forecasting model based on the variables — aphid population, minimum temperature and mean temperature, has been suggested to determine its incidence (Phadke, 1986):

$$Pt = 3954.5 + 0.80\,P\,(t-1) - 261 - 3\,\text{Min. temp.}\,(t-1) - 88.8\,\text{mean temp.}\,(t-1)$$

The pest follows an aggregated or negative binomial distribution on Indian mustard crop with an overall average value of the depression parameter "K" at 3.0968. This type of aggregated nature of distribution of the pest is suggestive of the need for a proper technique to make correct assessment of its population on the crop to formulate management schedule (Ramkishore & Phadke, 1988a).

Table 3.2. Incidence of aphid infestation on Brassica spp. in different regions of India.

Locality	Initiation of infestation	Peak period of infestation	Decline in infestation	Reference
1. Kalyani (West Bengal)	Early-November	Mid-December	February	Ghosh & Mitra (1983)
2. Sabour (Bihar)	3rd week-December	Mid-February	End-February	Sinha *et al.* (1989)
3. Kanpur (Uttar Pradesh)	Early-January	February	End-March	Uttam *et al.* (1993)
4. Delhi	Mid-December	Mid-February	Mid-March	Prasad and Phadke (1986)
5. Hissar (Haryana)	End-November	End-January	End-Feb.	Kalra and Gupta (1989)
6. Himachal Pradesh	Early-January	End-February	Early-March	Devi *et al.* (1995)
7. Madhya Pradesh	Early-January	3rd week-Feb.	Mid-March	Singh and Rawat (1983a)

As the temperature rises during March, the aphid population goes on decreasing and a generation of winged adults appears for their dispersal. During April, aphid population drops to the lowest level, when a few winged aphids can be seen flying about in the warm evening (Narayanan, 1954a). Overcrowding, low availability of food and moisture due to hardening of the host tissues and dry conditions due to the prevailing high temperature and low humidity provide the stimulus for wing formation in aphids (Lal, 1952, 1955; Roy, 1975a).

The mustard aphid has been reported to tide over the summer on wild and/or cultivated crucifers in cool, damp places (Sidhu & Singh 1964) which was later corroborated by Roy (1975a). On the contrary, Sachan and Srivastava (1972) could not detect the aphid on cabbage in Rajasthan from July to October. Lal (1977) observed that the aphid was not traceable in the plains during summer. Clearly, this vital aspect remains unresolved and serious studies in different agroclimatic regions are badly needed to bridge up this gap.

3.3.1.6 Integrated aphid management practices

3.3.1.6.1 Cultural practices

a. Date of sowing Adjustment in the date of sowing is one of the effective means of minimizing aphid infestations on crops provided it does not adversely affect the yield. Infestation by aphids is a major factor in yield reduction in late sown crops of Indian mustard and those sown early have a better chance of escaping the damage (Pal *et al.* 1976). Rapeseed and mustard sown by the middle of October suffer less damage because peak infestation is reached after the crucial growing and flowering periods are over, and the plants remain for longer duration in the field for maturity resulting in higher seed yield (Bhattacharjee, 1961; Kalra & Gupta, 1989; Phadke & Prasad, 1987a; Rawat & Singh 1983; Sachan *et al.* 1983; Singh *et al.* 1984b; Singh *et al.* 1992). It has been observed that every 10 days' delay in sowing after 15th October, results in an increase of 35.8 aphids/5 cm apical shoot and a reduction of 93.1 kg/ha in seed yield (Bhadauria *et al.*1992). In West

Bengal, the attack by injurious pests like aphid, saw-fly and diamond-back moth becomes less on mustard crop sown in early October in comparison to those sown in November (Ghosh & Ghosh, 1981).

b. Fertilization Available reports on the effect of fertilizer doses on the intensity of aphid infestations are at variance with one another. Increasing nitrogen levels or various combinations of nitrogen, phosphorus and potash did not have any significant effect on the population-build up of aphids on oilseed brassicas in a number of fertilizer trials (Kundu & Pant, 1967b; Rawat & Singh, 1983; Sachan *et al.* 1983). Similarly, the population level of *L. erysimi* and *M. persicae* was not affected when nitrogen doses upto 80 kg/ha was applied to the crop of *Eruca sativa* according to Bakhetia and Sharma (1979).

In contrast, the population build up of *L. erysimi* became much higher on Indian mustard fertilized with 40 and 60 kg N/ha as compared to that on crop without nitrogen fertilization (Rawat *et al.* 1968). Higher nitrogen doses to rapeseed and mustard result in higher aphid infestation (Kalra *et al.* 1983; Sidhu & Kaur, 1977) because of higher succulence of the plants, while significant reduction in infestations is observed due to the addition of phospohorus and potassium. Application of 40 kg N/ha together with 80 kg P_2O_5 and 40 kg K_2O/ha resulted in considerable reduction in aphid infestation with a resultant increase in crop yield (Singh *et al.* 1995). Thus it appears that, response to fertilizer application on aphid infestation and crop yield will, naturally, be largely influenced by irrigation doses and initial fertility status of the soil, besides other factors.

c. Irrigation Aphid infestation and the loss in crop yield can be minimized by judicial use of irrigation water. For instance, application of one irrigation to *B. campestris* var. Brown sarson after 45 days of sowing did not influence the population build-up of *L. erysimi* (Singh, 1982). On the other hand, rain-fed crop of *B. carinata* suffered heavily, and almost all varieties succumed to aphid attack (Bakhetia & Brar, 1988). Similarly, unirrigated crop of Indian mustard (cv. RVLM 619) at Ludhiana, India, supported higher aphid population throughout the season, followed by the crop irrigated once. The crop irrigated 2 and 3 times supported lower aphid populations than the crop receiving 4 irrigations although the differences between them were non-significant. The crop irrigated 2 times produced the greatest yield (Singh *et al.* 1994). It is considered that a moderate moisture stress in plants benefits the aphids through enriched levels of soluble nitrogen and sucrose in phloem sap, while a continuous moisture stress inhibits aphid activity due to hampered uptake of nutrients resulting from reduced turgidity and increased sap viscosity (Bakhetia, 1991). Further, aphids feeding on water stressed plants were found more susceptible to insecticides than those on the unstressed plants (Arora & Sidhu, 1991; Brar *et al.* 1991).

3.3.1.6.2 *Trap crops and adhesive traps*

Growing a susceptible variety as trap crop around or in between the main crop may often reduce the magnitude of aphid infestation on the main crop. Likewise, use of adhesive traps in the field from the very beginning would result in the mortality of winged migrants reducing in turn the intensity of initial colonisation. Adhesive yellow traps also hinder the population build-up on new plantings by the winged migrants that move around in search of host plants (Phadke, 1980). However, the practical and economic feasibility of these measures should be worked out before putting them into practice.

3.3.1.6.3 Host resistance

Resistance in plants against pests and diseases may often be correlated with their morphological, anatomical and biochemical characteristics.

a. Morphological and anatomical characters   The hardy slender inflorescence, and loosely packed flower buds in *B. napus* and *B. juncea* are comparatively less susceptible to *L. erysimi* as compared to tender inflorescence and thickly packed flower buds of Toria and Sarson (*B. campestris* var. Toria and *B. campestris* var. Yellow sarson) (Desh Raj *et al.* 1996; Rai & Sehgal, 1975). Waxiness prevents mustard aphids from reaching the undersurface of the leaves for feeding in plants that are in the vegetative stage (Ahman, 1990). Four *B. juncea* accessions, moderately resistant to mustard aphid, had thicker and smoother leaves and their surfaces had higher concentrations of long carbon chain waxes as compared to those of the susceptible ones (Talekar, 1980). Aphid multiplication is hindered on *B. juncea* strain B-85 with glossy surface as compared to that on the normal waxy B-85 strain (Chatterjee & Sen Gupta, 1987). In the same way, *B. carinata*, *B. alba* and *Eruca sativa* are less preferred hosts of mustard aphids because their stylet cannot easily probe the densely packed hard cell layers of these plants (Malik, 1981). Use of Brassica varieties that are either resistant or non-preferable to aphid attack should be encouraged.

b. Biochemical characters   Information on the relation of biochemical traits of Brassica crops to aphid resistance is limited. No correlation was found between total nitrogen, total sugars, free amino acids and amides in cell sap of Yellow sarson T-83 (*B. campestris* var. Yellow sarson), Rai T 151 (*B. juncea*) and *Eruca sativa,* and the developmental period of the mustard aphid (Kundu & Pant, 1967b).

Contrarily, *B. juncea* varieties having higher sugar and protein content act as susceptible hosts for growth and development of aphids as compared to those having lower amounts of these compounds (Malik, 1978; Sachan & Sachan, 1991). Reducing and total sugars present in cruciferous plants are believed to act as phagostimulant to mustard aphid (Malik, 1978). On the other hand, phenol content was found to be negatively correlated with aphid population (Desh Raj *et al.* 1996; Gill & Bakhetia, 1985; Sachan & Sachan, 1991). Again, phagostimulatory effect of phenols on *L. erysimi* as well as higher reduction in phenol content due to aphid attack in susceptible Brassica cultivars as compared to resistant and tolerant groups have also been observed (Malik, 1978).

The growth of *L. erysimi* does not appear to be significantly affected by low nitrogen content of its host (Sekhon & Ahman, 1993). There are certain amino acdis which are negatively correlated with the performance of aphid species, *Brevicoryne brassicae* and *Myzus persicae* (Van Emden, 1973). Significant negative correlation between the contents of proline and r-amino butyric acid (GABA) and relative growth rates of *M. persicae* in Brussels sprouts has also been observed (Van Emden & Bashford, 1971). Thus, the composition of amino acids in Brassica plants seems to be an important factor for the performance of *L. erysimi* (Sekhon & Ahman, 1993).

3.3.1.6.4 Screening for resistance

Different methods may be employed for the evaluation of Brassica germplasm for resistance against *L. erysimi*. The criteria used for screening include seedling survival, aphid injury, aphid population at a given growth stage, population increase in a given period, development fecundity and longevity of aphid and crop yield (Bakhetia & Sandhu, 1973; Bindra & Deole, 1962; Jarvis, 1969, 1970; Kundu & Pant, 1967a, 1968; Pathak, 1961; Rajan, 1961; Singh *et al.* 1965; Teotia & Lal, 1970). Although the reaction of cultivars to *L. erysimi* can be evaluated at any stage of plant growth with comparable results, screening is made either at the seedling or adult plant stage, the first method is more advantageous but is rarely used while the second method, though more laborious and time-consuming, is most practical and popular (Bakhetia & Bindra, 1977; Bakhetia & Sandhu, 1973; Sekhon & Ahman, 1993).

a. Screening at the seedling stage   In this technique, the insect population levels of 10, 20, 20 and 30 apterae, and 1 ml and 3 ml aphid colony (1ml = 600 nymphs + apterae) per plant are considered optimum for resistance screening at the cotyledonary, 2-leaf, 4-leaf, 6-leaf, flower bud initiation and flowering stages, respectively. The results of screening at cotyledonary, 2-leaf, 4-leaf and flowering stages for aphid resistance are highly comparable when tested under optimum level of aphid population per plant. The effect on the survival and fecundity of aphids is also similar at all these stages of plant growth (Bakhetia & Bindra, 1977).

b. Screening at the adult stage   Screening of adult plant reaction is based on symptoms of aphid injury on plants. The varieties/strains are classified into six grades using scoring system as under:

Score description

0   Completely free form aphid infestation
1   Normal growth, no visible symptoms of injury like curling or yellowing of the leaves, only a few aphids present
2   Average growth, curling and yellowing of a few leaves, average flowering and pod setting on almost all the branches
3.   Growth below average, curling and yellowing of leaves on some of the branches, poor flowering and pod setting
4.   Very poor growth, heavy curling and yellowing of the leaves, little or no flowering with very few well formed pods, heavy aphid colonies on plants
5.   Severe stunting of the plants, curling, crinkling and yellowing of almost all the leaves, no flowering and pod formation, plants full of aphids.

Every plant observed for aphid injury is given a specific grade (score) and then the aphid infestation index is worked out as under:

$$\text{Aphid infestation index} = \frac{0xa + 1xb + 2xc + 3xd + 4xe + 5xf}{a + b + c + d + e + f}$$

where *a*, *b*, *c*, *d*, *e* and *f* are the number of plants (frequencies) falling in each grade (0 to 5). The aphid infestation index is taken as the estimate of aphid resistance in the test entry, higher the index number, lower is the host resistance (Bakhetia & Sandhu, 1973).

c. Resistant cultivars   A good number of strains/varieties of different Brassica species has been reported tolerant or, resistant against aphids. *Brassica napus*, *B. alba* (*Sinapis alba*), *B. carinata*, *B. integrifolia*, *B. tourneforti*, *B. nigra* and *Eruca sativa* support relatively low population of aphids (Bakhetia, 1985; Bakhetia & Sandhu, 1973; Jarvis, 1970; Kher & Rataul, 1991; Kundu & Pant, 1967a; Singh *et al.* 1965; Teotia & Lal, 1970).

The cultivars Pusa Kalyani, IB 787, Torpe and CDA-Span of *B. campestris* (Bakhetia, 1985; Prasad, 1983; Singh *et al.* 1982); *B. juncea* such as Laha 101, T 6342, RL-18, RLM-29, RLM-84, RLM-171, RLM-528, Rai T3, Pant Rai 34, B 85, KRV Tall, RH 7846 and RH 7847 (Bakhetia, 1985; Bakhetia & Sandhu, 1973; Brar *et al.* 1976; Phadke & Prasad, 1987b; Singh *et al.* 1990; Teotia & Lal, 1970); *B. napus* strains, Gullivar, GSL-1, Regent, Karat, GSB, GSC and GS-47 (Bakhetia, 1985; Gill & Bakhetia, 1985); *B. nigra*-tall (Phadke & Prasad, 1987b); *B. carinata* var. HC-2; *B. tournefortii* var. local (Aggarwal *et al.* 1996); *E. sativa* var. ITSA, TMH-52 (Aggarwal *et al.* 1996; Bakhetia & Bindra, 1977); and *Crambe abyssinica* var. PI 247310 (Jarvis, 1969) are resistant to aphid attack.

Among the three commercially cultivated Brassica species, non-preference and tolerance is the mechanism of resistance in *B. napus* and *B. juncea,* respectively whereas, *B. campestris* is the most preferred host of *L. erysimi* (Kher & Rataul, 1991). Colchicine induced tetraploid Toria (*B. campestris* var. Toria) has an antibiotic effect on the life process of *L. erysimi* (Rajan, 1961) while the three principal components of resistance viz., non-preference, antibiosis and tolerance with a cumulative action, operate in the variety Laha 101 (Teotia & Lal, 1970).

3.3.1.6.5 Natural enemies

A number of natural predators, parasites and fungal pathogens cause death of mustard aphid but no serious attempt has so far been made to test their effectiveness as bio-agents against the pest under field conditions.

a. Predators   *Aspidolopha* sp. and *Monolepta signata* (Oliv.) are the two Chrysomelids (Coleoptera) that predate on mustard aphid in India (Ghosh *et al.* 1981).

Among the Coccinellids (Coleoptera) or the Lady bird beetles that predate on *L. erysimi* are: *Coccinella septumpunctata* (L.), *C. repandata* (Thub.), *C. transversalis*, *Menochilus sexmaculatus* (Fab.), *Brumoides suturalis* (Fab.), *Brumus* sp., *Oenopia luteopustulata* (Mulsant), *Pullus* sp. nr. *Pyrochilus* (Mulsant) and *Verania discolor* (Fab.) (Agarwala & Roy Chaudhari, 1981; Atwal & Sethi, 1963; Ghosh *et al.* 1981; Mathur, 1983; Modawal, 1941; Rao, 1962; Sethi & Atwal, 1963).

Coccinellids do not play any significant role in the natural suppression of aphid population. These predators become active in the field towards March, the end-season of the crop (Fig. 3.3), when aphid population is already declining. Generally, the aphids flourish at a temperature below 20°C, whereas *C. septumpunctata*, the most important among the Coccinellids that feed on aphids,

Fig. 3.3. Lady bird beetle, *Coccinella septumpunctata* feeding on aphid colony

flourishes at temperatures above 20°C (Sethi & Atwal 1963) and have little role in checking the population build up of aphids.

Syrphids (Diptera) or the hover flies that feed on mustard aphids include:

Syrphus spp., *S. serarius* (Wied.), *S. issaci* (B&S.); *Scaeva albomaculata, S. latimaculata* (Brunetti), *S. latifasciatus; Sphaerophoria scutellaris* (Fab.), *S. seripta* (L.), *S. indiana* (Big.); *Eristalis obscuritarsis* (de Meig.), *E. quinquelineatus* (Fab.), *E. tenax; Episyrphus balteatus* (De Geer.); *Metasyrphus confrater* (Wied.), *M. latilunulatus* (Coll.), *M. corollae, M. alligatus; Melanostoma orientalis; Diplazon* sp., *D. lactatorius* (Fab.); *Lasiopticus seleneticus; Leucopis* spp. (this also predates on *Myzus persicae* and *Bravicoryne brassicae*); *Baccha* sp.; *Paragus serratus* (Fab.); *Ischiodon scutellaris* (Fab.) and *Xanthogramma* sp. (Anand *et al.* 1967; Bakhetia & Sidhu, 1983; Bhatia & Shaffi, 1932; Cherian, 1934; Kumar *et al.* 1988 a,b; Kundu *et al.* 1966; Lal & Haque, 1955; Mathur *et al.* 1988; Roy & Basu 1977; Singh *et al.* 1990; Singh & Yadava, 1988).

Chrysopids (Neuroptera) or the lace wings which actively predate upon the mustard aphids are:

Micromus timidis; Chrysoperla sp.; *Chrysopa* sp. and *Chrysopa sceletes* (Banks). Both adult and larvae of *C. sceletes* feed on the aphids (Ghosh *et al.* 1981; Mathur, 1983; Nasir, 1947; Singh & Yadava, 1988).

b. Parasites *Aphidius* (Diaeretiella) *rapae* (Curtis.), *Aphidius* sp.; *Lipolexis gracilis; Aphelinus* sp.; *Aphidencrytus* sp., *A. aphidivorus; Diaeretus rapae* (McIntosh); *Ephedrus plagiator* and *Trioxys* (Binodoxys) *indicus* (Bakhetia & Sidhu, 1983; Chandra, 1981; Kundu *et al.* 1966; Mathur *et al.* 1988; Men *et al.* 1997; Sharma & Subba Rao, 1964).

c. Diseases *Entomophthora aphids, E. coronata* and *Cephalosporium aphidicola* have been recorded on the mustard aphid. The latter two fungi also infect *Myzus persicae* and *Brevicoryne brassicae* (Ramaseshiah, 1967; Ramaseshiah & Dharmadhikari, 1968; Singh, 1982).

3.3.1.6.6 Development of fore-warning system

Aphid infestation of oilseed brassicas is an annual feature in India, though the intensity of attack varies according to the meteorological conditions of the region and the growth stage of the crop variety. Once the initial infestation is established, aphid multiplication continues at a tremendous rate. This calls for a long range fore-warning system by which either the intensity of aphid attack can be predicted well before the crop is established or at least the onset of initial infestation determined for efficient management strategy - correlation of meteorological data of several years with both the time of occurrence and the number of catches on adhesive traps before the crop season, will indicate the possible initial pick up and subsequent aphid intensity (Phadke, 1980).

3.3.1.6.7 Economic-injury Level (EIL)/Economic-Threshold (ETH) and time of pesticide application

Determination of EIL and ETH of *L. erysimi* is a pre-requisite for achieving cost-effective and eco-friendly control measure. The ETH of the aphid on *B. juncea* var. RLM 198 was reported at 30 per cent plant infestation under Ludhiana, Punjab conditions (Bakhetia *et al*. 1983), while the EIL ranged from 9.42 to 30.60 aphids/10 cm terminal shoot and/or 2.60 to 6.90 per cent plant infestation of Indian mustard under Varanasi, UP conditions (Misra & Singh, 1986). The AICORPO. (1987) considered that the ETH for the mustard aphid is 50-60 aphis/10 cm terminal shoot and/or 40-45 per cent plants infested with the aphid. Singh and Sachan (1995) determined the EIL for *L. erysimi* on sarson (*B. campestris*) at Pantnagar, UP during 1986-88 witner seasons. The highest cost: benefit ratios, 1:9.50 and 1:9.26 were obtained after 3 weeks exposure to aphids during 1986-87 and 1987-88, respectively when the EIL was 28 and 26 aphids/plant, indicating that control measures should be initiated 3 weeks after aphid occurrence at flowering (76 DAS during 1st year) and/or pod initiation (83 DAS during 2nd year) for greatest benefit. Thus, success in achieving highest cost/benefit ratio from pest management measures will largely depend upon the accuracy with which the EIL/ETH of *L. erysimi* on the particular crop variety is determined. They are greatly influenced by a variety of interacting abiotic and biotic factors including the cropping systems, cultural practices, nature and cost of pesticides and the protection methodology used, etc. (Headley, 1972; Newson *et al*. 1980; Stern, 1973). The ETH will be more efficient, if it is made flexible, and both pest monitoring and forecasting systems are well developed (Headley, 1972).

3.3.1.6.8 Chemical control

Application of chemicals would continue to remain the most effective and quick method of combating the aphid menace, despite their possible hazardous effect on human health, ecological imbalance, pest resurgence and residual toxicity. A large number of chemicals of diverse nature has been used for the control of mustard aphid. Synthetic contact insecticides were used by early workers but they have been gradually replaced by systemic chemicals because of their greater efficiency in knocking down pests with sucking mouth parts, such as aphids.

Malathion, diazinon, pestox, systox and pyrocolloid (pyrethrum) are some of the contact insecticides used earlier against mustard aphid with considerable success (Ponnuswami, 1960; Pradhan *et al.* 1957; Singh & Sidhu, 1957, 1959).

Synthetic pyrethroids like cypermethrin, deltamethrin, decamethrin, fenvalerate and fluvalinate are the broad spectrum insecticides which are effective against *L. erysimi* (Bhadoria *et al.* 1982; Khurana & Batra, 1989; Nagia *et al.* 1991; Singh & Sircar 1980), but they should not be used in sub-lethal concentrations to prevent resurgence of pest problem (Tripathi & Sachan, 1990).

Significant reduction in aphid population can also be achieved through soil application (in furrows or as broadcast) of granular systemic insecticides, often supplementing with a spray chemical for better results (Bakhetia, 1986; Chaudhary & Roy, 1975; Gupta & Kavadia 1977; Hazarika & Saharia, 1981; Singh *et al.* 1984a; Prasad 1979). Furrow application of 10% phorate @ 15 kg/ha at sowing followed by a foliar spray of dimethoate @ 0.5 kg a.i./ha when the plants are at 20 per cent flowering resulted in higher yield compared to control (Chaudhary & Roy, 1975). Similarly, in experiments conducted both at the IARI, Delhi and Punjab, soil application of all the four granular insecticides viz., 10% aldicarb, 10% phorate, 5% disulfoton and 3% carbofuran significantly increased the crop yield and lowered aphid infestation, aldicarb gave better results than others (Bakhetia, 1986; Prasad, 1979). However, soil application of systemic granular chemicals, though proved much more effective against aphid than some spray chemicals, their use was found to be uneconomical (Hazarika & Saharia, 1981).

Relative efficacy of the systemic insecticides viz., dimethoate, menazon, phosphamidon, methyl-o-demeton, chlorpyriphos, monocrotophos, endosulfan, thiodicarb and quinalphos, etc. against *L. erysimi* has been well documented by several workers (Bakhetia, 1984; Butani, 1974; Kumar *et al.* 1996; Mathur & Upadhyay, 1980; Prasad, 1978a; Roy, 1975b; Saini, 1967; Saini & Chhabra, 1966). The insecticide, chlorpyriphos was reported to be the best among phosphamidon, methyl-o-demeton and monocrotophos both in checking aphid infestation and increasing seed yield (Kumar *et al.* 1996; Mathur & Upadhyay, 1980; Prasad, 1978b).

Spray schedule of six insecticides (0.25 kg/ha) for control of *L. erysimi* on Indian mustard cv. Varuna were evaluated in a field trial during 1981-83 at Bihar, India. Phosphamidon proved most effective both against the aphid and in resulting highest yield. The insecticides in descending order of efficacy were phosphamidon > dimethoate > lindane > thiometon > carbaryl > melathion > chlorpyriphos > endosulfan > quinalphos (Sinha *et al.* 1997). Baral and Sethi (1997) confirmed the high efficacy of chlorpyriphos, endosulfan and phosphamidon against *L. erysimi* infesting mustard (*B. campestris*) in West Bengal during 1995-96. The highest seed yield was obtained using chlorpyriphos (0.05%) followed by phosphamidon (0.04%), and the highest cost:benefit ratio was obtained by using phosphamidon.

Therefore, for effective control of aphids any recommended insecticide such as oxydemeton methyl 0.025%, phosphamidon 0.02-0.04%, dimethoate 0.03%, quinalphos 0.025%, endosulfan 0.03-0.04% and chlorpyriphos 0.02-0.05% @ 800 to 1000 l/ha may be used (Baral & Sethi, 1997; Gupta, 1971; Kumar *et al.* 1996; Phadke, 1980; Prasad, 1978b; Ramkishore & Phadke, 1988b; Singh *et al.* 1984 a,b; Singhvi *et al.* 1974; Sinha *et al.* 1997). To avoid the problem of insecticidal resistance more than one of the recommended insecticides should be used in rotation (Bakhetia, 1991).

Oxydemeton methyl, quinalphos, phosphamidon, menazon and endosulfan are relatively safer to the predator, lady bird beetle (*Coccinella septumpunctata*) and the pollinator honey bee (*Apis cerena indica* F.) besides being quite effective against mustard aphid (Bakhetia & Singh, 1992; Bhattacharjee *et al.* 1982; Thomas *et al.* 1994; Verma, 1980). Application of aldicarb granules @ 1 kg a.i./ha, after 45 days of sowing followed by irrigation also provides effective control of mustard aphid and is very safe to the pollinators (Singh *et al.* 1984a). All these chemicals will be useful in formulating integrated management schedule for aphid control on rapeseed and mustard.

Time of application rather than the choice of insecticides should be the more important consideration. Pesticides should be sprayed after the appearance of aphids in the field, preferably on the basis of economic threshold value (Bakhetia, 1984). They should be applied at fortnightly intervals towards the afternoon when pollinator bee activities are minimum (Sihag, 1988). Initiation of spray operations is recommended, say under the Punjab conditions, during the first fortnight of January when the economic injury level of *L. erysimi* reaches 9 to 19 aphdis (nymphs and adults)/plant and more than 10 per cent twigs get infested (Singh & Singh, 1988). Similarly, the application of pesticides should be abandoned during February-March as soon as the population of lady bird beetles, syrphids and crysopa, etc. become active (Bakhetia, 1986; Saini & Chhabra, 1966).

No one single control measure but judicial use of all of them in a complementary manner will ensure efficient management of this notorious pest.

3.3.2 Green Peach Aphid, *Myzus persicae* Sulzer.

(Homoptera: Aphididae)

The green peach aphid, *Myzus persicae* Sulzer is also known as potato aphid or spinach aphid. It is a cosmopolitan and highly polyphagous insect which attacks more than 40 different plant families, mostly of high economic value (Blackman & Eastop, 1984; Van Emden *et al.* 1969). The aphid also acts as vector of over 100 plant viruses (Rataul & Kishore, 1980). Under green-house conditions, it develops colonies on several cruciferous species such as radish, turnip, mustard (*B. alba*), chinese cabbage, cauliflower, Brussels sprouts and colza (MacKauer & Way, 1976). *Myzus persicae* was found infesting potato — February to March; radish — July to August; cauliflower — August to March; cabbage — October to March; and Indian mustard — November to March under Udaipur (Rajasthan) conditions (Chandra & Kushwaha, 1986). At Palampur (Himachal Pradesh), it infested oleiferous crucifers from December to first week of March with maximum population build up on Toria, followed by Sarson and Indian mustard (Desh Raj & Kumar, 1994).

3.3.2.1 Life history

Generally, *M. persicae* reproduces by means of viviparous parthenogenesis in the plains of India (Das, 1918; Lal, 1950). The average instar period ranges between 1.50 to 3.50 days, total nymphal period 8.25 to 12.40 days, the pre-laying period 1.00 to 2.80 days and the total generation period 10.00 to 14.67 days. The alatoid nymphs have an average duration of 9.88 days, the average pre-laying period is 1.88 days and the total generation period is 11.75 days. The developmental temperature threshold is 6.80°C for apterae and 7.20°C for alate (Rajendran, 1989). In a greenhouse study on the comparative biology of *M. persicae* on Taramira (*Eruca sativa*) and Raya (*B. juncea*), the duration of various nymphal instars and the pre-reproductive period was same on the two hosts but the reproductive and post-reproductive periods, adult life span and generation time were longer on *E. sativa* than on *B. juncea*. Fecundity was higher on *B. juncea* than on *E. sativa* (Singh & Singh, 1986). *Myzus persicae* exists in two distinct colour morphs viz., greenish yellow and red (pink), the former was more abundant (82%) than the latter in its population at Hissar (Haryana) (Singh & Singh, 1989). The alatae of *M. persicae* have a distinctive trapezoidal black patch on the mid-abdominal dorsum.

3.3.2.2 *Population dynamics*

Green peach aphid co-exists with *L. erysimi* (Kalt.) on cruciferous crops both in India (Banerjee & Basu, 1955a; Batra & Kumar, 1961; Fletcher, 1921) and other countries (Daiber, 1971). Earlier *M. persicae* was not considered to cause serious yield loss in oilseed brassicas (Blackman & Eastop, 1984) but recent reports show that it is also a pest to reckon with. It is gaining in importance and replacing *L. erysimi* particularly in irrigated crops or where Indian mustard is intercropped with potato, Toria with Gobi-sarson (*B. napus*) or there is simultaneous cultivation of different species/varieties of cruciferous oilseeds and vegetables (Bakhetia, 1991). It is more important on *E. sativa* than mustard aphid, *L. erysimi* (Bakhetia & Sharma, 1979).

At the IARI Farm, New Delhi, mixed infestation of Indian mustard due to the two aphids was 37 per cent plants, *L. erysimi* alone infested 42 per cent, while attack by *M. persicae* alone was 21 per cent plants. The colonization of *M. persicae* took place mainly on the upper portion of the plant, the lower portion of the plant had always their lowest number (Rajendran, 1989).

Colonies of mustard and green peach aphids were seen to co-exist upto a ratio of 53:47 and 62:38, respectively on rapeseed and mustard plants (Mathur & Singh, 1986; Singh & Singh, 1989). *Myzus persicae* appeared in low numbers on oilseed brassicas after a week following the attack of mustard aphid, when the plants were in advanced stage of flowering (Chandra & Kushwaha, 1986; Singh & Singh, 1989). The colony size of *M. persicae* was smaller than that of *L. erysimi*. *Myzus persicae* did not attack rapeseed at foliage stage of the plant. Its population showed two distinct peaks viz., the first in mid-January, and the second towards the end-February to early-March, when the average temperature was 13-17°C and the relative humidity was 64-74%. Population declined sharply after the first week of March with the rise in temperature. Too low (2.8°C) or too high (above 27°C) temperature, decreased relative humidity (55%), production of alates, water stress due to crop maturity, action of parasites and predators, and rainfall and wind velocity have adverse effect on its population (Desh Raj & Kumar, 1994; Singh & Singh, 1989).

Myzus persicae exhibits wide genetic variability in its population. Study of field populations of *M. persicae* in Scotland indicated the existence of different gene clones, rapid changes in the proportion of these clones and presence of different gene clones in *M. persicae* populations of different areas. There are also clones which are either resistant or susceptible to organophosphates. Individual aphids collected in samples of populations taken from rape or mustard had a different range of clone compositions than those in samples collected from swede, cabbage or calabrese (Baker, 1979). Further, immunoassay of field populations of *M. persicae* collected from Brassica crops showed that 85% of individuals had an elevated level of carboxyl esterase (E 4) — the enzyme that confers resistance in this aphid to a wide range of insecticides — above that of a standard susceptible clone and upto 12% had E 4 levels higher than a standard resistant clone. Proportion of these highly resistant aphids was different in different places (Little, 1987).

3.3.3 Cabbage Aphid, *Brevicoryne brassicae* L.

(Homoptera: Aphididae)

Brevicoryne brassicae L. is a cosmopolitan insect (Bonnemaison, 1965) that flourishes in temperate regions all over the world (Blackman & Eastop, 1984). The pest is present in India and may attack the newly introduced cultivars of *B. napus*. At present, it is not a problem for rapeseed and mustard, the principal oleiferous Brassica species of the country (Bakhetia & Singh, 1992).

3.3.3.1 Damage

Brevicoryne brassicae is a crucifer specialist and the glucoside sinigrin, produced by oilseed Brassicas, acts as specific stimulus in the selection of its host (Wensler, 1962). It causes serious losses to broccoli, Brussels sprouts, cabbage, cauliflower, oilseed rape and swede (Graham, 1979). In Britain, it attacks both winter and spring rape crops but is more important in the latter (Winfield, 1986). Prevalence of warm, dry weather conditions in spring is very conducive for the large scale infestation of winter rape by *B. brassicae*. The yield losses are most serious when the crop is infested at the beginning of flowering (Daebeler & Hinz, 1983; Sedivy, 1981). Infested plants produce shorter pods, fewer seeds/pod, a lower weight/1000 seeds and lower seed germinability. The reduction in number of seeds/pod is most pronounced in plants colonized by aphids immediately after anthesis (Sedivy, 1981).

When feeding on oilseed rape (*B. napus*), the cabbage aphid excretes low concentrations of glucosinolates and retains them in its body (Weber *et al.* 1986) because it has a glucosinolase system which hydrolyses these chemicals (MacGibbon & Allison, 1968). The polyphagous *M. persicae*, on the other hand, excretes a high concentrations of glucosinolates when feeding on *B. napus* (Weber *et al.* 1986). Consequently, these aphids are not deterred from attacking oilseed rape plants by glucosinolates and their fission products (Lamb, 1989). The cabbage aphid is also more active on waxy Brassica cultivars than on low waxy ones (Thompson, 1963; Way & Murdie, 1965) but opposite is the case with the green peach aphid, *M. persicae* (Way & Murdie, 1965).

Six species of Brassica were evaluated for resistance against *B. brassicae* in Pakistan. *Brassica napus*, supporting shortest nymphal stage and highest adult aphid density proved to be the most preferred host plant of the insect pest, followed in order of decreasing preference by *B. campestris*, *B. nigra*, *B. juncea*, *B. trilocularis* and *B. carinata*. The last named host species indicated the phenomenon of antibiosis by supporting reduced nymphal weight, nymphal survival and fecundity (Hussain, 1983).

Colony formation and aggregation behaviour of *B. brassicae* differ from that of *M. persicae*. *Brevicoryne brassicae* formed compact aggregates, whereas *M. persicae* formed aggregations with 1-2 mm distance between the nearest neighbours. Neonate nymphs of *B. brassicae* showed a strong tendency to remain in contact with the mother, whereas those of *M. persicae* moved away and settled at a distance of about 2 mm. Most individuals of *B. brassicae* remained in contact even at low densities, but few individuals of *M. persicae* were in contact with each other, even at high densities (Hyamizu, 1982).

3.3.3.2 Chemical control

A number of chemicals are effective against *B. brassicae*: Soil application of disulfoton granules @ 2 kg/ha (Lammerink & Banfield, 1980); foliar application of oxydemeton-methyl @ 0.5 lb/ha, methyl parathion @ 1 lb/ha, parathion @ 0.5 + endosulfan @ 1 lb/ha (Carlson, 1973) and menazon @ 0.035% (Hameed & Sud, 1978). At Karnataka, India, only one spray of oxydemeton-methyl (0.04%) or acephate (0.01%) was effective in integrated pest management programmes for aphid pests (mainly *L. erysimi, B. brassicae* and *M. persicae*) in Indian mustard (Basavaraju *et al*. 1995).

3.4 DIAMOND-BACK MOTH, *Plutella xylostella* L.

(Lepidoptera: Yponomeutidae)

Syn. *Plutella maculipennis* Curtis

Diamond-back moth, believed to have originated in the Mediterranean area (Harcourt, 1954), is probably the most universally distributed of all lepidopteran insects (Meyrick, 1928). It is a small insect, nearly half an inch long when wings are folded, with an expanse of two-thirds of an inch across the open wings. The colour of the wings and body is generally brownish-grey; the fore-wings have darker spots and a light line along the inner edge. When the fore-wings are folded, the light marks on the wings come together forming the characteristic diamond marks along the upper surface, from which the moth takes its name (Lefroy, 1906).

3.4.1 Damage

Diamond-back moth is one of the most destructive insect pests of cruciferous plants throughout the world (Talekar & Shelton, 1993). In India, it is a minor pest of rapeseed and mustard but is most serious on cauliflower, turnip, cabbage and radish. It prefers cauliflower for egg laying and feeding over cabbage, Indian mustard, turnip, chinese cabbage, broccoli or radish, although eggs are laid on all these plants (Abro *et al*. 1992; Singh & Singh, 1982; Verma & Sandhu, 1967).

The first- and second-instar larvae mine into the leaves and feed on the spongy mesophyll tissue. Later, they feed externally from the lower surface and usually consume all tissues except the wax layer on the upper surface, making small holes into the leaves and giving a shot-hole effect all over the plant (Fig. 3.4). The remaining leaf tissue shrivels and turns brown giving the affected plant a withered appearance. In case of severe infestation, the leaves are eaten up almost completely, except the veins and upper epidermis (Abro *et al*. 1992; Verma & Sandhu, 1967).

3.4.2 Host range

A large number of cruciferous and non-cruciferous plants have been reported to be the hosts of diamond-back moth (Li, 1981; Singh & Singh, 1982) but according to Talekar and Shelton (1993), the host range of the pest is limited only to the members of the family Cruciferae. Cultivated crops

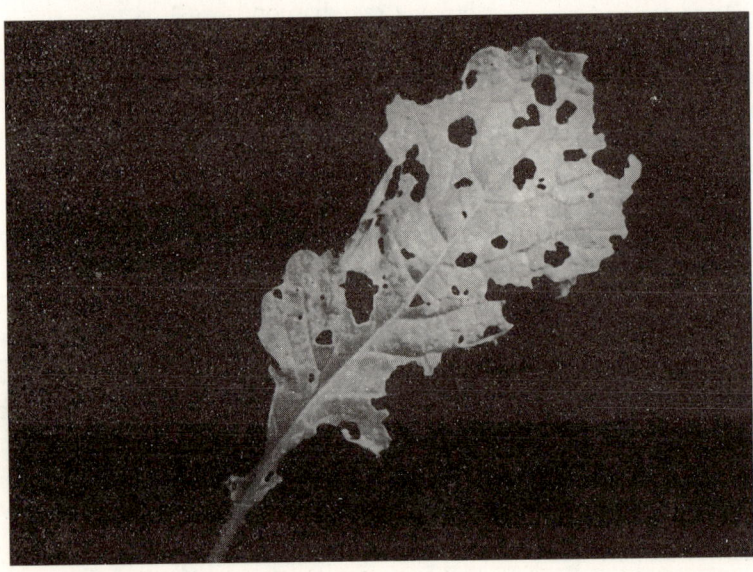

Fig. 3.4. Indian mustard leaf eaten up by Diamond-back moth, *Plutella xylostella*

on which the diamond-back moth feeds include cabbage, cauliflower, broccoli, radish, turnip Brussels sprouts, chinese cabbage, Kohl rabi, mustard (*B. juncea*), rapeseed, collard, pak choi saishin (*B. rapa* cv. gr. *saishin*), watercress, and Kale.

Cruciferous weed hosts/plants that sustain feeding of diamond-back moth in the absence of more favoured cultivated hosts are: *Arabis glabra, Armoracia lapathifolia, Barbarea stricta Barbarea vulgaris, Basela alba, Beta vulgaris, Brassica caulorapha, Brassica kaber (Sinapi. arvensis), Brassica napobrassica, Bunias orientalis, Capsella bursa-pastoris, Cardamine amara Cardamine cordifolia, Cardamine pratensis, Cheiranthus cheiri, Conringa orientalis, Descurainie sophia, Erysimum cheiranthoides, Galinsoga ciliata, Galinsoga parviflora, Hesperis matronalis Iberis amara, Isatis tinctoria, Lepidium perfoliatum, Lepidium virginicum, Lobularia maritima Mathiola incana, Norta (Sisymbrium) altissima, Pringlea antiscorbutica, Raphanus raphanistrum Rorippa amphibia, Rorippa islandica, Sinapis alba, Sisymbrium austriacum, Sisymbriun officinale*, and *Thlaspi arvense* (Craford & Chown, 1987; Ghesquiere, 1939; Harcourt, 1957 Kanervo, 1936; Louda, 1986; Mills, 1942; Rai & Tripathi, 1985).

Cruciferous plants containing mustard oils or allyl isothiocyanates and their glucosides ar only the hosts of diamond-back moth and the above named compounds provide the stimulus fo their oviposition (Gupta & Thorsteinson, 1960a,b; Hillyer & Thorstelnson, 1971, Nayar & Thorsteinson, 1963; Reed *et al.* 1989; Thorsteinson, 1953, 1955). Many glucosinolates stimulat feeding in diamond-back moths, but two of these, 3-butenyl and 2-phenylethyl, are toxic to them a high concentrations (Nayar & Thorsteinson, 1963). The glucosides sinigrin, sinalbin, an glucocheirolin act as specific feeding stimulants for diamond-back moths, and 40 plant specie containing one or more of these chemicals act as hosts. Plants containing these feeding stimulant are non-hosts when they also contain feeding inhibitors or toxins (Gupta & Thorsteinson, 1960a)

Presence of unidentified olfactory stimuli that attract diamond-back moth to crucifers has also been detected (Palaniswamy *et al.* 1986; Pivnick *et al.* 1990b).

3.4.3 Life history

Adult diamond-back moths emerge during the first 8 h of photophase (Pivnick *et al.* 1990a), start mating at dusk of the same day and continue to remain active into the night. The mean duration of copulation was 36.7 min. and insects mated on average 2.45 times per night (Abro *et al.* 1992). Female moths start laying eggs soon after mating and the oviposition period lasts 4 days (Harcourt, 1954). One female may lay out 200 minute (0.5 mm) yellowish-white eggs on the leaves singly or in clusters (Abraham & Padamanaban, 1968; Verma & Sandhu, 1967). The majority of eggs are laid before midnight of the first day with peak oviposition occurring between 7.00 and 8.00 P.M. (Abro *et al.* 1992; Asian Veg. Res. and Dev. Cent. 1987, 1985 Prog. Rept.; Pivnick *et al.* 1990a). More eggs are laid on the upper leaf surface than on lower leaf surface and very few are laid on stems and leaf petioles (Asian Veg. Res. and Dev. Cent. 1987, 1984 Prog. Rept.; Harcourt, 1954). Leaf concavities are more preferred for laying eggs than smooth surfaces (Gupta & Thorsteinson, 1960b).

Lack of normal day light stimulates oviposition but light during night hours does not completely inhibit it (Asian Veg. Res. and Dev. Cent. 1987, 1985 AVRDC Prog. Rept.; Tabashnik, 1985). Oviposition is influenced by plant volatiles, secondary chemicals, temperature, trichomes, and waxes on leaf surfaces (Asian Veg. Res. and Dev. Cent. 1986, 1985 AVRDC Prog. Rept. Summaries; Lu *et al.* 1988; Pivnick *et al.* 1990b; Tabasnik, 1985; Uematsu & Sakanoshita, 1989). Host plants influence the calling behaviour and egg maturation of diamond-back moths. In the presence of Indian mustard (*B. juncea*) seedlings, female moths start calling at younger age, begin calling earlier in the night and spend more time in calling than those not exposed to plants. Presence of plants accelerates egg maturation, both before and after the onset of calling (Pittendrigh & Pivnick, 1993).

Hatching of eggs is mainly influenced by temperature and takes place in about 4 to 6 days. There are 4 larval instars (Beri, 1961). The larval period varies from 8 to 21 days in India depending upon weather conditions. Newly hatched larvae are greyish-green with black head, with growth their head turns light-yellow and the body becomes pale-yellow. A full-grown larva is moderately stout with bristly hairs and measures about 10 mm long. The full-fed 4th instar larva constructs a very beautiful, transparent cocoon of white silk in which it remains quiescent for about one week, gradually becomes a little darker in colour to enter the pre-pupal stage. The pupa is about 6 mm long. The pupal stage lasts for about a week. Diamond-back moth completes its larval and pupal development in shortest time (16.9 days) on cauliflower, followed by Brown sarson and turnip (18.1 days). Indian mustard, Toria, cabbage and radish rank next with 19.5-19.9 days as the period of development (Abraham & Padmanaban, 1968; Lefroy, 1906; Singh & Singh, 1982; Stapathi, 1990; Verma & Sandhu, 1967). Adult moths emerge mostly between 1.00 and 4.00 PM with a peak at 2.00 PM (Pivnick *et al.* 1990a; Sakanoshita & Yanagita, 1972). Adults feed on water drops or dew and are short-lived (Talekar & Shelton, 1993). The life-cycle varies from 24 to 35 days (Abraham & Padmanaban, 1968). Diamond-back moth has several broods in a year, overlapping irregularly, so that insects of all ages are found at the same time. In India, there may be atleast 8 to12 generations in a year (Lefroy, 1906) and the pest is most active from August-October (Verma & Sandhu, 1967).

Cold weather is detrimental for its survival (Singh & Singh, 1982; Talekar & Shelton, 1993). It is not knwon whether the pest diapauses or hibernates in any of its life stages. In tropics and sub-tropics, where crucifers are grown throughout the year, all life stages of the moth can be found any time. In temperate regions, where crucifers are not grown the year-round, it's perennial occurrence is due to immigration of adult moths effected by favourable wind currents and/or the introduction of its different stages through contaminated seedlings. Diamond-back has the remarkable ability to remain in continuous flight for several days, cover distances of 1000 km per day and disperse over long distances (Talekar & Shelton, 1993).

3.4.4 Control

a. Chemicals

Pesticides are mainly used for the control of diamond-back moth since early days. Spraying with 0.025% diazinon (Basudin) emulsion, 0.1% trichlorphon (Dipterex) solution, 0.2% carbaryl (Sevin) suspension or 0.08% malathion emulsion is effective against this moth (Verma & Sandhu, 1967). According to Brar and Singh (1992), fenvalerate at 50 and 37.5 g a.i./ha, deltamethrin at 10.5 and 7.5 g a.i./ha and fluvalinate at 81.2 g/ha are most effective against diamond-back moth followed in order of efficacy by quinalphos at 500 g/ha, endosulfan at 525 g/ha, and cypermethrin at 37.5 g/ha, respectively.

Diamond-back moth, because of its high fecundity and reproductive potential, rapid generation build-up, long growing season and presence of cruciferous hosts over extensive areas, has developed resistance to every insecticide used extensively against it (Magaro & Edelson, 1990; Sun *et al.* 1978; Yamada & Koshihara, 1978).

b. Bio-pesticides

Insect-growth regulators and pathogens are useful alternatives to common classes of insecticides in resistance management against diamond-back moth. Benzoyl phenyl urea and teflubenzuron, which act as chitin synthesis inhibitor, are highly effective against diamond-back moth though the pest develops resistance afterwards (Ong & Ng, 1988; Perng *et al.* 1988).

Granulosis viruses cause high mortality in diamond-back moth (Su, 1987). The bacterium, *Bacillus thuringiensis* Berliner is highly effective and specific against this moth (Georghiou, 1990). However, low efficacy or resistance to, and control failures of *B. thuringiensis* ssp. *aizawai*, *B. thuringiensis* ssp. Kurstaki and HD-1 isolate of the Kurstaki serotype in field application against diamond-back moth have also been reported (Hama, 1992; Kirsch & Schmutterer, 1988; Shelton & Wyman, 1992).

Sex pheromone emitted by adult female moths is effective against mating disruption of the pest in the field. The pheromone consisting of three components, (Z)-11-hexadecenal, (Z)-11-hexadecenyl acetate, and (Z)-11-hexadecenyl alcohol, now available commercially, can be used along with natural enemies against diamond-back moth (Ando *et al.* 1979; Chisholm *et al.* 1979; Chow *et al.* 1977; Talekar & Shelton, 1993).

c. Biological control

Polyphagous predators like birds and spiders destroy adult moths (Talekar & Shelton, 1993). Out of 90 parasitoid species that attack diamond-back moth (Goodwin, 1979), about 60 are important, of which 6 species attack eggs, 38 attack larvae, and 13 attack pupae (Lim, 1986). Natural parasitoids reported from India are: (a) Larval parasites — (i) eulophid, *Tetrastichus sokolowskii* Kurdujmov (Cherian & Basheer, 1939; Patel & Patel, 1968); (ii) ichneumonids, *Diadegma fenestralis* (Holmgren) (Dutt, 1914; Fletcher, 1919a; Thompson, 1946) and *Casinaria* sp. (Simmonds & Rao, 1960); (iii) braconids, *Cotesia (Apanteles) plutellae* Kurdujmov (Bhatnagar, 1948; Patel & Patel, 1968), *Cotesia (Apanteles)* sp. (glomeratus group) and *Chelonus (Microchelonus) versatilis* Wilkinson (Patel & Patel, 1968); (iv) chalcids, *Hockeria testaceitarsis* Cameron, *Euchalcidia* sp. (Patel & Patel, 1968), (v) tachinid fly, *Voria rurlalis* Fall (Simmonds & Rao, 1960); (b) Pupal parasites — *Barchymeria excarinata* Gahan (Cherian & Basheer, 1937; Mani, 1940) and *B. plutellophaga* Girault (Mani, 1940).

Larval parasites belonging to the genera, Diadegma and Cotesia, and a few *Diadromus* spp., most of which are pupal parasitoids, play important role in keeping down the population of diamond-back moth in nature. Several countries have introduced one or more of the parasitoid spp., *Diadegma semiclausum*, *Diadromus collaris*, *Cotesia plutellae* and *Tetrastictus sokolowaskii* for the control of diamond-back moth with considerable success (Talekar & Shelton, 1993). *Dolichogenidea sicaria*, *D. litae*, and *D. appellator* are also important parasites of *P. xylostella* (Avci & Ozbeck, 1990).

Additional management measures required are: cultivation of resistant host-plant, release of efficient parasitoids and their conservation, use of pesticides that are compatible with natural enemies and use of yellow sticky traps to capture adult moths and thereby to reduce their oviposition and subsequent damage by larvae (Rushtapakornchai *et al.* 1992). The cultivars Rahangala and Cutlas represent the first source of resistance to *P. xylostella* identified in *B. juncea* and these may be used in varietal improvement programme (Andrahennadi & Gillott, 1998).

3.5 BIHAR HAIRY CATERPILLAR, *Spilosoma obliqua* Walker

(Lepidoptera: Arctiidae)

Syn: *Spilarctia obliqua* Walker

Diacrisia obliqua Walker

The Bihar hairy caterpillar, *Spilosoma obliqua* Walker is a polyphagous insect that causes serious damage to a variety of vegetables, cereals, oilseeds, pulses and medicinal plants. Brassica crops are infested only occassionally. Humid climate is probably the most important factor for the abundance of this pest (Deshmukh *et al.* 1979; Katiyar *et al.* 1975; Mathur, 1962; Ram & Pathak, 1980; Srivastava & Pandey, 1981). In Manipur, India, it remains active throughout the year and damages the germinating plants of mustard during November-December. Prevalence of humid climate with mean annual temperature and relative humidity range of about 14.5-26.6°C and 77-84 per cent, respectively play a vital role in multiplication and survival of the pest (Ram & Pathak, 1980).

3.5.1 Damage

Spilosoma obliqua damages the crop only in the larval stage. The young caterpillars are voracious eaters, they congregate in large numbers in a small area of the foliage, eat away the chlorophyll bearing tissues, leaving the veins and other tissues to give a meshed appearance to the leaf. As a result, the leaves turn yellow and crumble up (Fig. 3.5). The older caterpillars destroy the entire leaf except the veins resulting in defoliation of the crop (Mathur, 1962).

Fig. 3.5. Indian mustard leaves damaged by Bihar hairy caterpillar, *Spilosoma obliqua*. Note the meshed areas on leaves due to loss of chlorophyll

Growth and development of *S. obliqua* are greatly influenced by the kind of food plant it colonizes upon. Some hosts favour larval growth and development, others favour pupal development, adult emergence, male and female ratio, and adult longevity (Ali *et al*. 1988; Pandey *et al*. 1968; Sachan, 1981; Tewari *et al*. 1989). Generally, plant species that are favourable for larval survival are also favourable for their rapid development (Deshmukh *et al*. 1979). The order of suitability of food plants for the development of young larvae are: Toria > Sunflower > Sugar beet > Castor bean > Urd (*Vigna mungo*) (Tewari *et al*. 1989).

3.5.2 Life history

The adult moth is brown in colour with reddish abdomen. The wings have scattered black spots whereas in the abdomen, they lie mid dorsally and laterally in straight rows (Mathur, 1962). Males usually start emerging late in the afternoon and females at dusk. The time of mating coincides very closely with that of emergence. Two mating peaks, at 18.30 and 0.400 h respectively, were recorded and more than 80 per cent of the pairs mated before midnight. Maximum mating occurs in one day old adults, and mating activity ceases after the second day following emergence (Islam & Alam, 1979).

Hundreds of pale green eggs are laid singly by the female moth, scattered all over the plant. The egg stage lasts for 8 to10 days in summer and 2 to 3 weeks in winter. There are seven larval instars (Bakhetia, 1991). The larval period is correlated with their efficiency of conversion of digested food to body matter (Srivastava & Pandey, 1981). The larval period varies between 23 to 32 days (Sachan, 1981). Pupation takes place on ground surface under dry foliage and debris. The pupa lies inside a thin silken cocoon formed by the interwoven shed hairs of the larva. Pupal stage lasts for 9 to12 days in September but the duratin may be prolonged considerably during hibernation and aes-tivation. The outbreaks of *S. obliqua* occur twice in a year, in the months of March-April and August-October. In Punjab, it usually completes three generations in a year (Bakhetia, 1991; Mathur, 1962) whereas, under laboratory conditions it had as many as 9 generations from April to December (Ali *et al*. 1988).

3.5.3 Natural enemies

Natural enemies reported on *S. obliqua* from India are: *Trichogramma evanescens minutum* Riley, *Apanteles creatonoti* Viereck (Krishnamurti & Usman, 1954); *A. jayanagarensis* Bhatnagar and *A. obliguae* Wilkinson (Bhatnagar, 1948); *A. flavipes* Cameron (Usman & Puttarudriah, 1955) and *Brachymeria campestris* (Hussain & Agarwal, 1982).

3.5.4 Control

Following measures may be adopted for the control of Bihar hairy caterpillar:

1. Collection and destruction of young gregarious larvae from the field (Bakhetia, 1991).
2. Use of recommended insecticides.

Quinalphos (0.05%), endosulfan (0.03-0.15%), monocrotophos (0.05%) and phosalone (0.5 kg a.i/ha) (Mrig & Singh, 1981; Senapati & Ghosh, 1992; Sidhu & Dhawan, 1980; Tewari & Singh, 1979); emulsifiable synthetic pyrethroids like Cypermethrin (0.005% or 60 g a.i/ha), decamethrin (0.002%), deltamethrin (15 g a.i/ha) and fenvalerate (0.01%) provide high larval mortality (Goel & Kumar, 1991; Singh, 1991).

3.6 CABBAGE WEB-WORM, *Crocidolomia binotalis* Zeller

(Lepidoptera: Pyralidae)

The cabbage web-worm, *Crocidolomia binotalis* Zell. is an important pest of cruciferous crops all over the country, causing serious damage to cabbage, cauliflower and mustard (*Brassica campestris* L.) (Patel, 1975; Rai & Nagesh Chandra, 1976; Rout & Pani, 1968; Sen 1920). Indian mustard (*B. juncea* L.) is the preferred host as compared to cabbage (Srinivasan & Moorthy, 1991). It also attacks radish, turnip (Lefroy, 1907; Lever, 1945), the non-cruciferous plant *Cleodendron fragrans peniflorum* Vent. and the ornamental plant *Thymus vulgaris aureus* (Lever, 1945; Raich, 1975). In south India, cabbage web-worm causes substantial losses in yield of cruciferous crops during its peak period of activity from November to February (Peter *et al*.1983). In Madhya

Pradesh it is a major pest of mustard (Patel, 1975; Rout & Pani, 1968), and caused 17.54-47.82 per cent (av. 27.55%) infestation of plants during November 1977 to March 1978 (Singh & Rawat, 1983b). It has also been recorded on rape seed (*B. napus* L.) in Haryana where it may become a serious threat to Brassica crops (Singh & Singh, 1983).

3.6.1 Damage

The freshly hatched larvae of *C. binotalis* first feed on the chlorophyll of young tender leaves and stems of mustard plants. Later, the leaves, buds and pods are infested. The larvae often fold and web the leaves, buds and flowers, and remain inside the web. Severely attacked plants become completely defoliated. The larvae bore the young pods and remain hidden inside. Patel (1975) found as much as 82 per cent plants to be affected.

3.6.2 Life history

The cabbage web-worms are pale orchreous coloured moths. Their forewings have black specks with dark-edged white spots, while the hind wings are pale white in colour. Under field conditions, an adult female lays eggs on the underside of tender mustard leaves and stems. Eggs are pale white, small and round, and are arranged longitudinally and covered with white yellowish transparent substance. A prominent spot is present in the centre of the egg. The incubation period varies from 5-7 days. A young larva is pale brown in colour with pale brown head and pubescent body. A full-grown larva is pale greenish-brown and flattened posteriorly. It has a medial and lateral yellowish white line with short hairs on the dark tubercles, and measures 13 to 16 mm in length. The larval period varies from 14 to 16 days and the larva undergoes 4 larval instars before turning into a pupa (Patel, 1975). Larvae show aggregated distribution on cabbage (Srinivasan & Rao, 1987).

Before pupation, the larva forms a web and pupates inside the folded leaves (Patel, 1975), about 4 to 7 larvae were observed inside the webbed leaves of *T. vulgare aureus* (Raich, 1975). The pupal stage lasts 10 to 12 days while the moth lives 6 to 8 days without food (Patel, 1975).

Under laboratory conditions, a female laid egg masses mainly on the ventral surface of leaves of Indian mustard. Each female laid 74.60 ± 14.99 eggs during her life span of 12.40 ± 3.78 days. The incubation period, larval period, pre-pupal and pupal period lasted 6.40 ± 0.54, 23.40 ± 3.12, 4.40 ± 1.34 and 11.20 ± 1.54 days, respectively. The pupation took place after 5 larval instars in an earthen cocoon in soil upto 10 cm depth. Male and female exhibit sexual dimorphism (Singh & Rawat, 1983b).

3.6.3 Natural enemies

Bracon greeni Ashmead (Usman & Puttarudriah, 1955), *B. melleus* Ayyar (Ayyar, 1928), *Palexorista solennis* Walker (Peter *et al.* 1986) and *Bessa remota* (Jayanth & Nagarkatti 1984) are the larval parasites, and the larvae of *Chrysopa sceletes* Banks are the predator of *C. binotalis* (Krishnamoorthy, 1988).

3.6.4 Chemical control

Crocidolomia binotalis can be controlled effectively by spray application of monocrotophos, quinalphos, phenthroate, chlorpyriphos, chlorfenvinphos, acephate, methamidophos or fenitrothion at usual concentration (Krishnaiah & Mohan, 1983), cyfluthrin at 0.5 kg a.i./ha, deltamethrin at 0.012 kg a.i./ha, fenvalerate at 0.1 kg a.i./ha or profenophos at 0.5 kg a.i./ha, at two week intervals commencing at the first appearance of pest larvae on hosts. These offer both protection and enhanced crop yield (Mohan, 1987). The insecticide, permethrin applied at 75 g/ha after 15, 30, 45 and 60 days of planting resulted in complete control of the pest on cabbage (Krishna Kumar *et al.* 1986). Spray application of diflubenzuron at 75-200 g a.i./ha also caused complete mortality of *C. binotalis* larvae on radish in Tamil Nadu, India (Peter & David, 1988).

3.7 BUTTERFLY

3.7.1 Cabbage Butterfly, *Pieris brassicae* L.

(Lepidoptera: Pieridae)

3.7.1.1 Distribution

The cabbage butterfly, *Pieris brassicae* L. is a pest of great economic importance whose distribution in the world appears to be restricted between the winter isotherm of –16°C to –20°C and the summer (July) isotherm of +28°C (Blunck, 1953; Feltwell, 1982). It is unable to withstand temperature below –13°C and above 28°C at 60 per cent relative humidity in the wild, and at lower humidity, the oviposition is inhibited (Klein, 1932).

In India, *P. brassicae* is found all along the Himalayan region during summer months. They migrate to the plains during winter reaching within 16 km of the Himalayas in eastern Bengal (Bangladesh), Bihar, Uttar Pradesh and eastern Punjab (Lefroy, 1909), and upto Cuttack (Orissa) in south (Narayanan, 1958). They frequent Pusa (Bihar) during February, complete 2-3 broods before returning to the hills in April (Fletcher 1921). In Punjab, they are active from early October to the end of April in the plains, and from March to September in the hills (Rataul 1959). They are present in Katrain (Kulu valley), Himachal Pradesh (Chandra & Lall, 1977) and act as serious pest of Brassica spp. in the State (Rawat *et al.* 1990).

Cabbage butterflies exhibit mass migration from the plains to the hills during summer and back to the plains during winter (Narayanan, 1958). One such mass migration of about 75,000 to 80,000 individuals of *P. brassicae*, considered only a small portion of its total population, in northerly direction at altitudes of 3800-40000 m in Kashmir, India and which took 36 h to pass one site, was sighted on May 28, 1988 (Jamdar, 1991). *Pieris brassicae* is also widespread in Pakistan and is the most serious pest of cruciferous vegetables in Sialkot area (Mushtaque, 1989).

3.7.1.2 Host range

Pieris brassicae is an oligophagous insect having an extraordinary large number of host plants, but by far the most important of these belong to the Cruciferae family. Five plant families, the Cruciferae, Tropaeolaceae, Capparaceae, Resedaceae and the Papilionaceae are mainly exploited by *P. brassicae*. These are the principal plant families since *P. brassicae* may also be found regularly in the wild on any of these species. This group contains 83 host species, of which the largest number of species belong to the genus Brassica. Wild Crucifers play a very important part in supporting the first generation larvae of *P. brassicae* in many countries. There are also a secondary and a somewhat doubtful category of food plants, comprising 8 species from seven other plant families, on which *P. brassicae* may be occassionally found in the wild. Besides, there are 15 other plant species belonging to ten families on which *P. brassicae* larvae have been induced to feed in the laboratory under artificial conditions (Feltwell, 1982).

In India, the caterpillars of *P. brassicae* feed on rapeseed and mustard, Taramira (*Eruca sativa*) and cole crops, besides gram, linseed and sugarcane (Fletcher, 1921). Cabbage is most susceptible to attack by *P. brassicae*, followed by cauliflower, Indian mustard, Sarson and Toria. Females oviposit only on cruciferous plants and no egg is laid on wheat, gram or pea (*Pisum sativum*) (Tiwari & Kashyap, 1988).

The close association between the butterfly and the Cruciferae is manifests in the highly specialized sensory system of the larva and imago, and their responses to chemical substances produced by the plant (Feltwell, 1982). Glucobrassicin (3-indoyl-methyl glucosinolate) extracted from the surface of cabbage leaves stimulates oviposition in females of *P. brassicae*. Sinigrin (slightly active) and glucoiberin (inactive) are the other glucosinolates identified in the leaf extract.

Possibly, a high sensitivity of *P. brassicae* for indole glucosinolates as host recognition factor may confer an advantage for these specialist crucifer-feeders. The nutritional significance of their precursor tryptophan, and the non-volatile nature of aglycones formed upon enzymic hydrolysis in damaged tissues are supposed to be the properties of indole glucosinolates that contribute to this advantage (Loon *et al*. 1992; Renwick *et al*. 1992).

3.7.1.3 Life history

Pieris brassicae is a fairly large beautiful snow-white butterfly with black spot in its wings. Before copulation, the male butterfly flutters over the female, the latter alights on the ground with its wings expanded and finally, the pair take up tail to tail position. After copulation, the female lays 47-74 eggs in clusters in about 5 days, on either surface of the leaves. A single egg is laid at a time. The eggs are creamy or light yellow, pear shaped, sticky and measure 1.12 mm long and 0.23 mm thick (Mukerji, 1961).

Pieris brassicae females seek out green surfaces for laying eggs and they lay eggs on plants which contain the mustard oil glucosides. Sinigrin applied even to green paper stimulates the females to lay eggs. When laying an egg, the female locates one previously laid with the tip of her abdomen and thus builds up the regularly arranged clusters. The females laid more eggs per day, and more eggs in a batch, at 30°C than at 20°C. Oviposition occurr at low light intensities.

Fertilized females lay many more eggs than virgin females. Generally, eggs are fertilized only just before oviposition. A fertilized female lays scarcely any infertile eggs (David & Gardiner, 1952). The eggs hatch out on the seventh day. The first instar larva is a greenish polypod caterpillar with a deep green large head and indistinctly segmented body. It scrapes the leaf surface, spins a white tissue paper-thin web over the scraped surface to remain hidden inside, and as many as four of them may be seen within a single web. There are 5 larval instars, each of 5 to 7 days' duration. In each moult, the form of the body remains the same except the change in colour and size. These caterpillars, upto the fourth instar, do not show much movement and consume very little food. The fifth or the final instar larva is blackish and measures 53 mm in length and 6.7 mm in width which does not spin web but lie exposed and feed actively. It is gregarious and sun loving, and frequently perforates the leaf as it bites. Being a voracious feeder, it damages the crop when in great numbers. After 6 days, it goes underground or sticks to some leaf surface for pupation (Mukerji, 1961).

The pupae of *P. brassicae* exhibit diapause and the incidence of diapause increases from 0 to 100% when the larvae experience an increasing number of long-night cycles during their sensitive period, while being kept in continuous darkness during the remainder of their development. About 5 long-nights are required to induce diapause in 50 per cent of the insects, 7 long-night cycles are needed to raise diapause incidence to 100 per cent. The inductive "strength" of nights of 16 and 40 h long appears to be the same, indicating that nights of 40 h long are not measured twice by the photoperiodic clock, which would be expected if the clock is a Circardian oscillator or a complex of circadian osillators. The photoperiodic clock in *P. brassicae*, therefore, seems to be hourglass rather than a self-sustained oscillator (Veerman *et al.* 1988).

The pupa is non-feeding, immobile, brown and has wing-cases, apendages and segments indistinctly marked. The pupation period is 11 days and the life-history is completed in about 50 days (Mukerji, 1961). The life span of adults is 4-5 days (Ghosh, 1914).

3.7.1.4 *Chemical control*

The chemicals recommended against cabbage butterfly are: Fenvalerate (-.01%), malathion (0.1%) and dichlorovos (0.1%) (Mumtaz *et al.* 1991).

3.7.2 Crucifer Butterfly, *Pieris brassicae nepalensis* Doubleday
(Lepidoptera: Pieridae)

The butterfly that attacks cruciferous plants in Nepal is *P. brassicae nepalensis* Doubleday. It is commonly found in the southern Himalayas and Tibet where large breeding grounds occur (Chuang-Lung, 1962). The adults of *P. brassicae nepalensis* emerge in early January from their over wintered pupae. In the field, the number of eggs laid per cluster ranged from 20 to 235 (mean 101), 88 per cent of egg masses were laid on the lower leaf surface, usually on the apical portion of the plant. Larval infestation in the field was highest in late March to early April when the population was at its peak. There were 4 generations of the butterfly from early January to late April. The adults survived for about 3 days (Thapa, 1987).

3.7.2.1 *Natural enemies*

Larval parasites: *Apanteles glomeratus* L. (*Cotesia glomerata*), *Pteromalus puparum*, *Diadegma pierisae* and *Anilastus ebeninus* (*Hyposter ebeninus*) (Mushtaque, 1989; Rawat *et al.* 1990; Thapa, 1987). The eulophid, *Eutetrastichus galactopus* (*Acanthocerus galeator*) hyperparasitizes *A. glomeratus* (Rawat *et al.* 1990). The larvae of cabbage bufferfly are also destroyed by birds (*Passer domesticus* and *Pycnonotus* sp.), lizards and spiders (Thapa, 1987).

3.8 FLEA BEETLES, Phyllotreta spp.

(Coleoptera: Chrysomelidae)

Flea beetles or the chrysomelid pests are of common occurrence in both the plains and hilly regions of India. They are prevalent in Assam, Bihar, Madhya Pradesh, Orissa, Punjab, West Bengal and Uttar Pradesh causing moderate to fairly serious damage to rapeseed and mustard at the seedling stage (Batra, 1969; Gupta, 1945; Narayanan, 1958; Pl. Prot. Bull. 1959). Flea beetles have not been studied in details in India.

A number of species of the genus *Phyllotreta*, in both larval and adult stage, attack cruciferous crops. In India, *Phyllotreta cruciferae* Goeze is the most important pest, though heavy infestation of the mustard crop at late stage of development by *P. chotanica* Duvivier in West Bengal has been observed (Banerjee & Basu, 1955b; Narayanan, 1958). *Phyllotreta cruciferae* is also a common pest in Europe, North Africa and the erstwhile USSR. Four species of Phyllotreta are known to attack oilseed rape (*B. napus* L. and *B. campestris* L.) in the Canadian prairie provinces. These, in order of abundance and seriousness as pest are: *P. cruciferae, P. striolata* F., *P. albionica* Lec., and *P. robusta* Lec. (Burgess, 1977). In America and Europe, both *P. cruciferae* and *P. striolata* are important (Feeny *et al.* 1970).

3.8.1 Damage

The flea beetles are very active pests. Adults feed on the cotyledons and slender stems of young cruciferous plants and make small holes in the leaves as the plants grow, giving them a very characteristic spotted effect (Lefroy, 1906). Feeding damage to cotyledons and tender leaves of young plants during spring is the major cause of crop loss in Canada. In case of severe attack, the seedlings may wilt and die, necessitating re-sowing. It delays crop maturity and reduces seed yield. When the beetles attack the green, semi-maturing rape crops in late summer, they quickly devour the epidermis of stems, leaves and pods, hindering development of seeds, and increasing their chlorophyll content and affecting oil quality. Pod feeding also causes shattering and fungal growth on them (Burgess, 1977; Lamb, 1980, 1984; Lamb & Turnock, 1982; Putnam, 1977). The larvae of most *Phyllotreta* spp. feed on roots but no major effect on plant vigour or growth due to such feeding has been reported except about 5 per cent yield loss resulting from larval density of $1600/m^2$ (Bracken & Bucher, 1986; Burgess, 1977). The flea beetles are most active under sunny, warm and dry weather while cool, damp weather or strong surface winds reduce their feeding intensity (Burgess, 1977). They are also the vectors of turnip crinkle and turnip yellows mosaic viruses (Bonnemaison, 1965).

3.8.2 Host range

Phyllotreta cruciferae causes serious damage to mustard beside attacking other cruciferous plants like cabbage, Brussels sprouts, cauliflower, radish, turnip, etc. in India (Narayanan, 1958). Adults of both *P. cruciferae* and *P. striolata* have more or less an identical host range, restricted only to plants belonging to the families Capparidaceae, Cruciferae, Tropaeolaceae, and Limnanthaceae (Fenny *et al.* 1970).

Phyllotreta cruciferae exhibits two distinctive leaf feeding patterns, the edge and random feeding. Edge feeding occurs in the monogenic diploid *B. oleracea* group and the digenic amphidiploid *B. napus* group of plants, due to physical and/or chemical factors, that render their leaf unpalatable or difficult to feed upon or both. The feeding rate was estimated to be about 1/10 of that observed from random feeding in all other agronomic groups (Bodnaryk, 1992).

The flea beetles usually feed more on the upper surfaces, bases and edges of cotyledons, and first true leaves, and the feeding patterns are not identical on the four species of Brassicaceae, *B. juncea* L. ("Cutlass"), *B. napus* L. ("Westar"), *B. rapa* L. (=*B. campestris* L.) ("Tobin"), and *Sinapis alba* L. ("Ochre"). *Phyllotreta cruciferae* shows a greater preference for the upper surface of *S. alba* cotyledons than the upper surfaces of *Brassica* species. No significant difference was observed in the amount of stem damage for the four species.

A chemical attraction, rather than response to colour, texture, toughness, pubescence or nutrient balance of plants, is considered to represent the basis for host plant selection by these flea beetles. The precise correlation between susceptibility of attack by both *P. cruciferae* and *P. striolata* and the occurrence of thioglucosides among the host plants suggest the possibility that these compounds or their metabolic relatives are the chemicals responsible for host plant selection (Fenny *et al*. 1970). On the other hand, the "Canola" cultivars of oilseed rape, with low levels of glucosinolates or erucic acid, were not found to have consistently lower or higher survival than cultivars with higher levels of these chemicals in their seeds. The reduced glucosinolates or erucic acid levels in the seed of oilseed rape do not affect the susceptibility of the crop to flea beetle damage. The attractants and feeding stimuli in Canola are not known, but obviously Canola seedlings produce them in sufficient quantity to allow the flea beetles to exploit effectively the chemically modified crop (Lamb, 1988). The feeding rate of *P. cruciferae* is not also affected when either the sinigrin content of cotyledons present at emergence declines during the growth of mustard seedlings or the glucobrassicin content of cotyledons increases during the growth of rape seedlings, all these indicate that glucosinolates do not influence the feeding rate of the flea beetle (Bodnaryk & Palaniswami, 1990). Possibly, the food plant preference of *P. cruciferae* is associated with both chemical and morphological differences between cultivars and between plants of different ages within cultivars (Vaughn & Hoy 1993).

3.8.3 Life history

Phyllotreta cruciferae measuring about 2 mm long, with enlarged hind fumora and having a habit of jumping, is black in colour with bright blue or brown lustre. Mating pairs of flea beetles are found on cruciferous plants on warm, sunny days (Burgess, 1977). The mating between adult male and female beetles occurs about 2-4 days after their emergence from pupae and eggs are laid within 1-2 days. Eggs are mostly laid singly, sometime in lots of 2-3 in soil near the food plant. *Phyllotreta cruciferae* may lay about 25 eggs in a batch (Newton, 1928). Life span of a female ranges from 45-60 days and it lays 50-80 eggs. The larvae hatch out in 5-10 days and feed on the roots of the host plant. There are 3 larval instars, each lasting 3-6 days. The larvae wriggle out of root holes and make earthen cells in the neighbourhood of infected roots. The duration of pre-pupal and pupal stages varies from 2-4 and 8-14 days, respectively. In India, the adult beetles are active in the field throughout the year except during the winter months of November to January, when they over-winter in the top soil, in litters and other available shelters. Adults emerge from hibernation in February and start feeding on cruciferous plants including mustard. Peak emergence of new generation of adults in India takes place during April to June, they thrive on cultivated or wild cruciferous plants during July to September and then migrate to mustard crop in October (Burgess, 1977; Varma, 1961). There is no difference in longevity between males and females feeding on the same host plant (Peng *et al.* 1992).

3.8.4 Natural enemies

The braconid, *Microctonus indicus* parasitizes adults of *P. cruciferae* in India (Narayanan *et al.* 1960). Adults and nymphs of *Nabis alternatus* (Hemiptera: Nabidae) (Burgess, 1982) and *Gryllus pensylvanicus* Burmeister prey on adults of *P. cruciferae* (Burgess & Hinks, 1987). Lace wing larvae, *Chrysopa carnea* Steph. (Neuroptera: Chrysopidae) attack the adults of both *P. cruciferae* and *P. striolata* (Burgess, 1980).

3.8.5 Control

a. Chemicals

Seed-dressing with chemicals is more economical and more effective than is pre-sowing soil treatment (Bonnemaison, 1965). However, furrow application of granular insecticides like carbofuran, phorate, and BPHC [2-(1-methyl proply) phenyl methyl carbamate] is recommended in India (Singh *et al.* 1980b).

Lindane, diazinon or endosulfan are also effective pesticides (Bonnemaison, 1965). Neem based formulations like Safer's Neem insecticide, RD-9 Repelin at 0.05-12.0% conc. a.i., are effective as repellent (Palaniswamy & Wise, 1994).

b. Sources of resistance

Line C8711, a selection of *B. rapa* cv. Tobin, the inbred line L 19 of *B. napus* (Lamb *et al.* 1993a,b) and yellow mustard, *S. alba* are resistant to flea beetle damage in Canada, and antixenosis (non-preference) and tolerance are considered to be the two mechanisms of host resistance (Bodnaryk & Lamb, 1991). Antixenosis is genetically controlled involving 2 or more genes (Lamb *et al.* 1993a). Adult *P. cruciferae* fed actively on leaves of *B. juncea*, *B. napus* and *B. rapa* (*B. campestris*) with low antixenosis, and *B. carinata* and *Sinapsis alba* with moderate antixenosis but not on *Thlaspi arvense* with high antixenosis. No antibiosis was detected in any of the Brassica species or in *S. alba*. *Phyllotreta cruciferae* did not fed on highly antixenotic leaves of *T. arvense* probably to avoid suffering from antibiosis. The level of antibiosis vary less among Brassica species and related plants than does antixenosis, and hence the latter is considered to be a more promising type of resistance for use against *P. cruciferae* in rape (Palaniswamy *et al.* 1997).

3.9 POLLEN BEETLE, *Meligethes aeneus* Fabricius

(Coleoptera: Nitidulidae)

Meligethes aeneus Fabricius, popularly known as the pollen or blossom beetle, is the most abundant and easily recognized insect pest found associated with oilseed rape (*Brassica napus*) in

Europe, North Africa, the erstwhile USSR, Western Asia and North America (Bonnemaison, 1965; Pimentel, 1961; Winfield, 1961a). It is not a pest of rapeseed and mustard in India.

Meligethes aeneus attacks both winter and spring rape, the time and degree of infestation being influenced by the maximum daily temperature. The adult insects emerge from hibernation in the spring (Williams, 1980) when the temperature, moisture content and the carbon dioxide level of the soil become suitable for the resumption of their activity (Bonnemaison, 1965). After emergence, they feed on different host plants during which their ovaries mature (Williams, 1980). The beetle is sensitive to three colour ranges. It shows positive responses to ultra violet to dark blue and light green to orange colour but is repellant to light blue to dark green colour (Nolte, 1959).

3.9.1 Damage

The chief injury to the plant is caused by over wintered adults which feed on the interior of un-opened flower buds and destroy the pistil resulting in loss of seed yield. Cabbage, cauliflower, swede, rape, radish, *Barbarea vulgaris* and wild mustard (*Sinapis arvensis*) are the food plants on which oviposition occurs. When the plants flower, the beetles feed chiefly on the pollens due to which some of the stamens and pistils are also destroyed (Aksenova, 1929), and only a small proportion of buds and flowers drop due to injury (Williams, 1980; Williams & Free, 1978). However, auxillary racemes that spring rape plants putforth (Tatchell, 1977) following pollen beetle damage, causes uneven ripening and difficulties at harvest time (Winfield, 1986).

The beetles show greater preference for cruciferous buds and stamens to petals and leaves; stamens laden with mature pollen are most preferred and anthers are preferred to filaments; stamens from spring cultivars of rape are preferred differently; stamens from *B. campestris* are preferred to those from rape (cv. Gullivar); stamens from Compositae are much less preferred than rape stamens but more preferred than those from *Rosa pimpinellifolia,* whereas stamens from *Papaver dubium* are less preferred to rape leaves (Charpentier, 1985).

3.9.2 Life history

The pollen beetle is a very shiny greenish-black, oval, 2.5 mm long univoltine insect with clubbed antennae. The life cycle from egg to adult lasts for about 33 days. The mass emergence of the over wintered adults from the soil occurs at the end of May to early June in Tomsk region, Russia. Pairing begins within 7-10 days of emergence from hibernation, and oviposition chiefly occurs at the end of June to early July. The eggs are very small, elongate and creamy white. They are laid in the uninjured flower buds between the anthers and the ovary, singly or in batches of 5-8, and are fixed on the stamens with a sticky secretion. A female lays an average of 40 eggs. About 62 per cent of them hatched on the third day at 18-19°C and the rest on the fourth day. The larvae, which are also creamy white, moult twice, as many as ten of the first instar larvae may develop in one bud (Aksenova, 1929).

As the flower buds open, the larvae feed on pollens but do not cause any damage to flower (Williams & Free, 1978). The larvae feed for about two weeks to become mature and then drop to the ground for pupation. The new generation of beetles emerges in late June to early July on winter rape, and in mid to late July on spring rape in Britain. After a few weeks of feeding, they enter over-wintering sites (Williams, 1980).

Infestation of winter rape by adults begins in early to second half of April or even in May before flowering or as the flower opens, and the maximum temperature exceeds 15°C. Infestation reaches maximum by mid-May with the appearance of larvae in the crops which are in full flowers. The pest population declines rapidly during late May to early June and the beetles leave the crop in search of new hosts though the plants may continue to flower for sometime (Williams, 1980; Williams & Free, 1978).

During spring, pest infestation keeps pace with crop growth, beetle population increases rapidly during early June before flowering and reaches the peak before mid June as the flower buds unfold (Free & Williams, 1979; Williams, 1980). In mid-June, the population of beetles declines rapidly till a new generation of adults emerge from pupation (Williams, 1980).

3.9.3 Trap crops

Sunflower, marigold, chinese cabbage and calabrese (Husberg *et al.* 1985) may be used as trap crop to reduce the population of pollen beetles in the field.

3.9.4 Natural enemies

Hymenoptera parasites, *Isorgus* spp., *Diospilus* spp., and *Aneulis* spp. parasitize the larvae of *M. aeneus*. Besides, the Coleopterous predators and nematodes also destroy the larvae and pupae of the pollen beetle (Jourdheuil, 1960).

3.9.5 Chemical control

For effective control, chemicals should be applied at the beginning of but not during flowering. Insecticides which are non-toxic to the bees such as endosulfan, pyrenone, methoxychlor and fenitrothion are preferable. Diazinon is also an effective chemical against pollen beetle (Bonnemaison, 1965; Hansen, 1984).

3.10 CABBAGE SEED WEEVIL *Ceutorhynchus assimilis* Paykull

(Coleoptera: Curculionidae)

The cabbage seed weevil, *Ceutorhynchus assimilis* Paykull is another important pest of oilseed rape (*Brassica napus*) in England as well as in continental Europe and North America (Alford *et al.* 1991). It has not been reported from India. The weevils are attracted towards the odours from both the flowering and green parts of rape plant. Isothiocyanates (3-butenyl, 4-pentenyl and 2-phenylethyl isothiocyanates), alongwith other volatiles from rape probably play a role in host plant recognition by the seed weevil (Bartlet *et al.* 1993).

3.10.1 Life history

The cabbage seed weevil is a black to gray insect with a long narrow snout and is about one-eighth inch long. It over-winters as a hibernating adult in debris and soil, and emerges in late March to early April depending on the flowering of cruciferous hosts under conditions of Central California (Carlson *et al.* 1951). They feed on the flower buds, flower ovaries, pods and stem tips without causing ovule abortion (Williams & Free, 1978) and their feeding/egg-laying punctures in the pods provide sites for laying eggs by brassica pod midge.

Mating takes place soon after emergence. Oviposition is accomplished through the puncture made in the developing seed pods by means of the female's snout and mouth parts. Each act of oviposition into a pod is followed by specific and fixed behaviour in which females brush the pod surface with a brush like structure in the ovipositor providing chemical marking of the pod surface to avoid repeated oviposition in the same pod (Kozolowski *et al.* 1983). The pearl-white, ovoid eggs are laid singly within the pods, adjacent to the seed embroys, and hatch within a few days. The small, white grubs feed on the seed embryos within the seed pods for about three weeks. About five to six seeds are eaten by each grub (Carlson *et al.* 1951). The grubs cut a hole in the pod and drop to the soil for pupation. They burrow into the soil to a depth of one-half to two inches and construct a small earthen cell; pupation lasts for about four weeks. The adults emerge from the soil and fly/crawl to the plants in early May where they feed till August. This new generation of adults along with their over-wintered parents continue to feed on the buds and flowers. Only one generation of weevils per season is known to occur, but there is overlapping of the two seasons' adults. The population of new generation of weevils is highest in June-July when seed pods are maturing. They feed primarily on the late succulent pods, stems, and foliage (Carlson *et al.* 1951; Hanson *et al.* 1948). After completion of feeding, the new generation of adults go into hibernation until the next season (Carlson *et al.* 1951).

3.10.2 Natural enemies

Xenocrepis pura Myar, *Amblymerus mayetiolae* Gahan, *Trimeromicrus maculatus* Gahan, *Trichomalus fasciatus* Thomson, and *Spilochalcis side* Walk. (Carlson *et al.* 1951; Heymons, 1921).

3.10.3 Control

The following measures may be adopted for its control:

a. Collection and destruction of adults and deep ploughing under of the stubbles after crop harvest.
b. Recommended insecticides like lindane (Carlson *et al.* 1951), traizophos @ 400 g/ha or phosalone @ 470 g/ha may be sprayed at the end of the flowering season (Alford *et al.* 1978).
c. Sources of resistance

Seed weevil larvae attack only plants of Brassica and Raphanus. *Brassica hirta (alba)* (white mustard) and *B. nigra* (black mustard) seem to be immune while *B. kaber (arvensis)* is highly resistant to the pest. Radish seed pods are relatively more tolerant than Brassica pods though there is considerable damage to their seeds. *Brassica juncea* and *B. campestris* are moderately susceptible, the latter species is the most important single host involved in natural spread of the weevil and in the maintenance of its population in areas where there is no commercial production of susceptible seed crops. Garden types of several Brassica species such as Chinese cabbage, turnip, Kohlrabi, Kale, Brussels sprouts and Rutabaga also show considerable variations in their susceptibility to the seed weevil attack (Doucette, 1947).

3.11 STEM WEEVIL, *Ceutorhynchus quadridens* Panzer.

(Coleoptera: Curculionidae)

Syn: *Ceutorhynchus pallidactylus Marsham.*

The stem weevil, *Ceutorhynchus quadridens* Panzer, though widespread in occurrence, is considered to be a minor pest of oilseed rape and mustard in England, but it facilitates the entry of disease causing organisms like *Leptosphaeria maculans* that may cause pre-mature lodging of plants. It is not known to occur in India. *Ceutorhynchus quadridens* has one generation in a year. The adults are about 3 mm long and brownish-black in colour with a small patch of white scales in the centre of the back. They over-winter near the surface of the soil or beneath the debris and appear in large numbers during April to May as the conditions become favourable with air temperature above 12°C (Dmoch, 1959; Gunthart, 1949). They start feeding on the rapidly growing early spring-sown crops and on the enlarging racemes of over-wintered rape. The eggs are preferably laid in clusters of 3-5 in blisters in leaf mid vein ribs, in the petioles and sometimes in stems over a period of weeks depending on temperature and crop stand, until about mid-June. The eggs are translucent, oval and are about 0.4×0.6 mm in size. The blisters rupture to expose the eggs and when hatched, the young learvae with a distinct yellow-brown head, tunnel in the leaf veins, stalks and main stem. Eventually, the larvae tunnel into the stem and destroy the pith. Later, they leave the host by conspicuous exit holes and pupate in the soil (Winfield, 1961b, 1992).

3.11.1 Chemical control

Treatment with carbofuran or phorate granules reduces larval infestation. Sprays of the mixture of azinophos methyl and demeton-S-methyl sulphone (Graham & Gould, 1980), triazophos and chlorpyriphos also reduce stem infestation. In fact, it often remains in check on spring rape and mustard due to treatment applied for other pests such as blossom beetle and seed weevil (Winfield, 1986).

3.12 *GUJHIA* WEEVIL

3.12.1 *Gujhia* Weevil, *Tanymecus indicus indicus* Faust.

(Coleoptera: Curculionidae)

Syn: *Tanymecus indicus Faust.*

Tanymecus indicus indicus Faust., known as the *Gujhia* weevil in Punjab or *Godela* in Uttar Pradesh, India, is a widely distributed polyphagous pest that attacks a wide variety of crop plants (Supare *et al.* 1990). The pest was first noted in 1891 damaging opium (*Papaver somniferum*) at Ghazipur in Uttar Pradesh (Cotes, 1896). Later, severe infestation of this weevil was noted on rice seedlings in West Bengal (Banerjee & Basu, 1954), on wheat, maize and millets in Bihar (Pant &

Kalode, 1964), and on gram, rape and mustard in Punjab where the infestation in some areas was so high that re-sowing was necessary (Singh & Singh, 1964). The *Gujhia* weevil was also reported as serious pest of germinating rabi crops and less frequently of barley and poppy in north India (Pradhan, 1969).

3.12.1.1 Damage

Both grubs and adults damage the crop by feeding on the roots and cutting the seedlings at or below the soil surface (Singh & Gurham, 1960). The adults of *T. indicus indicus* start emerging from early June and are seen in the field till December. The adult weevils are few in June, followed by their mass emergence in July after the monsoon rains, and the population continues to increase till the beginning of August. The seasonal variation in population is governed by soil temperature, hiding places on food plants or ground, food condition and temperature. The adults feed on aerial parts of various kharif crops upto October. Then they come down to the soil surface, migrate to the rabi crops, live beneath the loose clods of soil and damage the mustard seedlings in their hypocotyl region above the ground level. Plants of about one week old are damaged by cutting off or puncturing holes into leaves. A single weevil can nibble two mustard seedlings within a week of their germination and the extent of damage to crops depends on the density of their population.

3.12.1.2 Life history

The adult weevils, which enjoy fairly long life, are incapable of flight. In Punjab, they emerge in June-July and start copulating around mid-October when they become sexually mature. Adults copulate day and night irrespective of temperature, and mating may be repeated 3-5 times a day. Oviposition starts towards the middle of November. The pre-ovipositon period ranges from 20-25 days (av. 23 days). Females oviposit both day and night. A female lays about 6-76 eggs (av. 40 eggs) singly on the soil surface, under loose clods and in crevices. On an average, the oviposition period lasts for 35 days and the post-oviposition period for 20 days. The females remain alive for 6-49 days (av. 20 days) after laying of eggs. The eggs are swollen, black and shining. The incubation period lasts for 43-50 days (av. 46 days). The grubs are found in the soil between 6-16″ (max.26″) depth and larval period varies from 11-16 weeks. Pupation takes place in the soil at depths of 6-24″ in specially constructed earthen cells. The pupation starts in mid-March, lasts for 7-9 weeks and is completed by the third week of April. The adults are formed by the third week of May and the weevils emerge on the soil surface in June in irrigated fields with the sowing of kharif crops and thus the insect passes through one generation in a year. The average life span of males and females is 215.80 ± 6.11 days and 212.35 ± 6.21 days, respectively and the average male and female ratio is 48:52 (Singh & Singh, 1964).

3.12.1.3 Chemical control

Soil application of 5% BHC or 5% aldrin dust @ 20 kg/ha in furrow and raking it into the soil or dusting the crop with 5% BHC @ 15-20 kg/ha were the early recommendations against the *Gujhia* weevil (Pradhan, 1969). Since the use of these chemicals is now banned (Farooqi, 1994), insecticides like aldicarb, carbofuran or phorate as soil applicant, and endosulfan, oxydemeton methyl, phosphamidon or quinalphos as foliar spray may be tried for its control.

3.12.2 *Gujhia* Weevil, *Tanymecus indicus assamensis* Supare, sub.sp. nov.

(Coleoptera: Curculionidae)

This new sub species has been described from Assam in 1990. Populations of *Tanymecus indicus assamensis* Supare differ from the populations of *T. indicus indicus* from other locations in their external morphology. Individuals of *T. indicus assamensis* are comparatively darker and smaller (av. body length and breadth 6.31 and 2.15 mm, respectively as against 7.78 and 2.55 mm, in *T. indicus indicus*); central carina on the prothorax complete; elytral vestiture with scales relatively fine and small; besides a few other genitalic differences in the two species (Supare *et al.* 1990).

3.13 SAWFLY

3.13.1 Mustard Sawfly, *Athalia proxima* Klug

(Hymenoptera: Tenthredinidae)

Syn: *Athalia lugens proxima* Klug

Athalia proxima is a major defoliating pest of mustard, rape and other young cruciferous plants throughout India. Mustard sawfly is probably a migrant from the mountains that has established itself in the plains of north India (Arora & Kaur, 1963). It is seen towards the middle of September and the pestilence persists upto the second week of March with peak period of activity during the months of November, December and January (Kelkar, 1977; Srivastava *et al.* 1972; Tripathi, 1963). It is a serious pest in Assam valley, West Bengal, Bihar, Madhya Pradesh, Bombay, Poona, Coimbatore and Mysore (Narayanan, 1958).

3.13.1.1 Damage

Athalia proxima causes serious damage to young seedlings, its grubs either riddle the entire leaves or cause numerous shot holes by excessive feeding. The grubs feed in the morning and evening, descending to the ground by day (Lefroy, 1906). The damage caused by mustard sawfly in certain years is so serious that re-sowing becomes a necessity (Narayanan, 1958). At Pantnagar, UP, higher grub population of sawfly was seen on 2-week old seedlings of all cultivars of rapeseed and mustard with maximum population on 30th October sown crops. Thereafter, the infestation declined substantially (Verma & Sachan, 1997). As the seedlings grow up, the damage due to the pest becomes insignificant.

3.13.1.2 Host range

The pest, though named mustard sawfly, is by no means restricted to feeding on mustard. It is a specific feeder and its grubs are known to complete development on 15 plant species belonging to the genera Brassica, Raphanus and Tropaeolum. It feeds on violet, cress (Fletcher, 1919b), lettuce (Gupta, 1956), *Senebiera didyma* Pers.(a weed) (Bindra & Mehra, 1964), candytuft and wallflower.

Non-cruciferous hosts are hardly of any importance as no economic damage is caused to these plants. (Bogawat, 1967).

Brassica campestris (vars. Toria, Brown Sarson and Yellow Sarson), *B. rapa* (turnip), *B. carinata*, *B. napus*, *B. juncea* and *B. oleracea* var. *capitata* suffer more feeding damage by *A. proxima* in the field as compared to *B. oleracea* var. *gongyloides*, *B. oleracea* var. *botrytis*, candytuft and Tropaeolum sp. (Sehgal *et al.* 1975).

All plant species on which grubs feed are not used by adult sawflies for laying eggs (Lal, 1953). Mustard (*B. nigra*) is the most preferred host both for feeding by the grub and oviposition by the adult, and the chemical factor, sinigrin in mustard acts as the phagostimulant (Bogawat & Srivastava, 1968). This is followed by Rai (*B. juncea*), turnip, radish, cauliflower and cabbage in order of host preferences by the pest (Bindra & Mehra, 1964; Bogawat, 1967; Srivastava, 1957). The pest shows very little attraction to candytuff and cress for oviposition and does not at all oviposit on lettuce and wallflower (Bogawat, 1967). However, plant species within the host range are exploited by the pest with varying degree of success, based on an assessment of oviposition preferences and survival of the adult stage. On the other hand, there is heavy pest mortality on distantly related species like *Eruca sativa*, *Tropaeolum majus*, candytuft, wallflower and *B. napus* indicating that these possess strong natural defences against exploitation by members of this insect species (Sehgal & Ujagir, 1977). This was evident from a study on the development biology and ovipositional preferences of *A. proxima* on *B. juncea* leaves treated with extracts containing glucosinolates and isothiocyanates prepared from the seeds of *B. campestris*, *B. juncea*, *B. napus*, *E. sativa* and *T. majus*. Treatment of *B. juncea* leaves with seed extracts from *B. napus*, *E. sativa* and *T. majus* acted as feeding depressants for the grubs and had more adverse effects on the development biology and ovipositional preferences as compared to effects obtained from treatment with extracts from *B. campestris* and *B. juncea* indicating that the members of this insect species have overcome the chemical barrier in *B. juncea* and *B. campestris* plants through more successful adaptations (Ahuja & Sehgal, 1982a,b). These observations are confirmed by the report that Toria (*B. campestris* var. Toria) was very suitable for rearing *A. proxima* whereas *B. napus* was the most unsuitable host. Larvae did not feed on *Camelina sativa* and complete larval mortality took place on *E. sativa* (Singh & Sachan, 1997). Further, consumption and utilization of protein, lipids and the C.A.D-protein (coefficient of apparent digestibility for protein) in the food consumed by the grub of *A. proxima* were higher on *B. campestris*, *B. juncea* and *B. rapa* than on any other plants tested showing that they are the more suitable host plants (Sharma *et al.* 1988).

3.13.1.3 Life history

Mustard sawfly is a very inconspicuous insect, the imago looks like a fly with a rather short thick-set body marked with black and orange, and with two pairs of dark wings (Lefroy, 1906). Adult mustard sawflies are not swift fliers, they take periodical rest on leaves between flights. The duration of the mating and the pre-oviposition period are short. Mating is frequent and lasts 1 to 4 minutes (Hussain & Chatha, 1981). About a week after the first mating, the females start laying eggs, which are inserted singly in the tissues of leaves around the periphery, within incisions made by their short, sharp saw-like ovipositor. The number of eggs laid by a single sawfly in her life span may vary widely and was 20 (Lefroy & Ghosh, 1908), 16-144 (av. 35) (Narayanan, 1958), 40.2

Fig. 3.6. Grubs of mustard sawfly, *Athalia proxima*. Note their cylindrical shape and markings on the body

(Bogawat, 1967; Tripathi, 1963) or 22.6 (Kapadia *et al.* 1980). *Athalia proxima* also shows differential preference in laying eggs on species and varieties of Brassica. It laid most eggs on *B. juncea* cvs. PR 18 (69.6/plant) and Porbiraya (57.6/plant), and on *Sinapis alba* (47.3/plant). Fewest eggs were found on *B. napus* (4.0-5.0/plant) and *B. carinata* (7.3/plant) (Sachan & Sumati, 1985). The average incubation period of eggs does not vary much, and was 5.05 days in mustard and 5.06 days in radish (Sumithramma *et al.* 1997). The newly-hatched grubs feed on the tender leaves of growing plants and have 6 larval instars. The first instar grub is grey-green, cylindrical in shape with shiny black head capsule but finally it turns black in colour (Fig. 3.6). The larval period varies and lasted from 9 days in summer to 30 days in November (Rai, 1976) or 12-20 days (av. 14.66 days) under laboratory conditions (Kapadia *et al.* 1980).

The fully grown grub enters the soil, spins an elongated oval cocoon of a parchment-like material secreted from its mouth and rests within it for 3-4 days before pupation. A thin layer of earth is cemented over the cocoon, making it water-proof (Verma, 1945). Sometimes these cocoons with pupae inside are formed in between two leaves, the latter held together by the silken strands of the cocoons. The pupal period together with the resting larval stage in cocoons lasted for about 9 days to 14 months in the soil (Narayanan, 1958) and under laboratory conditions for 10-15 days (Kapadia *et al.* 1980). The grub undergoes metamorphosis and emerges as adult completing the life cycle. A temperature range of 25-30°C is favourable for oviposition, and the best development of eggs and larvae takes place at 28°C. The most suitable temperature for the development of pupae and maximum longevity of adult is 25°C (Bogawat *et al.* 1966). In the absence of a clear-cut winter, the pest may pass through as many as ten overlapping generations in a year, depending on climatic factors (Narayanan, 1958). The longevity of females and males was 15.9 and 13.2 days, and 12.5 and 9.6 days on mustard and radish, respectively (Sumithramma *et al.* 1997). The maximum incidence of *A. proxima* was seen in Kanpur, Uttar Pradesh at 22-26°C, 60-82% R.H. and with plant heights at 2.0-5.7 cm (Srivastava & Srivastava, 1972).

3.13.1.4 Natural enemies

A number of natural enemies keep down the population of *A. proxima* by causing mortality of its grubs. The grubs are parasitized by the ichneumonid, *Perilissus cingulator* Morley (Dutt, 1914; Fletcher, 1919a). They are also attacked by the last instar nymphs and adults of *Cantheconidia furcellata* Wolff (David & Basheer, 1961). The mortality of grubs is also caused by the bacterium *Serratia marcescens* Bizio (Bogawat *et al.* 1966).

3.13.1.5 Control

Hand-picking of sawfly grubs in the morning and at dusk offers most effective method of its control if the area affected is small. The grubs can be easily collected and killed by shaking the seedlings over small containers filled with Kerosenized water (Jotwani & Phadke, 1982). Ploughing up of the soil in between the rows of plants exposes the hibernating pupae to prey for birds and predators, etc. (Narayanan, 1958).

Treatment of mustard seeds with lindane and phorate at 2.5 kg and 1.0 kg/100 kg seeds, respectively protects the seedlings against sawfly grubs upto 28 days after germination (Jotwani *et al.* 1968). Pre-sowing soil treatment with granular phorate or mephosfolan (Cytrolane) at 2 kg/ha is also very effective against the grubs of *A. proxima* (Pareek & Gupta, 1977). Similarly, soil application of 5% granular disulfoton at the rate of 1.5 kg/ha and irrigating the crop at the seedling stage considerably minimize the pest incidence and increase the crop yield by accelerating the plant growth (Singh *et al.* 1979). Alternatively, phorate applied at the rates of 1.15 and 2.25 g/m in furrows at a depth of 6 cm at the time of sowing remains very effective against the grubs of *A. proxima* for 24 and 29 days, respectively (Verma, 1980). Spray application of phosphamidon at 0.04% a.i./ha after 20 and 50 days of crop growth reduced the incidence of both *A. proxima* and *Lipaphis erysimi* on Chinese cabbage (Ram *et al.* 1987). Quinalphos (0.025%) also provides effective control of the pest (Patel *et al.* 1994).

Soil amendment with phosphorus (P_2O_5) and potassium (K_2O) at 75 kg/ha and 45 kg/ha, respectively reduced the incidence of sawfly whereas a high dose of nitrogen (75 kg/ha) increased its incidence (Ram & Gupta, 1992).

3.13.2 Rape Sawfly, *Athalia rosae* L.

(Hymenoptera: Tenthredinidae)

Syn: *Athalia colibri* Christ.

Athalia rosae L. is an important pest of turnip and many other cruciferous crops like swede, cabbage, rape and mustard (*Sinapis alba*), the latter being one of the most infested crop in Berlin (Reich, 1961a). *Athalia rosae* is a destructive insect pest of cruciferous plants in many countries but it has not been reported from India.

3.13.2.1 Life history

Generally, *A. rosae* has 2-3 generations in a year (Reich, 1961a; Riggert, 1939). Females predominate but the males fly actively and pair more than once. Oviposition began two days after emergence of adults at 30°C, and after a longer period at lower temperature. At an average daily temperature of 18°C, oviposition normally began 7 days after emergence and continued throughout the life of the female. Plentiful supply of mustard flowers are necessary for high rate of oviposition. Oviposition or larval feeding was observed only on crucifers (Reich, 1961a).

Eggs are laid on both wild and cultivated crucifers. They are laid singly at the edge of the leaf between the parenchyma and epidermis of the lower surface, with upto 35 eggs in a single leaf (Riggert, 1939; Verzhutskii, 1967). The females live somewhat longer than males, and they laid more eggs (average 131.7) at 18-20°C than at higher temperatures. Eggs laid by unfertilized females give rise to males only (Riggert, 1939). The duration of egg stage ranged from about 10 days at 16° to about 3 days at 25°C (Reich, 1961a) and at an average temperature of 17-18°C, it lasted 7-10 days (Verzhutskii, 1967).

Eggs hatch in 4-7 days in the field and in 4-12 days in the laboratory depending on the temperature. The newly hatched larvae feed on the lower surface of the leaves, but towards the end of the feeding period they migrate to the upper surface and feed at the edges. The larvae are always present in numbers and damage the leaves of plants. After the fifth moult, they spin cocoons in the soil and enter the eonymphal stage, in which they over winter (Riggert, 1939). Entry of larvae into the soil occurred almost rapidly at soil humidities of 4-15 per cent. Temperatures are the determining factor for the entry of *A. rosae* into prolonged diapause in the eonymphal stage, dryness of soil has no effect (Reich, 1961b). Day-length or photoperiod also profoundly affects the release of diapause of *A. rosae*. The critical daily photoperiod of larvae reared at 18 or 20°C was 14-15 hours, below which all individuals entered into eonymphal diapause, complete or near complete darkness precluded it and diapause became less frequent. At 28°C, the critical day-length was about 13 hours, but few individuals entered diapause (Saringer 1964).

In spring, the larvae develop to the pronymphal stage and then pupate, the actual pupal stage lasting about 4-8 days at 16°C. In cases of delayed development in the cocoon stage, the adults emerged about 20 months after the cocoons were formed (Riggert, 1939; Verzhutskii, 1967). The weather is very important in regulating the population, cool damp conditions being highly unfavourable to the pest at all stages (Reich, 1961b).

3.13.2.2 Natural enemies

Parasites bred from *A. rosae* comprised the tachinids, *Tachina rustica* Mg., and *Meigenia mutabilis* Fall.; the ichneumonids, *Mesoleius ciliatus* Hlmgr., *Perilissus lutescens* Hlmgr., *Acanthocryptus flagitator* Grav. and *Anilastus* sp.; the perilampid, *Perilampus italicus* F.; and the nematode, *Mermis albicans*, but their economic importance is insignificant (Riggert, 1939). The adults of *A. rosae* are also attacked by *Formica picea* Nyl., *Tenthredo fulva* Klug and *T. omissa* Forst, and the larva is parasitized by Diptera (Verzhutskii, 1967).

3.13.2.3 Chemical control

Dusts of derris or pyrethrum are preferable insecticides against *A. rosae* for vegetables or fodder plants (Riggert, 1939). Dust of diazinon, and sprays of malathion, chlorithion and trichlorphan (Dipterex) are effective (Reich, 1962). Borg (1956) obtained high larval mortality of *A. rosae* by soil treatment with 50% malathion and 1% Diazinon.

Application of light exposure for 30 minutes, 3 and 8 hours after the onset of night darkness in autumn from source such as military flare suspended above the field markedly reduced the number of diapausing larvae. Since non-diapausing larvae are unable to overwinter, this type of control measure can be adopted in a situation where the area under the crop is very large (Saringer, 1983).

Ploughing in of volunteer rape plants at the end of July and beginning of August destroys the developing larval population and acts as a green manure (Saringer, 1989) but deep ploughing may not produce the desired effect, since adults emerge even when the cocoons are at a depth of 1 ft (Reich, 1961b).

3.14 LEAF MINER

Cruciferous plants are infested by numerous Diptera of which two flies, *Chromatomyia horticola* Goureau and *Liriomyza brassicae* Railey, the pea leaf miner and the cabbage leaf miner, respectively are the important leaf-mining pests of oilseed brassicas (Sehgal & Trehan, 1963; Trehan & Sehgal, 1963).

3.14.1 Pea Leaf Miner, *Chromatomyia horticola* Goureau (Diptera: Agromyzidae)

Syn: *Phytomyza atricornis* Meigen

Phytomyza horticola Goureau (Singh *et al*. 1991)

Chromatomyia horticola Goureau is the most common and widespread leaf miner that attacks more than 300 known species of plants, both cultivated and wild, in different parts of the world (Spencer, 1973). This pest was first noticed in India in 1909 by Lefroy as a cruciferous leaf miner. Earlier it was identified as *Phytomyza atricornis* Meigen (*Chromatomyia atricornis* Meign) in 1937 causing severe injury to peas and other plants (Ahmad & Gupta, 1941).

Chromatomyia horticola is the commonest polyphagous species of leaf miner in northern India that attacks 105 host plants from among 21 families, out of which 11 hosts belong to the cruciferous family. Its host range includes *Brassica campestris*, *B. juncea*, *B. napus*, *B. oleracea* var. *botrytis* and *Eruca sativa* (Ghani, 1941; Gokulpure, 1966, 1972; Trehan, 1940; Trehan & Sehgal, 1963).

3.14.1.1 Damage

The pest appears in the field during December to early January but is most active during February to April when it causes the most serious damage to Brassica crops (Trehan & Sehgal, 1963). Serious incidence of *C. horticola* on Brown sarson (*B. campestris*) cv. BSH-1 was observed at Himachal Pradesh, India during 1990 and 1992. In both years, the infestation was greatest during the fourth week of February, when the mean maximum temperatures were 15°C and 17.7°C, mean minimum temperatures were 5.5 and 6.5°C and mean relative humidities were 65 and 44 per cent, respectively during 1990 and 1992. Presence of green, succulent foliage combined with a moderate temperature and humidity range are the most favourable conditions for pest infestation (Desh Raj *et al.* 1995).

It is the adult female agromyzid that inflicts the injury to plants. The female punctures the young leaves at several places with its ovipositor for laying eggs and for feeding on the leaf exudates. Serious damage is, however, done by the larva which mines on the upper or lower surface of leaf. The mine starts from the periphery with the insertion of an egg and terminates in a pupal blister (Trehan & Sehgal, 1963). More than 35 per cent of the leaves may be mined and there may be as many as seven mines in a leaf (Narayanan, 1958). Each mine is distinct and contains only one miner although it may anastomose with the adjacent ones. The mines are irregular, zigzug, whitish and linear. Generally, a larva feeds and grows in isolation in its own gallery. It mines into the mesophyll and feeds indiscriminately on pallisade and spongy mesenchymatous tissue of the leaf, but does not consume the entire tissue between the upper and the lower epidermis (Trehan & Sehgal, 1963). Leaf mining flies belonging to genera Chromatomyia and Liriomyza are responsible for an average of 38 per cent of crops loss, which often reaches upto 80 per cent (Singh, 1988).

3.14.1.2 Life History

The adult flies mate 36-48 hours after their emergence from pupal stage. The pre-oviposition period is 4 days. An adult female makes a kind of triangular wound by its ovipositor under the epidermis to lay eggs. Eggs are deposited singly under these scars, and a single female lays about 329-358 eggs in her life time under laboratory conditions. The eggs are colourless, oval to elongate and measure 0.28-0.33 mm × 0.13-0.15 mm. The incubation period is 2 days, larval period 5 days and pupal period 7 days (Ahmad & Gupta, 1941). The puparia are mostly found on the lower surface of leaves in the broader terminal end of the gallery and occassionally near the mid-rib of leaves (Gokulpure, 1966).

3.14.1.3 Natural enemies

The role of parasitism in checking the build up of the population of various agromyzid pests has not yet been seriously investigated. Not much is known about the biology and ecology of their parasites in India (Singh *et al.* 1991). However, a number of hymenopterous parasites are known to parasitise *C. horticola* and to exert a pronounced influence in maintaining the equilibrium of leaf miner population in India. These are:

Solenotus sp. (Ahmad & Gupta, 1941; Ipe, 1987), *Neochrysocharis* sp. (Kaurava *et al.* 1969), *Chrysocharis* sp., *Cirrospilus* sp., *Clostorocerus agromyzae, Hemiptarsenus* sp., *Pediobius* sp., *Tetrastichus* sp. (Gokulpure, 1972; Ipe, 1987), *Diglyphus* sp. (Kumar, 1990; Singh, 1982), *D. isaea, Chrysonotomyia formosa, Chrysonotomyia thakeri, P. acantha, Eulophus* sp. (Singh & Kumar, 1985), *P. indicus, D. horticola, D, mandibularis, D. funicularis* (Khan, 1985) and *Chrysocharis horticola* (Ipe, 1987) *(Fam. Eulophidae); Sphegigaster* sp. (Singh, 1982; Kumar, 1990), *S. stepicola* (Singh & Kumar, 1985) and *Callitula* sp. (Kumar, 1990) *(Fam. Pteromalidae); Opius* sp. (Gokulpure, 1972; Odak *et al.* 1968), *O. phaseoli, O. lantanae* (Gokulpure, 1972; Singh,

1982), *O. turcicus, O. exiguus* (Singh & Kumar, 1985), *Apanteles* sp. and *Bracon* sp. (Kumar, 1990) (*Fam. Braconidae*); and *Afrostilba* sp. (Singh, 1982) (*Fam. Eucoilidae*).

Chrysonotomyia formosa, D. isaea, O. turcicus, O. exiguus and *Sphegigaster* sp. are the dominent larval and pupal parasites of *C. horticola* on *B. campestris* var. Sarson and their overall parasitism rate of host larvae has been estimated at 65.8 to 86.6 per cent (Kumar, 1985).

3.14.1.4 Control

a. Chemicals

It is difficult to control leaf miner pests by means of insecticides since their larvae remain inside the host tissues and that they also develop resistance towards these chemicals after sometime (Singh *et al.* 1991). However, foliar application of formothion, thiometon and phosphomidon at 0.5% conc. is very effective against *C. horticola*. Formothion 4%, phorate 3%, methyl-o-demeton 4% and thiometon 4% are also effective as soil applicant (Kakar & Dogra, 1977). Phorate provided effective control of leaf miner infestation of *B. campestris* var. Toria (Singh & Bhati, 1990).

b. Sources of resistance

Brassica species differ in their reaction to leaf miner attack. The average pre-mating period of the pest was 2.46 days on *B. campestris* var. Sarson and 3.14 days on *B. juncea* var. Raya. It did not mate on *B. tournefortii* (Singh & Mavi, 1982). *Brassica juncea* (cv. Blaze), *B. napus* (cv. Regent) and a strain each of *B. tournefortii, B. carinata, B. alba* and *Crambe abyssinica* reacted moderately to highly resistant while *B. juncea* cvs RC 512, RC 978 and RLM 198, KB1, rai 231, rai 236, rai 219, RL 18, TG 342 and *B. campestris* cv. BSH-1 were susceptible to the leaf miner attack (Bakhetia, 1991; Bakhetia and Sandhu, 1977; Singh *et al.* 1987).

3.14.2 Cabbage Leaf Miner, *Liriomyza brassicae* Riley

(Diptera: Agromyzidae)

The genus *Liriomyza* contains more than 300 species of which only five are truely polyphagous (Spencer, 1965) and the cabbage leaf miner is one of them. *Liriomyza brassicae* Riley is economically important and cosmopolitan in habit. Severe infestation of the pest in the field is seen only during December-January (Dorge & Dalaya, 1964). It is mostly associated with winter plants in the Gangetic plains besides being found in the higher elevations of Western Ghats (Singh *et al.* 1991). The presence of *L. brassicae* was first noticed in this country on cauliflower in 1961 (Spencer, 1961). The other host plants on which it is active are *Brassica campestris, Tropaeolum majus* (Sehgal & Trehan, 1963); radish, safflower, cucumber, fenugreek (*Trigonella foenum gracium*) (Dorge & Dalaya, 1964), pea, cauliflower and many other wild plants (Singh *et al.* 1991).

3.14.2.1 Damage

Like the peach leaf miner, the adult female of the cabbage leaf miner makes several minute holes along the margin of young tender leaves with its ovipositor for laying eggs and for feeding on exudates with the result that attacked portions of leaves dry up. The larva of *L. brassicae* makes serpentine mines into the upper epidermis of leaf and heavy infestation results in the death of seedlings.

3.14.2.2 Life history

The adult leaf miner is a minute fly with yellowish body, dark brown head and legs, and about 2.5 mm in length with a wing expanse of 3.00 mm. The female differs from the male by the presence of a broad and dark ovipositor. Copulation takes place immediately after their emergence. The male dies after copulation, while the female continues to live for 6-9 days (av. 7.21 days). Pre-oviposition period is 24 h. Eggs are laid singly inside the host tissues, along the upper margin of tender leaves. They remain completely embedded in the leaf tissues. On an average, a female lays about 36 eggs within a period of 5 days, the maximum recorded being 55 eggs per female under laboratory conditions. Eggs are elongate, translucent, shinning, smooth and measure 0.25 mm × 0.1 mm. Incubation period is 3-5 days (av. 3.5 days). Freshly hatched larva is whitish but turns yellowish when fully developed and measures 2.1 mm in length. Larval period is 3-6 days (av. 4.12 days). For pupation, the larva cuts a triangular opening on the upper surface of leaf and drops down on the ground. Pupation takes place in the last larval moult in soil crevices at a depth of about 1/2″ to 3/4″ from the surface. Freshly formed pupa is yellowish in colour which gradually turns dark yellow and finally becomes dark brown when it emerges as adult. Pupa measures 1.8 mm × 0.6 mm. Pupal period is 9-11 days (av. 10 days). Adult emerges after breaking open the anterior end of the puparium. A generation is completed in about 16-23 days. (Dorge & Dalaya, 1964). Biology of the genus Liriomyza has been reviewed by Parrella (1987).

3.14.2.3 Natural enemies

Hymenoptera parasites that attack *L. brassicae* in nature in India are:
Diglyphus sp. (Singh, 1982), *D. indicus* (Ipe, 1987) (Eluphidae) and *Opius phaseoli* (Singh, 1982) (Braconidae). The incidence of combined parasitism by *D. indicus* and *O. phaseoli* was recorded at 60.0 per cent in March 1982 (Singh, 1982).

3.14.2.4 Control

The following are the recommended measures:

a. Flooding

Flooding destroys the pupae of *L. brassicae* in the soil, 3-4 days flooding at the appropriate time before sowing can destroy almost 95% of the pupae (Singh *et al.* 1991).

b. Chemicals

Control of *Liriomyza* leaf miners through the use of insecticides is difficult to achieve because of peculiar biology of these insects, i.e. fast development time, smallness and high mobility of adults, long duration pupal stage in the soil, high reproduction rate, and egg and well protected larval stages within leaf tissue. It is also very difficult to prevent yield reduction because mines once made by the larva cannot be eradicated by pesticides (Parrella, 1987). However, soil treatment with granular insecticides as recommended against *Chromatomyia horticola* (Gour) may also be tried against cabbage leaf miner.

3.15 BRASSICA MIDGE

3.15.1 Pod Midge, *Dasineura brassicae* Winn.

(Diptera: Cecidomyidae)

The pod midge, *Dasineura brassicae* Winn. is a delicate fly that infests the oilseed rape crops in end May to early June and July in UK when the crops are in full flowers (Free & Williams, 1979). It has two generations on winter crops, and a third generation on spring crops when grown in nearby locations (Williams, 1980). It is not present in India.

Dasineura brassicae adults live for only a few days. The females produce a sex pheromone from their ovipositor that attracts the males. Males are not attracted to live mated females or to other live or crushed males (Williams & Martin, 1986). The ovipositor of the female is too weak and cannot pierce the walls of undamaged cruciferous pods to lay eggs (Barnes, 1946; Williams, 1978; Winfield, 1986). For feeding and egg-laying, the Cecidomyid utilizes holes in Brassica pods most of which are made by the cabbage seed weevil although other types of pod damage may also be used. Holes made in spring rape pods with an insect pin received more eggs of pod midge than did weevil feeding punctures when both types of holes occurred in the same pod. Freshly made pin holes were used less by *D. brassicae* than were day old holes because sap exuding from the former may drown or be toxic to the eggs. The females laid more eggs when seeds were present in the vicinity of oviposition sites than when seeds were absent (Ahman, 1987).

Brassica species differ in their reaction to pod midge. *Brassica nigra*, *B. juncea* and *B. carinata* with greater resistance to *D. brassicae* support lower rates of oviposition and of larval growth as compared with the susceptible *B. campestris* and *B. napus*. *Capsella bursa-pastoris* and *Thlaspi arvense* also show reaction similar to resistant Brassica hosts. Glucosinolate products, of which more are produced by resistant than by susceptible Brassica hosts, are toxic to *D. brassicae* but there was no difference in oviposition on low glucosinolate and high glucosinolate oilseed rape varieties (Ahman, 1986). The females exhibit a higher landing rate and more repeated ovipositions on the preferred summer oilseed rape than on non-preferred mustard (Ahman, 1985). The pest probably survives on wild crucifers in smaller population in an area in the absence of favourable Brassica hosts (Ahman, 1988).

The larvae feed on sap that exudes from seed and pod walls. Infested pods ripen prematurely, swell and split, releasing the larvae, which fall to the ground to pupate below the soil surface. The weight of seeds produced per plant decreases with the increase in the proportion of pods that split (Williams, 1980).

3.15.1.1 Control

The following measures are useful:

1. Control of seed weevil will also minimize pod midge infestation.

2. Recommended chemicals:

Post-blossom sprays with triazophos (Graham, 1981), Pyrethroides (Hansen, 1984), fenvalerate (70g/ha) and phosalone (2.3-3.0 l/ha) (Nilsson, 1985) are effective.

3.15.2 Gall Midge, *Dasineura hisarensis* sp. nov.
(Diptera: Cecidomyidae)

This cecidomyid fly was described from Hissar (Haryana), India in 1990 as a pest for major rapeseed growing Asian countries (Nepal, Pakistan, Bangladesh and China) (Sharma & Singh, 1990). The male fly is 2.20 mm long, light yellowish-brown, wings hyaline, 2.36 × as long as broad. The female is 2.28 mm long (including the ovipositor). Larvae are whitish when young but turn pink with age. Females outnumber the males (Female: male:: 58: 42). The pest is multivoltine.

Dasineura hisarensis breeds in the buds of *Brassica campestris* var. Toria, *B. rapa* var. glauca and *B. juncea*. The female lays eggs in flower buds by inserting its ovipositor. At the site of ovipositon, an eye-shaped spot is developed which gradually widens. This midge does not form any complex gall. The infested buds inflate in size. Each bud may harbour 2-15 larvae inside. The inflated buds do not form pods but retain their normal colour till the larvae drop out for pupation in the soil. The buds gradually die, turn black but remain attached to the plant till harvest.

The pest incidence in the field varied from 2-5 per cent depending on the different agroclimatic zones of Haryana. Their population declined sharply after the first week of March. The larvae of *D. hisarensis* are parasitized by an unidentified chalcid and the extent of parasitism varied from 8.70-18.75 per cent during December to March.

3.16 PESTS OF NURSERY-BED

A number of insect pests appear early in the crop season, October-December and attacks the emerging seedlings and young plants of Brassica injuring and causing their death (Rai, 1976). Grass hoppers *Chrotogonus trachypterus* (Kevan, 1954), *Chrotogonus* sp. (Sachan, 1959), *Neorthacris simulans* (*Orthacris simulans*) and *Atractomorpha crenulata* (Nagalingam & Punnaiah, 1980) (Orthoptera: Acrididae), and brightly coloured beetles *Cassida exilis* (Kalra, 1987) (Coleoptera: Cassidae), both the larvae and adults, damage plants by scraping and biting leaves, etc.; Termites (Indian Cent. Oilseeds Comm. Rept. 1962) (Isoptera) cut off the roots of young seedlings; the phytophagous *Nezara viridula* (Nagalingam & Punnaiah, 1980) (Hemiptera: Pentatomidae) and the white fly *Bemisia tabaci* (Sarup *et al.* 1966) (Hemiptera: Aleyrodidae) devitilize seedlings by sucking cell sap; the semi looper *Plusia orichalcea* (Fletcher, 1921), army worm *Mythimna loreyi*, the cut worms *Ochropleura flammatra*, *Agrotis ipsilon* (Singh and Sinha, 1965), *A. segetum* (Singh & Singh, 1983), the ball worm *Heliothis armigera* (Nagalingam & Punnaiah, 1980) (Lepidoptera: Noctuidae), and *Hellula undalis* (Mehta & Purohit, 1957) (Lepidoptera: Pyralidae) cause defoliation, cut the young plants and feed on the leaves; and the *Melanagromyza* sp. and *Japanagromyza* sp. (Kalra, 1987) (Diptera: Agromyzidae) mine the leaves and bore the stems. Better sanitary practices and pre-sowing treatment of soil with insecticides like carbofuran and phorate, etc. may reduce their infestation.

REFERENCES

Abraham, E.V., Padmanabam, M.D. 1968. Bionomics and control of the diamond-back moth, *Plutella maculipennis* Curtis. *Indian J. Agric. Sci.* 28: 513-519.

Abro, G.M., Soomro, R.A. and Syed, T.S. 1992. Biology and behaviour of diamond-back moth, *Plutella xylostella* L. *Pakistan J. Zool.* 24: 7-10.

Agarwala, B.K. and Raychowdhari, D.N. 1981. Notes on some aphids affecting economically important plants in Sikkim. *Indian J. Agric. Sci.* 51: 690-692.

Aggarwal, N., Rohilla, H.R. and Singh, H. 1996. Effect of mustard aphid, *Lipaphis erysimi* (Kalt.) infestation on the yield contributing traits of some rapeseed-mustard genotypes. *Ann. Agric. Res.* 17(1): 18-21.

Ahmad, I. and Kamaluddin, S. 1981. A revision of the subgenus Bagrada Stal, 1862 (Heteroptera: Pentatomidae) from Pakistan with special reference to Zoogeography and phylogeny. *Acta Entomologica Musci Nationalis Prague.* 40: 377-397.

Ahmad, T. and Gupta, R.L. 1941. The pea leaf miner *Phytomyza atricornis* (Meigen) in India. *Indian J. Ent.* 3: 37-39.

Ahman, I. 1985. Oviposition behaviour of *Dasineura brassicae* Winn. on a high versus a low quality Brassica host. *Entomol. Exp. Appl.* 39(3): 247-253.

Ahman, I. 1986. Resistance in Brassica to *Dasineura brassicae* Winn. *Rev. Appl. Entomol.* 75: 390, 1987 (Abstr.)

Ahman, I. 1987. Oviposition site characteristics of *Dasineura brassicae* Winn. *J. Appl. Entomol.* 104(1): 85-91.

Ahman, I. 1988. Wild and cultivated crucifers as hosts for *Dasineura brassicae* Winn. *J. Appl. Entomol.* 105(4): 420-424.

Ahman, I. 1990. Plant surface characteristics and movements of two Brassica-feeding aphids, *Lipaphis erysimi* and *Bravicoryne brassicae. Symp. Biol., Hung* 39: 119-125.

Ahuja, D.B. and Sehgal, V.K. 1982a. Effect of seed extracts containing mustard oil glucosides on feeding responses of mustard sawfly grubs, *Athalia proxima* Klug. *Indian J. Ent.* 44: 34-40.

Ahuja, D.B. and Sehgal, V.K. 1982b. Effect of seed extracts containing mustard oil glucosides on the biology of mustard sawfly, *Athalia proxima* Klug. *Indian J. Ent.* 44: 264-272.

AICORPO. 1987. *Annu. Prog. Rept.* 1987. All India Coord. Res. Proj. Oilseeds, Direct. Oilseeds Res., ICAR, Hyderabad, India.

Aksenova, E.N. 1929. The biology of the rape blossom beetle (*Meligethes aeneus* F.) and its economic importance under the conditions of Tomsk region. *Rev. Appl. Entomol.* 18: 49, 1930 (Abstr.).

Alford, D.V., Cooper, D.A. and Williams, I.H. 1991. Insect pests of oilseed rape. *Rev. Appl. Entomol.* 78(11): 1097, 1990 (Abstr.).

Alford, D.V., Gould, H.J. and Graham, C.W. 1978. Chemical control of seed weevil (*Ceutorhynchus assimilis*) of winter oilseed rape in the UK, 1975-78. *Rev. Appl. Entomol.* 69(4): 234, 1981 (Abstr.).

Ali, M.S., Yazdani, S.S. and Hameed, S.F. 1988. Biology and seasonal history of Bihar hairy caterpillar, *Spilosoma* (*Diacrisia*) *obliqua* Walker. *J. Res. Rajendra Agric. Univ.* 6(1-2): 5-9.

Anand, P.K., Rai, S. and Sharma, V.K. 1967. Notes on hover flies (Diptera: Syrphidae) from Delhi and adjoining areas. *Indian J. Ent.* 29: 307-308.

Ando, T., Koshihara, T., Yamada, H., Vu, M.H. and Takahashi, N., *et al.* 1979. Electroantennogram activities of sex pheromone analogues and their synergistic effect on field attraction in the diamond-back moth. *Appl. Entomol. Zool.* 14: 362-364.

Andrahennadi, R. and Gillott, C. 1998. Resistance of Brassica, especially *Brassica juncea* (L.) Czern., genotypes to the diamond-back moth, *Plutella xylostella* (L.). *Crop Prot.* 17(1): 85-95.

Arora, G.L. and Kaur, D. 1963. The biology of the larvae of *Athalia proxima* Klug. (Hymenoptera: Symphyta). *Res. Bull. Punjab Univ. (Sci.)* 14 pt 1-2: 145-152.

Arora, R. and Sidhu, H.S. 1991. Efficacy of dimethoate against mustard aphid, *Lipaphis erysimi* Kalt. in relation to water stress in the host plants. *J. Insect Sci.* 4: 138-140.

Asian Vegetable Research and Developent Center. 1986. *1985 AVRDC Prog. Rept. Summaries* p. 96. Shanua, Taiwan.

Asian Vegetable Research and Development Center. 1987. *1984 AVRDC Prog. Rept.* p. 480. Shanua, Taiwan.

Asian Vegetable Research and Development Center. 1987. *1985 AVRDC Prog. Rept.* p. 471. Shanua, Taiwan.

Atwal, A.S. 1959. The oviposition behaviour of *Bagrada cruciferarum* Kirkaldy (Heteroptera: Pentatomidae) and the influence of temperature and humidity on the speed of development of eggs. *Proc. Ntn. Inst. Sci. India* B25: 65-67.

Atwal, A.S., Chaudhary, J.P. and Ramzan, M. 1971. Mortality factors in the natural population of cabbage aphid, *Lipaphis erysimi* Kalt. in relation to parasites, predators and weather conditions. *Indian J. Agric. Sci.* 41: 507-510.

Atwal, A.S. and Sethi, S.L. 1963. Predation by *Coccinella septumpunctata* L. on the cabbage aphid, *Lipaphis erysimi* Kalt. in India. *J. Anim. Ecol.* 32: 481-488.

Avci, V. and Ozbeck, H. 1990. Lepidepterous cabbage pests and their parasitoids in Erzurum. In: *Proc. 2nd Turkish Ntn. Cong. Biol. Cent. Izmir*, Turkey, Ege Universitesi: 319-330.

Ayyar, T.V.R. 1928. A contribution to our knowledge of South Indian Braconidae. *Mem. Dep. Agric. India* 10(3): 29-60.

Baker, J.P. 1979. Electrophoratic studies on populations of *Myzus persicae* in Scotland from October to December, 1976. *Ann. Appl. Biol.* 91(2): 159-164.

Bakhetia, D.R.C. 1983. Losses in rapeseed/mustard due to *Lipaphis erysimi* (Kaltenbach) in India: *A literature study.* pp. 1142-1147. *Proc. Sixth Int. Rapeseed Conf.*, May 1983, Paris.

Bakhetia, D.R.C. 1984.. Chemical control of *Lipaphis erysimi* (Kaltenbach) on rapeseed and mustard crops in Punjab. *J. Res. Punjab Agric. Univ.* 21: 63-75.

Bakhetia, D.R.C. 1985. Summary report 1979-85 and invited papers. pp. 83-90. *Joint Review Meet, Indo-Swedish Collab. Res. Prog. Rapeseed-Mustard Improv.*; I.A.R.I., New Delhi, Feb. 28-March 3, 1985.

Bakhetia, D.R.C. 1986. Pest management in rapeseed and mustard. *Pesticides* 20(5): 32-38 & 51.

Bakhetia, D.R.C. 1991. Insect pests. pp. 211-240. In: V.L. Chopra and S. Prakash eds., *Oilseed Brassicas in Indian Agriculture,* Vikas Publishing House, New Delhi.

Bakhetia, D.R.C. and Bindra, O.S. 1977.. Screening technique for aphid resistance in Brassica crops. *SABRAO J.* 9: 91-107.

Bakhetia, D.R.C. and Brar, K.S. 1988. Effect of water stress in Ethopian mustard (*Brassica carinata*) and Indian mustard (*Brassica juncea* sub. sp. *juncea*) on infestation by *Lipaphis erysimi*. *Indian J. Agric. Sci.* 58: 67-70.

Bakhetia, D.R.C., Brar, K.S. and Sekhon, B.S. 1986. Seasonal incidence of *Lipaphis erysimi* (Kaltenbach) on the Brassica species in the Punjab. pp. 29-36. In: B.K. Agarwala ed., *Aphidology in India*. A.R. Printers, Calcutta 1986.

Bakhetia, D.R.C., Labana, K.S., Sukhija, H.S. and Brar, K.S. 1983. Studies on the economic threshold of mustard aphid, *Lipaphis erysimi* (Kalt.) on *Brassica juncea* L. pp. 288-294. In: B.K. Behura ed., *The Aphids*, The Zoological Society of Orissa, Utkal Univ., Bhubaneshwar, India.

Bakhetia, D.R.C. and Sandhu, R.S. 1973. Differential response of Brassica species/varieties to the aphid, *Lipaphis erysimi* (Kalt.) infestation. *J. Res. Punjab Agric. Univ.* 10: 272-279.

Bakhetia, D.R.C. and Sandhu, R.S. 1977. Susceptibility of some Brassica species and *Crambe abyssinica* to the leaf miner, *Phytomyza horticola* (Meigen). *Crop Improv.* 4: 221-223.

Bakhetia, D.R.C. and Sekhon, B.S. 1984. Review of the research work on insect pests of rapeseed-mustard in India. *All India Annu. Rabi Oilseeds Workshop on Rapeseed-Mustard, Safflower and Linseed,* Sukhadia Univ., Reg. Res. Stn., Durgapura (Jaipur), Rajasthan, Aug.6-10, 1984.

Bakhetia, D.R.C. and Sharma, A.K. 1979. Preliminary observations on the aphid infestation on *Eruca sativa* Mill. *Indian J. Ent.* 41: 288-289.

Bakhetia, D.R.C. and Sidhu, S.S. 1983. Effect of rainfall and temperature on the mustard aphid, *Lipaphis erysimi* (Kalt), *Indian J. Ent.* 45: 203-205.

Bakhetia, D.R.C. and Singh, Joginder. 1992. Technological advances in pest management in rapeseed and mustard. pp. 120-149. In: D. Kumar and M. Rai eds., *Advances in Oilseeds Research* Vol.1, 1992. Scientific Publishers, Jodhpur, India.

Banerjee, S.N. and Basu, A.N. 1954. *Tanymecus indicus* Fst., a new Curculionid pest of paddy with suggestions for its control. *Curr. Sci.* 23(1): 22.

Banerjee, S.N. and Basu, A.N. 1955a. Aphididae of West Bengal. *Curr. Sci.* 24: 61.

Banerjee, S.N. and Basu, A.N. 1955b. *Phyllotreta chotanica* Duvivier, a new pest of mustard in West Bengal. *Curr. Sci.* 24: 14-15.

Baral, K. and Sethi, H. 1997. Study of insecticidal persistence of mustard aphid, *Lipaphis erysimi* (Kalt.). *J. Interacademicia* 1(4): 311-314.

Barnes, H.F. 1946. *Gall midges of economic importance.* I. *Gall midges of root and vegetable crops.* London: Crosby, Lockwood & Sons.

Bartlet, E., Blight, M.M., Hick, A.J. and Williams, I.H. 1993. The responses of the cabbage seed weevil (*Ceutorhynchus assimilis*) to the odour of oilseed rape (*Brassica napus*) and to some volatile isothiocyanates. *Entomol. Exp. Appl.* 68: 295-302.

Basavaraju, B.S., Sheriff, R.A., Rajagopal, D. and Rajagopal, B.K. 1995. Integrated pest management of aphids on mustard. *Curr. Res.* 24(8): 148-149.

Basu, A.N. and Honda, A. 1987. Aphid transmission of plant viruses in India. *J. Aphidology* 1: 5-17.

Batra, H.N. 1958. Bionomics of *Bagrada cruciferarum* Kirkaldy (Heteroptera: Pentatomidae) and its occurrence as a pest of mustard seeds. *Indian J. Ent.* 20: 130-135.

Batra, H.N. 1969. Food plants, bionomics and control of flea beetles. *Indian Fmg.* 19: 38-40.

Batra, H.N. and Kumar, K. 1961. Occurrence of green peach aphid, *Myzus persicae* Sulzer as a serious pest of pansy flower and its control. *Indian J. Ent.* 23: 149-151.

Beri, Y.P. 1961. Studies on the application of Dyar's law to larval stages of *Plutella maculipennis* Curtis. *Indian J. Ent.* 23: 69-70.

Bhadauria, N.S., Bahadur, J., Dhamdhere, S.V. and Jakhmola, S.S. 1992. Effect of different sowing dates of mustard on infestation by the mustard aphid, *Lipaphis erysimi* (Kalt.). *J. Insect Sci.* 5(1): 37-39.

Bhadoria, U.S., Dole, J.Y. and Dhamdhere, S.V. 1982. Efficacy of some foliar insecticides against mustard aphid, *Lipaphis erysimi* (Kalt.). *Pesticides* 16: 23-25.

Bhai, B.D. and Singh, Sardar. 1961. On the biology of Painted bug, *Bagrada cruciferarum* in the Punjab. p. 494. *Proc. 48th Indian Sci. Congr., Part 3.*

Bhatia, H.L. and Shaffi, M. 1932. Life-histories of some Indian Syrphidae. *Indian J. Agric. Sci.* 2: 543-570.

Bhatnagar, S.P. 1948. Studies on Apanteles Forester (Vipionidae: parasitic Hymenoptera) from India. *Indian J. Ent.* 10: 133-203.

Bhattacharjee, N.S. 1961. Control of mustard aphid by cultural practices. *Indian Oilseeds J.* 5: 133-138.

Bhattacharjee, P.B., Samui, R.C., Ghosh, M.R., Das Gupta, S.K. and Roy, Y. 1982. Sunflower seed yield as influenced by pollination and insect pests. *Proc. 10th Int. Sunflower Conf.*, Australia. March 14-18, 1982.

Bhattacharya, S., Datta, N. and Agarwala, B.K. 1995. Immigration, population development and dispersal of *Lipaphis erysimi* (Kaltenbach) in relation to phenology and quality of mustard crop. *Proc. Indian Natn. Sci. Acad.* B61: 265-274.

Bindra, O.S. and Deole, J.Y. 1962. Investigations on the cultural control of mustard aphid, *Lipaphis erysimi* (Kalt.) (Hemiptera: Aphididae). *Proc. Second All India Congr. Zool.*, Pt.2, Varanasi (Publ. Oct.1966).

Bindra, O.S. and Mehra, C.K. 1964. A note on host preference by *Athalia proxima* Klug., the mustard sawfly. *Indian J. Ent.* 26: 284-288.

Blackman, R.L. and Eastop, V.F. 1984. *Aphids on the world's crops: An introduction and information guide.* Chichestr: John Willey & Sons, N.Y. pp. 413.

Blunck, H. 1953. *Tiersche Schadlinge an Nutzpflanzen.* I. *Tiel*; 2. *Lief. Lepidopteren und Trichopteren.* (Cited from J. Feltwell ed., 1982. *Large White Butterfly, the biology, biochemistry and physiology of Pieris brassicae* L. pp. 535).

Bodnaryk, R.P. 1992. Distinctive leaf feeding pattern on oilseed rape and related Brassicaceae by flea beetles *Phyllotreta cruciferae* (Goeze.). *Can. J. Pl. Sci.* 72: 575-581.

Bodnaryk, R.P. and Lamb, R.J. 1991. Mechanisms of resistance to the flea beetle, *Phyllotreta cruciferae* (Goeze.) in mustard seedlings, *Sinapis alba* L. *Can. J. Pl. Sci.* 71: 13-20.

Bodnaryk, R.P. and Palaniswamy, P. 1990. Glucosinolate levels in cotyledons of mustard, *Brassica juncea* L. and *B. napus* L. do not determine feeding rates of flea beetle, *Phyllotreta cruciferae* (Goeze). *J. Chem. Eco.* 16: 2735-2746.

Bogawat, J.K. 1967. Biology of mustard sawfly on different host plants. *Indian J. Ent.* 29(3): 270-274.

Bogawat, J.K., Rangarajan, M. and Chakravarti, B.P. 1966. Bacterial mortality of the grubs of mustard sawfly, *Athalia proxima* Klug. (Hymenoptera: Tenthredinidae). *Indian J. Ent.* 28: 417-421.

Bogawat, J.K. and Srivastava, B.K. 1968. Discovery of sinigrin as a phagostimulant by *Athalia proxima* Klug. (Hymenoptera: Tenthredinidae). *Indian J. Ent.* 30: 89.

Bonnemaison, L. 1965. Insect pests of crucifers and their control. *Ann. Rev. Entomol.* 10: 233-255.

Borg, A. 1956. An experiment on the control of *Athalia rosae* L. in unfavourable weather. *Rev. Appl. Entomol.* 45: 457, 1957 (Abstr.)..

Bracken, G.K. and Bucher, G.E. 1986. Yield losses in Canola caused by adult and larval flea beetles, *Phyllotreta cruciferae* (Coleoptera: Chrysomelidae). *Can. Ent.* 118: 319-324.

Brandt, R.N. and Lamb, R.J. 1993. Distribution of feeding damage by *Phyllotreta cruciferae* (Goeze) (Coleoptera: Chrysomelidae) on oilseed rape and mustard seedlings in relation to crop resistance. *Can. Ent.*125: 1011-1021.

Brar, K.S., Bakhetia, D.R.C. and Sekhon, B.S. 1987. Estimation of losses in yield of rapeseed and mustard due to mustard aphid. *J. Oilseeds Res.* 4(2): 261-264.

Brar, K.S., Rataul, H.S. and Labana, K.S. 1976. Differential reaction of mustard aphid, *Lipaphus erysimi* (Kalt.) to different rapeseed and mustard varieties under natural and artificial infestations. *J. Res. Punjab Agric. Univ.* 13: 14-18.

Brar, K.S. and Singh, B. 1992. Efficacy of insecticides against diamond-back moth, *Plutella xylostella* on cauliflower. *J. Insect Sci.* 5: 51-53.

Brar, K.S., Singh, Inderjit and Ahjla, T.S. 1991. Water stress induced effects of Raya crop on the efficacy of oxydemeton methyl for the control of mustard aphid. *J. Insect. Sci.* 4: 141-144.

Burgess, L. 1977. Flea beetles (Coleoptera: Chrysomelidae) attacking rape crops in the Canadian prairie provinces. *Can. Ent.* 109: 21-32.

Burgess, L. 1980. Predation on adults of the flea beetle *Phyllotreta cruciferae* (Goeze) by lace wing larvae (Neuroptera: Chrysopidae). *Can. Ent.* 112: 745-764.

Burgess, L. 1982. Predation on adults of the flea beetle *Phyllotreta cruciferae* (Goeze.) by the western damsel bug, *Nabis alternatus* (Hemiptera: Nabidae). *Can. Ent.* 114: 763-764.

Burgess, L. and Hinks, C.F. 1987. Predation on adults of the crucifer beetle, *Phyllotreta cruciferae* (Goeze) by the northern fall field cricket, *Gryllus pensylvanicus* Burmeister (Orthoptera: Gryllidae). *Can. Ent.* 119: 495-496.

Butani, D.K. 1974. Effect of various insecticides on the mustard aphid, *Lipaphis erysimi* (Kalt.) and yield of rape, *Brassica campestris* Linn. *Indian J. Ent.* 36(3): 243-246.

Carlson, E.C. 1973. Cabbage and turnip aphid and their control and damage on rape and mustard. *J. Econ. Entomol.* 66(6): 1303-1304.

Carlson, E.C., Lange Jr., W.H. and Sclaroni, R.H. 1951. Distribution and control of the cabbage seed pod weevil in California. *J. Econ. Entomol.* 44: 958-966.

Chander, S. and Phadke, K.G. 1995. Intra-plant distribution of aphids infesting rapeseed. *J. Insect Sci.* 8(2): 151-153.

Chandra, J. and Lal, O.P. 1977. Mating behaviour of cabbage butterfly, *Pieris brassicae* (Linn.). *Indian J. Ent.* 38(2): 197-198.

Chandra, S. 1981. Management of the aphid species infesting mustard, cabbage and cauliflower at Udaipur, Ph.D. Thesis, University of Udaipur, Rajasthan, pp. 218.

Chandra, S. and Kushwaha, K.S. 1986. Impact of environmental resistance on aphid complex of cruciferous crops under the agroclimatic conditions of Udaipur. I. Abiotic components. *Indian J. Ent.* 48(4): 495-514.

Charpentier, R. 1985. Host plant selection by the pollen beetle *Meligethes aeneus*. *Entomol. Exp. Appl.* 38(3): 277-285.

Chatterjee, S.D. and Sengupta, K. 1987. Observations on reaction of mustard aphid to white petal and glossy plants of Indian mustard. *J. Oilseeds Res.* 4: 125-127.

Chaudhary, R. and Roy, C.S. 1975. Evaluation and economics of some insecticides for the control of mustard aphid, *Lipaphis erysimi* Kalt. on Rai (*Brassica juncea* L.). *Indian J. Ent.* 37(3): 264-268.

Cherian, M.C. 1934. Notes on some South Indian Syrphids. *J. Bombay Nat.* Hist. Soc. 37: 697-699.

Cherian, M.C. and Basheer, M. 1937. *Brachymaria excarinata* Gahan (Fam. Chalcididae), a pupal parasite of *Plutella maculipennis* Curtis in South India. *Proc. Indian Acad. Sci.* 7: 289-299.

Cherian, M.C. and Basheer, M. 1939. *Tetrastichus sokolowskii* (Fam. Eulophidae), a larval parasite of *Plutella maculipennis* Curtis in South India. *Proc. Indian Acad. Sci.* 9: 87-89.

Chisholm, M.D., Underhill, E.W. and Steck, W.F. 1979. Field trapping of the diamond-back moth *Plutella xylostella* using synthetic sex attractants. *Environ. Entomol.* 8: 516-518.

Chow, Y.S., Lin, M.Y. and Hsu, C.L. 1977. Sex pheromone of diamond-back moth (Lepidoptera: Plutellidae). *Rev. Appl. Entomol.* 67(3): 153, 1979 (Abstr.).

Chuang-Lung, L. 1962. Results of the Zoologico-Botanical expedition to south-west China. 1955-57 (Lepidoptera, Rhopalocera). *Acta En. Sinica* 11: 172-198.

Cotes, E.C. 1896. *Miscellaneous notes from the Entomological section of the Indian Museum*, Calcutta, 3(6): 1-22.

Crafford, J.E. and Chown, S.L. 1987. *Plutella xylostella* L. (Lepidoptera: Plutellidae) on Marion Island. *J. Entomol. Soc. South Africa.* 50: 259-260.

Daebeler, F. and Hinz, B. 1983. Effects of an early infestation of winter rape by *Brevicoryne brassicae* L. *Rev. Appl. Entomol.* 72: 2164, 1984 (Abstr.).

Daiber, C.C. 1971. Population changes in cabbage aphids in South Africa. *Zeitschrift Fur Pflanzenkrankheiten und Pflazenschutz.* 78: 586-594.

Das, B. 1918. The aphididae of Lahore. *Mem. Indian Mus.* 6: 188.

David, B.V. and Basheer, M. 1961. Mass occurrence of the predatory stink bug [*Cantheconidia* (*Canthecona*) *furcellata* Wolff.], on *Amsacta albistriga* Walk. in South India. *J. Bombay Nat. Hist. Soc.* 58: 817-819.

David, W.A.L. and Gardiner, B.O.C. 1962. Oviposition and the hatching of the eggs of *Pieris brassicae* L. in a laboratory culture. *Bull. Ent. Res.* 53: 91-109.

Deshmukh, P.D., Rathore, Y.S. and Bhattacharya, A.K. 1979. Larval survival of *Diacrisia obliqua* Walker on several plant species. *Indian J. Ent.* 41: 5-12.

Desh Raj, Devi, Nirmla., and Chandel, Y.S. 1995. Infestation of leaf miner, *Chromatomyia horticola* Gourean on *Brassica campestris* in mid-Hill zone of Himachal Pradesh (India). *J. Entomol. Res.* 19(2): 107-110.

Desh Raj, Devi, Nirmala., Singh, A.B. and Verma, S.C. 1996. Relative susceptibility of germplasms of three cruciferous oilseed crops to three different aphid species and chemical basis of their differential reactions. *J. Entomol. Res.* 20(2): 115-120.

Desh Raj and Kumar, S. 1994. Population build up of *Myzus persicae* Sulzer on oilseed crucifers and its correlation with abiotic factors. *J. Insect Sci.* 7(1): 16-17.

Devi, Nirmala., Desh Raj and Chandel, Y.S. 1995. Population dynamics of *Lipaphis erysimi* Kaltenbach on rapeseed in mid-Hill zone of Himachal Pradesh (India). *J. Entomol. Res.* 19(4): 367-371.

Dilwari, V.K., Kumari, Anita and Dhaliwal, G.S. 1998. Mechanism of host specificity of mustard aphid. In: G.S. Dhaliwal, R. Arora, N.S. Randhawa and A.K. Dhawan eds. *Ecological agriculture and sustainable development: Vol.I. Proc. Inter. Conf. Ecological Agriculture: Towards Sustainable Development*, Chandigarh, India, 15-17th Nov. 1997.

Dmoch, J. 1959. 'Badania nad chowaczem czterozebnym (*Ceutorhynchus quadridens* Panz.)'. *Prace nauki Institutu Ochrony Roslin* 1: 37-74.

Dorge, S.K. and Dalaya, V.P. 1964. Studies on cabbage leaf miner (*Liriomyza brassicae* Riley). *Curr. Sci.* 18: 560-562.

Doucette, C.F. 1947. Host plants of the cabbage seed pod weevil. *J. Econ. Entomol.* 40: 838-840.

Dutt, G.R. 1914. An annotated list of Ichneumonidae in the Pusa collection. *Mem. Dep. Agric. India* 8(2): 13-28.

Farooqi, S.I. 1994 Editorial diary. *Shashpa* 1(1): 1-6.

Feeny, P., Paauwe, K.L. and Demong, N.J. 1970. Flea beetles and mustard oils: Host plant specificity of *Phyllotreta cruciferae* and *P. striolata* adults (Coleoptera: Chrysomelidae): *Ann. Entomol. Soc. Amer.* 63: 832-841.

Feltwell, J. 1982. *Large white butterfly, the biology, biochemistry and physiology of Pieris brassicae* L. pp. 535. Dr. W. Junk Publishers, The Hague-Boston-London.

Fletcher, T.B. 1919a. *Second hundred notes on Indian insects. Bull.No.89*, Agric. Res. Inst. Pusa, pp. 1-102.

Fletcher, T.B. 1919b. *Annotated list of Indian crop pests. Proc. 3rd Entom. Mtg.*, Pusa, pp. 37.

Fletcher, T.B. 1921. *Annotated list of Indian crop pests. Bull. No.100*, Agric. Res. Inst. Pusa, pp. 1-238.

Free, J.B. and Williams, I.H. 1979. The infestation of crops of oilseed rape (*Brassica napus* L.) by insect pests. *J. Agric. Sci.* Camb. 92: 203-218.

Georghiou, G.P. 1990. Resistance potential to biopesticides and consideration of control measure. pp. 409-420. In: J.E. Casida ed., *Pesticides and Alternataives*, Amsterdam: Elsevier Science.

Ghani, M.A. 1941. Some host plants of *Phytomyza atricornis* Meigen in the Punjab. *Indian J. Ent.* 3: 143.

Ghesquiere, J. 1939. The diamond-back moth of crucifers in Belgian Congo. *Bull. Cercle Zool. Congol.* 16: 61-66.

Ghosh, A.K. and Ghosh, M.R. 1981. Effect of time of sowing and insecticidal treatments on the pests of Indian mustard (*Brassica juncea* L.) and on seed yield. *Entomon* 6: 1347-1352.

Ghosh, C.C. 1914. *Life-histories of Indian insects. Mem. Dep. Agric. India* 5(1): 1-72.

Ghosh, D., Poddar, S. and Raychaudhuri, D.N. 1981. Natural enemy complex of *Aphis craccivora* Koch. and *Lipaphis erysimi* Kalt. in and around Calcutta, West Bengal. *Sci. & Cult.* 47(2): 58-61.

Ghosh, M.R. 1980. Spread of infestation of *Lipaphis erysimi* Kalt. and its population composition at different growth phases of Indian mustard plant. *Indian J. Agric. Sci.* 50(11): 869-872.

Ghosh, M.R. and Mitra, A. 1983. Incidence pattern and population composition of *Lipaphis erysimi* (Kaltenbach) on mustard and radish. pp. 43-51. In: B.K. Behura ed., *The Aphids*, The Zoological Society of Orissa, Utkal University, Bhubaneswar, India.

Gill, R.S. and Bakhetia, D.R.C. 1985. Resistance of some *Brassica napus* and *B. campestris* strains to *Lipaphis erysimi* Kalt. *J. Oilseeds Res.* 2: 227-239.

Goel, S.C. and Kumar, S. 1991. Efficacy of synthetic pyrethroids and quinalphos against Bihar hairy caterpillar, *Spilosoma obliqua* Walker and sesamum sphinx, *Acherontia styx* Westwood infesting sesamum (*Sesamum indicum* L.). *J. Entomol. Res.* 15: 15-19.

Gokulpure, R.S. 1966. Host plants and larval feeding of *Melanagromyza theae* Green. (*Atomella* Mall) and *Phytomyza atricornis* Meigen (Diptera: Agromyzidae) in Domoh, Madhya Pradesh. *Indian Forester* 92: 687-689.

Gokulpure, R.S. 1972. Note on the hosts and parasites of *Phytomyza atricornis*. *Indian J. Agric. Sci.* 42(7): 638-640.

Goodwin, S. 1979. Changes in the numbers in parasitoid complex associated with diamond-back moth, *Plutella xylostella* L. (Lepidoptera) in Victoria. *Aust. J. Zool.* 27: 981-989.

Graham, C.W., 1979. *Cabbage aphid. Advisory Leaflet.* Minis. Agric. Fisheries and Food. No.269, pp. 8, ADAS, Reading, UK.

Graham, C.W., 1981. Pests of oilseed rape and their control. pp. 97-105. *Oilseed Rape Book*. Cambridge Agricultural Publishing, UK.

Graham, C.W. and Gould, H.J. 1980. Cabbage stem weevil (*Ceutorhynchus quadridens* Panz.) on spring oilseed rape in southern England and its control. *Ann. Appl. Biol.* 95: 1-10.

Gunthart, E. 1949. Beitrage zur hebensweise und Bekampfung von *Ceutorhynchus quadridens* Panz. und *Ceutorhynchus napi* Gyll. *Mitt. Schweiz. Entomol. Ges.* 22: 441-591.

Gupta, H.C.L. and Kavadia, V.S. 1977. Insecticidal trials against mustard aphid, *Lipaphis erysimi* Kalt. (Aphididae: Homoptera). *Entomon.* 2(1): 67-69.

Gupta, J.C. 1971. Studies on the efficacy of various insecticides against mustard aphid, *Lipaphis erysimi* Kalt. *PANS* 17(2): 206-208.

Gupta, K.M. 1945. *Phyllotreta cruciferae* Goeze (Halticinae: Chrysomelidiae) a pest of cultivated cruciferous crops in U.P. *Indian J. Ent.* 7: 239-240.

Gupta, P.D. and Thorsteinson, A.J. 1960a. Food plant relationship of diamond-back moth (*Plutella maculipennis* Curt.). I. Gustation and olfaction in relation to botanical specificity of larva. *Entomol. Exp. Appl.* 3: 241-250.

Gupta, P.D. and Thorsteinson, A.J. 1960b. Food plant relationship of diamond-back moth (*Plutella maculipennis* Curt.). II. Sensory relationship of oviposition of the adult female. *Entomol. Exp. Appl.* 3: 305-314.

Gupta, R.L. 1956. *Consolidated report on research on pests of oilseeds in Madhya Pradesh.* pp. 110. Govt. Press, M.P., Nagpur.

Hama, H. 1992. Insecticide resistance characteristics of the diamond-back moth. pp. 455-463. In: N.S. Talekar ed. *Management of Diamond-back Moth and other Crucifer Pests. Proc. 2nd Int. Workshop* Shanhua, Taiwan, AVRDC. pp. 603.

Hameed, S.F. and Sud, V.K. 1978. Persistence of toxicity of some insecticides against *Bravicoryne brassicae* L., on *Brassica campestris* L. var. Sarson Prain. *Indian J. Agric. Res.* 12: 89-91.

Hansen, K.E. 1984. Trials on the control of blossom beetles (*Meligethes aeneus* Fab.), brassica seed weevils (*Ceutorhynchus assimilis* Payk.) and Brassica pod midges (*Dasineura brassicae* Winn.) in witner and spring rape. *Tidsskrift for Planteavl*, 88(1): 91-100.

Hanson, A.J., Carlson, E.C., Breakey, E.P. and Webster, R.L. 1948. Biology of the cabbage seed pod weevil in north west Washington. State Coll. Wash., *Agr. Exp. Sta. Bull.* pp. 498.

Harcourt, D.G. 1954. The biology and ecology of the diamond-back moth, *Plutella maculipennis* Curtis in Eastern Ontario. Ph.D. thesis. Cornell Univ., Ithaca, N.Y., pp. 107. (Cited from N.S. Talekar and A.H. Shelton. 1993. *Ann. Rev. Entomol.* 38: 275-301).

Harcourt, D.G. 1957. Biology of diamond-back moth, *Plutella maculipennis* Curtis (Lepidoptera: Plutellidae) in Eastern Ontario. II. Life-history, behaviour and host relationship. *Can. Entomol.* 89: 554-564.

Hazarika, J. and Saharia, D. 1981. Control of mustard aphid, *Lipaphis erysimi* Kalt. by soil and foliar application of certain insecticides. *J. Res. Assam Agric. Univ.* 2(1): 108-110.

Headley, J.C. 1972. Economics of agricultural pest control. *Ann. Rev. Env. Ent.* 17: 273-286.

Heymons, R. 1921. Communications on the Rape weevil, *Ceutorhynchus assimilis* Payk. and its parasite, *Trichomalus fasciatus* Thoms. *Ztschr. Angew. Ent.* 8: 93-111.

Hillyer, R.J. and Thorsteinson, A.J. 1971. Influence of host plant or males on programming of oviposition in the diamond-back moth (*Plutella maculipennis* Curtis: Lepidoptera). *Can. J. Zool.* 49: 983-990.

Husberg, G.B., Granlund, H. and Hokkanen, H. 1985. Control of rape beetles with the aid of trap crops. *Vaxtskyddsnotiser.* 49(5): 98-101.

Hussain, R. and Agarwal, M.M. 1982. Indian species of Brachymeria Westwood (Hymenoptera: Chalcididae). *Oriental Insects*, 16: 491-509.

Hussain, T. 1983. Evaluation of oleiferous brassicas for resistance to cabbage aphid, *Bravicoryne brassicae*. *Pakistan J. Zool.* 15(1): 95-99.

Hussain, T. and Chatha, N. 1981. Mating behaviour and oviposition of *Athalia proxima* Klug (Hymenoptera: Tenthredinidae). *Pakistan J. Zool.* 14(1): 117-118.

Hyamizu, E. 1982. Comparataive studies on aggregations among aphids in relation to population dyanmics-colony formation and aggregation behaviour of *Bravicoryne brassicae* and *Myzus persicae*. *Appl. Entomol. Zool.* 17(4): 519-529.

Indian Cent. Oilseeds. Comm. Rept. 1962. *Informations collected from Indian States regarding pests of oilseeds, their status, time of apperance and control*, etc. Indian Cent.Oilseeds Comm., Hyderabad.

Ipe M. Ipe. 1987. Biosystematic studies on Agromyzidae from India. *Proc. Indian Acad. Sci. (Anim. Sci.).* 96: 573-581.

Islam, B.N. and Alam, M.Z. 1979. Mating behaviour of jute hairy caterpillar, *Diacrisia obliqua* Walker (Lepidoptera: Arctiidae). *Appl. Entomol. Zool.* 14(3): 303-309.

Jagdis and Dhingra, S. 1990. Residual toxicity of some important pestsicides to the adults of *Bagrada cruciferarum* Kirk. (Hemiptera: Pentatomidae). *J. Ent. Res.* 14(1): 12-15.

Jamdar, N. 1991. On the migration of the large cabbage white butterfly, *Pieris brassicae* in Kashmir. *J. Bombay Nat. Hist. Soc.* 88(1): 128-129.

Jarvis, J.L. 1969. Differential reaction of introductions of Crambe to the turnip aphid and the green peach aphid. *J. Econ. Ent.* 62(3): 697-698.

Jarvis, J.L. 1970. Relative injury to some cruciferous oilseeds by the turnip aphid. *J. Econ. Ent.* 63(5): 1498-1502.

Jayanth, K.P. and Nagarkatti, S. 1984. Testing of *Besa remota* (Dip: Tachinidae) against *Opisina arenosella* (Lep: Cryptophasidae) and other lepidopterous hosts in India. *Entomophaga* 29(4): 415-419.

Jotwani, M.G. and Phadke, K.G. 1982. Prospects and possibilities of increasing rapeseed and mustard production through insect-pest control. pp. 191-195. *Research and Development Strategies for Oilseed Production in India*. Indian Coun. Agric. Res., New Delhi.

Jotwani, M.G., Yadav, T.D., Sircar, P. and Mookherjee, P.B. 1968. Treatment of mustard and radish seeds for the control of mustard sawfly, *Athalia proxima* Klug., at seedling stage. *Indian J. Ent.* 30: 133-136.

Jourdheuil, P. 1960. Influence de quelques facteurs ecologiques sur les fluctuations de population d'une biocenose parasitaire; etude relative a quelques Hymenopteres (Ophionidae, Diospilinae, Euphorinae) parasites de divers coleopteres infeodes aux cruciferes. *Ann. Ephiphyties*, 11: 445-658.

Kakar, K.L. and Dogra, G.S. 1977. Comparative efficacy of soil and foliar applications of some systemic insecticides against *Phytomyza atricornis* Meigen infesting mustard. *Indian J. Agric. Sci.* 47(8): 405-407.

Kalra, V.K. 1987. Some new records of insect pests on oilseed crops in India. *Indian J. Pl. Prot.* 15(1): 85.

Kalra, V.K. and Gupta, D.S. 1989. Integrated control of *Lipaphis erysimi* Kalt. on Indian mustard, *Brassica juncea (L.)* Czern & Coss. *J. Entomol. Res.* 13(1-2): 26-37.

Kalra, V.K., Gupta, D.S. and Yadava, T.P. 1983. Effect of cultural practices and aphid infestation on seed yield and its component traits in *Brassica juncea* (L.) Czern and Coss. *Haryana Agric. Univ. J. Res.* 13: 115-120.

Kanervo, V. 1936. The diamond-back moth (*Plutella maculipennis* Curt.) as a pest of cruciferous plants in Finland. *Rev. Appl. Entomol.* 25: 281, 1937 (Abstr.).

Kapadia, M.N., Bharodia, R.K. and Vora, V.J. 1980. Biology and larval and post-larval development of *Athalia proxima* Klug. on different host plants. *Gujarat Agric. Univ. Res. J.* 6: 13-16.

Katiyar, O.P. Laksman Lal and Mukharji, S.P. 1975. Response of newly hatched caterpillar of *Diacrisia obliqua* Walker to certain host plants. *Indian J. Ent.* 37: 57-59.

Kaurava, A.S., Odak, S.C. and Dhamdhere, S.V. 1969. Preliminary studies on the biology of *Neochrysocharis* sp. (Eulophidae: Hymenoptera) a parasite of *Phytomyza atricornis* Meigen. *J. Bombay Nat. Hist. Soc.* 66(2): 396-398.

Kelkar, R.V. 1977. Field incidence and spatial distribution of *Athalia proxima* Klug. and *Lipaphis erysimi* Kalt. together with estimation of yield losses due to *Lipaphis erysimi* Kalt. (Cited from M.M. Sharma, V.K. Sehgal and A.K. Bhattacharya 1988. *Indian J. Ent.* 50(1): 100-106).

Kennedy, J.S., Day, M.F. and Eastop, V.F. 1962. *A conspectus of Aphids as vectors of Plant Viruses*. Common. Inst. Entomol., London, pp. 114.

Kevan, D.K. 1954. A study of the genus Crotogonus Audinet-Surville, 1839 (Orthoptera: Arcididae). III. A review of available informations on its economic importance, biology, etc. *Indian J. Ent.* 16: 145-172.

Khan, M.A. 1985. New descriptions of Eulophid parasites (Hymenoptera: Eulophidae) of Agromyzidae in India. *J. Bombay Nat. Hist. Soc.* 82(1): 149-159.

Kher, S. and Rataul, H.S. 1991. Investigations on the mechanism of resistance in oleiferous Brassicae against mustard aphid, *Lipaphis erysimi* Kaltenbach. *Indian J. Ent.* 53(1): 141-154.

Khurana, A.D. and Batra, G.R. 1989. Bioefficacy and persistance of insecticides against *Lipaphis erysimi* Kalt. on mustard under late sown conditions. *J. Insect. Sci.* 2: 139-145.

Kirsch, K. and Schmutterer, H. 1988. Low efficacy of a *Bacillus thuringiensis* Berl. formulation in controlling the diamond-back moth, *Plutella xylostella* L. in the Philippines. *J. Appl. Entomol.* 105: 249-255.

Klein, H.Z. 1932. Studien zur Oekologie und Epidemiologie der Kohlweisslinge-I. Der Einflus der Temperatur und Luftfeuchtigkeit auf Entwicklung und Mortalitat Von *Pieris brassicae* L. *Z. Angew Ent.*19: 395-448.

Kozolowski, M.W., Lux, S. and Dmoch, J. 1983. Oviposition behaviour and pod marking in the cabbage seed weevil, *Ceutorhynchus assimilis*. *Entomol. Exp. Appl.* 34(3): 277-287.

Krishnaiah, K. and Mohan, N.J. 1983. Control of cabbage pests by new insecticides. *Indian J. Ent.* 45(3): 222-228.

Krishnakumar, N.K., Srinivasan, K., Suman, C.L. and Ramchander, P.R. 1986. Optimum control strategy of cabbage pests from chemical control trial. *Prog. Hort.* 18: 104-110.

Krishnamoorthy, A. 1988. Biology of *Chrysopa scalestes* Banks (Neuroptera: Chrysopidae). *Bull. Ent.* 29: 69-72.

Krishnamurthi, B. and Usman, S. 1954. Some insect parasites of economic importance noted in Mysore State. *Indian J. Ent.* 16: 327-344.

Kumar, A. 1985. Incidence of parasitism of *Diglyphus isaea* Walk. on *Chromatomyia horticola* Gour., a pest of *Pisum sativum* in northern India. *Entomon.* 10(1): 55-58.

Kumar, A. 1990. Records of some new hymenopteran parasites of *Chromatomyia horticola* Gour. (Diptera: Agromyzidae) from India. *Entomon.* 15(1&2): 135-136.

Kumar, A., Kapoor, V.C. and Mahal, M.S. 1988a. Population build-up and dispersion of immature stages of aphidophagous syrphids (Syrphidae: Diptera) on Raya, *Brassica juncea* Coss. *J. Insect Sci.* 1(1): 39-48.

Kumar, A., Kapoor, V.C. and Grewal, J.S. 1988b. Biology of aphidophagous Leucopis species (Diptera: Chamaemyiidae). *J. Insect Sci.* 1(1): 102-103.

Kumar, S. Krishna Mohan, Tripathi, R.A. and Singh, S.V. 1996. Comparataive efficacy and economics of some insecticides against mustard aphid, *Lipaphis erysimi* Kalt., on mustard. *Ann. Plant Protc. Sci.* 4(2): 160-164.

Kundu, G.G., Anand, R.K., Sharma, V.K. and Rai, S. 1966. New host records of some Hymenopterous parasites. *Indian J. Ent.* 28: 560-561.

Kundu, G.G. and Pant, N.C. 1967a. Studies on *Lipaphis erysimi* Kalt. with special reference to insect-plant relationship. I. Susceptibility of different varieties of Brassica and *Eruca sativa* to the mustard aphid infestation. *Indian J. Ent.* 29(3): 241-251.

Kundu, G.G. and Pant, N.C. 1967b. Studies on *Lipaphis erysimi* Kalt. with special reference to insect-plant relationship. II. Effect of various levels of N, P and K on fecundity. *Indian J. Ent.* 29(4): 285-289.

Kundu, G.G. and Pant, N.C. 1968. Studies on *Lipaphis erysimi* Kalt. with special reference to insect-plant relationship. III. Effect of age of plants on susceptibility. *Indian J. Ent.* 30(2): 169-172.

Lal, K.B. 1953. *Consolidated report of the scheme for research on pests and diseases of til and other oilseed crops—Uttar Pradesh,* pp. 75. U.P. Govt. Press, Allahabad.

Lal, O.P. 1977. *Lipaphis erysimi* (Kalt.). pp. 335-336. In: J. Krantz, H. Schmutterer and W. Koch eds., *Diseases, Pests and Weeds in Tropical Crops.* Paul Parey, Berlin and Hamburg.

Lal, R. 1950. Biology and control of *Myzus persicae* Sulzer as a pest of potato at Delhi. *Indian J. Agric. Sci.* 20: 87-100.

Lal, R. 1952. Effect of malnutrition due to crowding and starvation of alate parents on the production of alate offspring among aphids. *Indian J. Ent.* 14: 9.

Lal, R. 1955. Effect of water content of aphids and their host plants on the apperance of alatae. *Indian J. Ent.* 17: 52-62.

Lal, R. and Haque, E. 1955. Effect of nutrition under controlled conditions of temperature and humidity on longevity and fecundity of *Sphaerophora scutellaris* Fabr. (Diptera: Syrphidae). *Indian J. Ent.* 17: 317-325.

Lamb, R.J. 1980. Hairs protect pods of mustard (*Brassica hirta* "Gisilba") from flea beetle feeding damage. *Can. J. Pl. Sci.* 60: 1439-1440.

Lamb, R.J. 1984. Effects of flea beetles, *Phyllotreta* spp. (Coleoptera : Chrysomelidae) on the survival, growth, seed yield and quality of Canola, Rape and Yellow mustard. *Can. Ent.* 116: 269-280.

Lamb, R.J. 1988. Susceptibility of low- and high-glucosinolate oilseed rapes to damage by flea beetles, *Phyllotreta* spp. (Coleoptera: Chrysomelidae). *Can. Ent.* 120: 195-196.

Lamb, R.J. 1989. Entomology of oilsed brassica crops. *Ann. Rev. Entomol.* 34: 211-229.

Lamb, R.J., McVetty, P.B.E., Palaniswamy, P., Bodnaryk, R.P. and Jeong, S.F. 1993a. Susceptibility of inbred lines of oilseed rape, *Brassica napus* to feeding damage by the crucifer flea beetle, *Phyllotreta cruciferae* (Coleoptera: Chrysomelidae) and its inheritance. *Can. J. Pl. Sci.* 73: 615-623.

Lamb, R.J., Palaniswamy, P., Pivnick, K.A.and Smith, M.A.H. 1993b. A selection of oilseed rape with resistance to flea beetles, *Phyllotreta cruciferae. Can. Ent.* 125: 703-713.

Lamb, R.J. and Turnock, W.J. 1982. Economics of insecticidal control of flea beetles (Coleoptera: Chrysomelidae) attacking rape in Canada. *Can. Ent.* 114: 827-840.

Lammerink, J. and Banfield, R.A. 1980. Effect of aphid control by disulfoton on seed yield components and seed quality on oilseed rape. *NZJ Exp. Agric.* 8(1): 45-48.

Lefroy, H.M. 1906. *Indian Insect Pests.* pp. 318. Reprint Edition 1971. Today and Tomorrow's Printers & Publishers, Faridabad.

Lefroy, H.M. 1907. *Mem. Dept. Agric. Indian Ent. Surv.* 1(2): 214.

Lefroy, H.M. 1909. *Indian Insect Life.* pp. 622-623. Thacker Spink & Company, Calcutta.

Lefroy, H.M. and Ghosh, C.C. 1908. The mustard sawfly. *Mem. Dept. Agric. India, Ent. Ser.* 1: 357-370.

Lever, R.J.A.W. 1945. Entomological notes. *Agric. J. Fizi.* 16(1): 8-11.

Li, C.W. 1981. The origin, evolution, taxonomy and hybridization of chinese cabbage. pp. 3-11. In: N.S. Talekar and T.D. Griggs eds., 1981. *Chinese Cabbage. Proc. 1st Int. Symp.* Shanhua, Taiwan, AVRDC, Taiwan.

Lim, G.S. 1986. Biological control of diamond-back moth. In: N.S. Talekar and T.D. Griggs eds., 1986. *Diamond Moth Management: Proc. 1st Int. Workshop.* Shanhua, Taiwan, AVRDC, Taiwan, pp. 471.

Little, E.J. 1987. The use of an immunoassay to determine the occurrence of insecticide resistant strains of *Myzus persicae* within Yorkshire and Lancashire in 1985. pp. 180-185. In: *Proc. Crop Protection in North Britain.* 1987

Loon, J.J.A.Van, Blaakmeer, A., Griepink, F.C., Beek, T.A.Van, Schoonven, L.M. and Groot, A. De. 1992. Leaf surface compound from *Brassica oleracea* (Cruciferae) induces oviposition by *Pieris brassicae* (Lepidoptera: Pieridae). *Chemoecology* 3(1): 39-44.

Louda, S.M. 1986. Insect herbivory in response to root-cutting and flooding stress on native crucifer under field conditions. (Cited from N.S. Talekar and A.M. Shelton, A.M. 1993. *Annu. Rev. Entomol.* 38: 275-301).

Lu, Z., Q., Chen, L.F. and Zhu, S.D. 1988. Studies on the effect of temperature on the development, fecundity and multiplication of *Plutella xyllostella* L. *Insect Knowl.* 24: 147-149.

MacGibbon, D.B. and Allison, R.M. 1968. A glucosinolase system in the aphid *Brevicoryna brassicae.* *NZJ Sci.* 11: 440-446.

MacKauer, M. and Way, M.J. 1976. *Myzus persicae* Sulz., an aphid of world importance pp. 51-119. In: V.E. Delucchi, ed., *Studies in Biological Control.* Cambridge Univ. Press.

Magaro, J.J. and Edelson, J.V. 1990. Diamond-back moth (Lepidoptera: Plutellidae) in south Texas: a technique for resistance monitoring in the field. *J.Econ. Entomol.* 83: 1201-1206.

Malik, R.S. 1978. Breeding for aphid resistance in Brassica. Ph.D. Thesis, Agra Univ., Agra and Div. Genetics, IARI, New Delhi, pp. 40.

Malik, R.S. 1981. Morphological, anatomical and biochemical basis of aphid, *Lipaphis erysimi* Kalt. resistance in Cruciferous species. *Sver Tidskr.* 91: 25-35.

Malik, Y.P. and Deen, B. 1998. Impact of aphid (*Lipaphis erysimi*) intensity on plant growth and seed characters of Indian mustard. *Indian J. Ent.* 60(1): 36-42.

Mani, M.S. 1940. Biological notes on Indian parasitic Chalcidoidae. *Misc. Bull. Indian Coun. Agric. Res.* 30: 4-5.

Mani, M.S. 1942. Studies on Indian parasitic Hymenoptera II. *Indian J. Ent.* 4: 153-162.

Mathur, A.C. 1962. Food plant spectrum of *Diacrisia obliqua* Wlk. (Arctiidae: Lepidoptera). *Indian J. Ent.* 24: 286-287.

Mathur, K.C. 1983. Aphids of agricultural importance and their natural enemies at Jullunder, Punjab, pp. 229-233. In: B.K. Behura ed., *The Aphids*, The Zoological Society of Orissa, Utkal Univ., Bhubaneswar, India.

Mathur, Y.K. and Singh, S.V. 1986. Population dynamics of *Myzus persicae* Sulzer and *Lipaphis erysimi* Kalt. on rapeseed and mustard in Uttar Pradesh. *J. Oilseeds Res.* 3: 246-250.

Mathur, Y.K., Singh, S.V., Singh, R.S., Agarwal, N. and Katiyar, R.R. 1988. Aphid management in mustard, *Brassica juncea* Czern and Coss. pp. 158-170. In: V.R. Rao and M.V.R. Prasad eds., *Proc. Natn. Seminar on Strategies for Making India Self-reliant in Vegetable Oils.* 5-9th Sept. 1988. Indian Soc. Oilseeds Res., Hyderabad, India.

Mathur, Y.K. and Upadhyaya, K.D. 1980. Evaluation and economics of some modern insecticides against mustard aphid, *Lipaphis erysimi* Kalt. *Pesticides* 14(1): 14-15.

Mehta, T.R. and Purohit, M.L. 1957. Research on diseases and pests of oilseeds. *Gwalior Coll. Agric. J.* 2: 1-16.

Men, U.B. and Kandalkar, H.G. 1997. Record of *Syrphophagus aphidovorus* Mayr (Hymenoptera: Encyrtidae), a hyperparasite of primary parasitoid, *Diaertiella rapae* McIntosh (Hymenoptera: Braconidae) on mustard aphid *Lipaphis erysimi* Kaltenbach (Homoptera: Aphididae). *P.K.V.Res. J.* 21 (2): 197-198.

Meyrick, E. 1928. *A revised handbook of British Lepidoptera*. London: Whatkins and Doncaster. pp. 803.

Mills, H.B. 1942. *Montana insect pests, 1941 and 1942. Twenty-ninth Rept. State Entomologist. Bull. Mont. Agric. Exp. Stn.* 408, pp. 36.

Misra, D.S. and Singh, W. 1986. Estimation of mustard yield and aphid, *Lipaphis erysimi* Kalt. infestation relationship and optimum protection. pp. 319-326. In: S.P. Kurl, ed., *Proc. 2nd Natn. Symp. Recent Trends in Aphidological Studies,* Modinagar, U.P.

Modawal, C.N. 1941. Biological note on *Chilomenes sexmaculata* Fabr. *Indian J. Ent.* 3: 139-140.

Mohan, N.J. 1987. Evaluation of new insecticides for the control of cabbage pests. *Pesticides* 21: 49-54.

Mrig, K.K. and Singh, R. 1981. Efficacy of insecticide dust against *Diacrisia obliqua* Walker on garden bean. *Pesticides* 15: 30-32.

Mukerji, G.P. 1961. On the biology of "Cabbage White" *Pieris brassicae* L. (Lepidoptera: Pieridae). *J. Zool. Soc. India* 13: 121-127.

Muller, F.P. 1986. The role of subspecies in aphids for affairs of applied entomology. *J. Appl. Entomol.* 101: 295-303.

Mumtaz, M., Rahim, A. and Hashmi, A.A. 1991. Insecticide efficacy trials in cauliflower fields against *Pieris brassicae* L. *Proc. 11th Pak. Congr. Zool.* 11: 15-18. Entomol. Res. Lab., Natn. Agric. Res. Cent., Islamabad, Pakistan.

Mushtaque, M. 1989. Control of large cabbage butterfly in Sialkot by local parasites. *Prog. Fmg.* 9(4): 38-40.

Nagalingam, B. and Punnaiah, K.C. 1980. Some new pests of mustard (*Brassica campestris* L.). *Curr. Res.* 9(1): 15.

Nagia, K.K., Kumar, S., Sharma, P., Meena, R.P. and Saini, M.L. 1991. Relative toxicity of some recommended and new insecticides against mustard aphid, *Lipaphis erysimi* Kaltenbach. *Pl. Prot. Bull. (India).* 43(3-4): 33-35.

Narayana, M.L. and Phadke, K.G. 1988. Bioefficacy of some insecticides for the control of *Bagrada hilaris* Burm. on rapeseed crop. *Pl. Prot. Bull. (India).* 40(3-4): 7-9.

Narayanan, E.S. 1954a. The mustard aphid. *Indian Fmg.* 3(1): 8-9 & 23.

Narayanan, E.S. 1954b. The painted bug, *Bagrada cruciferarum* Kirk. *Indian Fmg.* 4: 8-9 & 27.

Narayanan, E.S. 1958. Insect pests of rapeseed and mustard, and methods of their control. pp. 87-97. In: D.P. Singh ed., *Rape and Mustard*. Indian Cent. Oilseeds Committee, Hyderabad.

Narayanan, E.S., Subba Rao, B.R., Rao, M.R. and Sharma, A.K. 1960. Biology and morphology of the immature stages of *Microtonus indicus* (Braconidae: Hymenoptera), a parasite of *Phyllotreta cruciferae* Goeze (Coleoptera: Chrysomelidae). *Proc. Indian Acad. Sci. B.* 51: 280-287.

Nasir, M.M. 1947. Biology of *Chrysopa scelestes* Banks. *Indian J. Ent.* 9: 177-189.

Nath, D.K. and Saha, G.N. 1974. Effect of infestation of *Lipaphis erysimi* Kalt. (Homoptera: Aphididae) on qualitative and quantitative characters of seeds of mustard (*Brassica juncea* Coss.). *Curr. Sci.* 43: 448-449.

Nayar, J.K. and Thorsteinson, A.J. 1963. Further investigations into the chemical basis of insect-host plant relationship in an oligophagous insect, *Plutella maculipennis* Curtis (Lepidoptera: Plutellidae). *Can. J. Zool.* 41: 923-929.

Newson, L.D., Kogan, M., Miner, F.D., Rahi, R.L., Turnipseed, S.G. and Whitcomb, W.H. 1980. General accomplishments towards better pest control in soybean. pp. 51-98. In: C.B. Huffakar ed., *New Technology of Pest Control.* Willey & Sons, New York.

Newton, H.C.F. 1928. The biology of flea beetles (Phyllotreta) attacking cultivated cruciferae. *J.S.- East. Agric. Coll. Wye,* Kent, 25: 90-115.

Nilsson, C. 1985. Control of the pod gall midge—trials in winter rape 1981-83. *Rev. Appl. Entomol.* 73(8): 638, 1985 (Abstr.).

Nolte, H.W. 1959. Untersuchungen Zum Farbensehen des Rapsglanzkafers (*Meligethes aeneus* F.). I. Die Reaktion des Rapsglanzkafers auf Farben und die Okologische Bedeutung des Farbensehens. *Biol. Zentr.* 78: 63-107.

Odak, S.C., Dhamdhere, S.V. and Kaurava, A.S. 1968. New records of hymenopterous parasites of *Phytomyza atricornis* Meigen, a serious pest of pea. *Indian J. Ent.* 30(3): 250.

Ong, K.H. and Ng, B.B. 1988. Field efficiency of teflubenzuron against diamond-back moth and webworm. *Singapore J. Prim. Indust.* 16: 66-75.

Pal, S.R., Nath, D.K. and Saha, G.N. 1976. Effect of time of sowing and aphid infestation on Rai. *Indian Agriculturist.* 20(1): 27-34.

Palaniswamy, P., Gillot, C. and Slater, G.P. 1986. Attraction of diamond-back moth, *Plutella xylostella* (Lepidoptera: Plutellidae) by volatile compounds of Canola (*Brassica campestris* cv. Tobin), white mustard (*Brassica hirta* cv.Ochre), and faba bean (*Vicia faba*). *Can. Entomol.* 118: 1279-1286.

Palaniswamy, P., Lamb, R.J. and Bodnaryk, R.P. 1997. Antibiosis of preferred and non-preferred host-plants for the flea beetle, *Phyllotreta cruciferae* (Goeze) (Coleoptera: Chrysomelidae). *Can. Ent.* 129(1): 43-45.

Palaniswamy, P. and Wise, I. 1994. Effects of need based products on the number and feeding activity of a crucifer flea beetle, *Phyllotreta cruciferae. J. Agri. Ent.* 11: 49-60.

Pandey, N.D., Yadav, D.R. and Teotia, T.P.S. 1968. Effect of different food plants on the larval and post larval development of *Diacrisia obliqua* Walker. *Indian J. Ent.* 30(3): 229-234.

Pant, N.C. and Kalode, M.B. 1964. Pests of wheat, maize and millets. pp. 279-281. In: *Entomology in India.* Entomol. Soc. India, New Delhi.

Pareek, B.L. and Gupta, H.C.L. 1977. Evaluation of some granular insecticides against *Athalia proxima* Klug. infesting mustard. *Indian J. Ent.* 39(4): 392-394.

Parrella, M.P. 1987. Biology of Liriomyza. *Ann. Rev. Entomol.* 32: 201-224.

Patel, C.C., Patel, J.R. and Patel, M.G. 1994. Bio-efficacy of insecticides against mustard sawfly, *Athalia lungens proxima* Klug. *Gujarat Agri. Univ. Res. J.* 19(2): 50-52.

Patel, R.K. 1975. Biological observations on the larger moth, *Crocidolomia binotalis* Zell. (Lepidoptera: Pyralidae) in Madhya Pradesh. *Indian J. Ent.* 37(1): 102-103.

Patel, V.C. and Patel, H.K. 1968. New records of parasites of *Plutella maculipennis* Curtis in Gujarat, India. *Indian J. Ent.* 30: 86.

Pathak, M.D. 1961. Preliminary notes on differential response of yellow and brown sarson, and rai to mustard aphid, *Lipaphis erysimi* Kalt. *Indian Oilseeds J.* 5: 39-41.

Peng, C.W., Weiss, M.J. and Anderson, M.D. 1992. Flea beetle (Coleoptera: Chrysomelidae) response, feeding and longevity on oilseed rape and crambe. *Environ. Entomol.* 21: 604-609.

Perng, F.S., Yao, M.C., Hung, C.F. and Sun, C.N. 1988. Teflubenzuron resistance in diamond-back moth (Lepidoptera: Plutellidae). *J. Econ. Entomol.* 81: 1277-1282.

Peter, C. and David, B.V. 1988. Studies on the efficacy and persistance of diflubenzuron against *Crocidolomia binotalis* (Lepidoptera: Pyralidae) on radish, *Curr. Res.* 17(3): 32-34.

Peter, C., Singh, I. and Channa Basavanna, G.P. 1983. Biological and seasonal incidence of *Palexorista solennis* Walker (Diptera: Tachinidae) in South India. *Entomon.* 8: 317-320.

Peter, C., Singh, I. and Channa Basavanna, G.P. 1986. Effect of host plant on the behaviour of *Plaexorista solennis* Walker (Diptera: Tachinidae). *Curr. Res.* 15: 7-8.

Phadke, K.G. 1980. Strategy for increasing rapeseed and mustard production through insect pest control. pp. 151-158. *Proc. FAI Group Discussion on Increasing Pulses and Oilseeds Production in India*, 4-5th Sept, 1980, New Delhi.

Phadke, K.G. 1986. Ecological factors influencing aphid, *Lipaphis erysimi* Kaltenbach incidence on mustard crop. pp. 37-42. In: B.K. Agarwal ed., *Aphidology in India.* A.R. Printers, Calcutta, India.

Phadke, K.G. and Prasad, S.K. 1987a. Effect of sowing dates on aphid incidence and yield in some varieties of rapeseed and mustard. *J. Aphidology* 1(1&2): 23-28.

Phadke, K.G. and Prasad, S.K. 1987b. Identification of Brassica genotypes least susceptible to mustard aphid, *Lipaphis erysimi* (Kalt.). *J. Aphidology* 1(1&2): 93-97.

Pimentel, D. 1961. Species diversity and insect population outbreaks. *Ann. Entomol. Soc. Am.* 54: 76-86.

Pittendrigh, B.R. and Pivnick, K.A. 1993. Effects of a host plant, *Brassica juncea*, on calling behaviour and egg maturation in diamond-back moth, *Plutella xylostella*. *Entomol. Exp. Appl.* 68(2): 117-126.

Pivnick, K.A., Jarvis, B.J., Gillott, C., Slater, G.P. and Underhill, E.W. 1990a. Daily patterns of reproductive activity, and influence of adult density and exposure to host plants on reproduction in the diamond-back moth (Lepidoptera: Plutellidae). *Environ. Entomol.* 19: 587-593.

Pivnick, K.A., Jarvis, B.J., Slater, G.P., Gillott, C. and Underhill, E.W. 1990b. Attraction of diamond-back moth (Lepidoptera: Plutellidae) to volatiles of oriental mustard; the influence of age, sex and prior exposure to males of host plants. *Environ. Entomol.* 19: 704-709.

Pl. Prot. Bull. 1959. Insects and other pests of agricultural importance in India. *Pl. Prot. Bull. (India)* 11: 1-70.

Ponnuswami, M.K. 1960. The mustard aphid and its control with modern insecticides. *Pl. Prot. Bull. (India)* 12(1-4): 43-45.

Pradhan, S. 1969. *Insect pests of crops.* pp. 208. National Book Trust of India, New Delhi.

Pradhan, S., Jotwani, M.G. and Rai, B.K. 1957. Relative toxicity of some organophosphorus insecticides to *Lipaphis erysimi* Kalt. (*Rhophalosiphum pseudobrassicae* Davis) (Homoptera: Aphididae). *Indian J. Ent.* 19(3): 217-220.

Prasad, S.K. 1978a. Chemical control of mustard aphid, *Lipaphis erysimi* Kalt. *Indian J. Ent.* 40(3): 328-332.

Prasad, S.K. 1978b. Control of mustard aphid, *Lipaphis erysimi* Kalt. *Indian J. Ent.* 40(4): 401-404.

Prasad, S.K. 1979. Control of mustard aphid, *Lipahis erysimi* Kalt by granular systemic insecticides. *Indian J. Ent.* 41(1): 39-42.

Prasad, S.K. 1983. Varietal susceptibility of rapeseed and mustard cultivars to aphid, *Lipaphis erysimi* Kalt. *Indian J. Ent.* 45: 501-503.

Prasad, S.K. and Phadke, K.G. 1979. Effect of mustard aphid, *Lipaphis erysimi* Kalt. infestation on seed yield of different varieties of Brassica species. In: "*The Aphids*", p. 34. *Proc. Symp. "Recent Trends in Aphidological Studies*", Bhubaneshwar, Orissa, 1979.

Prasad, S.K. and Phadke, K.G. 1984. Yield loss in some improved varieties of rapeseed and mustard by aphid, *Lipaphis erysimi* Kalt. *Indian J. Ent.* 46(2): 250-253.

Prasad, S.K. and Phadke, K.G. 1986. Variability in the incidence of mustard aphid, *Lipaphis erysimi* Kaltenbach on different varieties/species of rapeseed and mustard crops. *Indian J. Ent.* 48: 222-225.

Prasad, Y.K. and Phadke, K.G. 1980. Population dynamics of *Lipaphis erysimi* Kalt. on different varieties of Brassica species. *Indian J. Ent.* 42(1): 54-63.

Putnam, L.G. 1977. Response of four brassica seed crop species to attack by crucifer flea beetle, *Phyllotreta cruciferae.* *Can. J. Pl. Sci.* 57: 987-989.

Rai, B.K. 1976. *Pests of oilseed crops in India and their control.* pp. 121, Indian Coun. Agric. Res., New Delhi, India.

Rai, B.K. and Sehgal, V.K. 1975. Field resistance of Brassica germplasm to mustard aphid, *Lipaphis erysimi* Kalt. *Sci. & Cult.* 4: 444-445.

Rai, J.P.N. and Tripathi, R.S. 1985. Effect of herbivory by the slug, *Mariella dussumieri*, and certain insects on growth and competitive success of two sympatric annual weeds. *Agric. Ecosyst. Environ.* 13: 125-137.

Rai, P.S. and Nagesh Chandra, B.K. 1976. Bionomics of cabbage leaf webbing caterpillar, *Crocidolomia binotalis* Zeller. *Indian J. Ent.* 38(3): 233-235.

Raich, R.V. 1975. *Thymus vulgaris aureus* (Fam. Labiatae), a new host plant of the cabbage web-worm, *Crocidolomia binotalis* Zeller (Lepidoptera: Pyralidae). *Indian J. Ent.* 37(3): 313-314.

Rajan, S.S. 1961. Aphid resistance to autotetraploid Toria. *Indian Oilseeds J.* 5: 251-255.

Rajendran, T.P. 1989. Incidence pattern and instar composition of the aphids infesting rapeseed crops. Ph.D. Thesis, pp. 110. IARI, New Delhi.

Rakshpal, R. 1949. Notes on the biology of *Bagrada cruciferarum* Kirk. *Indian J. Ent.* 11: 11-16.

Ram, S. and Gupta, M.P. 1992. Role of fertilizer (N, P & K) in insect management of mustard meant for fodder production. *Indian J. Agric. Res.* 26: 35-39.

Ram, S., Gupta, M.P. and Patil, B.D. 1987. Incidence and avoidable losses due to insect pests in green fodder yield of Chinese cabbage, *Indian J. Agric. Sci.* 57(12): 955-956.

Ram, S. and Pathak, K.A. 1980. Record of host plants of Bihar hairy caterpillar, *Diacrisia obliqua* Walker in Manipur. *Bull. Ent.* 21: 138-140.

Ramkishore and Phadke, K.G. 1988a. Distribution of aphid, *Lipaphis erysimi* on mustard crop. *J. Aphidology* 2(1&2): 72-75.

Ramkishore and Phadke, K.G. 1988b. Effect of number of insecticidal applications for aphid control on mustard crop yield. *J. Aphidology* 2(1&2): 56-58.

Ramaseshiah, G. 1967. The fungus, *Entomopthora coronata* parasitic on three species of aphids infesting crucifers in India. *J. Invert. Path.* 9: 126-128.

Ramaseshiah, G. and Dharamadhikari, P.R. 1968. Occurrence of fungus, *Cephalosporium aphidicola* on some aphids in India. *Tech. Bull. Commonw. Inst. Biol. Control.* 10: 150-155.

Rao, V.S. 1962. Status of *Coccinella septumpunctata* L. and its varieties *divaricata* Oliv. and *confusa* Wied. *Can. Ent.* 94: 134-143.

Rataul, H.S. 1959. Studies on the biology of cabbage butterfly. *Indian J. Hort.* 16: 255-265.

Rataul, H.S. and Kishore, R. 1980. Development of *Myzus persicae* Sulzer on winter hosts at Simla. *Indian J. Ent.* 42: 535-536.

Rawat, R.R., Misra, U.S., Thakur, A.U. and Dhamdhere, S.V. 1968. Preliminary study on the effect of different doses of nitrogen on the incidence of major pests of mustard. *Madras Agric. J.* 55: 363-366.

Rawat, R.R. and Singh, O.P. 1983. Effect of different dates of sowing and combinations of fertilizers on the incidence of the mustard aphid, *Lipaphis erysimi* and the grain yield of mustard. *Pranikee* 4: 295-302.

Rawat, U.S., Singh, R. and Pawar, A.D. 1990. Record of a hyperparasitoid on *Apanteles glomeratus* Linn. from Himachal Pradesh. *Pl. Prot. Bull. (India).* 42(3&4): 228.

Reed, D.W., Pivnic, K.A. and Underhill, E.W. 1989. Identification of chemical oviposition stimulants for the diamond-back moth, *Plutella xylostella* present in three species of Brassicacae. *Entomol. Exp. Appl.* 53: 277-286.

Reich, R. 1961a. Contributions to the bionomics of the turnip-rape sawfly, *Athalia rosae* L. On the dispause of the turnip rape sawfly, *Athalia rosae* L. *Rev. Appl. Entomol.* 51: 202, 1963 (Abstr.).

Reich, R. 1961b. Investigations on the epidemiology of *Athalia rosae* L. *Rev. Appl. Entomol.* 51: 625, 1963 (Abstr.).

Reich, R. 1962. On the possibilities of control of *Athalia rosae* L. from the economic point of view. *Rev. Appl. Entomol.* 52: 137, 1964 (Abstr.).

Renwick, J.A.A., Radke, C.D., Sachdeve-Gupta, K. and Stadler, E. 1992. Leaf surface chemicals stimulating ovipositon by *Pieris rapae* (Lepidoptera: Pieridae) on cabbage. *Chemoecology* 3(1): 33-38.

Riggert, E. 1939. Investigations on *Athalia rosae* L. *Z. Angew. Ent.* 26 pt. 3: 426-516.

Rout, G. and Pani, S.C. 1968. Insecticidal trials to control mustard aphid, *Lipaphis erysimi* Kalt. and the larger moth *Crocidolomia binotalis* Zell., affecting mustard crop. *Indian J. Agri. Sci.* 38(5): 828-831.

Roy, P. 1975a. Population dynamics of mustard aphid, *Lipaphis erysimi* Kaltenbach (Homoptera: Aphididae) in West Bengal. *Indian J. Ent.* 37(3): 318-321.

Roy, P. 1975b. Chemical control of mustard aphid, *Lipaphis erysimi* (Hemiptera: Aphididae). *Sci. & Cult.* 41: 37.

Roy, P. and Basu, S.K. 1977. Bionomics of aphidophagous syrphid flies. *Indian J. Ent.* 39: 165-174.

Rushtapakornchai, W., Valtanatangum, A. and Saito, T. 1992. Development and implementation of yellow sticky trap for diamond-back moth control in Thailand. pp. 523-528. In: N.S. Talekar ed. 1992. *Management of Diamond-back Moth and other Crucifer Pests. Proc. Second Int. Workshop.* Shanhua, Taiwan, AVRDC, Taiwan, pp. 603.

Sachan, G.C. 1981. Growth and development of *Diacrisia obliqua* Walker on some vegetables. *Indian J. Agric. Sci.* 51(8): 579-582.

Sachan, G.C., Pathak, P.K. and Chibber, R.C. 1983. Effect of nitrogen levels and date of sowing on the incidence of *Lipaphis erysimi* and yield of mustard. p. 78. A. Report Res., Direct. Expt. Stn., G.B. Pant Univ. Agric. & Tech., Pantnagar, India.

Sachan, G.C., Singh, C.P. and Tripathi, N.L.M. 1985. Entomology. pp. 84-93. In: *Oilseeds Research at Pantnagar, Expt. Stn. Bull.* 111, Direct. Expt. Stn., G.B. Pant Univ. Agri. & Tech., Pantnagar, India.

Sachan, G.C. and Sumati 1985. Incidence of *Athalia proxima* Klug on spp. and vars. of Brassica. *Cruciferae Newsl.* 10: 128-129.

Sachan, J.N. 1959. Common insect pests of crops and vegetables of Jobner. *Rajasthan Agriculture* 7: 39-44.

Sachan, J.N. and Srivastava, B.P. 1972. Studies on the seasonal incidence of insect pests of cabbage. *Indian J. Ent.* 34 : 123-129.

Sachan, S.K. and Sachan, G.C. 1991. Relation of some biochemical characters of *Brassica juncea* (Cossan) to suscepti-bility to *Lipaphis erysimi* Kaltenbach. *Indian J. Ent.* 53(2): 218-225.

Saini, M.L. and Chhabra, K.S. 1966. Control of mustard aphid, *Lipaphis erysimi* Kalt. by systemic insecticides. *Pl. Prot. Bull. (India).* 18: 4-8.

Saini, R.S. 1967. Evaluation of the effectiveness of some organophosphorus insecticides against two species of aphids. *Indian J. Ent.* 29(1): 34-43.

Sakanoshita, A. and Yanagita, Y. 1972. Fundamental studies on the reproduction of diamond-back moth, *Plutella maculipennis* Curtis. I. Effect of environmental factors on emergence, copulation and oviposition. *Proc. Assoc. Plant Prot. Kyushu* 18: 11-12. (Cited from N.S. Talekar and A.M. Shelton 1993. *Ann. Rev. Entomol.* 38: 275-301).

Samuel, C.K. 1942. Biological notes on egg parasites of *Bagrada picta* Fabr. (Pentatomidae). *Indian J. Ent.* 4: 92-93.

Saringer, G. 1964. The role of the photoperiod in releasing the diapause of *Athalia rosae* L. *Ann. Inst. Prot. Pl. hung.* 9: 107-113.

Saringer, G. 1983. Light exposure in the scotophase of the photoperiod as an ecological control method against *Athalia rosae* L. *Novenyvedelem* 19(7): 294-298.

Saringer, G. 1989. Insecticide free method of controlling turnip sawfly, *Athalia rosae* L. (Hymenoptera: Tenthredinidae). *Anzeiger fur Schadlingskunde, Pflanzenschutz, Umweltschutz.* 62: 31-32.

Sarup, P., Wadhwa, S., Singh, D.S. an Lall, R. 1966. Testing of pesticides against cabbage aphid, *Bravicoryne brassicae* L. *Indian J. Ent.* 28: 369-374.

Sedivy, J. 1981. Damage by the cabbage aphid (*Bravicoryne brassicae* L.) to winter rape. *Ochrana Rostlin* 54(4): 273-280..

Sehgal, V.K., Bhattacharya, A.K. and Singh, K.N. 1975. Food preferences of mustard sawfly grubs, *Athalia proxima* Klug (Hymenoptera: Tenthredinidae). *Sci. & Cult.* 41(9): 430-433.

Sehgal, V.K. and Trehan, K.N. 1963. On some dipterous leaf miners from India (Diptera: Agromyzidae). *Indian J. Ent.* 25: 17-20.

Sehgal, V.K. and Ujagir, Ram 1977. Plant's natural defences in Cruciferae and Tropaeolaceae against mustard sawfly, *Athalia proxima* Klug. *Indian J. Ecol.* 4(2): 199-203.

Sekhon, B.S. and Ahman, I. 1993. Insect resistance with special reference to mustard aphid. pp. 207-221. In: K.S. Labana, S.S. Banga and S.K. Banga, eds., *Breeding oilseed Brassicas, Theor. Appl. Genet.*, Vol.19, pp. 251.

Sen, P.C. 1920. *Annual report of the Entomological Collector, Bengal for the year 1918-1919.* pp. 104-106. Rept. Dept. Agric. Bengal.

Senapati, S.K. and Ghosh, S. 1992. Persistency of toxicity of insecticides in jute leaves against lepidopteran pests. *Crop Res.* (Hissar) 5(2): 363-369.

Sethi, S.L. and Atwal, A.S. 1963. Influence of temperature and humidity on the development of different stages of lady-bird beetle, *Coccinella septumpunctata* L. (Coleoptera: Coccinellidae). *Indian J. Agric. Sci.* 34: 166-171.

Sharma, A.K. and Subba Rao, B.R. 1964. A further contribution to the knowledge of the taxonomy and biology of Aphididae (Hymenoptera: Ichneumonoidea) with particular reference to Indian forms. *Indian J. Ent.* 26: 458-460.

Sharma, M.M., Sehgal, V.K. and Bhattacharya, A.K. 1988. Utilization of nutrients by the grubs of *Athalia proxima* Klug. *Indian J. Ent.* 50(1): 100-106.

Sharma, R.H. and Singh, H. 1990. A new species of Dasineura (Diptera: Cecidomyiidae) injurious to buds of Brassica spp. (Cruciferae) in Haryana. *J. Bombay. Nat. Hist. Soc.* 87(3): 429-432.

Shelton, A.M. and Wyman, J.A. 1992. Insecticide resistance of diamond-back moth in North America. pp. 447-454. In: N.S. Talekar ed. 1992. *Management of Diamond-back Moth and other Crucifer Pests: Proc. Second Int. Workshop*, Shanhua, Taiwan, AVRDC, Taiwan, pp. 603.

Sidhu, A.S. and Dhawan, A.K. 1980. Chemical control of Bihar hairy caterpillar infesting cotton. *Entomon* 5(4): 295-300.

Sidhu, H.S. and Kaur, P. 1977. Influence of nitrogen application to the host plant on facundity of mustard aphid, *Lipaphis erysimi* Kalt. *J. Res. Punjab Agric. Univ.* 14(4): 445-448.

Sidhu, H.S. and Singh, S. 1964. Biology of the mustard aphid, *Lipaphis erysimi* Kalt. in Punjab. *Indian Oilseeds J.* 8: 348-359.

Sihag, R.C. 1988. Effect of pesticides and bee pollination on seed yield of some crops in India. *J. Apicultural Res.* 27(1): 49-54.

Simmonds, F.J. and Rao, V.P. 1960. Records of *Plutella maculipennis* Curtis and some of its parasites in Kashmir, India. *Can. Ent.* 92: 278.

Singh, A., Sodhi, N.S. and Gupta, V. 1990. Notes on some syrphids from Chandigarh and adjoining areas. *Indian J. Ent.* 54(4): 719-721.

Singh, B., Singh, R., Mahal, M.S. and Brar, H.S. 1983a. Assessment of loss in yield of *Brassica juncea* by *Lipaphis erysimi* Kalt. I. Influence of varying levels of aphid population. *Indian J. Ecology* 10(1): 97-105.

Singh, B., Singh, R. and Mahal, M.S. 1983b. Assessment of loss in yield of *Brassica juncea* by *Lipaphis erysimi* Kalt. II. Economics of aphid control. *Indian J. Ecology* 10(2): 279-284.

Singh, C.P. and Pandey, M.C. 1996. Differential response of rapeseed-mustard to *Lipaphis erysimi* Kalt. infestation. *Pestology* 20(1): 32-34.

Singh, C.P. and Sachan, G.C. 1995. Economic injury level of mustard aphid on yellow sarson, *Brassica campestris*. *J. Insect Sci.* 8(2): 171-175.

Singh, D.S. and Singh, S. 1964. Notes on the bionomics of *Tanymecus indicus* Faust. (Coleoptera: Curculionidae). *Pl. Prot. Bull. (India)* 16(3-4): 28-33.

Singh, D.S. and Sicar, P. 1980. Relative toxicity of pyrethroids to *Lipaphis erysimi* Kalt. and *Aphis craccivora*. *Indian J. Ent.* 42: 599-605.'

Singh, G. and Singh, G. 1986. Biology of *Myzus persicae* (Sulzer) on two oilseed hosts at Ludhiana. *J. Res., Punjab Agric.Univ.*, 23(4): 599-602.

Singh, H. 1982. Studies on insect-pest complex in *Brassica campestris* L. var. Brown "sarso". Ph.D. Thesis, Haryana Agric. Univ., Hissar, pp. 192.

Singh, H. 1992. *Bagrada trilobata* Ahmad and Kamaluddin: First appearance in India. *Crop Res.* (Hissar). 5(1): 172-173.

Singh, H., Gupta, D.S., Yadava T.P. and Dhawan, K. 1980a. Post-harvest losses caused by painted bug (*Bagrada cruciferarum* Kirk.) to mustard. *Haryana Agric. Univ. J. Res.* 10(3): 407-409.

Singh, H., Gupta, D.S., Yadava, T.P. and Rohilla, H.R. 1984a. Efficacy and economics of some insecticidal granules and oxydemeton methyl against mustard aphid, *Lipaphis erysimi* Kalt. (Homoptera: Aphididae). *Indian J. Agric. Sci.* 54(6): 496-499.

Singh, H., Rohilla, H.R., Kalra, V.K. and Yadava, T.P. 1984b. Response of Brassica varieties sown on different dates to the attack of mustard aphid, *Lipaphis erysimi* Kalt. *J. Oilseeds Res.* 1: 49-56.

Singh, H., Singh, D., Singh, H. and Kumar, V. 1990. Basis of aphid tolerance and combining ability analysis in Indian mustard. p. 15. *Natn. Semin. Genet. Brassica.* (Cited from Sekhon, B.S. and Ahman, I. pp. 203-221. In: K.S. Labana, S.S. Banga and S.K. Banga eds. *Breeding Oilseed Brassicas, Theor. Appl. Genet.* Vol.I. pp. 251).

Singh, H. and Singh, Z. 1983. New records of insect pests of rapeseed. *Indian J. Agric. Sci.* 53(9): 870.

Singh, H. and Singh, Z. 1988. *Crop Productivity*. IBH and Oxford Ltd. New Delhi, pp. 445-450.

Singh, H. and Singh, Z. 1989. Population dynamics of green peach aphid (*Myzus persicae* Sulz.) on rapeseed cv. BSH-1. *Crop Res.* 2(2): 194-199.

Singh, H. and Yadava, T.P. 1988. Integrated management of aphid pest in rapeseed-mustard crops. pp. 150-157. *Proc. Nat. Seminar on Strategies for making India self-reliant in vegetable oils.* Indian Soc. Oilseeds Res., Hyderabad, 5-9th Sept., 1988.

Singh, I., Brar, K.S. and Ahuja, T.S. 1994. Effect of irrigation on the incidence of mustard aphid, *Lipaphis erysimi* (Kalt.). *Indian J. Ent.* 56(1): 63-66.

Singh, I.P. 1988. Ecotaxonomy and biology of Liriomyza Mik. from Indian faunal limits (Diptera: Agromyzidae). Ph.D. Thesis, Agra Univ., Uttar Pradesh (unpublished).

Singh, I.P., Agnes, Ipe and Ipe, M. Ipe. 1991. Control of *Liriomyza brassicae* Riley by flooding. *Entomon.* 16(1): 83-85.

Singh, K.J. and Singh, O.P. 1988. *Lipaphis erysimi* Kalt. infestation on the roots of mustard in Madhya Pradesh. *J. Aphidology* 2(1&2): 90-92.

Singh, M.P. and Sinha, M.H. 1965. Some cut-worm pests new to Bihar. *Indian J. Ent.* 27: 113-114.

Singh, O.P. 1991. Efficacy of some new insecticides against the Bihar hairy caterpillar, *Spilosoma obliqua* Walker and estimation of losses to soyabean in Madhya Pradesh. *Indian J. Agric. Res.* 25(4): 189-193.

Singh, O.P., Dhamdhere, S.V. and Neema, K.K. 1983c. Effect of different parts of mustard plant on the development of mustard aphid. *Lipaphis erysimi* Kalt. *Agric. Sci. Digest* 3(1): 5-7.

Singh, O.P. and Rawat, R.R. 1983a. Seasonal incidence and toxicological studies on *Lipaphis erysimi* and its parasites. *Aphidius* sp. (?) in Madhya Pradesh, India. *Pranikee* 4: 259-167.

Singh, O.P.and Rawat, R.R. 1983b. Bionomics of the cabbage web-worm, *Crocidolomia binotalis* Zell. on mustard at Jabalpur. *Bull. Ent.* 24(2): 75-82.

Singh, O.P., Rawat, R.R. and Choudhary, B.S. 1980b. Efficacy of some granular insecticides against the flea beetle, *Phyllotreta crucifearae* on mustard. *Indian J. Pl. Prot.* 8: 54-56.

Singh, P., Bhakhetia, D.R.C. and Sindhu, H.S. 1987. Plant apparency and chemical defences in Brassicas against the leaf miner, *Chromatomyia horticola* Goureau (Diptera: Agromyzidae), pp. 102-103. In: K.S. Gill, A.S. Khehra, M.M. Verma and K.S. Bains eds., Abstracts, *First Symp. Crop Improvement*, 23-27th Feb., 1987. Crop Improv. Soc. India, Ludhiana.

Singh, P. and Mavi, G.S. 1982. A study of the mating behaviour of the leaf miner, *Phytomyza horticola* Goureau on brassicas. *UP J. Zool.* 2(1): 27-31.

Singh, R.N., Dass, R., Saran, G. and Singh, R.K. 1982. Differential response of mustard varieties to aphid, *Lipaphis erysimi* Kalt. *Indian J. Ent.* 44: 408.

Singh, Rajwant and Singh, Balraj 1982. Influence of simulated rainfall on the population of mustard aphid, *Lipaphis erysimi* Kalt. *Indian J. Ecol.* 9: 344-345.

Singh, Rajwant, Singh, Balraj and Mahal, M.S. 1984c. Rainfall as a mortality factor of *Lipaphis erysimi* Kalt. on mustard. *Indian J. Ecol.* 11: 327-329.

Singh, R.P., Yazdani, S.S., Verma, G.D. and Singh, V.N. 1995. Effect of different levels of nitrogen, phosphorus and potash on aphid infestation and yield of mustard. *Indian J. Ent.* 57(1) : 18-21.

Singh, S. 1982. Ecology of the Agromyzidae (Diptera) associated with leguminous crops in India. *Mem. Sch. Ent.* 8: 1-126.

Singh, S. and Bhati, D.P.S. 1990. Effect of thimet on agromyzid pest, *Chromatomyia horticola* Gour. on *Brassica campestris* L. *Recent researches in Ecol., Env. & Polluation* No. 5: 185-192.

Singh, S. and Gurham, M.S. 1960. Occurrence of Tanymecus weevil in pest form in Punjab and its control. *Curr. Sci.* 29(7): 286.

Singh, S. and Kumar, A. 1985. Records and distribution of some Homoptera parasites of *Chromatomyia horticola* Goureau (Diptera: Agromyzidae) from India. *Indian J. Curr. Biosci.* 79-81.

Singh, S. and Sidhu, H.S. 1957. Control of mustard aphid by synthetic insecticides. *Indian Oilseeds J.* 1: 24-31.

Singh, S. and Sidhu, H.S. 1959. A schedule for control of mustard aphid by some insecticides. *Indian Oilseeds J.* 3: 170-178.

Singh, S., Singh, R.N., Singh, K.M., Singh, N.P. and Singh, S.N.1979. Effect of insecticides and irrigation on the incidence of pests, crop growth and yield of mustard. *Indian J. Ent.* 41(3): 267-271.

Singh, S., Singh, S.P., Suresh Babu, S. and Sabastian, P.C. 1991. Bioecology of Hymenoptera parasites of Agromyzidae (Diptera) pest species in India. *Mem. School Ent., India.* 11: 1-238.

Singh, S.P. and Sachan, G.C. 1997. Effect of different temepratures and host plants on the developmental behaviour of mustard sawfly, *Athalia proxima. Indian J. Ent.* 59(1): 34-40.

Singh, S.P. and Sachan, G.C. 1998. Food preference of grubs of mustard sawfly, *Athalia proxima*. *Indian J. Entomol.* 60(1): 103-105.

Singh, S.P. and Singh, D. 1982. Influence of cruciferous host plants on the survival and development of *Plutella xylostella* L. *J. Res. Punjab Agric. Univ.* 19: 100-104.

Singh, S.R., Narain, A., Srivastava, K.P. and Siddiqui, Q.A. 1965. Fecundity of mustard aphid on different rape and mustard species. *Indian Oilseeds J.* 9: 215-219.

Singh, V.K., Thakur, B.S. and Bajpai, R.P. 1992. Influence of sowing dates and incidence of aphids on yield of mustard. *Curr. Res.* 21: 97-98.

Singhvi, S.M., Verma, A.N. and Yadava, T.P. 1974. Crop spraying schedules against rapeseed and mustard pests. *Oilseeds J.* 4 : 15-19.

Singhvi, S.M., Verma, N.D., Yadava, T.P. 1973. Estimation of losses in rapeseed (*Brassica campestris* L. var. Toria) and mustard (*Brassica juncea* Coss.) due to mustard aphid (*Lipaphis erysimi* Kalt.). *Haryana Agric. Univ. J. Res.* 3(1): 5-7.

Sinha, R.P., Yazdani, S.S., Kumari, K. and Hameed, S.F. 1997. Evaluation of different spray schedules for control of mustard aphid. *Indian J. Ent.* 59(2): 179-186.

Sinha, R.P., Yazdani, S.S. and Verma, G.D. 1989. Population dynamics of mustard aphid, *Lipaphis erysimi* Kalt. in relation to ecological parameters. *Indian J. Ent.* 51(3): 334-339.

Spencer, K.A. 1961. A synopsis of the oriental Agronizidae (Diptera), *Trans. Rept. Ent. Soc.* London, 113: 55-100.

Spencer, K.A. 1965. The species-host relationship in the Agromizidae (Diptera) as an aid to taxonomy. *Proc. 12th Int. Cong. Entomol. London*, 1964, 1: 101-102, R. Entomol. Soc. London.

Spencer, K.A. 1973. Agromizidae (Diptera) of economic improtance. *Ser. Entomol.* 9: 1-418.

Srinivasachar, D. and Malik, R.S. 1972. An induced aphid resistant non-waxy nutrient in turnip, *Brassica rapa*. *Curr. Sci.* 41: 820-821.

Srinivasan, K. and Moorthy, P.N.K. 1991. Mustard plants trap major cabbage pests. *Indian Fmg.* 40(11): 11-12.

Srinivasan, K. and Rao, G.P.S. 1987. Distribution patterns of diamond-back moth and cabbage leaf-webber larvae on cabbage. *Int. J. Trop. Agric.* 5(3&4): 203-208.

Srivastava, A.S., Nigam, P.M. and Awasthi, B.K. 1972. Survey of pests on mustard crop. *Labdev. J. Sci. Tech. B. Life Sci.* 10: 165-166.

Srivastava, A.S. and Srivastava, J.L. 1961. Note on the life history of mustard aphid, *Lipaphis erysimi* Kalt. *Proc. Natn. Acad. Sci. India, B.* 31: 422-424.

Srivastava, A.S. and Srivastava, J.L. 1972. Ecological studies on the aphid, painted bug and sawfly attacking mustard and rape in India. *Pl. Prot. Bull.*, FAO 20(6): 136-140.

Srivastava, P.D. 1957. Studies on the choice of food plants and certain aspects of the digestive physiology of the larvae and adults of *Athalia lugens proxima* Klug. *Bull. Entom. Res.* 48: 289-291.

Srivastava, S.C. and Pandey, P.N. 1981. The effect of crucifers on growth, development, nutrition and reproduction of *Diacrisia obliqua* Walker (Lepidoptera: Arctidae). *Indian J. Zootomy* 22: 35-46.

Stapathi, C.R. 1990. Biology of diamond-back moth, *Plutella xylostella* L. *Environment and Ecology* 8(2): 784-785.

Stern, V.M. 1973. Economic Thresholds. *Ann. Rev. Entomol.* 18: 259-280.

Su, C.Y. 1987. The evaluation of granolosis viruses for the control of *Plutella xylostella* and *Artogeia rapae* at different time intervals. *Pl. Prot. Bull. Taiwan* 29(4): 397-399.

Sumithramma, N., Rajagopal, B.K. and Rajagopal, D. 1997. Comparative biology of mustard sawfly *Athalia lugens proxima* Klug (Hymenoptera: Tenthredinidae) on mustard and radish in south India. *Mysore J. Agri. Sci.* 31(2): 164-169.

Sun, C.N., Chi, H. and Feng, H.T. 1978. Diamond-back moth resistance to diazinon and methomyl in Taiwan. *J. Econ. Entomol.* 71(3): 551-554.

Supare, N.R., Ghai, S. and Ramamurthy, V.V. 1990. A revision of *Tanymecus* from India and adjacent countries (Coleoptera: Curculionidae). *Oriental Insects* 24: 1-26.

Suri, S.M., Singh, Darshan and Brar, K.S. 1988. Estimation of loss in yield of brown sarson due to aphids in Kangra Valley. I. Effect of crop growth stage and aphid exposure. I. *Insect Sci.* 1(2): 162-167.

Tabashnik, B.E. 1985. Deterence of diamond-back moth (Lepidoptera: Plutellidae) oviposition by plant compounds. *Environ. Entomol.* 14: 575-578.

Talekar, N.S. 1980. Search for host plant resistance to major insect pests in Chinese cabbage. pp. 164-173. *Proc. Symp. Production: Insect Control Crucif. Vegetables.* Taiwan, April, 1980. Plant Prot. Cent. Taiwan.

Talekar, N.S. and Shelton, A.M. 1993. Biology, ecology and management of the diamond-back moth. *Ann. Rev. Entomol.* 38: 275-301.

Tatchell, G.M. 1977. Oilseed rape (*Brassica napus*)—pest crop relationships. Ph.D. Thesis, Univ. London. (Cited from A.L. Winfield 1986. Field pests of oilseed rape. pp. 237-281. In: D.N. Scarisbrick, and R.W. Daniels eds., *Oilseed Rape.* Collins, 8 Graften St., London WI).

Teotia, T.P.S. and Lal, O.P. 1970. Differential response of different varieties and strains of oleiferous Brassicae to aphid, *Lipaphis erysimi* Kalt. *Labdev J. Sci. Tech.* 8-B: 219-226.

Tewari, R.K. and Singh, O.P. 1979. Evaluation of some insecticides for the control of hairy caterpillar, *Diacrisia obliqua* on sugar beet. *Indian J. Pl. Prot.* 7(1): 110-111.

Tewari, R.K., Prakash, O. and Singh, O.P. 1989. Effect of certain food plants on growth potential of *Spilosoma obliqua* Walker. *Bull. Entomol.* (New Delhi) 30(2): 195-199.

Thapa, R.B. 1987. Biology of *Pieris brassicae nepalensis* Doubleday (Lepidoptera: Pieridae) in Chitwan valley. *Pesticides* 21(6): 30-33.

Thomas, J., Phadke, K.G. and Verma, S. 1994. Efficacy of some insecticides against mustard aphids, safety to predator, pollinator and persistence of residues on rapeseed-mustard crop. *Shashpa* 1(2): 39-44.

Thompson, K.F. 1963. Resistance to cabbage aphid (*Bravicoryne brassicae*) in Brassica plants. *Nature* 198: 209.

Thompson, W.R. 1946. *A catalogue of the parasites and predators of insect pests. Part 8. Parasites of the Lepidoptera (N.P.),* pp. 475-477.

Thorsteinson, A.J. 1953. The chemotactic responses that determine host specificity in an oligophagous insect (*Plutella maculipennis* Curt., Lepidoptera). *Can. J. Zool.* 31: 52-72.

Thorsteinson, A.J. 1955. The experimental study of the chemotactic basis of host specificity in phytophagous insects. *Can. Entomol.* 33: 49-57.

Tiwari, S.N. and Kashyap, N.P. 1988. Feeding and observation preference of cabbage butterfly, *Pieris brassicae. Rev. Appl. Entomol.* 77(9): 752, 1989 (Abstr.).

Trehan, K.N. 1940. Hosts of *Phytomyza atricornis* in the Punjab. *Indian J. Ent.* 2: 95.

Trehan, K.N. and Sehgal, V.K. 1963. Range of host plants and larval feeding in *Phytomyza atricornis* Mg. (Diptera: Agromyzidae). *Ent. Mon. Mag.* 99: 1-3.

Tripathi, N.L.M. and Sachan, G.C. 1990. Effect of concentration of insecticides on the growth and development of mustard aphid, *Lipaphis erysimi* Kalt. *Indian J. Ent.* 52(1): 63-68.

Tripathi, R.L. 1963. Further studies on the biology of *Athalia proxima* Klug (Hymenoptera: Tenthrinidiae). *Indian J. Ent.* 24: 179-180.

Tripathi, R.L. and Singh, V.S. 1964. Effect of sowing date variations on the incidence of mustard aphid, *Lipaphis erysimi* Kalt on *Brassica campestris* var. sarson (Brown and yellow) and *B. juncea. Indian J. Ent.* 26: 251-252.

Uematsu, H. and Sakanoshita, A. 1989. Possible role of cabbage leaf wax bloom in suppressing diamond-back moth, *Plutella xylostella* (Lepidoptera: Yponomeutidae) oviposition. *Appl. Entomol. Zool.* 24: 253-257.

Usman, S. and Puttarudriah, M. 1955. *A list of insects of Mysore, including the mites.* p. 194. *Bull. No.16, Ent. Ser. 4,* Dept. Agric. Mysore, India.

Uttam, S.K., Mohan, K. and Tripathi, R.A. 1993. Studies on population dynamics of mustard aphid, *Lipaphis erysimi* Kalt. *Ann. Pl. Prot. Sci.* 1(1): 34-37.

VanEmden, H.F. 1973. Aphid-host plant relationships. pp. 54-64. In: H.J. Lowe ed., *Perspective in aphid biology. Entomol. Soc. N.Z. Bull.*

VanEmden, H.F. and Bashford, M.A. 1971. The performance of *Brevicoryne brassicae* and *Myzus persicae* in relation to plant age and leaf amino acids. *Entomol. Exp. Appl.* 14: 349-369.

VanEmden, H.F., Eastop, V.F., Hughes, R.D. and Way, M.J. 1969. The ecology of *Myzus persicae. Ann. Rev. Entomol.* 14: 197-270.

Varma, B.K. 1961. Bionomics of *Phyllotreta cruciferae* Goeze (Coleoptera: Chrysomelidae) reared on radish in India. *Indian J. Agric. Sci.* 31: 59-63.

Vaughn, T.T. and Hoy, C.W. 1993. Effect of leaf age, injury, morphology and cultivars on feeding behaviour of *Phyllotreta cruciferae. Environ. Entomol.* 22: 418-424.

Veerman, A., Beekman, M. and Veenendaal, R.L. 1988. Photoperiodic induction of diapause in the large white butterfly, *Pieris brassicae*: evidence for hourglass time measurement. *J. Insect. Physiol.* 34(11): 1063-1069.

Verma, A.N. and Sandhu, G.S. 1967. Diamond-back moth and its control. *Prog. Fmg.* 4: 6.

Verma, R.K. and Sachan, G.C. 1997. Impact of sowing time on the occurrence of *Athalia proxima* Klug. on three Brassica cultivars. *Ann. Pl. Prot. Sci.* 51(1): 44-49.

Verma, R.M. 1945. Prepupal and pupal changes in the mustard sawfly, *Athalia proxima* Klug. *Indian J. Ent.* 7: 238.

Verma, S. 1980. Evaluation of insecticides against pests and predators of mustard crop. *Indian J. Ent.* 45: 582-591.

Verzhutskii, B.N. 1967. The sawfly, *Athalia rosae* L. as a weed eliminator. *Rev.Appl. Entomol.*57: 467, 1969 (Abstr.).

Way, M.J. and Murdie, G. 1965. An example of varietal variation in resistance of Brussels sprouts. *Ann. Appl. Biol.* 56: 326-329.

Weber, G., Oswald, S. and Zollner, U. 1986. Suitability of rape cultivars with a different glucosinolate content for *Bravicoryne brassicae* L. and *Myzus persicae* Sulzer (Hemiptera: Aphididae). *Z. Pflanzenkr. Pflanzenschutz* 93: 113-124.

Wensler, R.J.D. 1962. Mode of host selection by an aphid. *Nature* 195: 830-831.

Williams, I.H. 1978. *Pests and pollination of oil-seed rape crops in England.* Illford, UK, Central Assocation of Bee-keeping.

Williams, I.H. 1980. Oil-seed rape and bee keeping, particularly in Britain. *Bee Wld.* 61(4): 141-153.

Williams, I.H. and Free, J.B. 1978. The feeding and mating behaviour of pollen beetles (*Meligethes aeneus* Fab.) and seed weevils (*Ceutorhynchus assimilis* Payk.) on oil-seed rape (*Brassica napus* L.). *J. Agric. Sci., Camb.* 91: 453-459.

Williams, I.H. and Martin, A.P. 1986. Evidence for a female sex pheromone in the brassica pod midge, *Dasineura brassicae. Physiol. Entomol.* 11(4): 353-356, UK.

Winfield, A.L. 1961a. Studies on the relationship between three species of Coleoptera and certain species of annual mustard and rape. *Entomol. Exp. Appl.* 4: 123-132.

Winfield, A.L. 1961b. Observations on the biology and control of the cabbage stem weevil, *Ceutorhynchus quadridens* Panz. on Trowse mustard. *Bull. Ent. Res.* 52: 589-600.

Winfield, A.L. 1986. Field pests of oilseed rape. pp. 237-281. In: D.H. Scarisbrick and R.W. Daniels eds., *Oilseed Rape.* Collins, 8 Grafton St. London WI.

Winfield, A.L. 1992. Management of oilseed rape pests in Europe, pp. 51-95. In: K. Evans ed., *Agricultural Zoology Reviews* Vol.5, Intercept Ltd., Andover, Hampshire, UK.

Yamada, H. and Koshihara, T. 1978. A simple mass rearing method of the diamond-back moth. *Plant Prot.* 28: 253-256.

Chapter 4

Non-insect Pests

4.1 INTRODUCTION

A number of non-insect pests damage oilseed brassicas but little is known about the identity of various species involved in their depredation, biology of these pests and measures to contain them. This lack of information about non-insect pests may be attributed mainly to three factors: lack of awareness about the type of depredation caused by these agents, absence of crop loss appraisal data and neglect of the crop itself. Now, with the growing demand for edible oil, the need to protect these crops and their yield has increased many fold. The present chapter provides information on plant nematodes, slugs and snails, birds, rodents and other animals that attack oilseed brassicas in India and measures to contain their damage.

4.2 NEMATODES

Nematode infestation is not a serious constraint in the growth and productivity of oilseed brassicas in India despite several reports of their association with roots of these crops. Plant parasitic and rhizosphere soil nematodes of oleiferous Brassicas reported from India include: *Aphelenchoides brassicae, A. taraii* (Edward & Misra, 1969) and *A. besseyi* (Gupta, 1986); *Meloidogyne* spp. (Rashid *et al.*1973), *M. incognita* (Roy, 1972; Roy & Das, 1980), *M. javanica* (Chandwani & Reddy, 1967; Jain, 1978) and *M. graminis* (Kaul & Chhabra, 1988); *Tylenchus* spp. (Rashid *et al.* 1973) and *T. microdorus* (Chawla *et al.* 1969); *Helicotylenchus* spp. (Rashid *et al.* 1973) and *H. elegans* (Prasad & Khan, 1990); *Hoplolaimus indicus* (Prasad & Khan, 1990; Rashid *et al.* 1973); *Tylenchorhynchus* spp. (Rashid *et al.* 1973; Sethi & Swarup, 1968), *T. mashhoodi* (Roy & Das, 1980; Sethi & Swarup, 1968) and *T. vulgaris* (Prasad & Khan, 1990; Upadhyay & Swarup, 1972); *Pratylenchus* spp. (Rashid *et al.*1973), *P. ranjani, P. cruciferous* (Bajaj & Bhatti, 1984; Khan & Singh, 1974) and *P. flakkensis* (Roy & Das, 1980); *Heterodera* spp. (Srivastava & Singh, 1967); *Rotylenchus reniformis* (Prasad & Khan, 1990; Rashid *et al.* 1973); *Xiphinema vulgare* (Roy & Das, 1980); and *Ecophydophora* spp. (Rashid *et al.* 1973). Besides, *Ditylenchus clarus, Geocenamus tenuidens* (Tylenchidae); *Eucephalobus arcticus, Chiloplacus saccatus* (Cephalobidae); *Primatolaimus primitivus* (Monhysteridae); *Aporcelaimellus obtusicaudatus* (Aporcelaimidae); *Eudorylaimus longicardius* (Dorylaimidae); and *Xiphinema capriviense*

(Longidoridae) were also found in soil around the roots of rapeseed at Jodhpur, Rajasthan (Rathore & Neema, 1991). Nothing is, however, known about the parasitic nature and economic importance of these eel worms in respect to Brassicas.

Tylenchorhynchus brassicae was reported parasitic on cabbage, cauliflower and other vegetables by Siddiqui *et al.* (1972) but not on sarson and rai though mentioned by Gupta (1986) and Chhabra (1992). Both, *B. alba* and *B. campestris* but not *B. campestris* var. Toria are the attractive hosts for *T. vulgaris* (Upadhyay & Swarup, 1972).

Among the phytoparasitic nematodes, two economically important root-knot nematodes, *Meloidogyne incognita* and *M. javanica* parasitize rapeseed and mustard crops. *Meloidogyne incognita* feeds on the root system, induces their swelling with egg sacs and brings about reduction in length and weight of shoots. Infested plants fail to produce any flower or pod. Plants artificially inoculated with *M. incognita* showed maximum reduction (50%) in shoot length and maximum number of galls per root system with 10,000 nematodes/pot, the highest level of inoculum used in the test (Prasad & Chawla, 1992). Likewise, *M. javanica* caused considerable reduction in length and weight of roots, number of branches, number of pods and seeds/pod of sarson (*B. campestris* var. Sarson) (Jain, 1978). It also caused similar damage to *B. campestris* ssp. *pekinensis* (Mangat & Bhatti, 1987).

Histopathological changes in the host due to infestation by *M. javania* are characterized by regions of hypertrophy and hyperplasia. Cells around the nematode body become either collapsed or compressed due to pressure exerted by tissue development or enlargement of the nematode (Hasan & Jain, 1985).

Brassicas may also interfere in the penetration of hosts and survival of nematodes in them. Co-culturing of Raya (*B. juncea*) cv. RLM-619, Toria (*B. campestris* var. Toria) cv. TLC-1 and Taramira (*Eruca sativa*) cv. ITSA seedlings with wheat cv. WL-711 caused significant reduction in the juvenile penetration of *Heterodera avenue* in wheat roots because of their mortality due to root exudates from Brassicas (Tanda *et al.* 1988). Indian mustard is an antagonistic trap crop that affects the biology of root-knot nematodes. In green-house experiments, the life cycle of *M. incognita* was reduced by 10 days besides drastic reduction in root galling and egg mass production in mustard as compared to that in susceptible tomato crop (*Lycopersicon esculentum* Mill.) because allyl isothiocynates present in the roots of mustard is inhibitory to nematode development. Leaf extract of mustard, and mustard cake have similar detrimental effect on the nematodes (Rangaswamy & Reddy, 1993a,b). Even application of 5% mustard cake reduced damage to *Phaseolus vulgaris* inoculated with *M. incognita* and *Fusarium solani* (Srivastava & Singh, 1991).

Rape crops are also affected significantly by other nematodes like *Helicotylenchus digonicus, H. vulgaris, Heterodera cruciferae, H. trifolii, H. schachtii, Merlinius brevidens, Pratylenchus neglectus, P. cruciferus, P. penetrans, P. pratensis, Trichodorus similis, Tylenchorhynchus brassicae* and *T. dubius* in different parts of the world (Gupta, 1986, Winfield, 1986). *Pratylenchus neglectus,* the root lesion nematode, is the most important parasitic nematode of rape in France, while *H. schachtii* (the beet cyst nematode) and *H. cruciferae* (Brassica cyst nematode) are important in UK and other European countries. These two have wide host range, attack all Brassicas and most other crucifers. *Heterodera schachtii* causes serious damage to sugar beet, mangels and red beet than to rape while *H. cruciferae* is a minor pest of rape, and produces patchy growth of stunted and sickly plants. Both the nematodes readily multiply on Brassicas but rarely cause any serious damage to them though they have the potentiality to do so (Winfield, 1986).

The reaction of 38 varieties and strains of *B. campestris* to *M. javanica* was evaluated in a green-house test. All the entries were susceptible to a varying degree and only four strains, No.107, 108, 110 and 18285 harbouring immature females showed small degree of resistance. The existence of nematode tolerant cultivars of Indian mustard was reported by Thakar and Patel (1986). Out of 30 cultivars tested, only the cultivars Varuna, Patan-67 and Kambli showed resistant reaction (root knot index = 1.56-1.88) to mixed infection by *M. incognita* and *M. javanica*.

In India, with the rapid increase in area under oilseed brassicas and their repeated cultivation in the same area year after year with higher inputs of manures and water, the population of parasitic nematodes may reach the threshold limit to warrant control measures. Regular crop survey and soil sampling are, therefore, necessary to monitor the population level of parasitic eel worms.

4.3 SLUGS AND SNAILS

4.3.1 Slugs

Little is known about these soft-bodied gastropods in India, except the taxonomic identity, distribution and food plants of only a few. The slug *Laevicaulis alte* Ferrusac is commonly seen in Delhi all the year round, and damages vegetable crops during the rainy months (Srivastava & Abbas, 1983).

There is, however, no report of slug damage to oleiferous Brassicas in India probably because the damage, if any, is too insignificant to attract attention and secondly, no one has yet seriously looked for it. Nevertheless, slugs do inflict damage to oilseed rape (*Brassica napus*) and cereals (wheat, barley and maize etc.) in Europe and other countries. One or more slug species may attack rape but the important ones involved in the U.K. are *Deroceras reticulatum, D. agreste* and *Arion intermedius* (Mabbett, 1991; Cedell,1989). Slugs cause serious damage to wheat that follows rape (Glen, 1989).

Rape plants are most vulnerable to slug attack from the time their cotyledons first come out of the soil surface until the successful formation of the first two leaves. Slugs cut holes in leaves of young seedlings, and seedlings in patches are mostly affected. The major factors that favour slug feeding activity are low glucosinolate content and retarded growth of hosts. Glucosinolates have an antifeedant property and their presence in rape seeds protect the seedlings from slug attack (Moens, 1989; Moens, *et al.* 1992a). In a trial, seedlings of commercial varieties of rape viz. Jet Neuf, Mikado, Rafal, Bienvenu, Cobra, Libravo, Ariana, Topas and Fido were exposed to the slug, *D. reticulatum* immediately after sowing in compost in trays. The number and leaf area of seedlings, and the damage symptoms were found to be strongly and inversely related to the total concentration of glucosinolates present in seeds and one-week-old seedlings (Glen, *et al.* 1990). Later in development, the antifeedant activity dissipates and the speed of development of the plant becomes important (Moens, *et al.*, 1992a).

4.3.1.1 Control

For control of slug infestation, one application of pellets containing 4% thiodicarb at 5 Kg/ha at seedling emergence stage provides good protection against species of Deroceras and Arion (Moens & Gigot, 1988). Mesurol (methiocarb) pellets at 3-4 Kg/ha is also effective (Cedell, 1989).

Slug control with methiocarb baits is more effective as compared to thiodicarb and metalde-hyde formulations in terms of numbers of slugs (*Deroceras* and *Arion* spp.) killed, persistence and prevention of crop damage (Kelly *et al.* 1993).

In addition to control through molluscicides, slug population can also be reduced by cultural methods based on five principles: crop rotation avoiding crops favourable to slugs; soil treatments including clearing after harvest, cultivation, compactation of coarse soils and improving soil structure; improving growth conditions of plants; seed dressing with fungicides; and use of resistant varieties (Moens, *et al.* 1992b).

4.3.2 Snails

Like slugs, not much is known about the role of snails as pest of oilseed brassica crops in India. According to Srivastava and Abbas (1983), and Srivastava (1992), the giant snail *Achatina fulica* Bowdich, *Opeas gracilis* Hutton, *Zootecus insularis* Ehrenberg, *Ariophanta bajadera* Pfeiffer, *A. solata* Benson, *A. ligulata* Ferrusac, *Cryptozona belangiri* Deshayes, *C. (Xestina) bistrialis* Beck, *C. (Nilgiria) semirugata* Beck, *Macrochlamys indica* Godwin-Austin and *Bensonia monticola* Hutton are the important land snail pests of vegetables, fruits, ornamental and other plants in India. An unusual outbreak of *Macrochlamys glauca* Pfeiffer infesting many vegetable, flower and cereal crops was observed at Katrain (Kullu valley), Himachal Pradesh in 1993. The snails congregated in wet places and climbed the host at dusk and fed there till morning (IARI News 9 (3), July-September 1993). According to preliminary observations of the author, *M. glauca* is also an important pest of rapeseed and mustard in Katrain and its adjoining areas.

Fig. 4.1. The snail, *Macrochlamys indica* devouring Indian mustard leaf

The author encountered heavy infestation of *Macrochlamys indica* (identity confirmed by P.D. Srivastava) on 30 to 45 day old seedlings of Yellow sarson cv. YS-8 (*Brassica campestris*) and Indian mustard cv. Pusa Bold (*B. juncea*) raised during June-August, 1988 at the IARI, New Delhi. They are flat and round with marks of grey-yellow band on the shell and measured about 1.0-1.5 inches in diameter (Bhowmik, 1988). These molluscs crawled up the seedlings in the afternoon and night, and devoured the foliage (Fig. 4.1). Seedlings maintained under moist and partly shadded conditions showed the highest infestation.

The presence of *M. indica* at Delhi, Pusa (Bihar) and Port Blair was reported by Srivastava (1992) who also found it to feed on money plant [*Scindapus* (*Pothos*) *aureus*]. This was earlier reported from Assam, Bihar, Orissa, West Bengal, Kerala and Tamil Nadu as garden pest of cucurbitaceous plants e.g. *Luffa* spp., beans, lettuce, cole crops, drum stick (*Moringa oleifera*), amaranth (*Amaranthus blitum*), okra (*Abelmoschus esculantus*), marigold (*Tagetes* spp.) and Chrysanthemum sp. (Raut & Ghose, 1984).

4.3.2.1 *Control*

Snail infestation is not a problem with rapeseed and mustard in India but in the event of any localized attack, they may be destroyed by hand-picking or through the use of 5% metaldehyde pellets (Srivastva, 1992).

4.4 BIRDS

Oilseed brassicas, like all grain and fruit crops, are also depredated by birds throughout the country but information on their avian pest complexes is scanty and precise damage estimates are wanting.

Bird damage to Brassica crops starts with the sowing of seeds when several avian species such as the blue-rock pigeon, *Columba livia* Gmelin, the ring-dove, *Streptopelia decaocto decaocto* Frivaldszky, the common house crow, *Corvus splendens* Vieillot, the common myna, *Acridotheres tristis* Lin. and the house sparrow, *Passer domesticus* Lin. etc., which are present throughout the country, visit the field. They usually come to the field in early morning for a few hours and then again in late afternoon for a shorter duration. Birds spoil much more than what they actually consume.

The pigeon and dove, both of which are vegetarian, pick out the germinating seeds of rapeseed (*Brassica campestris* L.) and mustard (*B. juncea* Czern and Coss.) from the soil and eat them, reducing the plant stand and ultimately the crop yield (Prasad, 1984). Ring-doves perch on trees and dwellings, and come to the threshing floors for food. Afzal Hussain and Bhalla (1937), as quoted by Ali and Ripley (1969), found ring-dove to eat Toria seeds (*B. campestris*) during threshing operations. Stomachs of dove examined at Pusa (Bihar) contained chiefly wheat, barley, and paddy grains, and seeds of mustard, linseed and various weeds according to Mason and Lefroy (1912).

The author noticed both house crow and myna to disturb the seed rows in the field while diging out the hibernating insects and insect grubs from the soil. But it could not be ascertained whether they also consumed the sprouting seeds, although these two birds are known to eat both grains and animal matters (Ali & Ripley, 1983). The house sparrows, the ubiquitous commensals of man, visit the nursery bed in the morning around 9-10 A.M. They come in large numbers and quickly nibble away the tender shoots and young leaves of emerging seedlings of rapeseed and mustard, and other crops. Prasad (1984) estimated that about 10% of sown seeds are destroyed by birds.

The common pea fowl, *Pavo cristatus* found in plentiful in north Indian states, feeds on grains, seeds, tender shoots, fruits and insects (Ali & Ripley, 1983). They eat away the emerging shoots and young seedlings of rapeseed and mustard, sometimes making it difficult to raise them in unprotected nursery beds or pots. During one morning in early January 1990, the author came across a group of five pea fowls that was nibbling the leaves of young Indian mustard plants (cv. Pusa Bold) at the IARI Farm, New Delhi. Ducks, *Anas strepera strepera* Lin, and domestic fowls damaging tender rapeseed and mustard seedlings in fields near the vicinity of village homesteads is a familiar sight and the damage is often considerable.

The great Indian bustard, *Choriotes nigricans* Vigors and the Bengal florican, *Eupodotis bengalensis* Gmelin are the other birds that prefer shoots of mustard (Bhatnagar, 1983).

The rose-ringed parakeet, *Psittacula krameri* Scopoli, because of its ubiquitous abundance and flocking habit, is considered to be the most destructive bird to agriculture. Parakeets are purely vegetarian and eat gregariously on grains and fruits of economically important plants. They attack Brassica crops when their flowering is nearly complete and the seeds in green siliquae are hardening. The parakeets reach the feeding area at dawn and feed for 2-3 hours (morning 6 to 9 a.m.). Their second feeding session begins by about 4 p. m. and lasts for 1.30-2.00 hrs after which they fly to night roost (Shivanarayan, 1982). It has been reported that in a field of Indian mustard (area 0.2 h a) in Punjab, the damage to pods by rose-ringed parakeets was so severe that the yield was reduced by 63%. (Simwat & Sidhu, 1973). Serious damage to rocket-salad (*Eruca sativa* Mill) and Sarson (*B. campestris*) besides other grains has also been observed (Sekhon, 1966), and the damage to pods of mustard and Toria was a high of 88% in one case (Toor, 1982).

The northern rose-ringed parakeets, *P. krameri borealis* Neumann sit on the plant, cut open the siliquae and feed upon seeds and dislodge them. They also cut the branches and take them to their roosting place. In case of severe infestation not even a single siliqua is left on the plant. The siliquae of Yellow and Brown sarson (*B. campestris*) are more preferred by parakeets than those of *B. juncea* and *B. nigra* Koch. varieties. The siliquae of *B. napus* L. shatter easily at maturity, and pigeons and doves feed on such fallen seeds (Prasad, 1984).

Depredation of oilseed brassicas by avian species is also common in other countries. In Britain, for example, grazing of oilseed rape (*B. napus*) by dark bellied brent geese (*Branta bernicola bernicola*) is a serious problem, especially in coastal areas of south-east Essex. Intensive grazing caused a mean yield loss of 11.1% during 1990-91 (McKay *et al.* 1993). Similarly, woodpigeon (*Columba palumbas*) is a pest of rape throughout Britain. The crop is vulnerable to attack from November but the most critical period for the birds is in February to early March when severe damage is done to the crop (Winfield, 1986).

4.4.1 Management

Recent increase in incidence of bird depredation to oilseed brassicas is considered to be due to a shift in their dietory habits as a result of deforestation and depletion of their natural food reserves.

Most birds are protected by national law (Rao, 1982). Birds should therefore, be managed in problem areas by traditional methods of scaring by human yelling, pelting stones, using noise makers and other frightening devices, etc. though these methods do not give the desired effect for long periods because birds become accustomed to them and continue feeding. Prasad (1984) suggested running of a wooden roller over the field immediately after sowing not only to reduce the loss of seeds but also to conserve the soil moisture essential for good germination. The other methods of bird management such as population reduction (by traps and nets, shooting and nest destruction, etc.) and chemical control (through repellants and poison baits) (Shivanarayan, 1982; Toor, 1982; Bhatnagar, 1983) are not appropriate for both ecological and economic considerations. In case of small crop area, the bird scaring metalised reflection ribbons or nylon nets may be used. The author found the latter one as very effective but costly.

4.5 RODENTS

Rodents damage oilseed brassicas from their sowing time to grown up stage in the field, and spoil stored seeds in godowns. They dig the soil and make burrows in the field disturbing the seed rows and later, damage the growing plants. In Rajasthan, mustard field showed high rodent population as indicated by 73.1 to 76.5 live burrows/ha affecting 33.2 to 45.2% reduction in plant population upto pre-flowering stage (AICRPRC. 1987). In Uttar Pradesh, mustard crop suffered only 2.66% loss in plant stand due to rodent attack during 1985-86 when it was grown with wheat as mixed crop since rodents are known to have higher preference for wheat (AICRPRC. 1986). Although there is no report of rodents consuming rapeseed and mustard seeds probably because of non-preference, they do spill them by making holes in storage bags and containers, and make them unfit for human consumption by their urine, hairs and droppings.

The rodent species that are found predominantly associated with rapeseed and mustard in Uttar Pradesh, Punjab and Rajasthan are: *Bandicota bengalensis*, *Rattus meltada*, *Mus booduga*, *Nesokia indica*, *Tatera indica* and *Meriones hurrianae* (Jain & Tripathi, 1992).

4.5.1 *Bandicota bengalensis* (Lesser bandicot, mole rat or field rat)

The mole rat is dark greyish brown in colour with greyish white belly and a bare tail. It is the most destructive to field crops and is found all over the country except the eastern desert. It is a nocturnal and fossorial rodent that occupies two types of habitats: in crop fields and godowns. In the field, it makes deep, large ramifying burrows and hoards large amounts of food in the burrow. It prefers wheat and rice crops, but is also responsible for losses in mustard and groundnut. The mole rat breeds all the year round and produces 2 to 18 young ones per litter (Prakash, 1983; David & Kumaraswami, 1988).

4.5.2 *Rattus meltada* (Soft furred grass rat or field rat)

The grass rat is dark brownish, grey above and pale grey below with soft fur, and is smaller in size than the mole rat (David & Kumarswami, 1988). This is another serious pest that lives in irrigated fields. It is nocturnal and lives in simple burrows, usually more than one adult rat occupy a single burrow. In Rajasthan desert, it breeds from March to September and produces 2-10 young ones per litter (Prakash, 1983; Rana & Prakash, 1984).

4.5.3 *Mus booduga* (Indian field mouse)

Field mouse is brown in colour with a white belly. It burrows in field bunds causing extensive damage and wastage of water. It is nocturnal and has the habit of cutting and removal of grains from the plant. The litter size ranges from 3 to 9 (David & Kumaraswami, 1988)

4.5.4 *Nesokia indica* (Short tailed mole rat)

This is common in Punjab, Haryana, Rajasthan, Delhi and Uttar Pardesh. It lives in cultivated fields and in areas under natural vegetation. It is also nocturnal and lives in burrows. The burrow is peculiar by being a small mole hill of sand which is accumulated by excavating the soil (Prakash, 1983). It breeds in January to March and August to October, and the litter size varies from 2-5 (Jain & Tripathi, 1992).

4.5.5 *Tatera indica* (Indian gerbil)

The Indian gerbil is reddish grey in colour with white underside (David & Kumaraswami, 1988), and is found throughout the country. It is also nocturnal in habit and lives in burrows of comparatively simple pattern (Prakash, 1983). The burrows are found in and around mustard and wheat-fields in Rajasthan (Jain & Tripathi, 1992). It breeds all the year round producing 1-9 (av. 4.78) young ones per litter (Jain, 1970).

4.5.6 *Meriones hurrianae* (Indian desert gerbil)

The desert gerbil is found mostly in the arid and semi-arid regions of Rajasthan, Gujarat, Punjab, Haryana and Delhi. It is diurnal and makes extensive burrows (Prakash, 1981). It shares its habitat with *T. indica* and causes extensive damage to young mustard seedlings (Jain & Tripathi, 1992). The desert gerbil breeds all the year round and shows two breeding peaks, from February to March and July to September. Litter size varies from 1-9 (av. 4.4) (Prakash, 1981,1983).

4.5.7 Common rodent control measures

Rodent infestation is not as serious problem with oleiferous Brassicas as with other oilseeds, pulses and cereals. Economic considerations should, therefore, be the deciding factor in rodent management programme.

4.5.7.1 *Cultural practices*

Practices like deep ploughing with mould board plough and reduction in bund size, destruction of rodent burrows and inducement of their migration from the crop field are useful. Clean cultivation and weed control reduce rodent infestation by depriving them shelter and food supply during lean periods. For limited areas and in storage godowns, the use of various live and kill types of traps such as wonder traps, sherman traps and snap traps etc. may provide effective rodent control. Trapping has also been suggested as a follow up measure after chemical control to eliminate residual rodent population (Jain & Tripathi, 1992).

4.5.7.2 *Fumigation*

Rodent control by fumigation is more effective in simple burrows, since the escape of poisonous gas is minimum, and the lethal concentration of gas is build up at a much faster speed than in complicated ones, and the rodents are unable to escape (Prakash & Mathur, 1987). The most used and recommended fumigant in India is Aluminium phosphide based compounds or tablets (Prakash,

1983). The chemical is especially effective in high moisture areas because soil moisture helps in releasing the lethal phosphine gas. The product is, however, highly inflammable and hazardous.

4.5.7.3 Baiting

The most common, effective and humane method of rodent control is through poisoning with rodenticides (Fitzwater & Prakash, 1978). Zinc phosphide and Barium carbonate, etc. are the single dose, acute poisons while compounds like warfarin and fumarin (the so-called first generation compounds), and bromadiolone, brodifacoum and flocoumafen (the second generation compounds), are the slow acting, multidose anticoagulants used against rodents. (Jain & Tripathi, 1992). Out of all these chemicals, Zinc phosphide is mostly used throughout the world for the preparation of baits for rodent control. The control procedure, as suggested by Prakash and Mathur (1987), consists in pre-baiting the active borrow openings in the field for three days at the rate of 6 g/rodent/day (with 97 parts Bajra flour + 3 parts groundnut oil). Next, on the fourth day, burrow openings are poison baited at the same rate (with 95 parts Bajra flour + 3 parts groundnut oil + 2 parts zinc phosphide).

4.6 OTHER ANIMALS

Young succulent rapeseed and mustard plants are palatable diet to grazing animals like cattle, buffaloes and goats, etc. Young seedlings of rapeseed and mustard that are thinned out from the field as well as plucked green leaves of adult plants, are fed to the milch animals by the farmers as they are believed to enhance milk production. These animals also often stray into the field and cause considerable damage if a watchful eye is not kept. Removal of leaves especially from the upper and middle position of plants at flower initiation stage and until a few days after flowering is detrimental to crop growth and yield (Paul & Saha, 1992; Raut & Ali, 1986; Tayo & Morgam, 1979).

The Indian hare, *Lepus nigricollis* Cuvier is found in almost every habitat throughout the country. During the winter months, it feeds mainly on green grass, wheat, barley and mustard crop (Prakash, 1983). The black buck (*Antelope cervicapra*) is another animal that destroys agricultural crops. A dramatic increase in the number of black bucks in recent years has posed as serious problem to agriculturists as well as for great Indian bustard (*Choriotis nigricans*) management in Karera bustard sanctuary in Madhya Pradesh. An extensive survey made to assess the extent of damage to crops in eight affected villages has shown lentil (*Lens esculenta*), as the most damaged crop, followed by mustard (*B. campestris*), taramira (*E. sativa*) and gram (*Cicer arietinum*). Wheat (*Triticum vulgare*) was the least damaged crop. The black buck damage problem has given rise to many factors inimical to bustard conservation, including hostality by farmers to the concept. Black bucks have emerged as a most important factor causing damage to bustard and its habitat (Sharma, 1994). There is, however, no report of crop damage by animals like Nilgai, *Boselaphus tragocamelus* Pallas and deers, etc. which are common in many parts of the country. In Britain, the double zero cultivars of oilseed rape (*B. napus*) are reported to be more palatable than other cultivars to rabbits, hares and deers grazing at night (Tapper & Cox, 1990).

Normally, damage to Brassica crops due individually to any of these animals may be negligible but when anyone of them invades the field in large numbers or when total damage due to all of them is considered, the reduction in crop yield must be considerable.

REFERENCES

AICRPRC. 1986. Annu. Prog. Rept., 1985-86, All India Coord. Res. Proj. Rodent Control (ICAR), Jodhpur.

AICRPRC. 1987. Annu. Prog. Rept., 1986-87, All India Coord. Res. Proj. Rodent Control (ICAR), Jodhpur.

Ali, Salim and Ripley, D. 1 969. *Handbook of the birds of India and Pakistan, Vol. 3.* Bombay Natural History Society. Oxford University Press, Delhi-Oxford. pp. 325.

Ali, Salim and Ripley, D. 1983. *A pictorial guide to the birds of Indian sub-continent.* Bombay Natural History, Centenary Publication. Oxford University Press, Delhi-Oxford. pp. 177.

Bajaj, H.K. and Bhatti, D.S. 1984. New and known species of Pratylenchus Filipjev (Nematoda: Pratylenchidae) from Haryana, India with remarks on intraspecific variation. *J. Nematol.* 16(4): 360-367.

Bhatnagar, R.K. 1983. Birds of agricultural importance. pp. 356-369. In: P.D. Srivastava, M.G. Jotwani, R.A. Agarwal, S.R. Wadhi, R.K. Bhanotar and R.K. Bhatnagar eds., *Agricultural Entomology, Vol. 11.* All India Scientific Writers' Society. A-2/78, Paschim Vihar, New Delhi, pp. 434.

Bhowmik, T.P. 1988. Annu. Prog. Rept. 1988. Project No.AR-14. Diseases of oilseed crops and their management with special reference to root rot of groundnut and foliar diseases of Brassica spp. Div. Mycol. & Plant Pathol., IARI, New Delhi.

Cedell, T. 1989. Slug attack on autumn seedlings. *Svensk-Frotidning.,* 58(7-8): 152-153, 163. (CAB Abstracts 1990-91).

Chandwani, G.H. and Reddy, T.S.N. 1967. The host range of root-knot nematode *Meloidogyne javanica* in tobacco nurseries at Rajahmundry, Andhra Pradesh. *Indian Phytopath.* 20: 383-384.

Chawla, M.L., Prasad, S.K., Khan, E. and Siya Nand. 1969. Two species of the genus Tylenchus Bastian (Nematoda: Tylenchidae) from Uttar Pradesh, India. *Labdev. J. Sci. & Technol.* 7B(4): 291-294.

Chhabra, H.K. 1992. Nematode pests of oilseed crops. pp. 149-158. In: D.S. Bhatti and R.K. Walia eds.: *Nematode Pests of Crops.* CBS Publishers and Distributors. 485, Jain Bhavan, Bhola Nath Nagar. Shahdara, Delhi-110032, India.

David, B.V. and Kumaraswami, T. 1988. *Elements of Economic Entomology,* 4th edition, pp. 537. Popular Book Depot, 29 Potters' Street, Saidapet, Madras-600015.

Edward, J.C. and Misra, S.L. 1969. Occurrence of some new species of Aphelenchoidea in the rhizosphere of certain field crops of Uttar Pradesh, India, with a note of an intersex. *The Allahabad Farmer* 43: 1-6.

Fitzwater, W D. and Prakash, I. 1978. *Handbook of Vertebrate pest control.* Indian Coun. Agri. Res., New Delhi, pp. 92.

Glen, D.M. 1989. Understanding and predicting slug problems in cereals. Monograph, BCPC, No. 41: 253-262. In: *Slugs and Snails in World Agriculture,* Guildford, 10-12 April, 1989. (CAB Abstracts 1987-89).

Glen, D.M., Jones, H. and Fieldsend, J.K. 1990. Damage to oilseed rape seedlings by the field slug *Deroceras reticulatum* in relation to glucosinolate concentration. *Ann. Appl. Biol.* 117(1): 197-207.

Gupta, D.C. 1986. Nematode pests of oilseed crops and their management. pp. 336-340. In: G. Swarup and D.R. Dasgupta eds: *Plant parasitic nematodes of India. Problems and Progress.* Allied Publishers Pvt. Ltd. A-104, Maya Puri, Phase II, New Delhi 110064. pp. 497.

Hasan, N. and Jain, R.K. 1985. Varietal screening and histopathological changes in *Brassica campestris* roots infected with root-knot nematode, *Meloidogyne javanica. Indian J. Nematol.* 15(1): 105-106.

Jain, A.P. 1970. Body weight, sex ratio, age structure and some aspects of reproduction in the Indian gerbil, *Tatera indica* Hardwicke in Rajasthan desert. *Mammalia* 34: 415-432.

Jain, A.P. and Tripathi, R.S. 1992. Management of rodent pests in oilseed crops. pp. 356-377. In: D. Kumar and M. Rai eds. *Advances in Oilseeds Research,* Vol. l, Scientific Publishers, Jodhpur.

Jain, R.K. 1978. Effect of root-knot nematode, *Meloidogyne javanica* on Japan sarson. *Indian J. Agric. Res.* 12: 92-93.

Kaul, V.K. and Chhabra, H.K. 1988. A new record of *Meloidogyne graminis* on Raya and occurrence of *Meloidogyne spp.* in Ludhiana, Punjab, India. J. *Oilseeds Res.* 5 (2): 200-205.

Kelley, J.R, Bolton, B.J.G., Gibbon, B. and Williams, G.H. 1993. Comparison of molluscicidal baits in cereals and oilseed rape. Crop Protection in Northern Britain. pp. 91-96. *Proceedings of a Conference,* Dundee Univ., 23-25 March, 1993.

Khan, E. and Singh, D.B. 1974. Five new species of Pratylenchus (Nematoda Pratylenchidae) from India. *Indian J. Nematol.* 4: 199-211.

Mabbett, T. 1991. Straw incorporation trials reveal arable slug damage will increase. *Agric.-Intern.* 43(11): 304-306 (CAB Abstracts 1992).

Mangat, B.P.S. and Bhatti, D.S. 1987. Pathogenicity of *Meloidogyne javanica* on *Brassica compestris ssp. pekinensis. Int. Nematol. Network Newsl.* 4(2): 14-15.

Mason, C.W. and Lefroy, H.M. 1912. The Food of Birds in India. *Mem. Agri. Dept. India, Entomological Series.* Vol. 3.

McKay, H.V., Bishop, J.D., Feare, C.J. and Stevens, M.C. 1993. Feeding by brent geese can reduce yield of oilseed rape. *Crop Prot.* 12(2): 101-105.

Moens, R. 1989. Factors affecting slug damage and control measure decisions. Monograph, BCPC, No. 41: 227-236, In: *Slugs and Snails in World Agriculture,* Guilford, 10-12 April, 1989 (CAB Abstracts 1987-89).

Moens, R, Couvreur, R. and Cors, F. 1992a. The influence of the content of glucosinolates of winter rape varieties on slug damage. *Bulletin-des-Rescherches-Agronomiques-de-Gembloux* 27(3): 289-301 (CAB Abstracts 1993-7/95).

Moens, R. and Gigot, J. 1988. A new slug bait containing 4% thiodicarb. *Revue-de-l'Agriculture* 41(5): 1213-1225 (CAB Abstracts 1990-91).

Moens, R, Latteur, G. and Fayt, E. 1992b. Contribution to an integrated slug control. *Parasitica* 48(3): 83-105.

Paul, N.K. and Saha, D.K. 1992. Effect of degree and time of defoliation and leaf sheding on yield and yield components of mustard. *Crop. Res.* 5(2): 249-255.

Prakash, I. 1981. *Ecology of Indian desert gerbil, Meriones hurrianae. CAZRI-Monograph* No. 10, pp. 87. Central Arid Zone Res. Inst., Jodhpur.

Prakash, I. 1983. Mammal pests of agricultural crops. pp. 371-386. In: P.D. Srivastava, M.G. Jotwani, R.A. Agarwal, S.R. Wadhi, R.K. Bhanotar and R.K. Bhatnagar eds. *Agricultural Entomololgy,* Vol-II, All India Scientific Writers' Society. A-2/78, Pashchim Vihar, New Delhi. pp. 434.

Prakash, I. and Mathur, R.P. 1987. *Management of rodent pests.* ICAR, Krishi Anusandhan Bhavan, Pusa, New Delhi 110012, pp. 133.

Prasad, D. and Chawla, M.L. 1992. Pathogenicity of *Meloidogynae incognita* on sunflower, safflower and mustard. *Curr. Nematol.* 3: 127-132.

Prasad, D. and Khan, E. 1990. Faunistic survey and ecology of plant parasitic nematodes infesting rabi oilseed crops. *Curr. Nematol.* 1(l): 73-76.

Prasad, S.K. 1984. Bird damage in oilseed crops. pp. 56-58. In: *Natn. Symp. : Impact of non-insect pests and predators of food production and environment.* Abstracts, 12-14 March, 1984. All India Scientific Writers' Society, A-2/78, Pashchim Vihar, New Delhi. pp. 117.

Rana, B.D. and Prakash, I. 1984. Reproductive biology of *Rattus meltada pallidior* (Ryley) in Rajasthan desert. *J. Bombay Nat. Hist Soc.* 81(1): 59-70.

Rangaswamy, S.D. and Reddy, P.P. 1993a. Effect of leaf extracts of trap crops on the growth of tomato and development of *Meloidogyne incognita* (Kofoid and White) Chitwood. *Curr. Nematol.* 4(1): 7-10.

Rangaswamy, S.D. and Reddy, P.P. 1993b. Effect of marigold and mustard as trap crops on the biology of *Meloidogyne incognita* (Kofoid and White) Chitwood. *Curr. Nematol.* 4(l): 77-80.

Rao, P.R.P. 1982. Bird strikes. pp. 41-54. In: R.A. Agarwal and R.K. Bhatnagar eds., *Proc.: Seminar on management of problem birds in aviation and agriculture,* 25-26 May, 1982. Aeronautics Research and Development Board, Min. of Defence, Govt. of India and Indian Agri. Res. Inst, New Delhi.

Rashid, A., Khan, F.A. and Khan, A.M. 1973. Plant parasitic nematode associated with vegetables, fruits, cereals and other crops in North India, 1. Uttar Pradesh. *Indian J Nematol.* 3(1): 8-23.

Rathore, S.S. and Neema, H.S. 1991. New records of nematodes from soil around roots of rapeseed *Brassica juncea* from India. *Indian J. Helminth.* 43(1): 9-18.

Raut, M.S. and Ali, M. 1986. Studies on defoliation and detopping in mustard under rainfed conditions. *Indian J. Agron.* 31: 252-255.

Raut, S.K. and Ghose, K.C. 1984. *Pestiferous Land Snails of India.* Z.S.I. Tech. Monog. No. 11, pp. 151. Zoological Survey of India, Calcutta.

Roy, A.K. 1972. Reaction of some plants to the attack of *Meloidogyne incognita* in Assam. *Indian J. Nematol.* 2(1): 86-89.

Roy, Sadasiv and Das, S.N. 1980. Nematode of saline soils in Orissa. *Indian J. Nematol.* 10(2): 231-260.

Sekhon, S.S. 1966. Studies on the nidification behaviour and damage by sparrows and parrots in the Punjab. M.Sc. Thesis, Punjab Agri. Univ., Ludhiana (Unpublished).

Sethi, C.L. and Swarup, G. 1968. Plant parasitic nematodes of north-western India. I. The genus Tylenchorhynchus. *Nematologia* 14: 77-88.

Sharma, R.D. 1994. Black buck damage - as a problem for sanctuary management in Bustard Sanctuary, Karera. *Indian Forester* (Special issue on biodiversity-II). 120: 10, 924-928.

Shivanarayan, N. 1982. The rose-ringed parakeet, the problem bird in agriculture and its management. pp. 154-158. In: R.A. Agarwal and R.K. Bhatnagar eds., *Proc.: Seminar on management of problem birds in aviation and agriculture.* 25-26 May, 1982. Aeronautics Research and Development Baord, Min. of Defence, Govt. of India and Indian Agri. Res. Inst., New Delhi.

Siddiqui, Z.A., Khan, A.M. and Saxena, S.K. 1972. Host range and varietal resistance of certain crucifers against *Tylenchorhynchus brassicae. Indian Phytopath.* 25: 275-281.

Simawat, G.S. and Sidhu, A.S. 1973. Note on the feding habits of rose-ringed parakeet, *Psittacula krameri (Scopoh). Indian J. Agric. Sci.* 43(6): 607-609.

Srivastava, A.K. and Singh, R.B. 1991. Use of organic amendments against *Fusarium solani* and *Meloidogyne incognita* on *Phaseolus vulgaris. New Agriculturist* 2(1): 63-64.

Srivastava, A. S. and Singh, B. 1967. Incidence and intensity of attack of plant parasitic nematodes on some important commercial crops and fruit trees in Uttar Pradesh. *Labdev. J. Sci. & Technol.* 3(4): 259-263.

Srivastava, P.D. 1992. *Problem of Land Snail Pests in Agriculture. A study of the Giant African Snail. pp.* 234. Concept Publishing Company, New Delhi 110059.

Srivastava, P.D. and Abbas, S.R 1983. Snails and slugs. pp. 340-355. In: P.D. Srivastava, M.G. Jotwani, R.A. Agarwal, S.R. Wadhi, R.K. Bhanotar and R.K. Bhatnagar eds. *Agricultural Entomology* Vol. II. All India Scientific Writers' Society. A-2/78, Paschim Vihar, New Delhi.

Tanda, A.S., Singh, I. and Sakhuja, P.K. 1988. Effect of crucifers on the penetration and survival of *Heterodera avenae* in wheat. *Nematologia Mediterranea,* 16(1): 143-144.

Tapper, S. and Cox, R. 1990. Selection of double zero oilseed rape crops by rabbits, hares and deer grazing at night. In: *Rapeseed 00 and Intoxication by wild Animals, pp.* 152-161, Report Commissioned by the European Communities EUR 11771, Luxembourg.

Tayo, T.O. and Morgan, D.G. 1979. Factors influencing flower and pod development in oilseed rape (*Brassica napus* L.). *J. Agric. Sci. Camb.* 92: 363-373.

Thakar, N.A. and Patel, C.C. 1986. Reaction of some mustard varieties to root-knot nematodes *Meloidogyne incognita* and *M. javanica. Indian J. Nematol.* 48(3) 359-360.

Toor, H.S. 1982. Problem birds and their management in Punjab. pp. 132-142. In: R.A. Agarwal and R.K. Bhatnagar eds., *Proc.: Seminar on management of problem birds in aviation and agriculture.* 25-26, May, 1982. Aeronautics Research and Development Board, Min. of Defence, Govt. of India and Indian Agri. Res. Institute, New Delhi.

Upadhyay, K.D. and Swarup, G. 1972. Culturing, host range and factors affecting multiplication of *Tylenchorhynchus vulgaris* on maize. *Indian J. Nematol.* 2 139-145.

Windfield, A.L. 1986. Field pests of oilseed rape. pp. 237-281. In: D.H. Scarisbrick and RW. Daniels eds: *Oilseed Rape.* Collins, 8 Grafton Street, London WI.

Chapter 5

Soil Salinity and Alkalinity

5.1 INTRODUCTION

High concentration of soluble salts in the top soil layer is detrimental to profitable agriculture. In India about 7 million hectares of land are known to have been degraded by salinity/alkalinity with varying degrees of salt accumulations. According to some estimates, the total salinity/alkalinity affected area will be around 12 million hectares although correct figure is difficult to obtain from coastal regions. The problem is acute in the semi-arid and arid tracts of Indo-Gangetic alluvial plains where about 40 per cent of the total affected area is concentrated (Agarwal *et al.* 1979). Besides, an additional area of about 15-20 million hectares of land in canal irrigated tracts runs the risk of being degraded through the influence of salts (Abrol, 1986). Loss of land to salt accumulation through irrigated agriculture has been estimated to be atleast several hundred km^2 a year in India (Flowers *et al.* 1977).

Rapeseed and mustard, the principal oilseed crops of the winter season, suffer serious damage due to toxicity of salts in irrigated areas of Rajasthan, western Punjab, Haryana, Delhi and Uttar Pradesh. In the Indo-Gangetic plains of northern India, Indian mustard is grown on about 3.8 m.ha out of which nearly 2.5 m.ha is sodic soil that affects their growth (Sharma & Singh, 1993; Singh *et al.* 1988). Increasing usage of poor quality underground water for irrigation because of erratic and insufficient rains in these areas has aggravated the problem of soil degradation. Corrective measures are needed not only to ensure optimum productivity of these oleiferous Brassicas but also to extend their cultivation into potentially arable lands of these tracts, presently lying unutilized due to excessive accumulation of salts.

5.2 SALT AFFECTED SOILS AND THEIR CHARACTERISTICS

Soils become degraded due to accumulation of different soluble salts in varying concentrations such that they adversely affect the growth and productivity of economic crops, since growth of crops is restricted when the conductivity of the soil saturation extract (ECe) or exchangeable sodium percentage (ESP) exceed the tolerable limit of plants. There are two main groups of salt affected soils, (a) Saline soil and (b) Sodic soil which may be either Non-saline sodic soil or Saline sodic soil.

Soils become saline when their ECe is more than 4dS/m (decisiemens/metre) at 25°C, the ESP is less than 15 and the pH is less than 8.5. Soils whose ECe is greater than 4 dS/m at 25°C and ESP greater than 15 are termed Saline sodic soils while those having ECe less than 4 dS/m at 25°C and ESP greater than 15 are the Non-saline sodic soils. The pH of Sodic soils, which are also called the Alkali soils, ranges from 8.5 to 10.0, though it may in some cases exceed 10.0 (U.S. Salinity Laboratory Staff, 1954). The salinity measurement unit is also expressed as mmhos/cm (millimhos/centimetre). 1dS/m is numerically equal to 1 mmhos/cm or is approximately equivalent to 640 mg salts/litre.

5.2.1 Saline soils

Plant tolerance to salinity differs from field to field and the type of salts they contain. Ions that contribute to soil salinity include Cl^-, SO_4^{2-}, HCO_3^-, Na^+, Ca^{2+}, Mg^{2+} and, rarely, NO_3^- or K^+. The salts of these ions occur in highly variable concentrations and proportions. They may be the natural constituents of these soils, but are also added to them through irrigation waters and waters coming from adjacent areas (Bernstein, 1975). Field soil salinity is governed both by the nature and quantum of salts present in a soil as well as by its water holding capacity. The water holding capacity of fine textured clay soil will be a few times higher than that of coarse textured sandy soil and hence at a given salt content on dry-soil basis, the concentration of soil solution of sandy loam soil will be a few times higher than that of the clay soil (U.S. Salinity Laboratory Staff, 1954). Many a times, a soil containing appreciable amounts of salts may not show salinity problem, if the salt, such as gypsum, is sparingly soluble and *vice versa*. The total soluble salt concentrations are high in saline soils and they may often give rise to nutrient deficiency such as that of Ca in plants (Bernstein, 1975).

5.2.1.1 Measurement of salinity

Generally, under saline field conditions in which Ca^{2+} and Na^+ concentrations are high, plant response is well correlated with osmotic potential of the soil water. Since the electric conductivity (EC) of the soil extracts is also well correlated with their osmotic potentials and can be easily measured, the EC of the soil saturation extract is commonly used as a measure of salinity. Soil salinity

Table 5.1. Crop response to salinity, measured as the electrical conductivity of the soil saturation extract, ECe.

Soil salinity class	ECe range in dS/m at 25°C	Crop response
Non-saline	0-2	Salinity effects mostly negligible
Slightly saline	2-4	Yields of very sensitive crops restricted
Moderately saline	4-8	Yields of most crops restricted
Highly saline	8-16	Only tolerant crops yield satisfactorily
Very highly saline	> 16	Only a few very tolerant crops yield satisfactorily

Source: Bernstein, 1975

in terms of electrical conductivity of the saturation extract (ECe) is usually grouped into five classes on the basis of crop response (Bernstein, 1975) (Table 5.1).

5.2.2 Sodic or Alkali soils

Non-saline sodic soils contain sodium salts, mostly sodium carbonate and is mainly responsible for high concentration of Na^+ ions on the soil exchange complex and in imparting high alkalinity to the soil solution. These soils may often be deficient in Ca and Mg resulting in their reduced availability to plants. Plant response is largely determined by the concentration of sodium ions in solution irrespective of their proportion on the exchangeable complex of the soil. They adversely effect plant growth and yield because of their poor physical condition, excess Na may also have direct toxic effects on plant. These soils deflocculate, are less permeable to water and air, and are sticky when wet and very hard when dry. They are often called Black alkali soil because of high proportion of dissolved organic matter in the surface soil (Bernstein, 1975; Maas, 1986).

Saline sodic soils, with ESP similar to Non-saline sodic soils, contain high concentration of different elements in soil solution and are nutritionally adequate. Their high salt concentrations promote flocculation, their permeability is normal and salinity effects predominate (Bernstein, 1975).

Besides the above major groups of salt affected soils, there exists soils with range of reactions which are intermediate between the major groups. There are also soils like acid sulphate, degraded alkali and those rich in a particular salt, etc. (Abrol, 1986).

5.3 FACTORS INFLUENCING SALT-TOLERANCE OF PLANTS

Crop species and even varieties within a species may vary in their tolerance to salts. Some crops may be quite tolerant to saline conditions but not to sodic conditions to the same degree and *vice versa*. Tolerance may also vary with the growth stage of crops, they are mostly sensitive at germination than afterwards. Some crop species are more salt sensitive than others (Abrol, 1986). Seed germination is affected more by soil salinity than by sodicity (Bansal & Bhattaryaryya, 1984).

Crop response to salinity is influenced by many interacting factors of environment and soil. Temperature, relative humidity and air pollution (eg. Ozone) influence crop tolerance to salinity. Adverse effects of salinity on crop plants become more pronounced under hot and dry weather than under cool and humid weather. Plants are likely to tolerate higher salinity levels when evapotranspiration is low, and lower salinity levels when evapotranspiration is high. Plants are more affected by salinity in nutrient deficient soils than in nutrient rich soils. Similarly, plants grown under depleted soil moisture condition suffer from both increasing salt and water stress.

Salt concentration of the surface soil layer gradually increases if the intervals between irrigations are increased because of loss of soil water due to evapotranspiration. Salinity also increases with soil depth and the salt concentration is much higher at the lowest end of the root zone as compared to that of the surface soil layer because of the increasing absorption of water by the plant. Under water-stress conditon, plants are forced to absorb salt solution of higher concentration from increasing greater depths (Maas, 1986).

5.4 MEASUREMENT OF PLANT TOLERANCE TO SALINITY

Assessment for relative tolerance of different crop variety to salinity is made by growing them under conditions of their recommended cultural and management practices for optimum production. Salt tolerance data of a crop variety are then calculated in terms of ECe at 25°C. Information obtained are then utilized in preparing yield response curve for individual crop variety to determine their tolerance to salinity up to threshold level above which yields decrease almost linearly with the . increase in salinity (Fig. 5.1).

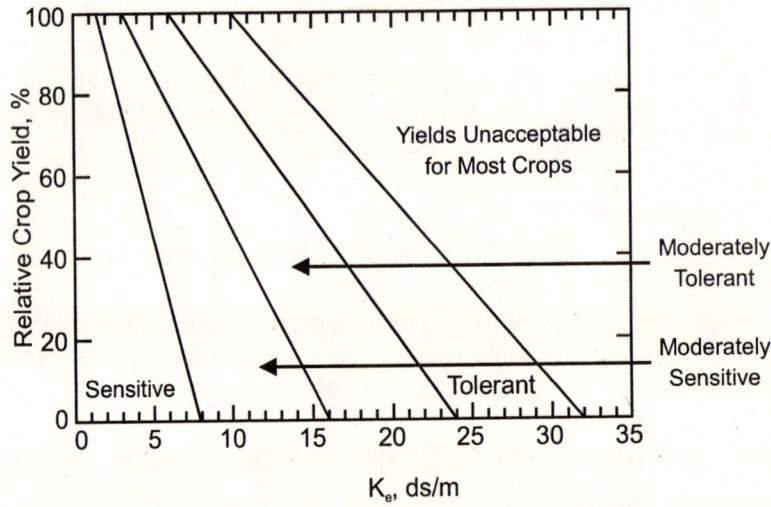

Fig. 5.1. Divisions for classifying crop tolerance to salinity. (*Source*: Mass, 1986)

The yield response curve provides two parameters for expressing salt tolerance of crops: (a) threshold or the maximum allowable salinity limit without yield reduction below that for non-saline or normal soil condition, and (b) slope or the per cent yield decrease per unit increase in salinity beyond the threshold level. The curve also provides four qualitative salt tolerance ratings limited by boundaries for quick comparison among crops (Maas, 1986).

The relative yield Y_r of a crop for any particular soil salinity exceeding the threshold limit can be obtained by the equation:

$$Y_r = 100 - B (ECe - A),$$

in which A = the salinity threshold, and B = the percentage yield decrease per unit of salinity increase above the threshold limit. For example, yields of *B. juncea* decrease approximately, say by 5% per dS/m, when *ECe* exceeds 24 dS/m, its threshold limit. Hence, at a soil salinity of 26 dS/m, the relative yield will be:

$$Y_r = 100 - 5 (26 - 24) = 90\%$$

5.4.1 Salt-tolerance of Brassica species

Information on the tolerance of oleiferous Brassicas to salts is limited. Appraisal of tolerance of Brassica plants to salinity/alkalinity has been based mostly on absolute plant growth and/or yield on problematic soil and the results obtained from different studies, in many cases, are at variance with one another.

The comparative performance of *B. carinata* over *B. juncea* to salinity stress at various growth stages was assessed through a sand culture experiment at the Central Soil Salinity Research Institute (CSSRI), Karnal during 1990-91 season. Early growth stages of the two species were more sensitive than later stages at the salinity levels of 2, 5, 10, 15 and 18d S/m. *Brassica carinata* made poor growth in the initial 50 days but later, the growth picked up and plants yielded higher than *B. juncea* at all the salinity levels indicating its better performance than the latter under saline water stress (CSSRI. 1991).

Superior performance of *B. carinata* over that of *B. juncea* and others to salinity was again confirmed when its 21 strains were compared with 5 varieties each of *B. juncea*, *B. napus*, *B. campestris* var. Yellow sarson, *B. campestris* var. Brown sarson and *B. campestris* var. Toria under saline, alluvial and sandy clay loam soils at the IARI Farm during 1984-85 and 1985-86 seasons. The soil pH ranged from 7.6 to 8.0 (1:2 soil:water suspension), ECe was 4.1 to 8.8 dS/m and water table ranged from a depth of 40 to 60 cm. Under such saline soil conditions, *B. carinata* performed much better than the other three species though it had the longest maturity days. In other species, seed germination was poor, a number of seedlings died after germination and those which survived did not grow normally, and produced seeds which were under-sized. *Brassica carinata*, on the other hand, showed rare mortality of plants, salinity had little effect on seed size, and higher number of primary and secondary branches of plants resulting from its longest vegetative growth phase contributed 22% more seeds and 25% more oil yield. *Brassica juncea* with short maturity days performed second best in respect to seed and oil yield while *B. napus* and *B. campestris* (vars. Yellow sarson, Brown sarson and Toria) ranked respectively third and fourth in respect to the two yield parameters (Malik, 1990) (Table 5.2).

Table 5.2. Response of Brassica species in saline soils.

Species	Maturity (days)	Seed yield (t/ha)		Oil yield (t/ha)
		1984-85	1985-86	
B. carinata	172	1.6	1.6	0.59
B. juncea	136	1.4	1.2	0.47
B. napus	163	1.1	0.9	0.37
B. campestris var. Yellow sarson	141	1.0	0.8	0.36
B. campestris var. Brown sarson	137	1.0	0.9	0.36
B. campestris var. Toria	98	0.3	0.4	0.25
LSD (5%)	6.5	0.24	0.21	0.07

Source: Malik, 1990.

Brassica juncea cultivars B-28, C-54 and T-59 showed moderate tolerance while *B. campestris* cultivars PBI-6, YSP b-24 and BSH-1 showed poor tolerance at seed germination under salinity range of EC 3 to 9 of irrigation water (Maliwal, 1973). This type of differential response of the two Bassica species is considered to be due to their genetic make up, *B. juncea* being a polyploid (4X) is more adaptive than its deploid (2X) counterpart, *B. campestris* (var. Yellow sarson, Brown sarson and Toria) on saline and sodic soils in respect to seed germination and seedling growth (Rana *et al.* 1980).

Brassica juncea showed better performance than *B. carinata* and *B. napus* in respect to seed germination on highly saline calcareous soils (ECe 16-20 dS/m) at Jodhpur, India. It recorded the highest seed germination of 13.91 and 6.75% and *B. napus* had the lowest seed germination of 3.40 and 0.60% at the salinity level of ECe 16 and ECe 20 dS/m, respectively. *Brassica carinata* was intermediate while Taramina (*Eruca sativa*) was superior to all the three Brassica species in this respect (Kumar, 1990) (Table 5.3).

Table 5.3. Per cent seedling emergence of Brassica and Eruca species on saline calcareous soil.

Species	Emergence (%)		
	ECe 3.4 dS/m	*ECe 16 dS/m*	*ECe 20 dS/m*
B. juncea	74.79	13.91	6.75
B. carinata	78.00	7.00	2.25
B. napus	70.80	3.40	0.60
E. sativa	83.00	27.00	22.66

CD (5%): Salinity - 2.40; Salinity × Species - 11.56
Source: Kumar, 1990.

Among the Brassicas, *B. juncea* is the major oilseed crop of the Indo-gangetic plains of India suffering from salinity (Kumar & Malik, 1983; Rai, 1977; Singh *et al.* 1979). Kumar (1992) categorized the general order of relative salt tolerance of Brassica spp. as *B. juncea* > *B. carinata* > *E. sativa* > *B. tournefortii* > *B. napus* > *B. campestris* var. Toria > Brown sarson > Yellow sarson and *B. alba*, though their comparative performance relative to individual control towards salt under uniform conditions of testing is not known. This aspect has been discussed in later part of this chapter.

5.4.2 Tolerance to NaCl

The four Brassica species, *B. campestris*, *B. carinata*, *B. juncea* and *B. napus* differ significantly ($P \leq 0.001$) in their responses to different concentrations of NaCl, increasing salt concentrations significantly reduce the fresh and dry biomass production of their root and shoot. In a sand culture study, *B. napus* produced more biomass and had a higher seed yield in both absolute and relative terms than the other three species when grown at 125 mol/m^3 NaCl. In contrast, *B. campestris* had the lowest biomass production, seed yield and oil content. It did not differ significantly from *B.*

juncea and *B. carinata* in biomass production for growth, and had lower leaf succulence than in other three species over the range of NaCl concentrations used. The seed yield of *B. napus* (1.74 g/plant) and *B. carinata* (1.60 g/plant) was higher than that of *B. juncea* (0.69 g/plant) and *B. campestris* (0.61 g/plant). *Brassica napus* and *B. carinata* accumulated lower amounts of Na^+ and Cl^- in their tissues and had significantly higher K selectivity ($S_{K,Na}$) in their shoots than did those of *B. campestris* and *B. juncea*. On the basis of these comparataive responses, *B. napus* and *B. carinata* were considered relatively tolerant whereas *B. campestris* and *B. juncea* relatively sensitive to NaCl (Ashraf & McNeilly, 1990).

He and Cramer (1992), on the other hand, found that the growth of six rapid-cycling lines of Brassica species, *B. napus*, *B. campestris*, *B. nigra*, *B. juncea*, *B. oleracea* and *B. carinata* was inhibited by sea water salinity. The relationship between salinity and growth is non-linear, and the growth response of a given species may be higher than the other species at one salt treatment but lower at another. This type of plant growth response to salinity makes it difficult to distinguish the difference between species in salt tolerance. However, on the basis of change in dry matter reduction relative to the control at varying concentrations of salts (4, 8 and 12 dS/m), the relative salt tolerance of the six Brassica species could be conveniently classified into three groups: (a) *B. napus*, showing a reduction in total dry matter content of 1%, 28% and 52% relative to control at 4, 8 and 12 dS/m respectively, as the most salt-tolerant, (b) *B. campestris*, *B. nigra*, *B. juncea* and *B. oleracea* with a mean decrease in their total dry matter production of approximately 23%, 48% and 68% relative to control at 4, 8 and 12 dS/m respectively, as moderately salt-sensitive species and (c) *B. carinata*, showing a reduction in total dry matter content of 39%, 56% and 71% relative to control at 4, 8 and 12 dS/m respectively, as the most salt-sensitive species. Thus, the most sensitive species *B. carinata* was earlier considered salt-tolerant (Ashraf & McNeilly, 1990) because the evaluation of salt-tolerance was then based on absolute fresh and dry weights and on seed yield of each species instead of the reducton in fresh and dry weights relative to control.

5.4.2.1 *Relationship between ion concentraton and salt-tolerance*

Salinity induces change in ion concentrations of plants and there exists a close relationship between ion concentrations in shoots and relative tolerance of Brassica species to salts. The relationship becomes apparent when categorization of plants into salt-tolerant and salt-sensitive is based on the reduction in biomass production and seed yield relative to their individual control.

The six rapid-cycling Brassica species, *B. napus*, *B. campestris*, *B. nigra*, *B. juncea*, *B. oleracea* and *B. carinata* showed increased concentration of Na in their shoots accompanied by a corresponding decrease in K concentration following increase in external concentration of salts. Determination of relationship between ion concentration and relative salt-tolerance of these six species through rank analysis indicated significant effect of salinity on the concentration of Ca, Mg, K, Cl, Na and total N in their shoots. Among all these elements, Ca was the only element that was significantly correlated with salt tolerance (Table 5.4).

The salt-tolerant *B. napus* had the highest Ca concentration at a given salinity level and the salt-sensitive *B. carinata* had the lowest, implying that Ca plays a regulatory role in the responses of Brassica species to saline conditions (He & Cramer, 1992).

Table 5.4. The relationship between the relative order (according to species) of salt tolerance and specific ion concentrations of the shoot. The rank scores of salt tolerance or ion concentrations were computed by first averaging the values of total dry weight expressed as % of the control or specific ion concentrations of the shoot expressed as mmole/g DW* at 4, 8 and 12 dS/m treatments and then ranking the mean values from the highest to the lowest among the six Brassica species as 1, 2, 3, 4, 5 and 6. The significant *r* value at P = 0.05 is 0.77.

Species	Salt Tolerance	The rank scores of ion concentration of the shoot							
		Na	*K*	*Mg*	*Ca*	*Cl*	*N*	*Na/Ca*	*Total cation content*
B. napus	1	5	4	1	1	4	5	6	4
B. campestris	2	1	5	4	2	2	1	1	1
B. nigra	3	3	3	3	3	3	3	3	2
B. juncea	4	4	2	2	4	1	2	4	3
B. oleracea	5	2	6	6	6	6	6	2	5
B. carinata	6	6	1	5	5	5	4	5	6
Rank Correlation coefficients (r)	1	0.26	–0.37	0.71	0.94	0.43	0.26	–0.029	0.66

Source: He and Cramer, 1992.　　　　　　　　*DW = Dry weight

These rapid-cycling Brassicas showed proportional decrease in K/Na ratio of their shoots with the increase in salinity from 4 dS/m to 12 dS/m. This decrease in K/Na ratio was correlated with salt induced growth reduction (expressed 'as percentage of control) within a species. The change in K/Na ratio with increasing salinity, however, was not correlated with K-Na selectivity. Both K/Na ratio and K-Na selectivity were not also correlated with relative salt tolerance of these Brassica species. Thus, a high shoot K/Na ratio or K-Na selectivity may not be reliable selection criterion for salinity resistance in some species (He & Cramer, 1992). Reliable and efficient screening criterion must, therefore, be used in determining relative salt tolerance in Brassica species under uniform conditions of soil and environment.

5.5 SALT-TOLERANT BRASSICA CULTIVARS

Brassica being the chief winter season oilseed crop of the salt affected regions, identification of intra-species variability in respect to salt tolerance through large scale screening of available germplasm is of tremendous economic significance.

5.5.1 Salinity tolerant cultivars

Indian mustard varieties T-59 (Varuna), Appress mutant and T-11 are some of the earliest ones identified as promising under saline water irrigation although salinity adversely affects their germination (Rai, 1977). The cv. T-58 is another saline water tolerant Indian mustard which can be raised with water up to EC 12 dS/m without any marked effect on yield. However, irrigation with EC 16 dS/m water significantly reduces its grain yield and dry matter production mainly due to adverse effects of high salinity on seed germination and plant stand (Narain *et al.* 1979) but this can be counteracted by increasing the seed rate.

In a micro-plot study on salt tolerance of six improved Indian mustard cultivars (RL-18, Pusa Bold, Prakash, Varuna (T-59), PR-10 and Laha-101), Varuna recorded the highest grain yield and proved most tolerant. The cv. RL-18 yielded the lowest and was the most salt-sensitive, the cv. Prakash reacted moderately tolerant and the rest three were salt sensitive (Kumar & Malik, 1983). Similarly, on loamy sand light textured soils at the salinity levels of EC 2.1, 6, 12 and 16dS/m, the cv.Appress Pod was superior to 9 other Indian mustards in respect of germinability of seeds and oil content (35.8%). Here again, the cv.Varuna surpassed all in respect to seed yield and oil yield/plant. Both Varuna and Appress Pod did not reflect any adverse effect of salinity on their oil content (Kumar & Kumar, 1985) (Table 5.5). Irrigation with saline water EC 12dS/m also did not have any

Table 5.5. Effect of saline water on seed germination, seed yield, oil content and oil yield of Indian mustard cultivars.

Treatments	Seed germination (%)	Oil content (%)	Seed yield/ plant (g)	Oil yield/plant (g)
Salinity (dS/m)				
2.1 (control)	88.8	28.3	5.2	1.4
6	58.6	31.5	6.2	1.9
12	41.2	34.6	10.6	3.6
16	32.7	25.0	7.8	1.9
S.Em.±	2.11	0.96	0.54	—
CD(5%)	7.20	NS	1.86	—
Cultivars				
T-11	52.7	29.4	7.2	2.1
T-56	56.5	33.5	8.1	2.7
Varuna	53.9	31.5	11.4	3.6
5422-2	54.6	30.2	9.6	2.9
5909	48.9	30.2	7.4	2.2
KB-2	60.5	28.8	8.5	2.4
Laha-101	57.5	31.3	8.1	2.5
T-6342	51.5	27.0	9.1	2.4
Appress Pod	61.2	35.8	6.0	2.1
Appress Mutant	59.6	32.4	9.3	3.0
S.Em.±	2.41	0.86	0.78	—
CD (5%)	6.80	2.41	2.19	—

Source: Kumar and Kumar, 1985.   NS = Not significant

adverse effect on the grain yield and dry matter production of Varuna, and it produced as good yield as that of control (EC 2 dS/m) in sandy loam soils at Agra (Chauhan *et al.* 1988).

Pusa Bold is the other popular high yielding Indian mustard which tolerated salinity up to ECe 15 dS/m without any difference in seed germination up to ECe 9dS/m (Girdhar, 1989). The cv. RSM 107 is another excellent strain of Indian mustard which ranked most tolerant in comparison to the genotypes Varuna (T-59), RW 4/86-452, RH-30, RSM-107-450, DIRA 367-419, RSK 5-445 and Kranti at salinity levels, EC 2.0 to 19.0dS/m. RSM-107 showed higher biomass production, grain yield and husk weight and lesser reduction in seed weight over others at higher salinity levels (Sharma & Gill, 1992). The highly salt-tolerant nature of Varuna was again evident from a trial with five Indian mustard varieties on medium-fine, red desertic loam to clay loam soil at Pali-Marwar, Rajasthan. Varuna yielded the maximum among five Indian mustard varieties when they were grown with EC 4.0 (control), 6.0, 9.0 and 12.0d S/m irrigation water application. It showed the least reduction in yield at 12 ECiw dS/m compared to control, highest mean salinity index, highest ECiw values for 50% yield decline and lowest reduction per unit increase in salinity (slope) (Table 5.6) indicating its superiority over othes (Chopra & Chopra, 1992).

Table 5.6. Relative salt-tolerance of Indian mustard varieties to salinity in terms of grain yield.

Variety	Mean yield at different salinity levels (q/ha)	Reduction at highest ECiw from control	Mean salinity index	*Slope	50% yield decline ECiw
Varuna	28.35	34.18	74.77	0.040	13.97
Kranti	27.74	47.71	60.97	0.050	10.64
RK-8501	25.41	44.10	62.27	0.049	11.16
RH-8311	26.53	51.17	56.87	0.057	9.80
RH-847	27.78	47.19	61.07	0.051	10.78

Source: Chopra and Chopra, 1992, partly rearranged.
*Slope — Yield reduction per unit increase in salinity beyond threshold value.

In the black soil area of Tungabhadra, Karnataka with medium ranged salinity, selection CS-416 and one "local" mustard with high yield potential and lower slope proved promising up to ECe 18dS/m compared to Varuna, Kranthi and seven other lines tested (Uma *et al.* 1992). Nevertheless, the variety Varuna (T-59), tested for seven consecutive years with no significant loss in grain yield (average reduction 23%) up to EC 12dS/m, should be preferred over others for cultivation in saline soil. Other improved varieties like PR-15, Prakash and RH-30 tolerate water salinity up to 12dS/m with less than 25% reduction in yield while PR-35, RIM + 524 and RH-7818 are medium tolerant to EC 8dS/m (Chauhan *et al.* 1993). According to Sinha (1993), Indian mustard cultivars do not yield significantly different between irrigation treatments of 0.8 EC dS/m (control) and saline water at 6 or 10 dS/m applied at different stages.

Sarson (*B. campestris* var. Sarson) is also fairly tolerant to saline water irrigation. The crop, however, suffered yield loss on a soil having initial EC 17.5 dS/m of the saturation extract (Ram Deo & Ruhal, 1971). In case of Toria (*B. campestris* var. Toria), the average germination percentage and early growth stage of six genotypes were adversely affected when exposed to variable salinity levels of 4.0 to 10.0 dS/m. Their germination decreased significantly with the increase in salinity levels and the reduction was more marked at and above EC 8.0 dS/m. Determination of relative germination percentage of these six genotypes at zero salinity level showed that the genotype TG-3 has the highest tolerance to salinity at germination over the salinity range of 4.0 to 10.0 dS/m followed by the genotypes TLC-2 and TLC-1, etc. while T-9 is the most salt sensitive (Singh & Prakash, 1984) (Table 5.7).

Table 5.7. Effect of various salinity levels on relative germination percentage of Toria genotypes on 10th day of sowing.

Genotypes	Salinity dS/m				
	0	*4*	*6*	*8*	*10*
Pant Toria 43	100.0	85.6	79.5	74.9	70.4
T-9	100.0	79.7	72.5	72.5	60.1
TH 68	100.0	85.6	80.1	78.0	78.0
TLC-1	100.0	96.4	90.0	84.7	77.8
TLC-2	100.0	96.4	87.5	84.7	82.5
TG-3	100.0	100.0	92.8	92.8	92.8

Source: Singh and Prakash, 1984.

Drastic reduction in seed germination at or above 8 dS/m was also noted in Indian mustard genotypes (Kumar & Singh, 1980; Paliwal, 1972; Rai, 1977). Both Yellow sarson (*B. campestris* var. Yellow sarson) cv. YSPb-24 and Brown sarson (*B. campestris* var. Brown sarson), cv. BSH-1 showed poor germination at the salinity range of EC 3 to 9 dS/m of irrigation water under Udaipur conditions (Maliwal, 1973). They, however, showed good germination up to salinity ECi 6 in a pot experiment at the IARI, New Delhi (Paliwal, 1972).

5.5.2 Alkalinity tolerant cultivars

Among the oleiferous Brassicas, *B. carinata* performs better than other species in alkaline soils. *Brassica carinata* cv. HC-6 with 40.6% germination performed well at soil pH 9.5 under Jodhpur condition (AICORPDA. 1987). In case of *B. juncea*, the cv. Varuna was superior to other Indian mustards in tolerance up to ESP 20-30 alkalinity under both Indore and Karnal conditions (CSSRI. 1986). Results of a field experiment at the CSSRI farm, Gudha during 1987-88 have clearly shown that Indian mustard is a semi-tolerant crop that can be grown successfully in sodic soil when the surface soil ESP is around 40 (CSSRI. 1989). Growth, yield attributes and seed yield of cultivars decrease and the maturity enhances with increasing levels of ESP, and the differences are significant beyond 38 (Table 5.8).

Among the four *B. juncea* cultivars tested, Pusa Bold produced significantly higher yield as compared to the three cultivars, Kranti, Pusa Barani and Varuna, which were at par (CSSRI. 1990).

Table 5.8. Effect of soil ESP on the yield attributes and seed yield of four Indian mustards.

Initial ESP (0-15 cm)	Plant height (cm)	Main branches/ plant	Pods/ plant	Grain/Pod	Grain weight (g/plant)	Test weight (g)	Seed yeild (t/ha)
64	123.9	3.89	149.5	12.6	5.81	4.34	0.70
38	137.6	4.39	192.3	13.5	9.58	4.74	1.18
28	140.7	4.38	196.3	13.6	9.62	4.82	1.19
26	143.6	4.41	201.2	13.8	9.88	4.89	1.26
23	145.1	4.58	209.4	13.9	10.12	4.99	1.28
CD 0.05	11.5	NS	47.9	NS	2.60	0.38	0.13
Cultivars							
Pusa Bold	135.8	4.31	205.3	13.8	10.67	5.03	1.26
Kranti	144.2	4.53	183.5	13.0	8.52	4.65	1.08
Pusa Barani	131.2	4.19	186.6	13.5	8.55	4.63	1.08
Varuna	139.3	4.29	178.2	13.6	8.56	4.74	1.07
CD 0.05	9.9	NS	NS	NS	NS	NS	0.07

NS = Not Significant
Source: CSSRI. 1990.

Rapeseed, Toria and Taramira can also be grown successfully in sodic soil up to about 44 ESP without any significant reduction in yield (Singh *et al.* 1988).

Thus, with the identification of a good number of salt-tolerant cultivars, there are great possibilities of increasing and stabilising productivity of oilseed brassicas in problematic areas besides incorporation of their salt-resistant trait(s) in breeding programme for enhanced tolerance to salt-stressed soils.

5.6 MANAGEMENT OF SALINE AND ALKALI SOILS

5.6.1 Reclamation of saline and alkali soils

Reclamation calls for in-depth understanding of the factors responsible for the impairment of physical/chemical properties of the soil due to salinity/alkalinity (sodicity), taking up of appropriate measures for removal of salts or alkali from the crop root zone to the desired level, amendment of the deteriorated soil and prevention of their future accumulation in the reclaimed soil profile (Agarwal *et al.* 1979; Kelley, 1951).

One of the most effective way for removal of excess soluble salts from the root zone of saline soil is through leaching with adequate good quality water and provision of proper drainage system for easy percolation of water through the soil layer. Generally, intermittent leaching is considered more advantageous than leaching at each irrigation (Meiri & Plaut, 1985). In case of alkali soil, a large part of the exchangeable sodium in the soil should be replaced by calcium to flocculate it and make the leaching process effective. This can be accomplished by adding directly calcium chloride, calcium salts like gypsum, lime stone, rock phosphate or basic slag. Addition of acidifying materials like sulphur and iron pyrites, etc., will also reduce the alkalinity. Amelioration of alkali soil can also be effected through biological means such as incorporation of organic matter, green manuring, etc. to improve water infiltration and release of CO_2 during decomposition to make Ca available for replacement of Na in the soil exchange complex (Agarwal *et al.* 1979; Singh, 1989).

Among the chemical amendments, gypsum is most commonly used and a 60-70% reduction in exch.Na is considered near economic application of the compound (Yadav & Agarwal, 1959). Iron pyrite is less effective than gypsum but is extensively used for calcareous alkali (*Usar*) soils in Uttar Pradesh and Bihar because of its ready availability and low cost (Singh, 1989). The availability and transportations of several nutrients in plants are strongly influenced by high pH levels of alkali soils, and plants readily respond to nitrogenous and phosphatic fertilizers (Abrol, 1968).

5.6.2 Land preparation

Deep ploughing, breaking the hard pan or compacted sub-soil layers and sometime even mixing of sand during ploughing improve water and air permeability of land. Loosening of the sub-soil also produces deeper root zone. If the sub-soil is more alkaline than the surface soil as is often the case in alluvial tracts, then turning over of the soil during ploughing should be avoided so that alkalinity from deeper layers is not added to the existing alkalinity problem at the surface. Sometimes, salts accumulate in high spots which is detrimental for plant growth. Hence, proper preparation of land and its precision levelling are essential for uniform spread of water and effective downward leaching of salts (Agarwal *et al.* 1979; Maliwal, 1973).

5.6.3 Planting

As a normal practice, sowing of oilseed brassicas under salt adversity conditions should be done with clean and certified seeds of the recommended cultivars when the maximum day temperature is around 25 to 30°C. Seed and oil yields are positively correlated with maximum temperature during vegetative growth, a mean daily temperature of 27°C usually gives best establishment and growth (Kumar & Singh, 1983). Genotypes which show greater tolerance than others under salt-stress condition should be preferred for sowing to avoid uneven or patchy crop stand and poor seed yield.

5.6.3.1 Effect of salinity on germination and growth of Brassica

Saline soil is unsuitable for germination and growth of rapeseed and mustard. Significant adverse effects of rising water salinity on seed germination and yield of six Indian mustard cultivars were observed in a micro-plot study during 1978-79 and 1979-80 (Table 5.9).

In 1979-80, seed germination occurred to some extent at EC 16 dS/m salinity level, but later there was complete mortality of plants. The cv. Varuna with maximum seed yield, minimum yield reduction at the abrupt salinity level over control during 1978-79 and maximum value on Mean Salinity Index (M.S.I.) was most tolerant while RL-18 with lowest yield and maximum yield reduction at the abrupt salinity level over control was most susceptible. The cv. Prakash was medium tolerant and others were susceptible (Kumar & Malik, 1983). In cv. Pusa Bold, seed germination does

Table 5.9. Effect of various salinity levels on relative germination percentage and grain yield of six cultivars of Indian mustard.

Treatments	Seed germination (%)		Grain yield (g/1.4 sq.m)		Reduction at abrupt salinity over control*		M.S.I. (%)	
	1978-79	1979-80	1978-79	1979-80	1978-79	1979-80	1978-79	1979-80
Salinity (dS/m)								
2.1(control)	86.4	73.6						
4.0	73.9	53.4						
8.0	48.4	38.6						
12.0	38.7	24.6						
16.0	31.2	11.7						
CD at 5%	32.4	7.0						
Variety								
RL-18	53.6	40.3	186.00	44.00	96.77	92.00	30.00	19.00
Pusa Bold	56.2	39.2	282.00	61.40	95.12	82.91	60.97	23.57
Laha 101	57.9	41.0	210.02	95.00	94.11	90.80	52.20	18.65
Varuna (T-59)	57.5	45.6	304.40	138.80	77.50	90.41	70.00	47.29
PR-10	52.1	40.3	274.00	57.80	82.05	89.28	62.82	28.98
Prakash	53.1	38.3	284.00	68.40	90.90	96.73	55.68	31.00
CD at 5%	3.1	6.5						

*16 and 12 dS/m salinity levels were considered abrupt in 1978-79 and 1979- 80, respectively.

$$\text{Mean Salinity Index (M.S.I.)} = \frac{\text{Mean yield at 4, 8, 12 and 16 ECe}}{\text{Yield of control}} \times 100$$

Source: Kumar and Malik, 1983.

not differ significantly due to root zone salinity up to ECe 9 dS/m but at salinity exceeding that value, the germination is greatly reduced (CSSRI. 1989).

High soil salinity is also detrimental to germination of seeds and growth of young seedlings in Toria (Ref. Table 5.7) (Singh & Prakash, 1984).

The reduction in germination under salinity condition is attributed to reduced absorption rate and moisture stress condition in the seed as a result of increased osmotic pressure of the soil solution. Salinity may also cause influx of ions in quantities large enough to make them toxic to the seed embryo (Rai, 1977).

5.6.3.2 Effect of alkalinity on germination and growth of Brassica

Alkali or sodic soils are also unsuitable for normal germination and growth of oilseed brassicas. Indian mustard cv. RL-18 when planted in a highly sodic soil at the CSSRI, Karnal, India during

1977-78, showed 2 to 4 days delay in the emergence of seedlings from soil with average ESP of 44.2 as compared to soil with average ESP value of 7.6. An ESP value of more than 23 delayed germination, emergence of flowers and pods but enhanced maturity (Singh *et al.* 1979). Similarly, five varieties of Indian mustard raised in six levels of sodicity in a replicated trial, showed significant varietal as well as sodicity level differences in respect to both percentage germination of seeds and time taken for their emergence from the soil. A drastic reduction in their germination took place when the ESP level changed from 45 to 57 (Roy & Khaddar, 1990) (Table 5.10).

Table 5.10. Effect of six sodicity levels of soil germination percentage of five Indian mustard varieties.

Soil condition (Initial)			Varieties					Treatment (Mean)
pH	Ece (d S/m)	ESP	RLM -632	Pusa Bold	RLC-1012	Varuna	RL3-1013	
8.4	2.1	5.9	90.0	90.0	92.5	85.0	92.5	90.0
8.6	2.2	8.7	87.5	82.5	92.5	85.9	90.0	87.5
8.7	1.9	15.0	85.0	77.5	87.5	80.0	90.0	84.0
8.7	1.9	29.4	82.5	75.0	82.5	80.0	77.9	79.5
8.7	2.1	44.8	70.0	65.0	80.0	70.0	70.0	71.1
8.8	2.1	56.7	57.5	57.0	67.5	30.0	52.5	53.0
Variety Mean			78.7	74.5	83.7	71.6	78.7	—

Cation exchange capacity (C.E.C.) 50 me/100 g of soil
C.D. (5%) Variety (V) = 5.33
C.D. (5%) ESP levels (E) = 5.84
Interaction V × E = Not significant.
Source: Roy and Khaddar, 1990.

Rising ESP gives lower plant N, P, K, Ca, Mg, Fe, Zn and Mn but higher Na concentration. Crops can be grown successfully up to approximately, 44 ESP level without any significant yield reduction (Singh *et al.* 1988). The inhibiting effect of sodicity on seed germination and delay in the emergence of seedlings (Roy & Khaddar, 1990) are due to the frequent formation of hard crust on the surface soil as it dries up. Substantial delay in emergence of seedlings was noted at almost every increase in ESP value beyond 8.7 point (Table 5.11).

In such a situation, better results may be obtained by applying irrigation in two equal splits, half before and half after sowing (Chauhan *et al.* 1993). To counter the effects of delayed emergence and slow growth of seedlings, the suggestion of advancing the sowing date by 2 to 5 days and even up to 10-15 days on saline and sodic soil conditions of EC 6 to 10d S/m, ESP 30 to 40; and EC 12dS/m, ESP 50 onwards respectively (Kumar, 1992) will be fruitful provided the diurnal temperature remains congenial for germination and seedling growth.

High concentration of salts in the soil close to the seedling row in furrow irrigated crops may seriously interfere seedling emergence and reduce final crop stand. In furrow irrigation, salt accumulation is much greater in the centre of the bed than near the shoulders. Therefore, double row

Table 5.11. Effect of six sodicity levels of soil on seedling emergence time (days) of five Indian mustard varieties.

Soil condition (Initial)			Varieties					Treatment (Mean)
pH	ECe (dS/m)	ESP	RLM-632	Pusa Bold	RLC-1012	Varuna	RL3-1013	
8.4	2.1	5.9	7.3	7.0	6.3	5.0	6.0	6.3
8.6	2.2	8.7	8.0	7.0	6.3	6.0	7.0	6.9
8.7	1.9	15.0	11.3	7.8	7.3	6.5	7.3	8.0
8.7	1.9	29.4	11.8	8.8	8.0	9.3	8.5	9.3
8.7	2.1	44.8	15.2	11.5	8.8	11.0	11.0	11.5
8.8	2.1	56.7	16.7	15.2	13.3	13.5	13.5	14.4
Variety mean			11.7	9.5	8.3	8.5	8.9	

Cation exchange capacity (C.E.C.) 50 me/100 g of soil.
C.D.(5%) Varieties (V): 5.33
C.D.(5%) ESP values (E): 5.84
Interaction V × E: Not significant.
Source: Roy and Khadder, 1990.

beds, sloping seed beds or suitable adjustment of the soil surface contour and seeding position will decrease salt accumulation around the root zone (Maliwal, 1973; Meiri & Plaut, 1985).

5.6.4 Irrigation and drainage

Adequate provision for good quality water to meet crop requirement, and practices that ensure efficient drainage of both surface and ground water, keeping in view the quality of drainage flows and their environmental impact, are important for optimum crop production (Abrol, 1988). Drainage followed by leaching with good quality water removes excess salts from the root zone creating favourable conditions for crop growth. In areas where underground water is of poor quality, provision should be made for horizontal drainage to avoid the problems of soil salinity and water logging (Singh, 1982). But when the underground water is of good quality, conjunctive use of underground and surface water should be preferred. In case of canal irrigation, complete cement lining of different components of water distribution system will not only prevent ground water recharge and rise in ground water table through leakage loss but will also help increased supply of irrigation water to additional areas. In water scarcity areas, high water application efficiency can be achieved through the use of sprinkler and drip irrigation devices. These help in providing the desired quantity of water in the field and reduce the risk of soil degradation (Joshi, 1987).

Irrigation with good quality water or low salinity water helps in preventing salinity build-up in the surface soil layer (0-15 cm), increase in irrigation frequency with non-saline water helps in pushing down the accumulated salts below the root zone and creates favourable conditions for plant growth. Use of high salinity water or reducing the frequency of irrigation have the opposite effect of increasing the salt concentration in the top soil layer.

Increase in crop density resulting from increased amount of seed sown under saline irrigation has a direct bearing on crop yield. Results of field experiment carried out on sandy loam soil at Bichpuri, Agra during 1976-77 and 1977-78 seasons on the effect of seed rates and saline irrigation water on the yield of Indian mustard cv. Appress Mutant showed significant increase in crop yield at low salinity levels of ECi 2.1 and 4.0dS/m with seed rates up to 5.0 and 5.5 kg/ha, respectively. Further increase in seed rates had negative effects due to over-crowding of plants. But at higher salinity levels of ECi 8 to 16 dS/m, the seed yield/ha increased with the increase in seed rate from 4.0 to 6.0 kg/ha (Table 5.12).

Table 5.12. Effect of saline water for irrigation and seed rates on seed yield (q/ha) of "Appress Mutant" Indian mustard during 1976-77 and 1977-78.

Salinity (d S/m)	Seed rate (kg/ha)											
	4.0			5.0			5.5			6.0		
	1976-1977	1977-1978	Mean	1976-1977	1977-1978	Mean	1976-1977	1977-1978	Mean	1976-1977	1977-1978	Mean
2.1 (control)	7.8	8.5	8.3	10.7	9.9	10.3	9.6	8.3	8.9	7.7	6.2	6.9
4.0	6.5	6.9	6.7	7.8	9.7	8.7	9.6	9.3	9.6	7.8	7.1	7.4
8.0	6.0	4.6	5.3	7.0	8.1	7.6	8.0	7.8	7.9	9.2	8.8	9.0
12.0	3.5	2.2	2.9	2.2	5.5	5.4	5.8	6.0	5.9	7.2	7.6	7.4
16.0	2.0	0.9	1.4	3.6	1.7	2.6	5.1	3.0	4.1	5.5	5.0	5.2

	1976-77	1977-78
CD$_1$ (5%) for comparing seed rates at same or different salinity levels =	1.10	1.50
CD$_2$ (5%) for comparing salinity levels with same or different seed rates =	1.24	1.11

Source: Kumar and Singh, 1980.

High seed rate at salinity levels > 8 dS/m increases seed yield by improving the plant stand but at salinity level < 8d S/m, it decreases seed yield due to over-crowding of plants (Kumar & Singh, 1980). However, increase in seeding rate should be in keeping with their row spacing because the total field yield is the product of crop density and yield per plant. Reduced intra-row spacing results in strong competition between plants for nutrition and sunshine, and have little effect on yield per unit area while reduced inter-row spacing does not cause much plant competition and thereby increases yield per unit area (Keren *et al.* 1983).

In situations where saline ground water is the only source for pre-sowing irrigation, sowing of pre-hydrated seeds has been found beneficial especially for relatively salt-sensitive Indian mustard cultivars like Dira-337 as compared to the tolerant cv. Kranti. Germination tests were carried out at the CSSRI, Karnal during 1989-90 with hydrated and unhydrated seeds of these two cultivars. In one set, seeds were hydrated in water for 8 hours before exposure to saline solution. The average moisture content of the hydrated seeds ranged between 50 $\pm$ 2% and the threshold moisture for germination was taken as 60 per cent. Germination counts of the two cultivars showed that for 50 per cent ($EC_{50\%}$) reduction in germination, the salinity limit was 21 and 26 d S/m, respectively for Dira-337 and Kranti. Hydration treatment of seeds shifted the germination vs. salinity curves of the cultivars to the right of respective controls. Hyderation alone enhanced seed germination particularly at higher salinity levels. The $EC_{50\%}$ germination limits for the hydrated Dira-337 and Kranti seeds were 29 and 32dS/m, respectively (Sinha & Gupta, 1990) (Fig. 5.2).

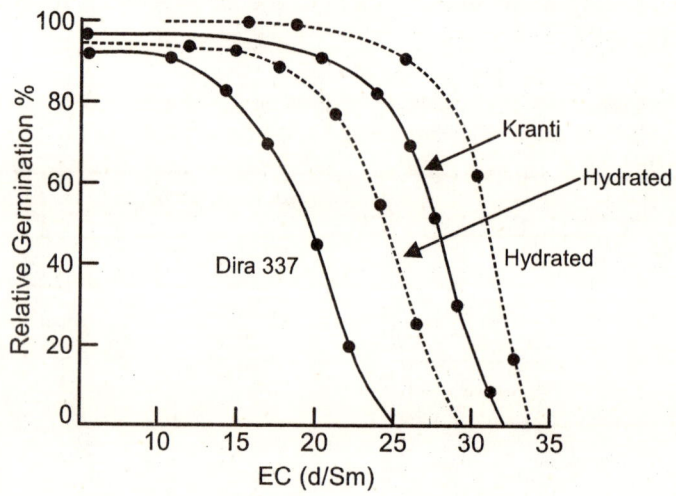

Fig. 5.2. Effect of salinity and hydration treatment on seed germination
(*Source*: Sinha and Gupta, 1990)

Plant tolerance to salts varies with the species, variety and its growth stages. Plants are usually more salt-sensitive at the seedling stage (Meiri & Plaut, 1985) and a sound knowledge on the sensitive growth stage(s) of recommended cultivars to saline irrigation will help in formulating irrigation schedule for better productivity. Per cent seed germination and seed yield per plot decrease linearly with the rise in salinity (ECi 8dS/m onwards) of irrigation water at pre-sowing of the crop (Kumar, 1984; Kumar & Kumar, 1990). Hence, pre-sowing irrigation with saline water should be avoided and instead, a bumper crop harvest can be expected if dry sowing is immediately followed by saline irrigation (Chauhan *et al.*1993). Replacement of saline water irrigation (EC 12dS/m) by non-saline water (Eci 0.3dS/m) at the pre-sowing, flowering and siliquae development stages resulted in 32, 29 and 10 per cent yield increase respectively, compared to yield obtained from saline water irrigation throughout the cropping period (Minhas *et al.* 1990). Similarly, two-year field studies conducted on sandy loam soil on the impact of saline water EC 16dS/m, applied at three growth stages of Indian mustard cultivars Varuna (T-59), Prakash and Pusa Bold, have confirmed that mean grain yield and dry matter production are significantly reduced when saline water irrigation is made at the pre-sowing stage of the crop and in all through the growth stages. On the other hand, saline water irrigation at flowrering and secondary branch initiation stages gives stimulatory effects for majority of the yield components (Kumar & Kumar, 1990).

A micro-plot study on the effect of 4 water salinity EC 4.0 (control), 6.0, 9.0 and 12dS/m on 5 Indian mustard cultivars during 1988-90 winters, showed significant decrease in yield and yield attributes of the cultivars with the increase in salinity levels of irrigation water. The average seed yield (pooled) was reduced by 45.05% at the highest level of saline water irrigation from control (Table 5.13).

Table 5.13. Effect of different salinity levels on the yield components of five cultivars of Indian mustard.

Treatment	Height (cm)		Branches/plant		Siliquae/plant		1000 seed weight (g)		Yield
	A	B	A	B	A	B	A	B	(q/ha)*
Salinity (dS/m)									
4.0	134.64	162.65.	24.81	34.93	288.00	465.81	4.42	3.73	37.69
6.0	120.37	126.90	24.52	23.29	265.46	302.35	4.27	4.70	26.64
9.0	101.67	121.35	18.00	19.15	199.83	233.27	4.66	4.58	23.86
12.0	101.67	126.10	17.23	16.63	198.68	195.59	4.45	4.52	20.71
CD (P=.05)	11.33	24.97	5.43	6.17	46.85	94.12	NS	NS	4.97
Variety									
Varuna	113.73	136.35	18.30	21.67	226.80	254.74	5.40	5.19	28.35
Kranti	119.12	132.51	18.57	23.08	252.71	288.49	4.08	4.37	27.74
RK-8501	119.98	119.28	26.16	24.34	278.38	224.47	4.35	4.48	25.41
RH-837	—	—	—	—	—	—	4.08	4.65	26.53
RH-847	123.20	142.40	21.48	24.86	213.82	327.22	4.35	4.68	27.78
CD	9.90	NS	3.97	NS	46.53	NS	0.77	4.68	—

A = 1988-89; B = 1989-90; *Pooled data of 1988-89 and 1989-90.
Source: Chopra and Chopra, 1992.

Reduction in yield components at saline water application of 12dS/m as compared with the control was 23.92, 30.55 and 31.01%, and 22.31, 52.39 and 58.01% in plant height, number of branches and siliquae/plant, respectively during 1988-89 and 1989-90 (Chopra & Chopra, 1992).

Saline water application at any stage of growth of Indian mustard (cv. Kranti) has no appreciable effect on the number of primary branches, but secondary branches decrease more when saline water is applied at early stages. The tertiary branches also decrease under salinity but they are not produced at EC 15.5 dS/m when stress is applied at germination stage, and at EC 18.0dS/m when stress is applied at later stages. The effect of salinity in reducing pod number is in the order: primary, secondary and tertiary branches, respectively (CSSRI. 1991).

In partially reclaimed sodic soil (pH 8.8 and ESP 23), Indian mustard sown after one pre-sowing irrigation, requires only one post-sowing irrigation at the rosette stage (28 to 30 DAS) giving maximum water use efficiency. Irrigation at the rosette stage stimulates root extension, gives significantly greater relative growth rate, branches and pods/plant, and seed and straw yield compared with one irrigation at pod formation stage and unirrigated treatments. The crop evapotranspiration peaks from 30 to 60 DAS (Sharma & Singh, 1993).

5.6.5 Fertilization

The use of fertilizers to augment crop productivity under saline irrigation should primarily be determined by the fertility cum salinity/sodicity status of the soil. Generally, saline soils are not nutrient deficient but high fertilization often leads to increased salt-tolerance in plants probably due to overcoming of nutritional imbalance or a reduction in toxicity. But in case, the soil suffers from low fertility or is deficient in certain specific nutrient, then application of fertilizer or the appropriate nutrient to the level required under normal situation is expected to be rewarding. On the other hand, in a situation where the problem of salinity is very acute, leaching and drainage of salts will be more effective than mere amendment with fertilizers. Conversely, if sodicity is the dominant problem, then crop response from fertilizer application will be substantial (Bernstein *et al.* 1974).

An improvement in soil properties in relation to salinity, pH and ESP takes place following application of fertilizers and manures in soils irrigated with different quality waters. Fertilizer and manures are more effective in increasing crop production on soils up to moderate salinity. Soils having higher levels of salinity and alkalinity can also be made favourable for crop growth with sufficient manuring (Maliwal, 1973). Application of nitrogen at 40 kg/ha on three mustard (*B. campestris* var. Sarson) cvs. BS-70, YS-42 and GBS-1, grown on saline soils with high ground water table, resulted in both higher grain yield as well as accumulation of N, P, K, Ca and Mg in their shoot, the performance of the cv. BS-70 was better than the other two cultivars in these respects (Panwar & Bhardwaj, 1976). A two-year field trial on P and N requirement of Indian mustard cv. Varuna under three levels of saline irrigation at Agra during 1982-84 seasons on sandy loam soil having surface layer (0-15 cm) ECe 2.8 dS/m, pH 8.6, ESP 16 and SAR 15, showed that irrigation with saline water (EC 12 dS/m) produced as good yield as with low salinity water (EC 2 dS/m). Application of phosphorus (15 to 45 P_2O_5 kg/ha) did not have significant influence on grain yield, whereas application of 60 and 90 kg N/ha caused 37 and 80 per cent more grain yield over 30 kg N/ha (control), the increase in yield with higher nitrogen dose being mainly due to more number of pods per plant than seed weight (Chauhan *et al.* 1988) (Table 5.14).

It may be said that, fertilization under saline conditions may follow the recommendations for crops under non-saline condition whenever the salinity is not high as to inhibit the response of its direct limiting effect on growth (Abrol, 1974).

Alkali soils with their high pH levels, readily respond to nitrogenous and phosphatic fertilizers. Application of nitrogen up to 120 kg/ha to alkali soils with 60-70 ESP level can be beneficial for reasons of high volatile losses, non-availability and nutrient deficiencies (Kumar, 1992). In a highly alkaline soil at CSSRI, Gudha, Karnal, seed yield of both Indian rape (*B. campestris* cv. Pusa Kalyani) and Indian mustard (*B. juncea* cv.Pusa Bold) increased following gypsum application from 6.25 to 25.0 t/ha, although there was no significant yield difference due to 12.50 to 25.0 t/ha of gypsum in case of cv. Pusa Kalyani or due to 6.25 to 25.0 t/ha of gypsum in case of cv. Pusa Bold (Table 5.15).

Table 5.14. Indian mustard (cv.Varuna) yield (q/ha) as influenced by salinity and fertilizers.

Treatments	1982-83		1983-84	
	Grain	Dry matter	Grain	Dry matter
Water salinity (dS/m)				
EC 2 (control)	10.0	50.3	10.5	50.9
EC 6	10.9	57.4	10.9	51.6
EC 12	10.0	55.1	11.6	56.6
CD (5%)	NS	NS	NS	NS
Nitrogen (N g/ha)				
30	7.2	38.1	7.9	39.4
60	10.0	53.3	11.7	52.9
90	13.8	71.1	13.4	66.7
CD (5%)	1.2	4.8	1.0	4.2
Phosphorus (P$_2$O$_5$ kg/ha)				
15	9.7	51.5	10.9	51.9
30	10.5	56.2	11.0	53.8
45	10.8	55.9	11.1	53.3
CD (5%)	NS	NS	NS	NS

Source: Chauhan et al. 1988. NS = Non-significant

Both the crops flourished well in alkali soil having surface soil (0-15 cm) ESP of about 30 and there was no adverse effect on their oil content due to different sodicity levels (CSSRI. 1985). Results of experimentation over a decade on normal (ECe 1.9 dS/m) sandy loam alkaline soil (pH 8.5) under semi-arid agroclimatic conditions have demonstrated that it is possible to grow Indian

Table 5.15. Effect of gypsum levels on mean seed yield of Indian rape (cv. Pusa Kalyani) and mustard (cv. Pusa Bold).

Gypsum level	ESP at sowing (cm)		Yield (t/ha)	
	0-15	15-30	Rape	Mustard
Control	77.0	88.5	0.30	0.58
6.25	45.5	81.0	1.05	1.33
12.50	32.0	69.5	1.17	1.45
18.75	28.0	58.0	1.23	1.49
25.00	25.0	49.0	1.24	1.52
CD at P=0.05			0.11	0.20

Source: CSSRI. 1985.

mustard with a marginal yield loss of about 15-20% even with high water salinity of about 21 dS/m by adopting recommended practices (Chauhan *et al.* 1993).

5.6.6 Breeding for salt-tolerance

Information on the genetic basis of salt tolerance in oilseed brassica is very limited. Little has been done on the identification of genetic variability available within the existing germplasm, and on incorporation of their useful traits in developing commercial varieties for improved yield under saline condition (Tal, 1984). Lack of reliable and efficient field and laboratory screening techniques at the practical breeding level for salt resistance (Srivastava & Jana, 1984) and fluctuations in the amount of salinity within small distances across the field and during the crop growing season (Stavarek & Rains, 1984) make the task of developing salt tolerant varieties difficult. Most of the present-day work on genetics of salt resistance is limited to aspects of breeding crop plants for better adaptability to high salinity in achieving the highest yield (Tal, 1984).

Indian mustard (*B. juncea* L.) genotypes growing in saline-sodic soil having a pH of 9.5, ESP 55.0 and EC (1:2) of 1.75 dS/m at 25°C, were differently affected in respect to different plant characters. Correlation between percentage reduction in oil yield and percentage reduction in other quantitative characters revealed that the reduction in yield was due mostly to lowered production of branches and siliquae, implying that genotypes having less decrement in these characters may be used for further breeding programme (Singh *et al.* 1974). Assessment of morphological traits in 48 cultivars of Indian mustard on normal (control) and sandy loam sodic soil with pH 9.2 and ESP 42, revealed that yield components are marked with less estimates of genetic coefficient of variability (GCV), heritability and genetic advance. The 1000-seed weight had higher heritability but moderate estimates of GCV and genetic advance under both the soil environments. On the contrary, attributes like seed yield per plant, leaf area and leaves per plant possessed high GCV (> 27%), heritability (> 55%) and genetic advance (> 40%) over the two environments. These traits can, therefore, be improved through selection in Indian mustard irrespective of the two environments (Kumar *et al.* 1983).

Jain *et al.* (1990) obtained salt tolerant plants of *B. juncea* cv. Prakash through *in vitro* screening of highly morphogenic cotyledon explant cultures on high NaCl media. Cotyledon explants were raised on high-salt medium and those which survived, made sustained growth and regenerated shoots. The somaclone plants retained salt tolerance following 3 months of growth and multiplication on salt free medium. R_1 segregating generation obtained from the seeds of these two fertile somaclone plants were evaluated in the field. Progenies from selected R_1 plants were evaluated for both agronomic performance under field conditions and salt tolerance in greenhouse tests. Most of the lines bred true for their specific characteristics. The selected salt-tolerant somaclones (SR-2 and SR-3) performed better for plant growth, yield and other agronomic traits at higher salt treatments. Thus, salt-tolerance trait selected *in vitro* is expressed in the whole plants, is genetically stable and is transmitted on the progeny.

Salt tolerance is a complex character and its expression largely depends on the genetic background of the cultivar and hence breeding plants with the highest possible yield under saline conditions, will be best achieved by recurrent selection. The method enables simultaneous selection of the character desired, with the favourable genetic background (Ramage, 1980). Selection should preferably be made for increased mean productivity (the average yield in stress and non-stress environments) instead of tolerance to stress (yield difference between stress and non-stress environments). If selection is made for increased mean productivity, then mean yields in both environments will generally increase making the crop more adaptable to varying environments (Roiella & Hamblin, 1981).

REFERENCES

Abrol, I.P. 1968. A study of the effect of added nutrients on plant growth on a sodic substrate. *Trans. 9th Int. Congr. Soil Sci.* 2: 585-595.

Abrol, I.P. 1974. Recent advances in fertilizer use in salt-affected soils. *Fert. News.* 19: 12-16.

Abrol, I.P. 1986. Salt-affected soils: An overview. pp. 132. In: V.L. Chopra and R.S. Paroda eds., *Approaches for incorporating drought and salinity resistance in crop plants.* Oxford & IBH Publishing Co., New Delhi.

Abrol, I.P. 1988. Salinity control and irrigated agriculture. In. I. Prakash ed., *Scientific Reviews on Arid Zone Research* Vol. 5. pp. 205-222. *Proc. National Symp. Desert Ecology,* Jaipur, 24-27th October, 1986 (Published 1988).

Agarwal, R.R., Yadav, J.S.P. and Gupta, R.N. 1979. *Saline and Alkali Soils of India,* ICAR, New Delhi.

AICORPDA. 1987. Annu. Prog. Rept., *All India Coord. Res. Proj. Dryland Agric.,* Main Centre, Jodhpur, Rajasthan.

Ashraf, M. and McNeilly, T. 1990. Responses of four Brassica species to sodium chloride. *Environ. Expt. Bot.* 30(4): 475-487.

Bansal, A.K. and Bhattacharyya, R.K. 1984. Germination of raya under salt stressed soil conditions. *J. Oilseeds Res.* 1: 211-215.

Bernstein, L. 1975. Effects of salinity and sodicity on plant growth. *Annu. Rev. Phytopathol.* 13: 295-312.

Bernstein, L., Francois, L.E. and Clark, R.A. 1974. Interactive effects of salinity and fertility on yields of grains and vegetables. *Agron. J.* 66: 687-689.

Chauhan, C.P.S., Singh, S.P., Pathak, D.C. and Bhudayal 1988. Nitrogen and phosphorus requirement for mustard crop under irrigation with saline water. *Ann. Arid Zone* 27(3&4): 293-296.

Chauhan, C.P.S., Chauhan, R.P.S., Singh, A.K. and Singh, S.P. 1993. Techniques for boosting mustard production with saline irrigation. *Indian Fmg.* 43(9): 5-6.

Chopra, N. and Chopra, N.K. 1992. Salt tolerance of raya (*Brassica napus* var. glauca) varieties. *Indian J. Agron.* 37(1): 93-96.

CSSRI. 1985. Annu. Prog. Rept., pp. 61-62. Cent. Soil Salinity Res. Inst., Karnal.

CSSRI. 1986. *Proc. Eleventh Workshop, Coord. Proj. Research on Management of Salt Affected Soils and Use of Saline Water in Agriculture,* pp. 13-15. Cent. Soil Salinity Res. Inst., Karnal.

CSSRI. 1989. Annu. Prog. Rept., pp. 80-84. Cent. Soil Salinity Res. Inst., Karnal.

CSSRI. 1990. Annu. Prog. Rept., pp. 114-117. Cent. Soil Salinity Res. Inst., Karnal.

CSSRI. 1991. Annu. Prog. Rept., pp. 79-80. Cent. Soil Salinity Res. Inst., Karnal.

Flowers, T.J., Troke, P.F. and Yeo, A.R. 1977. The mechanism of salt tolerance in halophytes. *Annu. Rev. Plant Physiol.* 28: 89-121.

Girdhar, I.K. 1989. Relative salt tolerance in wheat and raya. Annu. Prog. Rept., p. 80. Cent. Soil Salinity Res. Inst., Karnal.

He, T. and Cramer, G.R. 1992. Growth and mineral nutrition of six rapid-cycling Brassica species in response to sea water salinity. *Plant and Soil* 139: 285-294.

Jain, R.K., Jain, S., Nainawatee and Chowdhury, J.B. 1990. Salt tolerance in *Brassica juncea* L. I. In vitro selection, agronomic evaluation and genetic stability. *Euphytica* 48: 141-152.

Joshi, P.K. 1987. Effect of surface irrigation on land degradation - Problems and Strategies. *Indian J. Agric. Econ.* 42(3): 416-423.

Keren, R., Meiri, A. and Kalo, Y. 1983. Plant spacing effect on yield of cotton irrigated with saline water. *Plant and Soil* 74: 461-465.

Kelley, W.P. 1951. *Alkali Soils: Their Formation, Properties and Reclamation.* Reinhold Publishing Corporation, New York, U.S.A.

Kumar, A. and Singh, R.P. 1983. Crop management strategy and role of non-monetary inputs in Indian rape (*Brassica campestris* var. Toria) p. 304 (Abstr.). *Sixth Int. Rapeseed Conf., Paris,* France, 1983.

Kumar, D. 1984. The value of certain plant parameters as an index for salt tolerance in Indian mustard (*B. juncea*). *Plant and Soil* 79: 261-272.

Kumar, D. 1990. Screening of related Brassica species for seedling emergence and seed yield under saline conditions. *Natn. Seminar Genetics of Brassicas,* Rajasthan Agric. Univ., Jaipur, August, 1990.

Kumar, D. 1992. Review on rapeseed and mustard for yield enhancement on saline and sodic conditions. pp. 201-243. In D. Kumar and M. Rai eds., *Advances in Oilseeds Research, Vol.I. Rapeseed and Mustard,* Scientific Publishers, Jodhpur 1992.

Kumar, D., Dhanda, S.S., Singh, M.P. and Bultar, B.S. 1983. Variability studies in mustard under normal and sodic soil conditions. *Curr. Agric.* 7: 25-29.

Kumar, D. and Malik, R.S. 1983. Salt tolerance in six Indian mustard cultivars. *Indian J. Agron.* 28(4): 325-331.

Kumar, D. and Singh, A.K. 1980. Effect of seed rate and saline irrigation on "Appress Mutant" Indian mustard. *Indian J. Agron.,* 25(2): 285-288.

Kumar, V. and Kumar, D. 1985. Effect of sodicity and seed rate on seed yield and oil content of Indian mustard. *Curr. Agric.* 9: 21-26.

Kumar, V. and Kumar, D. 1990. Response of Indian mustard to saline water application at different growth stages. *Trans. ISDT,* 15: 121-125.

Maas, E.V. 1986. Salt tolerance of plants. *Appl. Agri. Res.* 1(1): 12-26.

Malik, R.S. 1990. Prospects of *Brassica carinata* as an oilseed crop in India. *Exptl. Agric.* 26 : 125-129.

Maliwal, G.L. 1973. Tolerance of field crops to salts. *Farmers and Parliament* 8(12): 17-18.

Meiri, A. and Plaut, Z. 1985. Crop production and management under saline conditions. *Plant and Soil* 89: 253-271.

Minhas, P.S., Sharma, D.R. and Khosla, B.K. 1990. Effect of alleviation of salinity stress at different growth stages of Indian mustard (*B. juncea* L.). *Indian J. Agric. Sci.* 60(5): 343-346.

Narain, P., Pal, B. and Singh, B. 1979. Effect of saline water irrigation on performance of Laha (var. T-59) and salinity status of soil. *Indian J. Agron.* 24(1): 1-6.

Paliwal, K.V. 1972. *Irrigation with Saline Water.* p. 127. *IARI, Monograph (New Series) No.2,* New Delhi.

Panwar, K.S. and Bhardwaj, R.B.L. 1976. Effect of nitrogen fertilization on the chemical composition and yield of varieties of oilseed crops under saline and high water table conditions. *Indian J. Agron.* 21: 503-504.

Rai, M. 1977. Salinity tolerance in Indian mustard and safflower. *Indian J. Agri. Sci.* 47(2) : 70-73.

Ramage, R.T. 1980. Genetic methods to breed salt tolerance in plants. pp. 311-318. In D.W. Rains, R.C. Valentine, and A. Hollaender, eds., *Genetic Engineering of Osmoregulation.* Plenum, New York.

Ram Deo and Ruhal, D.V.C. 1971. Effect of salinity on yield and quality of Indian rape and linseed. *Indian Agric. Sci.* 41: 134-136.

Rana, R.S., Singh, K.N. and Ahuja, P.S. 1980. Chromosomal variation and plant tolerance to sodic and saline soils. pp. 487-493. *Proc. Int. Symp. Salt Affected Soils,* Cent. Soil Salinity Res. Inst., Karnal.

Roiella, A.A. and Hamblin, J. 1981. Theoretical aspects of selection for yield in stress and non-stress environments. *Crop Sci.* 21: 943-946.

Roy, N. and Khaddar, V.K. 1990. Response of mustard varieties to graded levels of exchangeable sodium percentage in black-cotton soil. *Indian Agric.* 34(4): 209-217.

Sharma, D.K. and Singh, K.N.1993. Effect of irrigation on growth, yield and evapotranspiration of mustard (*Brassica juncea*) in partially reclaimed sodic soils. *Agric. Water Manage.* 3: 225-232.

Sharma, P.C. and Gill, K.S. 1992. Salinity induced effects in biomass, yield, yield attributing characters and ionic content in mustard genotypes. *Natn. Seminar on Plant Physiol. Physiological Approaches for Crop and Plant Production under Environmental Stress.*, Rajasthan Agric. Univ., ARS, Durgapura, Jaipur (Rajasthan) Jan. 15-17, 1992.

Singh, H. and Prakash, J. 1984. Effect of salinity on germination and early growth of Toria (*Brassica campestris* var. Toria) genotypes, *Seed Res.* 12(2): 22-24.

Singh, K.N., Sharma, D.K. and Chillar, R.K. 1988. Growth, yield and chemical composition of different oilseed crops as influenced by sodicity. *J. Agric. Sci. Camb.* 111: 459-463.

Singh, K.N., Singh, T.N., Mishra, B. and Joshi, Y.C. 1974. Effect of saline-sodic soil on some quantitative characters of different genotypes in Indian mustard [*Brassica juncea* (L.) Czern & Coss]. *Indian J. Agric. Res.* 8(4): 249-255.

Singh, N.T. 1989. *Salt affected soils: Some reflections on the state of knowledge.* pp. 621-643. *The Seventh Prof. J.N. Mukherjee—ISSS Foundation Lecture.* 54th Annu. Conven. of the Indian Soc. Soil Sci., S.V. Agric. College, Tirupati, A.P.

Singh, S.B., Chhabra and Abrol, I.P. 1979. Effect of exchangeable sodium on the yield and chemical composition of raya (*Brassica juncea* L.). *Agron. J.* 71: 767-770.

Singh, O.P. 1982. "Studies on Hydrological Aspects of Saline Soil Reclamation in Gohana Region of Haryana", Annu. Rept. 1979-1982, Cent. Soil Salinity Res. Inst., Karnal.

Sinha, T.S. 1993. Grow a good crop of Raya with saline drainage water. *Indian Fmg.* 43(8): 4-5.

Sinha, T.S. and Gupta, R.K. 1990. Seeding practice of Indian mustard using saline waters. pp. 114-115. In: Annu. Prog Rept., Cent. Soil Salinity Res. Inst., Karnal, 1989-90.

Srivastava, J.P. and Jana, S. 1984. Screening of wheat and barley germplasm for salt tolerance. In: R.C. Staples and G.H. Toenniessen eds., *Salinity Tolerance in Plants: Strategies for Crop Improvement.* John Wiley and Sons, New York.

Stavarek, S.J. and Rains, D.W. 1984. Cell Culture Techniques: Selection and Physiological Studies of Salt Tolerance. pp. 321-334. In: R.C. Staples and G.H. Toenniessen eds., *Salinity Tolerance in Plants: Strategies for Crop Improvement.* John Wiley and Sons, New York.

Tal, Moshe 1984. Physiological genetics of salt resistance in higher plants: Studies on the level of the whole plant and isolated organs, tissues and cells. pp. 301-320. In: R.C. Staples and G.H. Toenniessen eds., *Salinity Tolerance in Plants: Strategies for Crop Improvement.* John Wiley and Sons, New York.

Uma, M.S., Srinivas, S., Hebbara, M. and Patil, S.G. 1992. Screening of Indian mustard (*Brassica juncea*) genotypes for saline Vertisols of Tungabhadra area of Karnataka. *Indian J. Agri. Sci.* 62(7): 486-488.

U.S. Salinity Laboratory Staff. 1954. *Diagnosis and Improvement of Saline and Alkali soils.* Handbk. U.S. Dep. Agric. No.60.

Yadav, J.S.P. and Agarwal, R.P. 1959. Dynamics of soil changes in the reclamation of saline alkaline soils of the Indo-Gangetic alluvium. *J. Indian Soc. Soil Sci.* 7: 213-222.

Chapter 6

Weeds

6.1 INTRODUCTION

Weeds act as yet another important constraint in the growth and productivity of oilseed brassicas in India. Weeds not only remove a great part of the available nutrients and water from the soil but also compete with the crop for light and space, besides serving as reservoir of many pests and diseases, which in turn, attack the crop. It has been estimated that the over-all yield depression due to weed infestation varies from 20 to 70% in the case of rapeseed and mustard depending upon the composition and density of weed flora and the time of their occurrence (Ghosh & Mukhopadhyay, 1981; Panchal *et al*. 1980; Saini *et al*. 1989; Sandhu & Walia, 1979). Infestation by weeds such as *Cuscuta reflexa* may reduce the seed oil content and bring about alteration in their lipid composition (Misra & Sanwal, 1992). Some weeds are poisonous. Green plants of *Phalaris tuberosa* cause death of cattle within a few hours of feeding. *Parthenium* sp., poison sumac, poison ivy and corn cockle are health hazards (Mazumder, 1995). Effective management of weeds at the critical growth period of the crop is a vital necessity for optimum productivity.

6.2 WEED FLORA

India with its great size, geographical position and unique physical features provides varied climates for diverse types of vegetation to flourish. Naturally, the composition and density of weed flora that infest oil yielding Brassica crops differ greatly not only from one region to another but also from one location to another within a region due to variations in climatic, edaphic and systems of cultivation, etc. Although no systematic survey for weed flora of these group of crops has been carried out in India, the major weeds of rapeseed and mustard reported from the states of Assam (Choudhary & Pathak, 1992; Gogoi & Kalita, 1995), West Bengal (Ghosh *et al*. 1988, 1993; Ghosh & Mukhapadhyay, 1981; Pradhan, 1993), Bihar (Pandey, 1980), Orissa (Tosh, 1982), Uttar Pradesh (Ali, 1993; Mehrotra *et al*. 1972; Singh *et al*. 1993), Haryana (Panwar *et al*. 1987; Sarmah *et al*. 1992), Punjab (Gill *et al*. 1984), Himachal Pradesh (Rana & Angiras, 1990), Gujarat (Kaneria & Patel, 1993) and Madhya Pradesh (Bhadoria & Chauhan, 1995; Rajput *et al*. 1993; Saraswat *et al*. 1993; Sharma & Chauhan, 1995; Tiwari & Kurchania, 1993; Tomar & Namdeo, 1991) are listed in Table 6.1.

Table 6.1. Principal weed species of rapeseed and mustard in India.

Family	Weed name
A. Dicotyledons (Broad leaved)	
Papaveraceae	*Argemone maxicana* L.
Cruciferae	*Brassica sinensis* L.
Caryophyllaccae	*Spergula arvensis* L.
Papilionaceae	*Desmodium trifolium* Dc.
	Lathyrus aphaca L.
	Medicago denticulata L.
	Medicago hispida (L.) Gaertn.
	Melilotus spp.
	Melilotus alba Medik ex.Desr.
	Melilotus indica All.
	Trigonella polycerata Benth.
	Trifolium alexandrinum L.
	Trifolium flagiferum
	(T. fragiferum ?)
	Vicia hirsuta (L.) S.F. Gray
	Vicia sativa L.
Oxalidaceae	*Oxalis corymbosa*
Primulaceae	*Anagallis arvensis* L.
Compositae	*Acanthospermum hispida*
	Ageratum conyzoides L.
	Blumea lacera (Burm.F.) D.C. Prodr.
	Cichorium intybus L.
	Cirsium arvense (L.) Scop.
	Cnicus arvensis Hoftn.
	Eclipta alba (L.) Hasak.
	Eupatorium glandulosum
Rubiaceae	*Borreria hispida* (L.) K. Schum.
Boraginaceae	*Heliotropium indicum*
Convolvulaceae	*Convolvulus* sp.
	Convolvulus arvensis L.
Solanaceae	*Solanum nigram* L.
Cucurbitaceae	*Melochia corchorifolium (M. corchorifolia ?)*
Nyctaginaceae	*Boerhaavia diffusa* L.
Amaranthaceae	*Amaranthus viridis* Hook, F.
	Amaranthus spinosus L.
	Digera arvensis Forsk.
Chenopodiacea	*Chenopodium* sp.
	Chenopodium album L.
	Chenopodium murale L.

Family	Weed name
Polygonaceae	*Polygonum* sp.
	Polygonum plebeium R. Br.
	Polygonum hydropiper L.
	Rumex maritimus L.
	Rumex dentatus
Portulacaceae	*Portulaca oleracea* L.
Euphorbiaceae	*Croton sperciflora* Morong
	Euphorbia hirta L.
	Phyllanthus niruri L.
Fumariaceae	*Fumaria parviflora* L.
Aizoaceae	*Trianthema portulacastrum* L.
Orobanchaceae	*Orobanche* sp.
	Orobanche aegyptica
	Orobanche ospera
	Orobanche nicotiana
B. Monocotyledons (Grasses)	
Liliaceae	*Asphodelus tenuifolium* Cav.
Graminae	*Avena fatua* L.
	Avena ludoviciana Dur.
	Brachiaria mutica Forsk.
	Cynodon dactylon (L.) Pers.
	Dactyloctenicum aegyptium (L.) Beauv.
	Digitaria sanguinalis (L.) Scop.
	Digitaria adscendens
	Echinochloa colonum (L.) Link.
	Echinochloa crus-galli (L.) Beauv.
	Eleusine indica (L.) Gaertn.
	Lolium temulentum L.
	Setaria glauca (L.) Beauv.
	Sorghum halepense L.
	Sporobolus diander (Retz.) Beauv.
	Paspalum distichum
	Phalaris minor Retz.
Cyperaceae (Sedge)	*Cyperus* sp.
	Cyperus iria L.
	Cyperus rotundus L.

Among the various weed species that occur in rapeseed and mustard fields, the broad leaved species such as the *Chenopodium album, Meliolotus indica, Convolvulus arvensis, Trianthema portulacastrum* and *Anagallis arvensis*; the grasses like *Cynodon dactylon, Phalaris minor* and *Asphodelus tenuifolium*; and the sedge, *Cyperus rotundus* are the most prominent ones. *Trianthema portulacastrum* offers a serious competition to Toria, especially during its early growth periods in Punjab (Brar & Walia, 1995). Similarly, *C. rotundus* is a serious problem in Indian mustard crop in West Bengal (Ghosh *et al.* 1988).

The broom rape or the *Orobanche* spp., notably the *O. aegyptica* Pers. is a common root holoparasite of rapeseed and mustard in Andhara Pradesh, Tamil Nadu (Saraswat, 1993), parts of Rajasthan (AICORPO. 1972) and Bihar (Narasimhan & Thirumalachar, 1954). It is of wide spread occurrence in Brassicas, tomatoes and faba beans in the adjoining Terai plains of Nepal and causes estimated yield losses upto 20 percent in Toria. *Orobanche aegyptica* is the predominant species on Brassicas in Nepal (Bharat, 1989).

Serious infestation of broom rape in Taramira (*E. sativa*) and mustard (*B. juncea*) crops at Sriganganagar area of Rajasthan; in rapeseed and mustard fields at Pusa, Bihar; Kalyanpur Farm, Kanpur, Uttar Pradesh and Berhampur Government Farm, Murshidabad, West Bengal is an annual feature. At Berhampur, rapeseed and mustard are sown between October to early November, and the epigeal stage of the broom rape is seen between mid-January to early February, when its seedlings emerge above ground and soon start flowering coinciding with that of the host species (Fig. 6.1). Host plants infested with broom rape become thin and sickly, remain stunted in growth and yield poorly, although data on crop yield losses have not been documented.

Fig. 6.1. Yellow sarson (cv. Benoy) crop heavily infested with broom rape, *Orobanche* sp. (*Courtesy*: A.K. Chattopadhyay)

6.3 CROP-WEED COMPETITION

As mentioned earlier, the area under oilseed brassicas in India has vastly increased since 1950's, and new crop species and varieties are now being grown with higher inputs of fertilizers and water to achieve higher productivity. This changed scenario has encouraged the emergence and multiplication of various weed species leading to intense crop-weed competition for available resources.

Weed competition in Indian mustard starts from weeds that emerge before and along with the crop, and persists as long as they are actively growing. Early emerging weeds are more competitive as the mustard crop grows slowly during the first 4-6 weeks after sowing (Gill *et al*. 1984). Weeds offer maximum competition at 30 days after sowing (DAS), and Kumar (1992) considers that the 4th leaf-stage is the critical period for crop-weed competition in Indian mustard. The maximum reduction in seed yield due to weeds takes place between 20 and 40 days of growth in mustard (Ambasht & Chakhaiyar, 1981). Early season weed control is, therefore, essential if the productive potential of the crop is to be fully realized. Later, the plants grow vigorously and the crop canopy offers a smothering effect on weeds (Dashora *et al*. 1990; Pandey, 1980), a characteristic feature of the Brassicas. Some *B. juncea* genotypes may suppress upto 70.4-76.6% weed population except *Cyperus* spp., and per cent suppression is more in dicot than in monocot weeds. The *B. juncea* cv. RH 8689 have the most smothering effect on all weeds. In general, all *B. napus* cultivars give good suppression of weeds because of early development of broad leaves. Early maturing varieties gave best results with suppression of ≤ 82%, while the late maturing cv. Midas gave 78.5% suppression. *Brassica carinata* genotypes gave weed suppression of only 44.6-65.6%, because their slow growth rate allowed weeds to develop although they have also broad leaves (Sarmah *et al*. 1992; Yadava & Narwal, 1997). Some double-zero cultivars of winter rape (*B. napus*) develop rapidly and compete with weeds so strongly that species such as *Capsella bursa-pastoris*, *Lapsana communis* and *Viola* spp. do not require control measures (Klischowski & Beyer, 1989). The most smothering genotypes of *B. napus* and *B. carinata* in India are HNS 8902 and BCCN-5, respectively (Sarmah *et al*. 1992)

Indian mustard sown during the first week of October produces vigorous growth and therefore, asserts a strong suppressing effect on weeds under north Indian conditions. In Pantnagar, Uttar Pradesh, planting of mustard in the first week of October usually have poor competition and lower weed density but the density becomes maximum when planting is delayed upto the 4th of November (Kumar & Singh, 1985).

6.4 WEED CONTROL

6.4.1 Hand and mechanical weeding

Indian farmers mostly prefer conventional methods of weed control namely, hand-weeding, hand-hoeing or use mechanical tillers/cultivators because of their high effectiveness and operational ease. Effectiveness of these methods in weed control and yield increase has been amply demonstrated in a number of field trials over the years. Rapeseed and mustard need at least two weedings at the 3rd and 5-6th week after sowing for normal growth and development.

In a trial on weed control in rapeseed and mustard crops during 1984-85 season at Kalyani, West Bengal, two manual-weedings at 25 and 45 DAS resulted in 58% yield increase of Indian mustard cv. Varuna over unweeded check (Ghosh *et al*. 1988). Similarly, in a two year field study in Terai tracts of North Bengal, manual weedings done twice at 21 and 35 DAS provided grain yield of mustard cv. Seeta similar to that obtained in weed-free check (Pradhan, 1993).

Effectiveness of maintaining weed-free condition and two hand-weedings at 25 and 45 DAS, in reducing both dry weight of weeds and removal of NPK nutrients by them, and in increasing seed yield of Indian mustard cv. Varuna by 80 and 69%, respectively over unweeded control was dem-onstrated in a field experiment during 1989-91 seasons at Navsari, Gujarat (Kaneria & Patel, 1993). At the IIT, Kharagpur, West Bengal during 1987-89 seasons, two hand-weedings at 20 and 40 DAS or one hand-weeding at 20 DAS followed by one mechanical weeding at 40 DAS reduced the dry matter of weeds by 55.5 and 61.6% (average of two years), respectively compared to the unweeded check (Ghosh *et al.* 1993). Further confirmation about the effectiveness of manual operation in weed control came from field studies conducted during 1990 and 1991 crop seasons at Gwalior, Madhya Pradesh. Significant reduction in dry matter of all types of weeds and weed densities, and increased seed yield of Indian mustard over unweeded control were observed following two hand-weedings at 30 and 40 DAS, though they were ineffective against *Cyperus rotundus* and *Cynodon dactylon* (Sharma & Chauhan, 1995). Hand-weeding was found more effective than using hand-hoe in eradicating weed flora of Indian mustard crop during 1991-92 at Gwalior (Bhadoria & Chauhan, 1995) but hand-weeding + hoeing at 30 DAS recorded the highest weed control effi-ciency, with maximum values of yield components and seed yield in mustard cv. Pusa Bold (Nair *et al.* 1996). At Jorhat, Assam during 1988-90 winter seasons, wheel-hoeing twice at 20 and 40 DAS registered 50.3% weed control efficiency and resulted in the highest seed yield (9.07 q/ha) of Indian mustard (cv. Pusa Bold) by improving the yield components. This was also at par with two hand-weedings (Gogoi & Kalita, 1995).

6.4.2 Chemical control

Chemicals or herbicides are vital to modern weed management practices. A large number of effec-tive pre-plant, pre-and postemergence herbicides are available to suit the requirements of particular areas/situations.

The herbicides eptam as pre-plant and lasso as pre-emergence treatment, respectively con-trolled 67.9% and 62.9% of *Cyperus rotundus* and *Chenopodium album*, the two most dominant weeds in Indian mustard fields of Uttar Pradesh during 1968-70 winter seasons. They increased the crop seed yield significantly by 32.9% and 27.9%, respectively during 1968-69 and 1969-70 over the weedy check but showed some phytotoxic effects which gradually disappeared (Mehrotra *et al.* 1972).

Fluchloralin and trifluralin as pre-plant; pendimethalin, terbutryn and thiobencarb as pre-emer-gence; and isoproturon both as pre- and postemergence treatment, are highly effective against all grassy and broad leaf weeds in Indian mustard. They increased the crop yield which was at par with that obtained after two hand-weedings in a field trial during 1981-83 at Ludhiana, Punjab (Gill *et al.* 1984).

Fluchloralin is highly persistent and provides season long control of weeds (Balayan *et al.* 1983). In sandy loam soil during 1987-89 seasons at Morena, Madhya Pradesh, fluchloralin (1.0 kg/ha) was more efficient than pendimethalin (pre-emergence), isoproturon and oxadiazon in reducing the population and dry matter accumulation of weeds like *Asphodelus tenuifolium*, *Chenopodium* sp. and *Convolvulus arvensis*, and was the best-substitute to repeated manual weedings (Tomar & Namdeo, 1991). It also performed well against weeds in Indian mustard and increased crop seed yield, and yield attributes both at Pusa, Bihar and Gwalior, Madhya Pradesh (Sharma & Chauhan, 1995; Singh *et al.* 1989). At Kalyani, West Bengal, fluchloralin (1.25 l/ha) confirmed its efficiency by recording nearly similar weed population and weed dry matter in rape-seed and mustard fields as with two hand-weedings at 25 and 45 DAS (Ghosh *et al.* 1988); at Udaipur, Rajasthan, fluchloralin resulted in saving of 9.6 Kg N/ha and provided the highest seed yield compared to all other herbicidal treatments used (Dashora *et al.* 1990).

Isoproturon (pre- and postemergence), oxadiazon (pre-emergence) and metoxuron (pre-emergence) applied @ 1.0 kg/ha, controlled 25-73% annual weeds in Indian mustard during 1987 and 1988 at Jabalpur, Madhya Pradesh and resulted in seed yields of 1549, 1517,1460 and 1467 Kg/ha, respectively. All these chemicals, and butachlor, oxyfluorfen, metolachlor and pendimethalin as pre-emergence application were at par with hand-weedings at 30 DAS (1401 Kg/ha) and were significantly superior to the weedy-control (821 Kg/ha). Post-emergence application of Fluazifop-P-butyl @ 0.5 kg/ha, controls the grassy weeds only but the perennial weeds, *Cynodon dactylon*, *Paspalum distichum* and *Cyperus rotundus* are not controlled by any of these herbicides (Tiwari & Kurchania, 1993). In further studies by these workers (Kurchania & Tiwari, 1994), isoproturon (1.0 kg/ha pre-emergence) has shown higher weed control efficiency of 76.1%, and *Phalaris minor*, *Trifolium flagiferum*, *Melilotus alba*, *Medicago hispida*, *Chenopodium album* and *Cichorium intybus* were controlled effectively as against weed control efficiency of 58.3, 50.2 and 81.4% shown by butachlor (2.0 kg/ha pre-emergence), fluchloralin (1.0 kg/ha pre-plant) and hand-weeding, respectively.

Both trifluralin and pendimethalin are highly toxic against annual weeds, particularly *Trianthema portulacastrum*, the predominant weed in Toria crop. They increased the crop seed yield significantly over both hand-weedings and weedy check on loamy-sandy soil at Ludhiana during 1990-92 seasons (Brar & Walia, 1995). High effectiveness of pendimethalin against grassy and broad leaf weeds was also observed during 1984-86 at Kalyani, West Bengal. Pendimethalin (1.25 l/ha) resulted in 46% more grain yield of rapeseed and mustard compared to unweeded check and gave the highest benefit-cost ratio among the various herbicides tested. It has been recommended for pre-emergence application against weeds in West Bengal (Ghosh *et al.* 1988). Under irrigated conditions, it performed next best to fluchloralin in increasing the seed yield of Indian mustard during 1985-86 at Udaipur (Dashora *et al.* 1990). Pendimethalin is, however, ineffective against *Avena* spp. and leguminous weeds (AICRPWC. 1984).

Both oxadiazon and isoproturon (post-emergence) cause temporary yellowing of leaves in the early stages of crop growth but they recover later. Oxadiazon also causes partial thinning of the crop but does not reduce the seed yield (Chauhan *et al.* 1993; Gill *et al.* 1984). Isoproturon, following its application, is taken up by the roots of plants and then translocated to their foliage. Pre-plant incorporation of isoproturon (1.0 kg/ha) was more effective in reducing weeds (92%) than any other treatment in Indian mustard during 1991-93 crop seasons at Morena. Pre-plant or pre-emergence application has better effect than its post-emergence (30 DAS) application. Pre-plant incorporation of isoproturon resulted in highest crop grain yield (mean 1.78 t/ha) followed by pre-emergence treatment (mean 1.77 t/ha). The same trend was observed for number of siliquae/plant and seed weight/plant (Yadav *et al.* 1995).

Basalin is also a good herbicide. During 1990-91 at Gwalior, pre-plant application of basalin was most effective in reducing weed density and weed biomass in Indian mustard cv. Pusa Bold compared to the herbicides, stomp, tolkan and ronstar, which were at par when applied at the same rate. Basalin and stomp were superior to other weed control treatments in providing both higher number of siliquae/plant and significantly higher yield/ha than weedy check (Bhadoria & Chauhan, 1995).

It is not always possible to effectively control the multitude of weed species that infest the oilseed brassicas during their critical growth period with a single herbicide. Sequential application of pre-sowing/pre-emergence and post-emergence herbicides with different toxicities or combination of herbicides with complimentary efficacies may provide the desirable result (Mazumder, 1995). Another practical approach should be the combined use of manual and herbicidal methods of control in a judicial manner as the situation demands.

6.4.3 Control of parasitic weeds

Many plant species are infested by dodder (*Cuscuta* spp.) in India and *C. reflexa* has been reported parasitic on rapeseed and mustard crops (Misra & Sanwal, 1992). But dodder infestation is not a problem with oilseed brassicas in India. Application of fluchloralin as pre-plant or pendimethalin as pre-emergence treatment at 1.0 Kg/ha reduces dodder infestation (Saraswat *et al.* 1993). Destruction of infested plants is essential to prevent its further spread.

Removal of broom rape (*Orobanche* spp.) by manual weeding before they flower and form seeds, is very effective in reducing their population in the field. Growing of trap crops such as brinjal and linseed also reduces their infestation but this is not always feasible. Satisfactory control of broom rape through herbicide application is difficult to achieve. However, application of 10% copper sulphate solution, growing resistant mustard variety such as Durgamati, and use of fluchloralin or pendimethalin (1.0-1.5 Kg/ha), respectively as pre-plant or pre-emergence application, are the other useful measures for the control of *Orobanche* spp. in mustard (Saraswat *et al.* 1993).

6.5 WEED MANAGEMENT IN INTERCROPPING SYSTEMS

Intercropping is a potential weed management practice where the weed suppressing efficiency depends largely on the nature of canopy of the component-crops besides the fertility and moisture status of the soil. A quick growing component crop with sufficient canopy cover, such that the total crop canopy at any time is higher than that in the sole crop is desirable for better result (Singh, 1993). Intercropping of rapeseed and mustard with a winter season base crop such as wheat, chickpea, potato and sugarcane, etc. is an age-old practice among the Indian farmers because it not only utilizes the unused inter-row or inter-plant space for added gain but also minimizes the risks at times of adversity such as the incidence of pests or diseases in epidemic form or unfavourable weather (Ali, 1993; Chatterjee & Ghosh, 1991; Dashora *et al.* 1990; Gautam, 1982; Panwar *et al.* 1987; Saraswat *et al.* 1993; Sawhney *et al.* 1983; Sidhu *et al.* 1988). Although, information on crop-weed competition are available in sole crop stand in most of these crops, very little is known about their impact on the nature and intensity of weed infestation when grown as intercrops except the effectiveness of various herbicides used and their yield performance. Nevertheless, a good deal of information on weed management in intercropping systems involving rapeseed and mustard, and a few other crops are available (Ali, 1993; Dashora *et al.* 1990; Gautam, 1982; Panwar *et al.* 1987; Saraswat *et al.* 1993; Sidhu *et al.* 1988; Tosh, 1982). A few illustrative cases are:

Field experiments on weed control in wheat-Indian mustard (10:1 row) intercropping system were carried out during 1982-84 crop seasons at Hissar, Haryana. Post-emergence application of isoproturon (1.0 Kg/ha) gave higher yields of wheat but lower yields of mustard when compared with the pre-emergence application of fluchloralin and pendimethalin. Isoproturon reduced the population and dry weight of weeds (mainly *Phalaris minor* and *Chenopodium album*) significantly more than by fluchloralin. All the three herbicides, however, resulted in significantly higher grain yield of mustard as compared to weedy checks in both the crop seasons except by isoproturon in 1983-84 (Panwar *et al.* 1987). In a similar study, the combination of two wheat-Indian mustard intercropping systems of 8:1 and 12:4 wheat:mustard rows, and nine treatments for weed control were examined. The treatments comprised two doses each of pre- and postemergence application of isoproturon, pre-emergence application of pendimethalin, two hoeings, one hoeing plus isoproturon application and weedy check (Table 6.2).

Table 6.2. Influence of various treatments on mean density & dry weight of weeds, and grain yield (kg/ha) of Indian mustard and wheat (Mean of 1983-84 & 1984-85 seasons).

Treatment	Rate (kg a.i./ ha)	Time of application	Weeds/m²	Dry matter (q/ha)	Indian mustard (kg/ha)	Wheat (kg/ha)
Intercropping systems						
Indian mustard: wheat						
1:8	—	—	85	9.3	185	4275
4:12	—	—	76	8.4	395	3503
CD 5%	—	—	NS	NS	25	214
Weed Control						
Isoproturon	0.70	pre-em.	99.0	9.4	277	3905
Isoproturon	0.94	pre-em.	81.5	6.7	332	3902
Isoproturon	0.70	post-em.	43.5	8.1	231	4120
Isoproturon	0.94	post-em.	39.0	5.5	274	4171
Pendimethalin	0.50	pre-em.	68.5	9.3	281	3787
Pendimethalin	0.75	pre-em.	52.0	9.5	250	3966
Two Hoeings	—	4 & 6 WAS	83.5	8.7	284	3771
One Hoeing + Isoproturon	0.70	4 WAS + 50 DAS	52.5	6.0	291	4045
Weedy check	—		190.0	16.2	229	3333
CD 5%			24.6	4.6	49	469

Pre-em. = Pre-emergence   WAS = Weeks after sowing
Post-em. = Post-emergence   DAS = Days after sowing
Source: Sidhu *et al.* 1988 (re-arranged).

The intercropping systems failed to influence the weed count and their dry weight, and the lowest yield of wheat and mustard was obtained from untreated control. On the other hand, all the herbicidal treatments reduced the weed population significantly in both the crop seasons. Isoproturon (0.94 Kg/ha) as post-emergence treatment was most effective against weeds, effected highest grain yield of wheat though it caused transient toxicity on mustard, the grain yield of the latter crop was highest only when the herbicide was incorporated at pre-emergence. Pendimethalin (0.05 and 0.75 Kg/ha) proved inferior to isoproturon. (Sidhu *et al.* 1988). Confirmation about the effective control of weeds in wheat-mustard intercropping systems through post-emergence application of either isoproturon (1.0 Kg/ha) or pendimethalin (1.5 Kg/ha) also came from the work of Saraswat and co-workers (1993).

Effectiveness of isoproturon in controlling winter weeds in autumn sugarcane-mustard intercropping systems also became clearly evident when its use as pre- and postemergence application (0.75 and 1.0 Kg/ha), pendimethalin as pre-emergence (0.75 Kg/ha), fluazifop-P-butyl as post-emergence (0.25 Kg/ha) and two hoeings at 25 and 40 DAS, were assessed in field trials during 1986-87 and 1987-88 at Ludhiana, Punjab. Post-emergence application of isoproturon at either 0.75 or 1.0 Kg/ha resulted in effective control of broad leaf weeds and *Phalaris minor*. The treatment gave 65.1 - 90.6% and 44.8 - 45.3% average increases in the yields of sugarcane cv. COJ 54 and intercropped mustard cv. RLM 619, respectively (Mehra *et al.* 1989).

The nature and magnitude of crop-weed competition in chickpea -Indian mustard intercropping systems (4:1 row) were evaluated during 1990-91 season at Kanpur, Uttar Pradesh. The

Table 6.3. Effect of crop-weed competition on grain yield and dry weight of weeds in chickpea-Indian mustard intercropping.

Treatments	Seed yield (kg/ha)			Dry weight of weeds at chickpea harvest (g/m^2)
	Chickpea	Indian mustard	Chickpea equivalent	
Unweeded check	417	1302	2291	319
Weed free check	1135	1962	3960	—
Weed free upto 20 DAS	552	1533	2759	286
Weed free upto 40 DAS	791	1709	3252	183
Weed free upto 60 DAS	1052	1799	3642	109
Weed free upto 80 DAS	1085	1874	3783	45
Unweeded upto 20 DAS	1025	1903	3765	—
Unweeded upto 40 DAS	894	1495	3046	—
Unweeded upto 60 DAS	727	1242	2515	—
Unweeded upto 80 DAS	625	1202	2356	—
L.S.D (P=0.05)	130	141	176	—

DAS = Days after sowing
Source: Ali, 1993.

pre-dominant weed flora were *Chenopodium album*, *Anagallis arvensis*, *Melilotus indica* and *Trifolium alexandrinum*. The loss in seed yield due to uncheced weeds till crop maturity was 63% in chickpea and 34% in mustard (Table 6.3).

The yield of chickpea increased significantly when weed free conditions were extended upto 60 DAS. In case of Indian mustard, weed free conditions beyond 40 DAS did not prove beneficial. On the basis of chickpea equivalent yield, unchecked weeds till maturity accrued 42% loss over weed free condition (Ali, 1993).

6.6 WEED AND FERTILIZER MANAGEMENT

Weeds grow at a faster rate and deprive the crop a large part of the applied nutrient resulting in lower fertilizer efficiency and poor crop yield (Rana & Angiras, 1990). Effective control of weeds in the critical growth period of the crop and adequate fertilization, particularly with nitrogen are essential for their optimum growth and productivity.

In a study conducted in calcareous soil at Dholi, Bihar during 1979-80, application of nitrogen upto 180 Kg/ha, in two splits, half at sowing and the remaining half after a month, and control of weeds through pre-emergence application of bifenox, fluchloralin or nitrofen proved essential for higher seed yield of Indian mustard cv. Varuna (Pandey, 1980). Similarly, control of weeds through pre-plant soil incorporation of fluchloralin (1.0 kg/ha) and application of nitrogen (60 kg/ha) were the most cost effective measures for the seed yield of cv. Varuna in a high nitrogen (0.085%) clay loam soil at Udaipur, Rajasthan during 1985-86 winter season (Dashora *et al.* 1990).

For sandy loam soil at Bulandshahar, UP, the effects of various nitrogen doses (50 and 100 Kg/ha, both applied as single dose and in two equal splits) and weed control measures (hand-weeding once 30 DAS, repeated weedings, pendimethalin at 1.0 Kg/ha and isoproturon at 0.75 Kg/ha) on weed population and seed yield in Indian mustard (cv. Pusa Bold) were assessed during 1985-87 crop seasons. All weed control measures decreased weed dry weight compared to untreated control values and increased crop yields. Repeated weedings resulted in greatest yields. Nitrogen gave higher seed yield of mustard, at lower dose (50 Kg N/ha) it gave higher weed biomass as compared to higher dose (100 Kg N/ha) because of quick initial growth of mustard at higher nitrogen level which suppressed the growth of weeds. However, application of 100 Kg N/ha in two equal splits combined either with repeated hand-weeding or post-emergence application of isoproturon was better in terms of weed control, grain yield and net profit (Singh *et al.* 1993).

The extent of NPK loss through weeds in Indian mustard (cv. Varuna) was estimated in clay soils during 1989-91 seasons at Navsari, Gujarat (Table 6.4).

Maintaining weed free conditions or two hand-weedings at 25 and 45 DAS were most effective in reducing both dry weight of weeds and removal of NPK by them, and resulted in higher nutrient uptake by the crop and increased seed yield. Infact, most of the weed management practices such as the pre-emergence application of pendimethalin at 1.0 Kg/ha plus one hand-weeding at 45 DAS or even pre-emergence application of pendimethalin at 1.0 Kg/ha alone, that control weeds at the critical growth period of the crop resulted in higher grain yield compared with unweeded control, the latter treatment showed the highest uptake of NPK by weeds, highest weed dry matter and lowest seed yield (Kaneria & Patel, 1994).

Table 6.4. Seed yield of Indian mustard and nutrient uptake by crop and weeds, as affected by weed-management practices and nitrogen levels.

Treatment	Dose (kg a.i./ha)	Seed yield (kg/ha)	Dry weight of weeds* (kg/ha)	Nutrient uptake by crop (kg/ha)			Nutrient uptake by weeds (kg/ha)		
				N	P	K	N	P	K
Weed management practices									
Pendimethalin	1.0	1250	11.21	86.2	30.3	113.5	1.79	0.45	2.66
Pendimethalin + one H.W. (45 DAS)	1.0	1340	10.67	97.6	33.4	122.3	1.58	0.35	2.37
Alachlor	1.0	1130	12.61	75.3	26.2	105.0	2.43	0.61	3.39
Alachlor + one H.W. (45 DAS)	1.0	1180	11.78	79.8	29.3	109.6	2.01	0.50	2.94
Two H.W. (25, 45 DAS)	—	1400	9.31	105.9	35.8	135.5	1.17	0.25	1.76
One interculture (25 DAS)	—	980	17.60	61.0	18.8	95.0	5.51	1.47	6.79
One H.W. (45 DAS)	—	1070	16.85	67.4	2.1	99.5	4.93	1.26	6.16
One interculture (25 DAS) +One H.W. (45 DAS)	—	1090	15.85	70.8	24.2	102.9	4.29	1.04	5.42
Weed free condition (H.W. at 25,45,65 DAS)	—	1490	8.35	122.7	42.9	144.9	0.88	0.19	1.40
Unweeded control	—	830	28.39	51.3	15.6	85.3	15.15	4.07	18.62
CD (P=0.05)	—	3.1	0.87	15.8	9.8	19.0	0.52	0.23	0.57
Nitrogen (kg/ha)									
60	—	1070	13.97	66.7	24.0	102.7	3.59	0.91	4.83
75	—	1190	14.26	83.3	28.0	112.3	3.97	1.01	5.11
90	—	1270	14.56	95.5	31.6	119.0	4.36	1.31	5.51
CD (P=0.05)	—	1.1	NS	6.9	3.6	8.2	NS	NS	NS

* Square-root-transformed values.   DAS = Days after sowing   H.W.= Hand-weeding
Source: Kaneria and Patel, 1994.

Judicious application of fertilizers to facilitate their maximum utilization by the crop and mini mize loss through weeds, and control of weeds provide higher crop yield. In a study during 1986-8 winter seasons at Madhopur, Bihar, the influence of various methods of fertilizer application (broad casting, broadcasting+band placement, band placement+broadcasting, and band placement) and weed control measures (no weeding, hand weeding at 25 DAS, and incorporation of thiobencarb a 1.0 Kg/ha at 2 DAS) on the yield of Indian mustard cv. Kranti were evaluated (Table 6.5).

Minimum depletion of the nutrients, and highest seed yield (13.2-15.2 q/ha), and yield attrib utes were obtained from band placement of 80 Kg N + 40 Kg P + 40 Kg/ha, with half of N applied at sowing and remaining half after first irrigation. Highest accumulation of weed dry matter and highest depletion of nutrients at 45 DAS took place under broad casting method of fertilizer appli cation. Control of weeds either through manual or herbicidal treatment also resulted in significan increase in yield (12.0-14.0 q/ha and 13.0-15.0 q/ha, respectively), and yield attributes ove unweeded control (10.0-11.6 q/ha) (Singh, 1992).

Table 6.5. Effect of fertilizer application methods and weed control measures on yield and yield attributes of Indian mustard.

Treatment	Siliquae/plant		Seeds/siliquae		1000 Seed weight (g)		Seed yield (q/ha)	
	1986-87	1987-88	1986-87	1987-88	1986-87	1987-88	1986-87	1987-88
Fertilizer application								
B	129.4	131.4	8.81	10.14	4.1	4.1	10.36	11.93
P	142.3	145.1	11.20	12.78	4.7	4.7	13.16	15.15
BP	134.8	136.6	9.70	11.32	4.3	4.3	11.47	11.08
PB	136.1	138.4	10.08	11.88	4.4	4.5	12.05	13.74
CD (P=0.05)	5.9	6.4	1.08	1.04	0.5	0.4	1.48	1.62
Weed-control								
No weeding	125.4	128.9	8.48	9.91	4.0	4.0	9.94	11.61
1-Handweeding (25 DAS)	138.4	140.3	10.23	11.83	4.7	4.6	12.02	13.86
Thiobencarb @@ 1.0 kg/ha (2 DAS)	142.6	143.3	11.34	12.46	4.7	4.6	13.33	14.95
CD (P=0.05)	7.2	6.8	1.19	1.12	0.4	0.3	1.58	2.14

B = Broadcasting   P = Bandplacement
BP = Broadcasting + band placement   PB = Band placement + broadcasting
DAS = Days after sowing
Source: Singh, 1992.

Side application of fertilizers also profoundly influences weed growth and crop performance. This was evident in field trials at Faizabad, Uttar Pradesh, during 1985-87 seasons. Side placement of NPK fertilizers (60 Kg N, 40 Kg P_2O_5 and 40 Kg K_2O/ha) near the crop-row at sowing and side-dressing of urea (60 Kg N/ha) in the standing crop of Indian mustard cv. Kranti, significantly reduced the dry matter production and NPK removal by weeds compared with their broadcast application at both the stages. Control of weeds either by mechanical means (one hand-weeding with or without hoeing) or through herbicide (pre-emergence application of either isoproturon at 0.75 Kg/ha or thiobencarb at 1.0 Kg/ha) considerably reduced the dry matter of weeds and NPK removal by them compared with the unweeded check, and had positive effect on mustard as regards dry matter production and NPK uptake (Singh & Singh, 1993). Furrow-application of NPK fertilizers was also effective both in reducing the weed biomass production by 17% and in increasing the seed yield of Indian mustard cv. Pusa Bold by 15.2% over broadcast method of application in a field experiment during 1988-90 crop seasons at Jorhat, Assam (Gogoi & Kalita, 1995).

Broadcast application of fertilizers results in their uniform distribution in the soil and divided availability to weeds and the crop, while band placement or placement of fertilizers in furrows or near the crop-rows, etc. ensure efficient utilization by the crop for better growth and higher seed yield with opposite effect on weeds.

6.7 INTEGRATED WEED MANAGEMENT

It is almost impossible to control or eradicate weeds in a crop through a single operation or treatment, be it manual/mechanical or herbicidal because of delayed emergence or regeneration of one or the other weed species. Manual or mechanical weeding is highly effective but laborious, time consuming and is often uneconomical due to high labour cost. Non-availability of labour at the critical period, unfavourable weather and soil condition, likely damage to densely populated or broadcast-sown crops may often delay or make the task of manual weeding difficult. Herbicidal or chemical method, on the other hand, is more convenient, quick, economical and effective means of weed control. Here again, most of the presently available herbicides are effective against a narrow spectrum of weed flora. Continued usage of the same or similar types of herbicides may give rise to the problem of soil and environmental pollution, residual toxicity and emergence/dominance of resistant weed biotypes. Use of a mixture of compatible herbicides with differing toxicity or sequential application of two or more herbicides against a multitude of weed species that emerge at different times of crop life is also not an economically sound proposition for annual crops like rapeseed and mustard in India. Hence, an integrated approach namely, judicial application of pre-plant, pre- or postemergence herbicides in conjunction with manual/mechanical or cultural practices may provide effective control of wider spectrum of weed species. Research is wanting on this aspect but a few reported studies are noteworthy.

In a field study during 1991-93 crop seasons at Hissar, Haryana, integration of either pre-plant incorporation of fluchloralin (0.75 kg/ha) or pre-emergence application of pendimethalin (0.75 Kg/ha) with one manual weeding at 30 DAS proved highly effective against dominant weeds in Indian mustard cv. RH-30 compared to application of herbicides alone. These measures resulted in yield and yield attributes of the crop which were at par with those of two hand-weedings at 30 and 45 DAS, and weed free check (Chauhan *et al.* 1993). In an earlier study from the same place, pre-plant application of fluchloralin (1.0 Kg/ha) + one hoeing resulted in significant control of weeds in Taramira (Jat *et al.* 1987). In Terai region of Eastern India (Cooch Behar, West Bengal), a field study on integrated weed management in Indian mustard cv. Seeta was conducted during 1988-90 winter seasons. Pre-emergence application of oxadiazon (0.75 Kg/ha) plus one manual weeding effected crop yield increase which was at par with two manual weedings at 21 and 35 DAS (Pradhan, 1993). Higher efficacy of integrated weed management in Indian mustard cv. Varuna, combining herbicidal treatment (isoproturon) + mulching (with 25 μm black polyethylene sheet) in between crop rows, than weed control with herbicide alone, was demonstrated in a two year field study during 1987-89 seasons at the IIT, Kharagpur, West Bengal (Table 6.6).

Table 6.6. Effect of different methods of weed control on dry weight of weeds at harvest and seed yield of mustard.

Treatment	Dry weight of weeds (kg/ha)		Seed yield (kg/ha)	
	1987-88	1988-89	1987-88	1988-89
Weedy check	1.58	1.20	190	630
Hand weeding (HW) at 20 and 40 DAS	0.59	0.62	440	820
Mulch with black polyethylene	0.93	0.69	420	970
Mechanical weeding (MW) at 20 and 40 DAS	0.97	0.85	280	800
Isoproturon (1.0 kg/ha) + Mulch	0.44	0.54	580	1030
Isoproturon (1.0 kg/ha)	1.06	1.05	210	630
Isoproturon (1.0 kg/ha) + MW at 40 DAS	0.96	0.92	270	680
HW at 20 DAS + MW at 40 DAS	0.52	0.53	390	750
L.S.D. (P=0.05)	0.40	0.21	100	240

DAS = Days after sowing
Source: Ghosh et al. 1993.

Pre-emergence application of isoproturon (1.0 Kg/ha) initially controlled the weeds but at later stages, the grassy weeds (particularly, *Digitaria sanguinallis, Cyperus rotundus* and *Cynodon dactylon*) re-infested the field. On the other hand, when isoproturon treatment was combined with mulching, the weeds were controlled most efficiently, the latter treatment also helped in conservation of soil moisture. The integrated measure gave the highest yield of seed and stalk as compared to all other treatments (Ghosh *et al.* 1993).

REFERENCES

AICORPO. 1972. Eighth Annu. Workshop Rept. 1971-72. Summary of research work conducted on oilseeds in Plant Pathology section, *All India Coord. Res. Proj. Oilseeds*. ICAR, August 27-31, Jaipur, 1972, Rajasthan.

AICRPWC. 1984. Final Tech. Rept. 1978-84. *All India Coor. Res. Prog. Weed Control*. G.B. Pant Univ. Agric. & Tech., Pantnagar, U.P., pp. 112.

Ali, M. 1993. Studies on crop-weed competition in chickpea (*Cicer arietinum* L.)/mustard (*Brassica juncea* (L.) Czern & Coss) intercropping. In: *Integrated Weed management for sustainable agriculture. Proc. Int. Symp.*, Indian Soc. Weed Sci., 2: 39-40, Hissar, November 18-20, 1993.

Ambasht, R.S. and Chakhaiyar, S.N. 1981. Weed and weed free duration effects on growth and yield of mustard (*Brassica juncea*) and gram (*Cicer arietinum*) crop. p. 9. (Abstracts). *Annu. Conf.*, Indian Soc. of Weed Sci., 1981. (Undated).

Balayan, R.S., Bhan, V.M. and Singh, S.P. 1983. Chemical and cultural weed control studies in cotton. *Tropical Pest Management* 29(1): 56-59.

Bhadoria, R.B.S. and Chauhan, D.V.S. 1995. Efficacy of herbicides in the control of weeds infesting Indian mustard (*Brassica juncea*). *Indian J. Agron.* 40(2): 327-329.

Bharat, M.P. 1989. Occurrence of Orobanche in Nepal. In: K. Wegmann and K.J. Musselman eds., *Progress in orobanche research. Proc. Int. Workshop Orobanche Res.*, Obermarchtal, Germany, August 19-22, 1989.

Brar, L.S. and Walia, U.S. 1995. Bioefficacy of herbicides against *Trianthema portulacastrum* in toria (*Brassica campestris* sub sp. *oleifera* var. toria). *Indian J. Agron.* 40(4): 647-650.

Chatterjee, B.N. and Ghosh, R.K. 1991. Agronomy. pp. 138-197. In: V.L. Chopra and S. Prakash eds. *Oilseed Brassicas in Indian Agriculture*. Vikas Publishing House, New Delhi.

Chauhan, D.R., Balayan, R.S., Kadian, V.S. and Dhankar, R.S. 1993. Integrated weed management studies in rai (*Brassica juncea* (L.) Czern & Coss). In: *Integrated Weed Mangement for sustainable agriculture. Proc. Int. Symp.*, Indian Soc.Weed Sci., 3: 114-116, Hissar, November 18-20, 1993.

Choudhary, J.K. and Pathak, A.K. 1992. Competition of wood-sorrel (*Oxalis corymbosa*) with rapeseed (*Brassica napus*) and oat (*Avena sativa*). *Indian J. Agron.* 37(2): 299-301.

Dashora, G.K., Maliwal, P.L. and Dashora, L.N. 1990. Weed crop competition studies in mustard (*Brassica juncea* (L.) Czern & Coss). *Indian J. Agron.* 35(4): 417-419.

Gautam, K.C. 1982. Weed management studies in wheat-mustard mixed crops (Abstracts). *Annu.Conf.*, Indian Soc.Weed Sci., December, 27-30. Div. Agron., I.A.R.I., New Delhi.

Ghosh, B.C., Mitra, B.N. and Pande, M. 1993. Effect of physical, mechanical and herbicidal methods of weed control in mustard (*Brassica juncea* L.) var. Varuna. In: *Integrated weed management for sustainable agriculture. Proc. Int. Symp.*, Indian Soc. Weed Sci., 3: 91-93, Hissar, November 18-20, 1993.

Ghosh D.C. and Mukhopadhyaya, S.K. 1981. Weed control studies in rapeseed and economics of chemical method. *Pestology* 5(4): 24-28.

Ghosh, R.K., Mandal, B.K. and Das Gupta, B. 1988. Weed control in rapeseed and mustard. *Oils, Fats and Feed Review* (1988). pp. 9-15.

Gill, H.S., Sandhu, K.S., Paul, S. and Singh, T. 1984. Efficacy of some herbicides for control of weeds in Indian mustard. *Indian J. Sci.* 16(3): 171-173.

Gogoi, A.K. and Kalita, H. 1995. Effect of weed control and fertilizer placement on weeds, yield components and seed yield of Indian mustard (*Brassica juncea*). *Indian J. Agron.* 40(4): 643-646.

Jat, N.L., Keshwa, G.L. and Singh, G.D. 1987. Efficacy of herbicidal weed control in Taramira (*Eruca sativa* Mills). *Haryana J. Agron.* 3: 92-93.

Kaneria, B.B. and Patel, Z.G. 1993. Effect of weed management practices and nitrogen on mustard yield and nutrient losses through weeds. *J. Oilseeds Res.* 10(2): 246-250.

Kaneria, B.B. and Patel, Z.G. 1994. Weed and nitrogen management in Indian mustard (*Brassica juncea*). *Indian J. Agric. Sci.* 46(1): 44-46.

Klischowski, B. and Beyer, H. 1989. Some considerations on weed control in winter rape. *Gesunde-Pflanzen*. 41(9): 311-313.

Kurchania, S.P. and Tiwari, J.P. 1994. Integrated weed management in mustard (*Brassica juncea* L.). *World-Weeds*, 1: 95-99.

Kumar, A. 1992. Production technology for yield enhancement of Indian mustard under irrigated condition. pp. 71-95. In: D. Kumar and M. Rai, eds. *Adv. Oilseeds Res*. Vol. 1. Scientific Publishers, Jodhpur, Rajasthan

Kumar, A. and Singh, R.P. 1985. Agronomy. pp. 63-83. In: Oilseed research at Pantnagar. *Expt. Stn. Tech. Bull*. 111., Direct. Expt. Stn., G.B.Pant Univ. Agric. & Tech., Pantnagar, India.

Mazumder, J.C. 1995. Strategy for weed management for improving crop productivity in India. pp. 247-262. In: D. L. Deb, ed. *Sustaining Crop and Animal Productivity — The Challenge of the Decade*. Associated Publishing Co., New Delhi.

Mehra, S.P., Kanwar, R.S. and Bhatia, R.K. 1989. Herbicidal control of winter weeds in autumn cane + Indian mustard intercropping system. *Indian J. Weed Sci*. 21(3): 37-41.

Mehrotra, O.N., Garg, R.C. and Sharma, A.P. 1972. Chemical control of weeds in mustard (*Brassica juncea* L.). *Indian J. Agron*. 17(3): 194-198.

Misra, S. and Sanwal, G.G. 1992. Alterations in lipid composition of seed oil from *Brassica juncea* upon infection with *Cuscuta reflexa. J. Agri. and Food. Chem*. 40(1): 52-55.

Nair, S.G., Patel, B.M., Karunakar, A.P. and Sethi, H.N. 1996. Weed control studies in irrigated mustard. *Ann. Plant Physiol*. 10(2): 182-185.

Narasimhan, M.J. and Thirumalachar, M.J. 1954. A Sclerotinia disease of *Orobanche cernua* in Bihar area. *Phytopath. Z*. 22(4): 421.

Panchal, Y.C., Ganesh Babu, M.S. and Patil, V.S. 1980. Chemical control of weeds in mustard. *Annu. Conf*., Indian Soc. Weed Sci., Orissa Univ.Agric. & Tech., Bhubaneswar, Orissa.

Pandey, J. 1980. Harvest high yield of rai (*Braissca juncea*) with herbicides and nitrogen in calcareous soil. *Indian J. Weed Sci*. 12(2): 178-180.

Panwar, R.S., Malik, R.S. and Bhan, V.M. 1987. Studies on weed management in wheat-raya and chickpea-raya intercropping systems. *Indian J. Agron*. 32(4): 365-369.

Pradhan, A.C. 1993. Integrated weed management in mustard (*Brassica juncea* (L.) Czern & Coss) in terai tract of eastern India. In: *Integrated weed management for sustainable agriculture. Proc. Int. Symp*., Indian Soc.Weed Sci., 3: 123-125, Hissar, November 18-20, 1993.

Rajput, R.L., Gautam, D.S. and Verma, O.P. 1993. Studies on cultural and chemical weed control in mustard (*Brassica campestris*). *Gujarat Agri. Univ. Res. Jr*. 18(2): 1-5.

Rana, M.C. and Angiras, N.N. 1990. Effect of weed control methods and phosphorus levels on phosphorus uptake, phosphorus use efficiency and quality of gobi sarson (*Brassica napus* var. *oleracea*). *Indian J. Weed Sci*. 22 (1-2): 71-77.

Saini, J.S., Sahota, T.S. and Dhillon, A.S. 1989. Agronomy of rapeseed and mustard and their place in new and emerging cropping systems. *J. Oilseeds Res*. 6: 220-267.

Sandhu, K.S. and Walia, U.S. 1979. Herbicides for controlling weeds in Indian mustard. *Indian J. Weed Sci*. 11: 78-80.

Saraswat, V.N. 1993. Major weeds of Indian agriculture — their distribution and ecology. In: *Integrated weed management for sustainable agriculture. Proc. Int. Symp*., Indian Soc.Weed Sci. 1: 35-41, Hissar, November 18-20, 1993.

Saraswat, V.N., Misra, J.S. and Radha, M.K. 1993. Status of weed management research in oilseed crops in India. In: *Integrated weed management for sustainable agriculture. Proc. Int. Symp*., Indian Soc.Weed Sci:, 3: 98-102, Hissar, November 18-20, 1993.

Sarmah, M.K., Narwal, S.S. and Yadava, J.S. 1992. Smothering effect of Brassica species on weeds. pp. 51-55. In: P. Tauro and S.S. Narwal eds. *Proc. 1st Natn. Symp. "Allelopathy in Agro-ecosystems"*. Indian Soc. Allelopathy, Haryana Agri. Univ., Hissar, India.

Sawhney, J.S., Narang, R.S., Mahajan, V.P. and Sidhu, M.S. 1983. Intercropping of *Brassica juncea* (Raya) with Wheat. *Proc. Symp. Agronomy 2000 A.D., Looking Ahead*, Nagpur. p. 16.

Sharma, M.L. and Chauhan, Y.S. 1995. Cultural and chemical weed control in Indian mustard (*Brassica juncea*). *Indian J. Agron.* 40(2): 235-238.

Sidhu, M.S., Sawhney, J.S. and Narang, R.S. 1988. Chemical weed control in wheat — Indian mustard intercropping system. *Indian J. Weed Sci.* 20(2): 92-95.

Singh, G. 1993. Integrated weed management in pulses. In: *Integrated weed management for sustainable agriculture. Proc. Int. Symp.,* Indian Soc. Weed Sci., 1: 335-342, Hissar, November 18-20, 1993.

Singh, J., Singh, H.B. and Gangasaran. 1993. Studies on the weed management and nitrogen fertilisation in mustard (*Brassica juncea* L. Czern & Coss.) In: *Integrated weed management for sustainable agriculture. Proc. Int. Symp.,* Indian Soc. Weed Sci., 3: 94-97, Hissar, November 18-20, 1993.

Singh, S.J., Sinha, K.K. and Misra, S.S. 1989. Effect of herbicides on Indian mustard (*Brassica juncea* Coss) in calcareous soil. *Indian J. Agron.* 34(4): 494-495.

Singh, S.S. 1992. Effect of fertilizer application and weed control on the yield of mustard (*Brassica juncea*). *Indian J. Agron.* 37(1): 196-198.

Singh, U.P. and Singh, S.P. 1993. Effect of method of fertilizer application and weed control on nutrient uptake by mustard (*Brassica juncea*) and associated weeds. *Indian J. Agron.* 38 (2): 277-281.

Tiwari, J.P. and Kurchania, S.P. 1993. Chemical control of weeds in Indian mustard (*Brassica juncea*). *Indian J. Agric. Sci.* 63(5): 272-275.

Tomar, S. and Namdeo, K.N. 1991. Studies on chemical weed control in mustard. *Indian J. Agron.* 36(1): 118-121.

Tosh, G.C. 1982. Herbicide evaluation for intercropped wheat with mustard and linseed (Abstract). *Annu. Conf.*, Indian Soc. Weed Sci.. December, 27-30, 1982. Orissa Univ., Bhubaneswar.

Yadav, R.P., Srivastava, U.K. and Yadav, K.S. 1995. Yield and economic analysis of weed-control practices in Indian mustard (*Brassica juncea*). *Indian J. Agron.* 40(1): 122-124.

Yadava, J.S. and Narwal, S.S. 1997. Weed suppression vs foliage role in rapeseed-mustard. *Cruciferae Newsl.* 19: 127-128.

Index